Henry George Raverty

A Grammar of the Pukhto, Pushto

Language of the Afghans

Henry George Raverty

A Grammar of the Pukhto, Pushto
Language of the Afghans

ISBN/EAN: 9783743394346

Manufactured in Europe, USA, Canada, Australia, Japa

Cover: Foto ©Paul-Georg Meister /pixelio.de

Manufactured and distributed by brebook publishing software (www.brebook.com)

Henry George Raverty

A Grammar of the Pukhto, Pushto

A

GRAMMAR

OF THE

AFGHĀN LANGUAGE.

A

GRAMMAR

OF THE

PUK͟HTO, PUS͟HTO,

OR

LANGUAGE OF THE AFG͟HĀNS;

IN WHICH

THE RULES ARE ILLUSTRATED BY EXAMPLES FROM THE BEST WRITERS, BOTH POETICAL AND PROSE:

TOGETHER WITH

TRANSLATIONS FROM THE ARTICLES OF WAR,

AND REMARKS ON THE

LANGUAGE, LITERATURE, AND DESCENT OF THE AFG͟HĀN TRIBES.

BY

MAJOR H. G. RAVERTY,

BOMBAY ARMY, RETIRED LIST.

AUTHOR OF A DICTIONARY OF THE PUS'HTO LANGUAGE; THE GULSHAN-I-ROH, OR SELECTIONS, PROSE AND POETICAL, IN THE PUS'HTO OR AFG͟HĀN LANGUAGE; THE POETRY OF THE AFG͟HĀNS, TRANSLATED FROM THE ORIGINALS IN THE PUS'HTO LANGUAGE; THE GOSPEL FOR THE AFG͟HĀNS; A THESAURUS OF ENGLISH AND HINDŪSTĀNĪ TECHNICAL TERMS, ETC. ETC.

فارسیوانو د حیرت گوتي په خولي کړي　　　چه حمید سخن سازي که په پښتو کښي

THIRD EDITION.

LONDON:

WILLIAMS AND NORGATE,

HENRIETTA STREET, COVENT GARDEN; AND 20, SOUTH FREDERICK STREET, EDINBURGH.

CALCUTTA:

W. NEWMAN AND CO.

MDCCCLXVII.

STEPHEN AUSTIN,

PRINTER, HERTFORD.

TO THE MOST NOBLE

JAMES ANDREW, MARQUIS OF DALHOUSIE, K.T.,

GOVERNOR-GENERAL OF INDIA,

ETC. ETC. ETC.

THIS GRAMMAR OF THE PUS̱H̱TO LANGUAGE

IS,

WITH THE GREATEST RESPECT,

DEDICATED

BY HIS LORDSHIP'S MOST OBEDIENT HUMBLE SERVANT,

H. G. RAVERTY, Captain

3rd Regiment, Bombay N. I.

PREFACE TO THE FIRST EDITION.

In offering this Grammar of the Pus̲hto to the Orientalist and the Student, as well as to those who may take an interest in the hardy, warlike, and independent race who speak the Afg̲hān language, I deem it necessary to state, that the idea of the following pages originated in my being under the necessity of making a Grammar for my own convenience, during the years 1849 and 1850, when stationed at Pes̲hāwer with my Regiment, which formed part of the Bombay Division of the Army of the Panjāb in the late campaign.

Having a deal of leisure time on my hands, and imagining that by studying the peculiar and little known language of the Afg̲hāns, an Officer *might* be considered in some measure qualified for employment where the Pus̲hto is spoken, I determined to try to acquire some knowledge of this dialect, the mastery of which had never been attempted, except by the late Major Leech, of the Bombay Engineers, and (as I have since found) Professor Bernhard Dorn, of St. Petersburgh.

Unable to obtain or discover anything like a guide to the grammatical rules of the language, a matter to which the Afg̲hāns of the present day appear to have paid no attention, I commenced my studies with the poems of Mullā Æabd-ur-Raḥmān. I did not find them very difficult, or even so much so as I had expected; for I had the advantage—if such there be in knowing Oriental languages—of possessing some proficiency in Persian, and some acquaintance with Arabic and other tongues.* Still there were difficulties to contend with; and I was obliged to make a sort of outline Grammar, which was filled in as I advanced, and examples compared and selected.

I had fortunately at the outset secured the services of an Afg̲hān of Hās̲htnagar, in the Doāba of Pes̲hāwer—a Molawī of the Muḥammadzo'e tribe—a

* By the Orders of the Government of India, I was awarded the sum of 1000 Rupees, by the Governor in Council of Bombay, for proficiency in the *Urdū*, *Persian*, *Murāṭī*, and *Guzerāṭī* languages; in all *four* of which I have passed the Presidency Examination as Interpreter on *four* different occasions—somewhat superior, I flatter myself, to the so-called test for the "Higher Standard" Civil Examination in the Panjāb. During twelve years' service, I have devoted ten to the study of the above, and to the Arabic, Pus̲hto, Sindī, Panjābī, and Multānī languages.

man well acquainted with his mother-tongue, and a first-rate Arabic scholar, and who was for some time Lieut. R. F. Burton's teacher. I had also in my service a clever Mīrzā,—a native of Kandahār, who is well acquainted with the Pus͟hto dialect, having been born and bred in the Western capital.

In 1850 I was obliged to leave Pes͟hāwer with my Regiment for the Dekhan, but my teachers accompanied me, and have remained in my service ever since. Although some portion of my time was taken up in preparing for the ordeal of the Presidency Examinations, as Interpreter in Murātī and Guzerātī, I continued to persevere in my Pus͟hto studies; and by Midsummer, 1852, I had prepared a somewhat copious Grammar of the language.

This humble effort I had the honour of submitting to the Most Noble the Governor-General in July, 1852; and, by His Lordship's command, it was sent to the late Panjāb Board of Administration for that body's opinion as to its publication. From thence I believe it reached the late Commissioner of Pes͟hāwer (by the Board's order) to be reported on by "competent Judges."

I was not aware that Pus͟hto had been made the subject of general study at Pes͟hāwer, nor that any parties, with the exception of those I have referred to in a former paragraph—one of whom died some ten years since, and the other, a resident in the Russian capital—had ever turned their attention to, much less pretended to such a knowledge of the Afg͟hān language, as to render them for a moment "competent judges." Who these "competent judges" were—who must have grown spontaneously in that district—and the opinion they arrived at, I have not yet discovered. What became of the MS. may be easily imagined.

The only copy which I had made was forwarded about the same time to the Government of Bombay, and laid before the Hon'ble the Court of Directors. Nine months afterwards I received a letter stating that the Hon'ble Court had been pleased to direct that my Grammar should be printed at Bombay at the public expense, provided no other work of a similar nature might have been already undertaken by the Supreme Government.

It appears that an Officer of the Bengal Army some time previously had offered to prepare a Grammar of the Pus͟hto language, and had obtained a promise from one of the late Lahore Board to the effect that it should be printed at the expense of Government. In January, 1853, the Officer here referred to and myself chanced to be at the same station, at which time he first became aware that I had been in the field before him; and, therefore, he lost no time in submitting his work to the Lahore Authorities. For the reasons above stated his work was printed, and has been before the public for some months;* and consequently the instructions of the Hon'ble Court as regarded my MS. could not be

* "A Grammar of the Pooshtoo Language, spoken in the Trans-Indus Territories under British Rule," 8vo., 101 pages, price Five Rupees. Calcutta, 1854.

carried out. *His* work, of course, had not to undergo the ordeal of the "competent judges."

Blessed, however, with some patience, and a good stock of perseverance and industry, I was not to be disheartened by this strange and significant procedure of the Lahore Board, or, at least, of one of its members, neither at the loss of the labour of a couple of years,—in truth, I rather rejoice now, for it has made me go deeper into Puṣhto than I might otherwise have done; and "he who entertains the hope of winning a decisive battle, will not mind the loss of a few skirmishes, in order to arrive at the end he aimed at." I again went to work with greater industry than before; and during the six years which I have devoted to the study of the language of the Afghāns, the materials have naturally accumulated, and have now assumed a somewhat bulky volume. Whether these six years have been spent profitably or not, remains to be seen. I have at least gained the satisfaction of having, I trust, rescued from oblivion, and shed some light on, the language of a manly race, "the literary exertions of whose authors, and some of whose odes, would stand the severest criticism of European judges."*

A short time since, two gentlemen connected with the Asiatic Society of Bengal offered, in the most handsome manner, to undertake the publication of this Grammar; and one of them (whose disinterested liberality I can never forget) volunteered to bear any loss that might be sustained, rather than the work should remain unpublished. The patronage of the Government of India, of the North-West Provinces, and of Bombay, who have subscribed for a number of copies; as well as the great support, as the list of subscribers will show, of the Officers of the United Service and others, will, however, preclude the possibility of any loss in a pecuniary point of view.

The work professes to be a Grammar of the language of the children of Afghānah—whether Eastern or Western—whether Saṛraban, Gharghaṣht, or Karlāṛṇī—Bar Pukhtūn or Lar Pukhtūn—Panjpā'o or Zīruk; and is not confined to the "Pooshtoo of the Trans-Indus Territories under British Rule," but applies wherever the Puṣhto may be the medium of communication.

I have endeavoured to lay down the clearest, and, at the same time, most simple rules, the whole of which I have illustrated by carefully selected examples from the works of the most elegant—as well as the most standard—authors, both poetical and prose, the greater number of whose works are seldom to be met with at the present day. I have adduced nothing but what has been proved by the extracts given, avoiding examples made up for the occasion, not wishing to make the work a mere category of provincialisms. Nothing has been advanced but what has been accounted for and explained, as well as tested and supported by the "*dictum*," not only of a "Mullā," but of every writer in the Puṣhto language.†

* Professor Dorn.

† This refers to some uncalled for remarks in the preface to the work before-mentioned.

The Introduction contains some remarks on the origin and affinity of the Afghān to the dead languages of Asia, and the Hebrew origin of the children of 'Abd-ur-Rashīd, Paṭṭān; together with remarks on the literature of the Afghāns, and other matter regarding the language.

In the Appendix will be found a specimen translation of the Articles of War for the Native Army; and a few difficult and idiomatical stories, intended to show the capabilities of the dialect, and the mode of construction.

The character used is that peculiar to the language—the Nasḵẖ character of the Arabic; and the types for the extra letters, exclusively Puṣẖto, have been cut expressly for this volume.

The particular parts of speech or matters referred to in the various examples in the following pages, are printed in small capitals in the English, and its corresponding Pushto word or words with a line over them. It was intended to have had these words printed in red ink, which, although an easy matter to an European, is an insuperable difficulty to an Indian Press.

I must crave the patience of my readers with respect to the long list of corrections; and I fear I shall scarcely be credited, when I state that each sheet has been revised no less than three times, and which has been the principal cause of the great delay in the publication of the work.

I propose giving a Persian translation of this Grammar, for the convenience of natives who may wish to acquire a knowledge of Puṣẖto, should a sufficient number of subscribers be forthcoming.

The opportunity for the renewal of friendly intercourse with the Afghāns, as advocated in the Introduction, page 25, has happened sooner than expected, and appears to have been cordially embraced. It cannot fail to be highly advantageous to both nations.

H. G. R.

MULTAN, 31ST MARCH, 1855.

PREFACE TO THE SECOND EDITION.

THE flattering manner in which the First Edition of this work was received by the public, and its rapid exhaustion, has rendered it necessary to print a New Edition, uniform with the Dictionary and Text Book.

I have taken the opportunity thus offered to correct the numerous press errors in the former edition, which was printed at Calcutta, and to improve the work materially.

The Chapters on the Nouns and Adjectives have been considerably extended.

H. G. R.

CAMP, NĀSAK,
21ST NOVEMBER, 1859.

CONTENTS.

INTRODUCTION.

CHAPTER I.—THE ALPHABET.

CHAPTER II.—THE PARTS OF SPEECH.

CHAPTER III.—THE NOUN.

CHAPTER IV.—THE ADJECTIVE.

CHAPTER V.—THE PRONOUN.

CHAPTER VI.—THE VERB.

CHAPTER VII.—THE SEPARATE PARTICLES.

CHAPTER VIII.—THE DERIVATION OF WORDS.

CHAPTER IX.—THE NUMERALS.

CHAPTER X.—THE SYNTAX.

APPENDIX.

INTRODUCTION.

"I am not willing that any language should be totally extinguished; the similitude and derivation of languages afford the most indubitable proof of the traduction of nations, and the genealogy of mankind; they add often physical certainty to historical evidence of ancient migrations, and the revolutions of ages which left no written monuments behind them."

DR. JOHNSON.

IN all investigations into the manners and customs of mankind, language has a strong claim to our attention and study. It will be found, in various ways, so unerring a guide that we may term it the barometer of a people's civilization or barbarity; whilst, on the other hand, the derivation and affinity of different tongues afford an indisputable proof of the origin and genealogy of the various families of the human race. It also adds a physical certainty to historical evidence; and no authority can so indubitably determine the peculiar habits and pursuits of a people as the manner in which their thoughts and ideas are articulated and expressed; for want of copiousness, or poverty of a language, as it may be termed, generally indicates an uncivilized state—ignorance and superstition.

By oral means alone can a dialect be formed or extended, but its subsequent cultivation must depend on writing and literature; and knowledge, on which civilization, refinement, and everything that tends to raise mankind above the level of the brute, depends, must naturally be confined within exceedingly narrow limits, until a written language has diffused it throughout all classes of mankind.

Before venturing to offer an opinion as to the origin of the Pus͟hto language, it will be necessary to make a few observations respecting the topography, as it may be termed, of the ancient languages of Asia, more particularly those from which we may naturally suppose the Pus͟hto or Afg͟hān language to have sprung: still all researches into high antiquity are more or less involved in darkness and perplexity, and every argumentative inquiry, however ingenious, must at last rest on the uncertain basis of conjecture and fancy.

We learn from the accounts given by Herodotus, and other ancient writers, that in certain countries of no great extent, various languages, totally distinct from each other, were used; whilst, on the other hand, the same language, with slight variations in its dialects, was spoken throughout vast regions. The first remarks are applicable to nearly all mountainous districts, inhabited, like Afghānistān, by different tribes, for the most part independent of each other.

Throughout the boundless steppes of the Asiatic continent were spread the more prevalent languages. The limits of the various dialects also were the same stupendous ranges of mountains, and the same noble and mighty rivers, which formed the boundaries of the different territories. Between the Attak or Indus, the Æmān or Oxus, and the banks of the Dajlah or Tigris, one language appears to have predominated; a second from the Tigris to the Halys or Kizil Irmāk; and a third between the Halys and the Ægean sea.

To commence with the language which appears to have been most widely prevalent in ancient times, we find that, from the Caucasian* range of mountains on the north to the Red Sea on the south, and from the banks of the Euphrates on the east to the Halys on the west, one mighty tongue was spoken, which, with some slight variations, retained a primitive and distinct character, known as the Semitic, and of which the Arabic, Assyrian, Chaldaic, Cappadocian, Hebrew, Sarmatian, and Phœnician were merely dialects.†

From the Tigris eastward, as far as the mountain range which forms the western barrier of the Indus, and from the Oxus to the Indian sea, another great language prevailed, the various dialects of which, both in elements and construction, as also in vocabulary and phraseology, were so totally distinct as to preclude the possibility of their being of the same family as the Semitic. One peculiar feature of the ancient dialects of the immense tract which constituted the Persian empire is, that every vowel, whether short or long, has a distinct character. We are indebted to the labours of several eminent scholars in Zend literature for much important information on this subject, particularly from the work known as the "Zend Avesta"—the sacred volume of the Parsīs or Gabrs, two English translations of which are about to be given to the world—one by a European Orientalist, the other by an Asiatic, and a disciple of Sapetmān Zoroaster. From these researches we find that three different languages, which followed each other successively, were spoken in Iran;‡—the Zend, in which the sacred books of their religion were written; the Pehlavī; and the ancient Persian, or Pārsī. The date from which the Zend ceased to be the medium of conversation is unknown; but, as early as the reign of Bahmān, the Pehlavī was considered rude, and on this account in disrepute at the court of that ruler;§ and in the reign of Bahrām Gūr,|| in the fifth century of our era, was

* [illegible] at present known as the Caucasian range, not the Koh-i-Ķāf of the ancient Arabian authors.

† [illegible] "Asiatic Nations."

‡ [illegible] for Persia, in contradistinction to Turan or Tartary.

§ [illegible], Bahmān, also called Ardashir, was son of Isfandiār, son of Kashtāsib, son of Lohrasp. [illegible] uprightness and justice; others, that it was from his precociousness as a child; and [illegible] of the length of his arms, which were so long that his hands reached his knees. There [illegible] word in the work I have quoted. Bahmān died A.D. 240.

|| He [illegible] A.D. 420, and reigned twenty years.

proscribed by edict, and soon after fell into total disuse. After this event the Pārsī became the idiom of Persia. It was divided into two dialects—the Derī, or court language, and the Pārsī, which was spoken by the people at large. The Shāh Nāmah of Ferdousī is almost entirely written in the former tongue.

If we compare these dialects with the modern Persian, divested of the Arabic and Turkish, which, during a period of several centuries have crept into it, we shall find them differing essentially in several respects; but at the same time, in phraseology and construction, bearing such a striking similarity, as to prove almost indubitably that the dialects themselves, as also the people who spoke them, must have sprung from one and the same original stock.

It is a striking fact that no convulsions of Government, no efforts of literature, can so alter a language as to destroy every atom of similarity between the speech of the present day and that of most ancient and remote origin. Nothing but the total extirpation of the aborigines of a country appears capable of accomplishing so singular and wonderful a change. For a striking instance of this we have merely to look to the present dialects of the peninsula of India, or, for a still more conclusive proof, to the modern European languages, amidst the polish and refinement of Latin and Greek.

It appears, therefore, that the principal languages of the Asiatic continent, or, of what was considered Asia by the ancients, were the Semitic, and the Irānīan or Persian: * the last was spoken as far as the western bank of the Indus, beyond which the Sanskrit and Prākrit commenced. †

In ancient times, as in the present day, the greatest diversity of language appears to have prevailed in mountain tracts, generally inhabited by a number of independent tribes, who may either have been aborigines of those mountains, or strangers compelled to seek in them refuge from powerful neighbours, or security from invasion and subjection to a foreign yoke. In the absence of facilities for communication with other races, the languages of these mountaineers have been less liable to be mixed up with other tongues; but as their more numerous tribes separated into smaller septs, a variety of dialects was naturally formed, which, in many points, differed from each other.

The ancient languages of Persia suggest other important facts not to be passed over without notice, and which also bring us to the point to which these straggling and imperfect remarks are intended to lead—that not merely in the modern Persian

* Heeren, "Asiatic Nations."

† "With regard to the affinity of the language from Bactria to the Persian Gulf, it would of course follow, that the country being that of the ancient Persians, the Persian language would be spoken in it, varied as to dialect, but radically the same. If the language of Persia was Zend, this would have been in use throughout Ariana; and its strong affinity to Sanskrit would justify the extension of Strabo's remarks even to the Indians of the Paropamisus and the west bank of the Indus. With all the other divisions of Ariana there is no difficulty, even if the Persian of ancient did not materially differ from that of modern times; for Persian is still the language of the inhabitants of the towns of Afghānistān and Tūrkistān—Kābul and Bokhāra."—Ariana Antiqua, pp. 122, 123.

territory do we find languages which still exist, mixed up with others, and only preserved from oblivion by a few written remains; but that in the present day there is also a language spoken immediately west of the Indus, which is totally different in phraseology and construction from any modern tongue, and in all probability derived from the Zend, Pehlavī, and the Hebrew. The language to which I refer is the Puk'hto, Pus͟hto, or Afg͟hān.

Languages, though they may be cultivated by writing and literature, can alone be fashioned and extended by oral use; and it is therefore certain that the dead languages of the Asiatic continent must at one time have been generally spoken,* because several living languages are evidently derived from them.† They may have ceased to be the medium of oral communication in various ways: intercourse with foreigners, subjugation to the yoke of others, and such like circumstances, so affect a language as to produce various new dialects, which, as proved in the case of our own mother-tongue, are capable of undergoing still further transformation.

There has, perhaps, never been a greater diversity of opinion respecting the descent of any people than in reference to that of the Afg͟hāns. Feris͟htah‡ traces their origin to the Copts, whilst most Oriental writers are of opinion that they are of the Jewish family. According to Klaproth, Gatterer considers the Afg͟hāns to be a Georgian race, and their language Georgian also. The Armenians hold the Afg͟hāns to be descended from themselves; and Krusinsky, Reineggs, and several other European historians, notwithstanding the want of proof, hold the same opinion. Major Keppel § (the late Earl of Albemarle) states that the people of S͟hīrwān and the adjoining countries consider the Afg͟hāns are descended from them. St. Martin,‖ in his account of the Armenian Arghowans, is of opinion that the Afg͟hāns cannot be identified with them. Other authors have declared them to be descendants of the Indū-Scythians, the Medians, the Sog͟hdians, Turks, Tārtars, and Mong͟hols.¶

The Afg͟hāns themselves persist in their descent from the Jews; and their traditions on the subject trace their ancestry to Saul, king of Israel.**

The best account I have met with on the subject has lately fallen into my hands quite unexpectedly. It is contained in a history of the house of Saddo or Suddozo'e tribe of the Afg͟hāns. The work itself is written in 8vo., 640 pages of 17 lines to a page, and entitled Taẕkirāt-ul-Mulūk. It is very rare, and I imagine there is not a copy to be found east of the Indus, even if it has ever been heard of before by Europeans. Two-thirds of the entire work are occupied in the detail of events which have happened since the death of Aḥmad S͟hāh, Abdālī. The commencement

* I have lately heard of a seal having been found near Pīnd Dādun K͟hān, in the Panjāb, bearing an inscription in the arrow-headed character.

† Heeren. ‡ "Tārīk͟h-i-Feris͟htah." § "Personal Narrative of Travels," vol. ii. page 194.

‖ "Memoires sur Armenie," vol. i. page 213 to 226.

¶ See "Tārīk͟h-ul-Yamīnī of Otbī," "Matlaa-us-Salāṭin," and "Jami-ul-Tawārīk͟h."

** See Sir G. Rose's "Afg͟hāns, the Ten Tribes, and the Kings of the East," etc. London, 1852.

alone is sufficient for my present purpose; on some future occasion I may give a translation of that part which terminates with the death of the founder of the Dūrānī monarchy. I may also add, that the work is written in Pus͟hto. The account is as follows :—

"The chief object of the author in writing this august work, was the compilation of a history of the ancestors of the tribe of Saddo, known as the Suddozo'es,* who, after the family of the last of the Prophets, (on whom be the blessing of the Almighty!) are the greatest and best, as well as the most generous and open-hearted of the children of Ādam.

"All traditions and histories agree, as to their exalted descent from the Ban-i-Isrā-īl, of whom their great ancestor is Malik Tālūt (Saul) of the tribe of Isrā-īl, who afterwards became the ruler of that people. From Malik Tālūt is descended Afg͟hān, one of the greatest of God's creatures, and who in the reign of Sūlīmān, was, by that monarch, made sovereign of the Jinns and Dīws.

"From Malik Afghān, Æabd-ur-Ras͟hīd bin Ḳais al Laiḳ, who was a contemporary of the prophet of God, and one of his most honoured associates, is a lineal descendant. He is the ancestor of the Sarrabands, who are considered the first of the Afg͟hān tribes, as also of the twelve *āstānas* or families who were formerly considered as hereditary devotees.†

"His Highness Saddo chief of the Afg͟hans, being the fruit of the tree of that garden, and a blossom of that rose tree, this account of his ancestry has been compiled, to the end that their fame may be known to posterity.

'What can we inherit but fame beyond the limits of the tomb?'

"The following histories and authorities have been consulted in the composition of the work, viz.:—Tārīk͟h-i-Salāṭīn-i-Sūreah; Ṭabaḳāt-i-Akbarī; Aæn-i-Akbarī; Mirāt-ul-Afāg͟hanah, which work was written by K͟hān Jehān, Lūdī, in the reign of the Emperor Jehāngīr; Tārīk͟h-i-S͟hāhān-i-Ṣafāwīah, Irānī; S͟hāh Jehān Nāmah; Tārīk͟h Ālamgīrī; Furuk͟h Seorī; Tārīk͟h-i-Maḥommed S͟hāhī; Nādir Nāmah; Tārīk͟h Aḥmad S͟hāhī; Rassālah Akbār, K͟hadakah; and other information has been collected from the narratives of trustworthy persons. I have entitled the work, TAẔKIRĀT-UL-MULŪK, of the ancestry of the tribe of Saddo, the chief of the Afg͟hāns. It consists of one *muḳaddamah* (preface), two *aṣals* (originals), and one *k͟hātimah* (epilogue)."‡

* From which the kings were chosen, as being the royal tribe.

† Both Mr. Elphinstone ("Caubul," vol. i. page 252) and Professor Dorn ("Neamut Ullah," Part ii. page 40) have fallen into error respecting this *fourth* grand division of the Afg͟hāns, called by them respectively the Betuee, and Botni, Baiṭni, or Bāṭinī. باطني is not the name of a tribe, but is derived from the Arabic باطن *bāṭin*, which means, *hidden*, or *knowing the hidden* or *concealed*; hence the Almighty is often termed الباطن *Al Bāṭin*.

‡ The contents of the whole work are:—MUḲADDAMAH. On the forefathers of Saddo, chief of the Afg͟hāns. FIRST AṢAL. On the subject of those of the tribe who have ever dwelt in Afg͟hānistān. This *Aṣal* is divided into two *Farua* or Parts. 1st. Respecting that branch who have ruled over the whole tribe. 2nd. On the other members of the tribe, who still dwell in their native country. SECOND AṢAL. On that branch of the clan who left their country and took up their abode at

"MUḲADDAMAH.

"On the Forefathers of Saddo, Chief of the Afg͟hān People.

"The great ancestor of this tribe is Malik Tālūt (Saul) who is mentioned in the Kur'ān and other works, as descended from Binyāmīn bin Yaæḳūb, bin Isḥ'āḳ, bin Ibrāhīm (may the blessing of the Almighty rest on them and on their house!) Tālūt was celebrated amongst his countrymen for his wisdom, knowledge, and mightiness in war; and the All-wise Creator of the Universe made him king over Isrā-īl, and commanded him to bring to perdition the infidel Jālūt (Goliath), the enemy of his people.*

"At this time Mehtar† Dā'ūd, who dwelt in the district situated between the territories of the rival princes, went and joined the army of his countrymen,‡ who were hard pressed by the superior army of Jālūt.§ The king on this account issued a proclamation to the effect, that whoever would go forth to fight with Jālūt and kill him, should receive the hand of the king's daughter in marriage, and be declared heir to the throne.

"When Tālūt went out to meet Jālūt, his troops being seized with a sudden panic, fled from the field with the exception of 313 persons, who by the will of God, took courage and remained with their king.‖ It was at this time that Dā'ūd

Multān. This is in five *Farae* or Parts. I. On the K͟hān Modud K͟hel. II. The history of the Bahādūr K͟hel. III. Account of the Kāmrān K͟hel. IV. Account of the Zafarān K͟hel. V. The K͟hwājah K͟hiẓr K͟hel, who are generally known as the Sulṭān Khel, Khadakah. K͟hātimah. Account of the remaining branches of the K͟hwājah K͟hiẓr K͟hel, the descendants of S͟hāh Dur-i-Dūrān, and their dispersion into various parts of India and the Panjāb.

* "And their prophet answered and said unto them, Verily God hath set Tālūt king over you, and hath enlightened his mind, and strengthened his arm: they answered, How shall he reign over us, seeing that we are more worthy of the kingdom than he, neither is he possessed of great riches? Samuel said, Verily God hath chosen him before you, and hath caused him to increase in knowledge and stature."—Al Ḳur'ān, chap. ii.

"Now there was a man of Benjamin, whose name *was* Kish, the son of Abiel, the son of Zeror, the son of Bechorath, the son of Aphiah, a Benjamite, a mighty man of power.

"And he had a son, whose name was Saul, a choice young man, and a goodly: and *there was* not amongst the children of Israel a goodlier person than he: from the shoulders and upwards *he was* higher than any of the people.—1 Samuel, chap. ix., verses 1, 2.

"So Saul took the kingdom over Israel, and fought against all his enemies on every side, against Moab, and against the children of Ammon, and against Edom, and against the kings of Zobah, and against the Philistines: and whithersoever he turned himself, he vexed them.

"And he gathered an host and smote the Amalekites, and delivered Israel out of the hands of them that spoiled them."—1 Samuel, chap. xiv., verses 47, 48.

† A lord, a prince, a great chief, a title generally applied to Israelites by Muḥammadans.

‡ "Wherefore Saul sent messengers unto Jesse, and said, Send me David thy son, which *is* with the sheep.

"And Jesse took an ass laden with bread, and a bottle of wine, and a kid, and sent them by David his son unto Saul."—1 Samuel, chap. xvi., verses 19 and 20.

§ "Now Saul, and they and all the men of Israel, were in the valley of Elah fighting with the Philistines.

"And David rose up early in the morning, and left the sheep with a keeper, and took, and went, as Jesse had commanded him; and he came to the trench, as the host was going forth to the fight, and shouted for the battle."—1 Samuel, chap. xvii., verses 19, 20.

‖ "And Tālūt said unto his soldiers, Verily God will prove you by the river, for he that drinketh thereof shall not be on my side (but he shall be on my side who shall not taste thereof) except he who drinketh a draught of the water out of his hand. And they drank thereof, except a few of them. And when they had passed over the river, he and those who believed with him, said, We have no strength this day against Jālūt and his host. But they who considered that they should meet God at the resurrection, said, How often hath a small army, by the will of God, defeated a greater one and discomfited it, for God is with those who patiently persevere. And when they went forth to battle against Jālūt and his forces, they said, Oh Lord, pour on us patience, confirm our feet, and help us against this unbelieving people. Therefore they discomfited them by the Almighty will, and Dā'ūd slew Jālūt."—Al Ḳur'ān, chap. ii.

killed the infidel Jālūt in single fight, after which, the small but brave band that had stood its ground, fought with such determined courage, that the enemy were entirely defeated and put to the rout.*

"After this action on the part of Mehtar Dā'ūd, it became incumbent on king Tālūt to fulfil the terms of the covenant which he had made, and accordingly he gave his daughter to Dā'ūd in marriage, and a patent of succession to the throne.

"During the life-time of king Tālūt, Dā'ūd served him faithfully, and at his death succeeded him. Armīah (Jeremiah) and Birkīya, Tālūt's sons, were raised to the highest honors, became the captains of his armies, and continued in his service during their life-time.

"In the common course of events, Dā'ūd himself set out on that journey from which no traveller returneth, and was succeeded by his son Sūlīmān. He appointed Afghānah, the son of Armīah, to the command of his armies, and the government of the Jinns and Dīws; whilst Āṣif, the son of Tālūt's son Birkīya, was made his principal minister.†

"One day king Sūlīmān seated on his throne, and accompanied by his minister, was journeying through the air,‡ when they passed the district of Rūdah, or Roh, in which is situated the lofty mountain of Kasoghar, which lies between Peshāwer and Kandahār, and Kābul and Multān. It is near the town of Darāban and west of the Sindhu (Indus) river.

"Pleased with the spot, and the salubrity of the climate, The Wisest of Men directed his minister to form a seat out of a stone which was at hand. This being almost immediately done, Sūlīmān sat in it for some time and enjoyed the beauty of the landscape which lay spread out at his feet. The mountain is known at present as the Takht, or Throne, of Sūlīmān.§ A portion of the throne still remains, to which the people of the surrounding districts are in the habit of making pilgrimages.

* "And the men of Israel and of Judah arose, and shouted, and pursued the Philistines, until they came to the valley, and to the gates of Ekron. And the wounded of the Philistines fell down by the way to Shaaraim, even unto Gath, and unto Ekron.

"And the children of Israel returned from chasing after the Philistines, and they spoiled their tents."—1 Samuel, chap. xvii., verses 52, 53.

† "This statement will not appear so fabulous if we compare it with 2 Samuel, chap. xxi., verses 15 to 22, for Dīw and Jinn mean a giant as well as a demon or genii; دیو *dīw*, a devil, a demon, genius, giant, spirit, ghost, hobgoblin. The Dīws or Dives, Jinns, Genii, or giants of eastern mythology, are a race of malignant beings." See جن also in Richardson.

‡ "No name is more famous among Muhammadans than that of Solomon. According to their belief, he succeeded David his father when only twelve years old; at which age the Almighty placed under his command all mankind, the beasts of the earth and the fowls of the air, the elements, and the genii. His throne was magnificent beyond description. The birds were his constant attendants, screening him like a canopy from the inclemencies of the weather, whilst the winds bore him whithersoever he wished to go. Every age and every nation have had their fooleries, and even many of the received opinions of modern times will not bear the touchstone of Truth. The sorcery laws of our country are a far more authentic disgrace to human nature, than all the wild, yet pleasing fables of the East."—Richardson.

§ "In the southern part of the Wuzeeree country, where this range is passed through by the river Gomul, it is low in both senses, and forms the lofty mountain of *Cussay Ghur*, of which the Takht of Sūlīmān, or Solomon's Throne, is the highest peak."—Account of the Kingdom of Cābul, vol. i. page 164.

"I was told that on the top there was a holy stone or rock, the seat of a Musalmān Faḳir, whose name it bears; but I venture to doubt the story."—Vigne's Ghuznī, Cābul, etc., page 61.

"The mountain tract of Kaseghar, and the district of Rūdah, were assigned in feudal tenure to Afghānah.

"The original meaning of the word Afghānah is *fighān*—a Persian word, which means 'complaint,' 'lamentation,' because he was a cause of lamentation to the devil, the jinns, and mankind. From the constant use of the word, the vowel point (ـِ) *kasrah* was dropped, after which the other letters could not be sounded without the aid of a vowel, and *alif-i-waṣl* was placed before the *gh*, and thus made Afghānah.

"Malik Afghān having taken possession of his new territory (to use the expressive words of the author), 'irrigated the land of that mountainous country with the water of the sword, and planted in the hearts of its inhabitants the seeds of his own faith. He fixed his residence at a place named Pusht or Pasht, situated in the mountains; and from the name of this place the people have derived the name of Pushtūn, or Pukhtūn, and their language Pushto, or Pukhto. Some traditions state that the Afghāns acquired their language from the Dīws; and others, that it is the original dialect of the aboriginal inhabitants of Kaseghar, and that the Afghans were in the habit of carrying off the wives and daughters of those infidels, and intermarrying with them,* thereby learning from them the Pushto language, and in course of time forgetting their own Ibrahāmī tongue." †

Again, to use the words of the author, "Malik Afghān having purified the face of the mistress of that country from the filth of the wicked infidels by the pure water of the sword; and having given unto her the rouge of beneficence, and decked her out in the bridal garments of religion and the ornaments of Islām, bestowed her in the marriage of possession to one of his sons; after which he returned to the court of king Sūlīmān, at Bait-ul-Muḳaddas, ‡ where at length he died at a very advanced age. His descendants, from generation to generation, and from tribe to tribe, continued to dwell round about the mountain of Kaseghar, and to rule over it; and were constantly at war with the infidels, as the neighbouring people were termed.

"At length, during the chieftainship of Æabd-ur-Rashīd bin Ḳais al Ḷaik, an event happened which was the cause of shaking the world to its very foundations§—the joyful tidings of the last and greatest of the Prophets, resounded both in Arab and in Ajam too; and Æabd-ur-Rashīd became desirous of making a pilgrimage to Makka for the purpose of seeing him:—

'Love ariseth not alone from seeing the object;
This wealth is often acquired by mere conversation.'

"In company with several of his kinsmen and friends, he set out for the Hedjāz; and having arrived at Makka, performed his pilgrimage according to the rites and

* See the "Khulāṣat-ul-Ansāb."

† Ibrahāmī means the Hebrew language.

‡ بيت المقدس The Sanctified or Holy Temple—the Arabic name for Jerusalem.

§ Allowance will of course be made for religious prejudice

tenets of the religion of his forefathers, Isrā-īl, Ish'āķ, and Ibrāhīm.* He now set out for Madīnah, and on the road fell in with the celebrated Khālid-ibn-Wālid, 'The Sword of God,'—to whom he explained the object of his journey. They travelled towards Madīnah in company, and on his arrival there, Æabd-ur-Rashīd became a convert to Islām. In the numerous struggles of that period, he became conspicuous for his intrepid bravery, which made the Prophet bestow on him the surname of بتان *baṭān* or پتان *paṭān*,† which in Arabic‡ means the *keel* of a vessel, without which it cannot sail, neither can the ship of war sail along without the keel of battle.

"Æabd-ur-Rashīd having acquired great renown, at length obtained his dismissal, and was allowed by the Prophet to return to his native land; but was at the same time enjoined to publish and diffuse the doctrines of Islāmism amongst his countrymen. He departed from Madīnah, and in due course reached his home in safety, after which he converted his family and tribe to the new faith, and taught them the Ķur'ān. He made war on the infidels with greater zeal than ever, and was celebrated for his piety. At length, finding his end approaching, he called his family and tribe around him, and enjoined them to keep their hearts fixed on the only true religion, and their feet firm in the path of Islām; to show friendship and obedience to the followers of Muḥammad; and to make war on the infidels, and convert them to the only true faith. After taking an affectionate leave of all, the swallow of his soul, having escaped from the wintry cage of this world, took its flight towards the summer mansions of eternal bliss.

"He was blessed with three sons—Sarī, Gharī, and Tabrī. The first, known as Sarraban, or Sarrabarn, succeeded his father in the chieftainship, and gave name to one of the two great divisions of the Afghāns, called Sarrabans. The second also, called Ghargh̲asht, gave name to the Ghargh̲ashts. The descendants of these three sons constitute the whole of the different Afghān clans, with their numerous branches and ramifications.

"The tribes which are included in the Sarraban division are:—Abdālī, Tarīn, Barech, Mabānah, Gharshīn, Shīrānī, Bābarr, Kānsī, Jamand, Kātanī, Kalīānī, Tarkānī, Khalīl, Muhmand, Dā'ūdzo'e,§ and Yūsufzo'e. The twelve *Astānahs*, or families, who are considered sacred by the other Afghāns, from their progenitors

* The temple of Mecca was a place of worship, and in singular veneration with the Arabs from great antiquity, and many centuries before Muḥammad. Though it was most probably dedicated at first to an idolatrous use, yet the Muḥammadans are generally persuaded that the Caaba is almost coeval with the world; for they say that Adam, after his expulsion from Paradise, begged of God that he might erect a building like that he had seen there, called Bait-al-Mamūr, or the frequented house, and al-Dorāh towards which he might direct his prayers, and which he might compass, as the angels do the celestial one."—SALE's INTRODUCTION TO THE ĶUR'ĀN, page 83.

† He (Muḥammad) conferred the title of Paṭān upon Æabd-ur-Rashīd, as the angel Gabriel had revealed to him, that the attachment of the newly-converted Afghāns to the Faith, would, in strength, be like the timber upon which they lay the keel when building a ship, which timber the seamen call Paṭān."—MIRĀT-UL-AFĀGHANAH, of Khān Jehān, Lūdī. (This is the work translated by Professor Dorn, under the title of "The History of the Afghāns, of Neamet Ullah.")

‡ Written بطان in Arabic, and probably signifying *keelson* instead of *keel*.

§ *Zo'e* in Pushto means "son"—*zāe* is a corruption of the word, and most generally used.

having been devotees, are also included amongst the Sarrabans. The Abdālī, Tarīn, Bābarr, Jamand, and Yūsufzo'e tribes have each one family; the Khalīls, three; and the Muhmands, four.

"The different branches of the Gharghasht division, or offspring of Gharī, are: the Surānī, Jailam, Worokzo'e or Orokzo'e, Afrīdī, Chakānī, Jankī or Jangī, Kerānī, Aormarr, Nīwat, Kākarr, Nāghir, Bābī, Mashwānī, and Tārrn tribes.

"The third son, Tabrī, is the progenitor of the Ghalzo'e, Lūdhī, Nīazī, Lohānī, Sorbanī, Sarwānī, and Klakpūr clans, the whole of whom are styled Tabrīns. It is said there was an illicit connection between one of the daughters of Tabrī and Mast-Æalī, Ghorī;* and, after a short time, the fruits of this amour becoming apparent, the father, to make the best of a bad matter, gave her to him in marriage. Three sons were the offspring of this marriage—Ghalzo'e,† of whom she was pregnant before the nuptial knot was tied, Lūdī, and Sarwānī.

"The tribes above-mentioned are the whole of those who are of pure Afghān descent—the offshoots of the three sons of Æabd-ur-Rashīd, Paṭān. He was buried at Kaseghar, and succeeded by his eldest son Sarī, who was constantly at war with the Kāfirs or infidels. He had two sons—Sharkabūn and Kharshabūn. The Sarrabans are the descendants of the former, and the Yūsufzoe's, Muhmands, Khalīls, and other tribes inhabiting the plain of Peshāwer, are the children of the latter.

"On the death of Sarī, Sharkabūn, his son, was acknowledged chief of the Afghānah. He was celebrated for his piety and wisdom. In his wars with the infidels he not only acquired great wealth, but also increased his territory, and brought many of the neighbouring tribes under his authority. During his chieftainship Kandahār and Kābul were conquered by Hūjāj bin Yūsuf, Saḳafī, who was governor of Khorāsān for the Khalīfah Abd-ul-Malik bin Mirwān, who reigned from the year of the Hijrah 73 to 79 (A.D. 692–698). This event greatly increased the authority of Sharkabūn, and established his power more firmly than before.

"He is said to have been succeeded by Abdāl, his son. Some accounts mention that he was the son of Sharkabūn, and others that he was his grandson, but neither of these accounts can be correct, as there is a space of three hundred years between them; Sharkabūn being a cotemporary of Hūjāj bin Yūsuf, Saḳafī, before referred to, whilst Malik Abdāl lived in the reign of Māhmūd bin Sabuktagīn, who succeeded his father to the throne of Ghaznī in the year of the Hijrah 387 (A.D. 997). This great hiatus between the reigns of these two chieftains may be accounted for in the following manner. It often happens that the names of those chiefs who have been celebrated for their wisdom, bravery, piety, or numerous progeny, have been alone handed down to posterity, and those of mediocrity set aside and forgotten.

* The ancestor of the Ghoriān Sulṭāns who conquered Ghaznī, in 1152.

† غل *ghal* in Pushto means 'a thief,' and زوي *zo'e* 'a son,' hence غلزوي *Ghalzo'e*, 'the son of a thief;' زاي *zāe* is a mere corruption of the word, and is often written زي *zī*.

There is an instance of this with regard to Hāsham* and Æabd-ush-Shams, who were both sons of Æabd-ul-Manāf. The descendants of the former are still styled Ban-i-Hāsham, whilst those of the latter are known as the Ban-i-Omeyah, from Omeyah the celebrated son of Æabd-ush-Shams, and thus the father's name has been dropped altogether. In the same manner Malik Abdāl, having acquired a great name for bravery, equity, and generosity, and having surpassed many of his predecessors in grandeur and dignity, his name has been handed down to us, whilst the very remembrance of those of little or no celebrity is now altogether lost in oblivion. This is the great cause of the confusion which so often takes place in the genealogical histories of different tribes and people, and hence the reason why Malik Abdāl has been called the son or grandson of Sharkabūn.

"Malik Abdāl thus became chief of the Afghānah—Sarrabans, Gharghashts, and Tabrīns. During his reign the people began to pay attention to agriculture, and the lands about Kaseghar were brought under cultivation. Abdāl, who was famed for his bravery, followed in the path of his ancestors by making war on the people of the surrounding parts, in the plundering of whose property his followers acquired great wealth. A number of the infidels who dwelt in the vicinity of the Kaseghar district was also, at this time, converted to the Muḥammadan faith. At length the Afghāns, having no infidels to plunder, and insufficient land to yield them a subsistence, began to take service under the Ghaznīwīd Sulṭāns, from whom they obtained the district of Bagrām, now known as Peshāwer, as a feudal fief.† Of the countries to the north, such as Suwāt and Bājawarr, which were in the hands of

* The great-grandfather of Muḥammad.

† The account contained in the رياض المحبت (Gardens of Friendship), by Maḥabbat Khān, differs in some respects from the preceding narration. He says, "Up to the time of the Prophet of Islām, the descendants of Afghānah dwelt in the Salmān mountains, at which period Ḳais was their chief. He subsequently went to Arabia to do homage to Muḥammad, taking with him eleven persons of his tribe, who with himself became converts to the new faith.

"He returned to his native land, but in the following year he again returned to Arabia with seventy of his tribe, and joined the followers of Muḥammad a short time previous to his attack on Makka, in which affair, and the subsequent operations, Ḳais behaved so well that the title of Æabd-ur-Rashīd was conferred on him, and he soon after returned to his home.

"After the death of Muḥammad, Ḳais Æabd-ur-Rashīd, with a number of his people, followed the two succeeding Khalīfs in their wars; and when the Khalīf Oṣmān determined on the conquest of Khorāsān, he requested Ḳais to obey the orders of Æabd-ullah bin Æāmir bin Kārez, who had been appointed to head the expedition. This chief had been directed to settle the Afghān tribe with their families, after the conquest of that province, between it and Hindūstān, that they might become a barrier against invasion from the latter country. Ḳais assisted in the conquest of Khorāsān, after which the tract of country lying between Hirāt and Ḳandahār was bestowed on him and his tribe, subject to the governor of the province.

"At the period of the struggles between the Omeyahs and Abbāsīs, which ended in favour of the latter, the Government of Khorāsān was administered by Hūjāj bin Yūsuf, Saḳafī, who sent an expedition into Hindūstān, under his nephew Ḳāsim bin Muḥammad bin Yūsuf, Saḳafī, who was accompanied by a strong body of Afghāns. They advanced through the district of Roh,[1] and at length reached Multān, after annexing the former district, which was made over to the Afghān tribes, with directions to keep under the refractory Hindūs. From the occupation of Roh by the Afghāns they obtained the name of Rohilas.

"Sabuktagīn, the founder of the Ghaznīwīd dynasty, and father of the great Māḥmūd, entertained a number of Afghāns in his army. When that ruler died, Ismāæīl, his son, by the daughter of Alta'kīn, the owner of Sabuktagīn--for the latter was originally a slave—succeeded his father; but Māḥmūd, another son by the daughter of the chief of Zābulistān (Kābul)

[1] The Belūchīs, and other inhabitants of the Derā Ghāzī Khān, and those of the southern part of the Derā Ismaæīl Khān districts, speak of the mountain range immediately west of the Indus, to the southern boundary of Afghānistān by the name of Roh. See my paper on Roh: "Journal of Asiatic Society of Bengal." 1856.

the Kāfirs, they got possession by force of arms. They also obtained grants of land at Ghaznī and Kābul, from Sulṭān Māḥmūd and his successors; and by degrees began to emigrate from the neighbourhood of Kaseghar, and settled in those places they considered best suited to themselves. Up to the time of Malik Abdāl, the whole of the tribes considered and obeyed him as their head and chief; but now each tribe and village began to choose their own governors, and ceased to pay that respect and obedience to his authority which they formerly did; in fact they fell headlong into the slough of arrogance and presumption.

"Abdāl was succeeded by his son, Malik Rajar. This prince—a second Nimrūd—was passionately fond of the sports of the field, in which he spent the best part of his days and nights. He was blessed with four sons—Æsau, Nūr, Khokār, and Mākou, the first of whom, a God-fearing and just personage, succeeded him in the chieftainship: the others gave name respectively to the Nūrzo'e, Khokārī, and Mākou tribes.

"The remainder of the Abdālīs, and other clans, which had up to the present period continued to dwell in the Kaseghar district, near the Takht-i-Sūlīmān, finding it too small to support so many families, began, in the hot season, to migrate with their flocks to the neighbourhood of Ḳandahār, returning again to their old haunts at Kaseghar in the winter.

"Malik Æsau had three sons—Zīrak, Is'ḥāḳ, and Æalī. At his death he bequeathed the turban of authority to Zīrak, his sword to Is'ḥāḳ, and his carpet for prayer to Æalī. From these two latter the Is'ḥāḳzo'e and Æalīzo'e branch of the Abdālīs are descended; and from them is also descended the only one of the twelve *āstānahs*, or families, who are devoted to the priesthood, as already referred to.

"Zīrak, who was a wise and able chief, governed his tribe with energy and ability. He completely rooted out the crimes of impiety, adultery, and dishonesty, which appear to have been but too prevalent at the period in question.

"The five tribes which have been already mentioned as the Abdālī clan, viz., Is'ḥāḳzo'e, Æalīzo'e, Nūrzo'e, Khwagānī, and Mākou, are known as the Panjpā'o branch.

"My own opinion is, that Malik Abdāl was a cotemporary of Sulṭān Māḥmūd, Ghaznīwīd, and Malik Zīrak of Shah Rukh Mīrzā, son of Amīr Tīmūr, Gūrgānī,*

opposed him in the succession, and a civil war ensued between them. The Afghāns, who were dependent in some measure on this chief, joined his son-in-law Māḥmūd, who defeated Ismāæīl, and confined him in a fortress.

"In gratitude for this effectual aid on the part of the Afghānah, Māḥmūd gave his sister in marriage to Sa'ho, the chief of the tribe, by whom he had three sons—Salār, Mas'æūd, and Ghāzī, who are buried at Barāj.

"When Sulṭān Māḥmūd set out on his expedition against Sanmāth, in Guzerāt, he took with him a body of Afghāns. Several times during the siege of that stronghold, fortune seemed to incline against the Muḥammadan arms; but at length the Afghāns were brought to the front, who, having fastened the skirts of their garments together, attacked the Hindūs with such fury that the latter were entirely defeated, but not until the victors, as well as the vanquished, had sustained immense loss. In reward for this important service the 'Breaker of Idols' bestowed on each of the Afghāns the Tūrkī title of Khān: their former title of Malik was derived from Malik Talūt."—Rī'āzu-l-Maḥabbat.

* Tīmūr-i-Lang, commonly written Tamerlane.

between whose reigns there is a period of some three centuries. As has been already noticed, the names of the most celebrated chieftains can alone have been preserved by their countrymen, whilst those of less fame have sunk into oblivion.

"The district of Rūdah and Kaseghar, as before stated, not being of sufficient extent to support the great number of people to which the Afghāns had by this time increased, Malik Zīrak was induced to send an agent to Shāh Rukh Mīrzā, at Hirāt, for the purpose of soliciting a grant of the districts round Kandahār. This request was favourably listened to by the Shāh, and Zīrak, in consequence, gave directions to the Abdālī, Barech, Tarīn, Jamand, Ghalzo'e, Kākarr, Kāsī, Bābarr, and other tribes—who were more numerous than the extent of their lands could support—to proceed to Kandahār, and settle on the lands granted by the Shāh in that district. To each tribe a portion of land was given, in proportion to the number of families of which it consisted, and for which they had to pay a small tax to the Governor of the province.

"Zīrak had three sons—Popul, Bārak, and Alako, from whom have sprung the Populzo'es, Bārakzo'es, and Alakozo'es. At his death Popul succeeded him in the chieftainship of the whole Afghān people. Being a sagacious and intelligent chief, and endowed with the tact of government, he kept the whole of the tribes under subjection and obedience. They also were generally well satisfied with his government; but, at the same time, those who showed any opposition to his authority were punished by the Kandahār Governors, and this tended still more to keep all under proper restraint.

"Popul had also three sons—Ḥabīb, Bādū, and Aiyūb. The two former were by one mother, and the latter by another wife. Some also say that Aiyūb was the son of the first wife by a former husband. Bādū was the ancestor of the Bādūzo'es, and Aiyūb of the Aiyūbzo'es.

"At length Popul, suddenly finding his end approaching, sent for his children; and, after giving them much good advice, and exhorting them to follow in the footsteps of their ancestors, departed this life, leaving the chieftainship of the tribes in the hands of his eldest son Ḥabīb.

"The children of Afghānah, who had now become a numerous people, and had, up to this time, generally paid obedience to the authority of their chiefs, began to show symptoms of restlessness and dislike to the yoke of Ḥabīb's supremacy. At length they commenced quarrelling amongst themselves, and the *khels* or clans of every village, having declared themselves independent, set about nominating their own chiefs. All was uproar and confusion; the rich tyrannized over the poor, and the strong plundered the property of the weak; might was right; and villany, impiety, and depravity, reigned supreme.

"Malik Ḥabīb endeavoured for a long time to stem this torrent of rebellion, and regain his lost authority over the people, but without success; and at length not one tribe remained on his side. The Tarīns, Barec̲h̲is, G̲h̲alzo'es, Kākaṟṟs, S̲h̲īranīs, and others, each set up one of their own tribe as pretenders to the chieftainship, raised the standard of revolt, and commenced a civil war. The life of Ḥabīb was spent in civil contentions, which were entirely without avail. He had three sons—Bāmī, Ismāʿīl, and Ḥasan, from whom are descended the clans of Bāmīzo'e, Ismāʿīlzo'e, and Ḥasanzo'e.

"Bāmī, who was of a mild disposition, and possessed of many excellent qualities, succeeded his father as nominal head of the Afg̲h̲āns. Sulṭān Bahlol, Lūdī, and his son Sikandar, emperors of Hindūstān, were on friendly terms with him, and sent him from time to time various costly presents. This produced great envy in the hearts of the pretenders to the chieftainship, and they despatched agents with presents to those potentates. Their agents, without being admitted to an audience even, were dismissed with the answer that the Sulṭāns neither knew of, nor recognized, any other head of the Afg̲h̲āns than Malik Bāmī. He had four sons—Ṣāliḥ, Æalī, Zaiyl, and Warūkah. They were fathers of large families, and their memory has been perpetuated in the separate clans bearing their respective names.

"Bāmī died at an advanced age, and the shadow of chieftainship which now alone remained descended to his eldest son Ṣāliḥ, who became head of the Ḥabībzo'e tribe, which consisted of the three smaller ones of Æalī, Zaiyl, and Warūkah, just mentioned, who acknowledged and supported his authority. He was a man of great piety and generosity; and his threshold was never clear from the crowds of poor, nor his table from the numerous guests. In his lifetime S̲h̲īr S̲h̲āh and Salīm S̲h̲āh, who were of the S̲h̲ork̲h̲el branch of the Afg̲h̲āns, sat on the throne of Dehlī; and the friendship which had sprung up between his father and the Lūdīah Emperors was renewed and kept up with the former princes also. At length the vicissitudes of fortune wrested the sovereignty from the grasp of the Lūdīahs, and placed it in the hand of the Mog̲h̲al; but when S̲h̲īr S̲h̲āh, in the year 951 of the Hijrah (A.D. 1544), sallied forth to regain the throne of his ancestors, the Afg̲h̲āns assisted him with a powerful force of their countrymen, and Hindūstān was regained. When the agents of Malik Ṣāliḥ presented his letter of congratulation to S̲h̲īr S̲h̲āh, the Emperor observed to his ministers and court, that Malik Ṣāliḥ was not only his own chieftain, but that his forefathers, from the time of Malik Afg̲h̲ān, were the chiefs of his forefathers also; and that the family of Malik Ṣāliḥ had no equal in rank amongst the whole of the Afg̲h̲ān tribes. S̲h̲īr S̲h̲āh, after thus acknowledging Ṣāliḥ as his head and chief, and treating his agents with great distinction, dismissed them with numerous presents for their master.

"At length, in the reign of S̲h̲āh Ṭahmāsib, Ṣufawī, in the year of the Hijrah 965, on the night of Monday, the 17th of the month Ẕū'lḥijjah, the bright orb of Saddo rose from the eastern horizon of the black goat's hair tent of Malik Ṣāliḥ, and diffused his refulgent beams on the surrounding world."

With the birth of Saddo, the ancestor of the great Aḥmad S͟hāh, Abdālī, the Introduction to the "Taẕkīrāt-ul-Mulūk" closes.

Sir John Malcolm's words on the origin of the Afg͟hāns are—"Although the right of the Afg͟hāns to this proud descent is very doubtful, it is evident, from their personal appearance, and many of their usages, that they are a distinct race from the Persians, Tartars, and Indians, and this alone seems to give credibility to a statement which is contradicted by so many strong facts, and of which no direct proof has been produced."

Sir William Jones was of opinion that the Afg͟hāns are the Paropamisadæ* of the ancients; but this is very improbable, for it is proved by the statements of many authorities, besides that of the work from which I have given an extract, and many other histories of undoubted authenticity, that the Afg͟hāns are not the aborigines of the country they at present inhabit, but have gradually advanced from the west of Asia; and it is not improbable but that, during the lapse of ages, they might have been forced, from various causes, to emigrate from the districts in the vicinity of Jerusalem, as stated in the tradition I have quoted. The Seāh-pos͟h Kāfirs are in all probability the Paropamisadæ of the writers of antiquity, respecting whom, on some future occasion, I hope to offer some remarks.†

According to the "Makhzan Afg͟hānī," after Ferīdūn's victory over Ẕoḥāk, the latter was subjected to such acts of tyranny that his children fled for safety to the mountain tract of G͟hor, which at that time was only inhabited by a few scattered tribes of the Israelites, Afg͟hāns, and others. If Jewish families could, at that period, have been inhabitants of G͟hor, it is equally possible that the Afg͟hāns themselves might have come originally from the Holy Land.‡

The mountain districts of Afg͟hānistān heard not the "Allāhu-Akbar" of the conquering Arabs until the fourth or fifth century of the Hijrah, by which time the sun of their power had commenced to wane. Up to this time even, we find that the Kāfirs or infidels inhabited the mountain districts of G͟hor, and continued to dwell there up to the thirteenth century of our era, when Marco Polo visited those regions.§

The Yūsufzo'e tribes, who now hold the whole of the districts to the north of the Landdacy Sind, or eastern half of the Kābul river,‖ were, even in the time of

* See Quintus Curtius's "Life of Alexander," Book vii.

† See my "Account of the Seāh-pos͟h Kāfirs," in the "Journal of the Bengal Asiatic Society" for the present year.

‡ In the reign of Saosduchinus, king of Babylon, called in Scripture Nebuchodonosor the First (A. M. 3335, Ant. J. C. 669), the prophet Tobit, who was still alive and dwelt among other captives at Nineveh, a short time before his death, foretold to his children the sudden destruction of the city, of which at that time there was not the least appearance. He advised them to quit the place before its ruin came on, and to depart as soon as they had buried him and his wife. The Jews, being at this time captives, would—if they had followed the advice of Tobit—have had, in the first place, to escape from Nineveh by stealth; and, having accomplished this much, where could they hope to find a more secure retreat than towards the east, and in the direction of the mountainous tracts now inhabited by the Afg͟hān tribes? See Tobit, c. xiv., v. 5–13.

§ "Travels of Marco Polo;" Marsden's Translation. Book I., chap. xxii., pp. 122.

‖ *Landdacy Sind*, in Pushto signifies the "Little river," in contradistinction to the *Aba Sind*, or "Father of rivers," as the Indus is termed.

Bāber, but new comers; and in this, his statement agrees with the account in the "Tazkirāt-ul-Mulūk." In another place Bāber mentions the people of Bājawarr as "rebels to the followers of Islām; and, besides their rebellion and hostility, they followed the customs and usages of infidels, while even the name of Islām was extirpated from among them."* From this it appears that the people of the country had been converted to Muhammadanism, and relapsed again to idolatry, but were *not* Afghāns.†

Nowāb Allah Yār Khān, son of the Nowāb Hāfiz Rahmat Khān,‡ in the preface to a lexicographical work of which he is the author, states that "there are two divisions of the Afghāns, whose language also differs in many respects, so that the words used by some tribes are not known to, or understood by, others. They are termed Pushtūn and Pukhtūn, and they speak the Pushto and Pukhto respectively.§ The former is the western dialect, having some affinity to the Persian; and the latter the eastern, containing many Sanskrit and Hindī words. The people who dwell about Kābul and Kandahār, Shorā'wak and Pishīn, are designated Bar Pushtūn, or Upper Afghāns, from بر *above*; and those occupying the district of Roh, which is near Hind (India), are called Lar Pukhtūn, or Lower Afghāns, from لر *below*.

He describes Roh—about which there has been great diversity of opinion—as "bounded on the east by Suwāt and Kashmīr, west by the Helmund river, north by Kāshkār or Chitrāl and Kāfiristān, and south by the river or sea of Bukker, called in Persian Nīlāb (the Blue Water), and Nīl'āow or Aba-Sīn (the Father of Rivers) by the Afghāns."

The author of the "Ferang-i-Jehāngīrī" gives a somewhat similar account of it. "Roh," he says, "is the name of a range of lofty mountains, in length extending from Suwāt and Bājawarr to Sīwnī, or Sīwa'ī, which is in the district of Bukker, in Sind; and in breadth from Hasan Abdāl (in the Sind Sāgur Doāba, of the Panjāb) to Kandahār: and in this highland range the latter city is situated."

I have been told by Afghāns in the vicinity of Peshāwer, and other places, that their ancestors first came from a district named Ghwārī Marghāb, which they said lies to the westward of Khorāsān. This is, however, a mistake; a small village, bearing that name, and the place referred to by them, is situated about mid-way between Kandahār, Shorā'wak, and Girishk, which is one of the old seats of the Afghān tribes who now occupy the Peshāwer valley. Ghor, supposed to have been the original district of the Afghānah, lies much to the north. It was from this latter place that the Ghoriān tribe issued in the year 1152 A.D., when they overturned the throne of the Ghaznīwīd Sultāns.

* "Bāber's Memoirs" page 248.

† "Although Bajour, Sewād, Peshour, and Hashnagar, originally belonged to Kābul, yet at the present time some of these districts have been desolated, and others of them entirely occupied by the tribes of Afghāns, so that they can no longer be properly regarded as provinces."—Ibid, page 141.

‡ The author of the "Khullāsat-ul-Ansāb."

§ Merely in substituting *sh* for *kh*, *z* for *g*, *jz* for *j*, etc.

The diversity of opinion regarding the origin of the Afg͟hānah, is not greater than that respecting their language, of which, at the time I write, with the exception of a small brochure by the late Major R. Leech of the Bombay Army, no grammar exists.* It is to be hoped that the present work, together with the Dictionary which is published consentaneously with it, will enable the learned both of Europe and India, to give a better, and more decided opinion than heretofore on the affinity of the Afg͟hān language to the languages of ancient Asia.†

Sir William Jones's opinion was, that the Pus͟hto or Puk͟hto language has a manifest resemblance to the Chaldaic, but Professor Klaproth vehemently denies this, and states, that nothing whatever is known regarding this dialect; ‡ that neither in words nor grammatical structure is there the slightest resemblance between Pus͟hto and any Semitic language, and that it is unquestionably a branch of the great Indū-Germanic division of languages.

I cannot refrain from remarking here, that it appears most astonishing that persons, who cannot possibly have had any opportunity of becoming practically acquainted with a language, or even with the correct pronunciation of its alphabet, can venture opinions, often very decided, as to its origin and similarity with other tongues, with which they may even be less acquainted, or of which they may have only a slight theoretical idea, derived at second-hand from translations alone; for surely no one would venture to give an opinion of a language from original MSS. which no one within a thousand miles can decipher!

"A little knowledge is a dangerous thing, Drink deep, or taste not the Pierian spring."

Professor Dorn of St. Petersburgh—who some few years since published a work on the Pus͟hto language §—in the preface to his translation of "Neamet Ullah," gives as his opinion, that the Pus͟hto language bears not the slightest resemblance to the Hebrew or Chaldaic, either in its grammar or vocabulary; ‖ and he imagines the Afg͟hāns may belong to the great Indū-Teutonic family of nations, and are aborigines of the country they at present inhabit. This latter opinion, however, is proved to be an erroneous one, from the writings of various authors, and many well authenticated facts.

The Baptist Missionaries of Serampūr consider that the Pus͟hto and the

* Since writing the above, Captain Vaughan, of the Bengal Army, has published a short "Grammar of the Pooshtoo."

† A copious Dictionary, and a Text-Book containing selections in prose and verse from the works of the most standard authors, is now published, uniform with this work.

‡ It is to be hoped the Professor will change his opinion now as regards the latter part of this sentence.

§ "A Chrestomathy of the Pŭshtŭ Language, with a Glossary." St. Petersburg, 1847. The work consists of extracts from a few of the best known Pus͟hto authors, amongst which the odes of Mullā Æabd-ur-Raḥmān predominate. The text appears to have been printed from a recent and incorrect MS., and consequently is full of errors. In the Glossary, the meanings of many of the Pus͟hto words are merely guessed at (!) and are very wide of the mark.

‖ If we are to take the Glossary of Prof. Dorn as a specimen of the vocabulary of the Pus͟hto, I should say the language bears more than a strong resemblance to Hebrew, Chaldaic, and other Semitic dialects, seeing that this Glossary contains *ninety per cent. of pure Arabic words.* See pages 388, 389, and 390, in which there is not *one* Pus͟hto word; with two or three exceptions, they are all pure Arabic.

Belūch* languages form the connecting link between those of Sanskrit and those of Hebrew origin;† but, if we are to take their so-called translation of the New Testament (see subsequent note) as a specimen of their knowledge of Pushto, they are not authorities in the matter.

M. Adelung, in his "Mithridates," vol. i. page 225, considers Pushto an original and peculiar dialect, but at the same time acknowledges his acquaintance with it to be very slight.

Mr. Elphinstone, in his work on Kābul, vol. i. page 302, with reference to the Afghān language, considers that its origin cannot be easily discovered. He remarks, "a large portion of the words that compose it, as also most of the verbs and particles, belong to an unknown root, and in this portion are included most of those words which, from the early necessity for designating the objects they represent, must have formed parts of the original language; yet some of this very class belong to the Zend and Pehlavī, such as the terms for father and mother, sister and brother." He also further states, that out of two hundred and eighteen Pushto words, not one had the smallest appearance of being deducible from any of the Semitic languages; but that a resemblance (five out of one hundred and ten words) can be traced between it and the Kūrdish, considered to be an Indū-Germanic tongue.‡

One of the most decided proofs against the erroneous idea that the Afghāns are the aborigines of the territory they at present inhabit, and that the Pushto is the original dialect of those countries, consist in the facts brought to light in the deciphering of the Bactrian and Indū-Scythian coins. M. Lassen, in his interesting and erudite work§ on this subject, very truly observes; "I indeed know that some have pretended to recognize the Afghāns in Eastern Kābul, even as early as Alexander's time; not so Mr. Elphinstone,|| who rather proves their immigration into Kābul at a much later period. This conjecture has originated with Professor Wilken,¶ who thinks he recognizes the Afghāns in the Assakanes. If these were indeed Afghāns, the Afghān language would have been spoken throughout Kābul, and the language of the coins must be the source of the Pushto. Without observing that neither ancient authorities nor modern Afghān history** admit or require this supposition, the correct assertion of the learned

* The Belūchkī is a mixture of Persian, Sindhī, Panjābī, Hindī, and Sanskrit, with some apparently exotic words, and cannot properly be called an original language.

† They also notice the numerous pure Hebrew roots to be found in Pushto, which is not astonishing, considering that those roots are alike cognate to the Arabic and other dialects of the Semitic, which, being the sacred language of Islām, has entered largely into every Muḥammadan tongue, and for which words there is generally no equivalent in them.

‡ This probably refers to the vocabulary contained in the work in question, in which about one quarter of the words, or more, may be identified with Arabic and its cognates, and many others with Persian and Sanskrit.

§ "Points in the history of the Greek and Indū-Scythian Kings in Bactria, Kābul, and India," p. 116.

|| "Account of Caubul," vol. ii., pp. 10, 33, 41, 50, and 56. ¶ "Abhandlg. der Berlin Acad.," 1818-19, p. 261.

** Bāber does not mention anything about Afghāns at Kābul, when he took that city in the month of October, 1504; but he notices the tribe of Tarkolārrnī Afghāns in Lamghān, a district on the northern bank of the Kābul river, and immediately west of Jelālābād. The Tarkolārrnī tribe now occupy the country of Bājawrr, much further to the west.

Academician himself, that the Afghāns belonged to the Medo-Persic tribe, is at variance with it: the Assakanes inhabited a country, where even, in the 7th century, A.D., an Indian language was spoken."

As the learned Professor urges—if the Afghāns were the aborigines of the countries they at present inhabit, the Afghān language must, as a matter of course, have been generally spoken. Had such been the case, the language on the coins must have been the source of the Pushto; but no similarity whatever exists between them.

The Afghāns, although subdivided into numerous tribes, are undoubtedly one race, and speak one original language. Had they been the aborigines of the country at present known as Afghānistān, we must have heard something of them from ancient writers, for we find that, even in the time of Herodotus, Darius had sent an exploring expedition under Scylax of Caryanda and others as far as the Indus.* That the whole of the regions west of Jelālābād, or even as far west as Kābul, were peopled by a Hindū race, most ancient writers agree to, as also that they were of different tribes and spoke different languages. Herodotus says: "There are many nations of Indians, and they do not speak the same language as each other; some of them are Nomades, and others not."†

Again the father of history observes: "There are other Indians bordering on the city of Caspatyrus and the country of Pactyica, settled northwards of the other Indians, whose mode of life resembles that of the Bactrians."‡ The country here referred to—the same as Scylax and his companions started from on their voyage down the river—is the present district of Paklī, north of Attak. The Indians here mentioned are, in all probability, the ancestors of the race who still occupy that district,—the Suwātīs, and the people of Astor and Gilgitt.

It is therefore evident that the Afghāns have immigrated into their present territories from the westward;§ and that the aborigines—the Seāh-posh Kāfirs,

* "A great part of Asia was explored under the direction of Darius. He, being desirous to know where the Indus, which is the second river that produces crocodiles, discharged itself into the sea, sent in ships both others on whom he could rely to make a true report, and also Scylax of Caryanda. They accordingly, setting out from the city of Caspatyrus and the country of Pactyica, sailed down the river towards the east and sunrise to the sea."—"MELPOMENE," iv., p. 44.

† "THALIA," iii., p. 98.

‡ IBID, iii., p. 102.

§ The empire of the Great Cyrus extended, according to the best authorities, from the Ægean to the Indus, and from the Euxine and Caspian to Ethiopia and the Arabian sea. As it was customary to transport a whole tribe, and sometimes even a whole nation, from one country to another, and as the Jews were ever a stiff-necked race, is it not possible that the Great King may have transported some of the most troublesome amongst them to the thinly-peopled provinces of the east, where they would be too far away from their native land and captive countrymen to give trouble in future? Or, as I have remarked in another place, is it not probable, as well as possible, that those of the Jews who could effect their escape might have fled eastward, preferring a wandering life in a mountainous country, with independence, to the grinding tyranny of Cyrus's successors and their Satraps? In fact, there was no other direction to which they could have fled, except towards the north, inhabited by the Scythians, who would have massacred, or at least made slaves of them, or have sold them as such; or eastward, which, being mountainous and but thinly peopled, was likely to afford them a permanent and secure retreat. According to Niæmatu-l-lah, Zohāk's children, to escape the exterminating vengeance of Ferīdūn, fled for refuge to the Kohistān of Ghor, and settled there; and, at his time, its only inhabitants were some scattered tribes of the Israelites, Afghāns, and others.

There are a number of Jews to be found in the south-west parts of India, and in the Bombay Army there are a great number. Where did they come from? and when did they come?

Again, in the fifth year of Darius (A.M. 3488; Ant. J. C. 516), Babylon revolted, and could not be reduced until after

or Black-clad Pagans; the Suwātīs; and the people inhabiting the hills to the north-east of Suwāt, on the one side, and possibly the Belūchīs and Jatts, on the other—have been forced, by the gradual advance of this powerful race, to move to the north-east and south-west respectively.

I formerly entertained an idea that some affinity might exist between Pushto and the language of that strange people, the Gypsies, but subsequent inquiries have convinced me to the contrary, and I find that no trace of similarity exists between them.

Whether the Afghān language be a dialect of the Semitic, of Zend, or Pehlavī origin, or of the Indian stock, I will leave for others better qualified to decide. Before entering into any investigation on the subject, it must be borne in mind that "no efforts of the learned can ever so far alter a language, as to deface every line of resemblance between the speech of the present day and that of even the remotest ancestry: nothing but the absolute extirpation of the aboriginal natives can apparently accomplish so singular a revolution."* As an instance of this, we have merely to examine the present language of Persia, and the different dialects of the continent of India; or for a still more convincing proof, to look into the Gothic and Celtic original of the modern European languages, amidst the polish and refinement of the Greek and Latin.

Before bringing these rambling remarks to a close, I must notice a few of the most striking peculiarities of the Pushto language, which will, in some measure, serve as a guide in investigations as to its origin and affinity to the other dialects of the Asiatic continent. It will, however, be well, first to point out the best and most effectual method of ascertaining the *real* affinity of Oriental languages.

Baron William Humboldt, in an essay on this highly important subject, remarks: "I confess that I am extremely averse to the system which proceeds on the supposition that we can judge of the affinity of languages merely by a certain number of ideas expressed in the different languages which we wish to compare. I beg you will not suppose, however, that I am insensible to the value and utility of the comparisons; on the contrary, when they are well executed, I appreciate all their importance; but I can never deem them sufficient to answer the end for which they have been undertaken. They certainly form part of the data to be taken into account in deciding on the affinity of

a siege of twenty months. It is therefore probable that the Jews, of whom a considerable number remained at Babylon, went out of the city before the siege was formed, as the prophets Isaiah and Jeremiah had exhorted them long before, and Zachariah very lately in the following terms: "Thou daughter of Zion, that dwellest with the daughter of Babylon, flee from the country and save thyself."—Isaiah, chap. xlviii., verse 20; Jeremiah, chap. l., verse 8, chap. li., verses 6, 9-45; Zachariah, chap. ii.

It also appears that Ochus, son of Artaxerxes Mnēmon, carried a number of Jewish captives into Egypt, and many others into Hyrcania, where he settled them on the coast of the Caspian (A. M. 3653, Ant. J. C. 351); might not some have been sent eastward also?—See "Solin. C." 35, "Euseb. in Chron." etc.

* Richardson's "Dissertation."

languages; but we should never be guided by them alone, if we wish to arrive at a solid, complete, and certain conclusion. If we would make ourselves acquainted with the relation between two languages, *we ought to possess a thorough and profound knowledge of each of them.* This is the principle dictated alike by *common sense* and by that precision acquired by the habit of scientific research.

"I do not mean to say that, *if we are unable to attain a profound knowledge of each idiom,* we should on this account entirely suspend our judgment: I only insist on it that *we should not prescribe to ourselves arbitrary limits,* and imagine that we are forming our judgment on a firm basis, while in reality it is insufficient.

"But further, I am convinced that it is only by an accurate examination of the grammar of languages, that we can pronounce a decisive judgment on their true affinities.

"If two languages, such, for instance, as the Sanskrit and the Greek, exhibit grammatical forms which are identical in arrangement, and have a close analogy in their sounds, we have an incontestible proof that these two languages belong to the same family.

"The difference between the real affinity of languages, which presumes affiliation, as it were, among the nations who speak them, and that degree of relation which is purely historical, and only indicates temporary and accidental connections among nations, is, in my opinion, of the greatest importance. Now it appears to me impossible ever to ascertain that difference merely by the examination of words, especially if we examine but a small number of them.

"But whatever opinion may be entertained with respect to this manner of considering the difference of languages, it appears to me at all events demonstrated: First, that all research into the affinity of languages, which does not enter quite as much into the examination of the grammatical system as into that of words, is faulty and imperfect; and, secondly, that the proofs of the real affinity of languages, that is to say, the question whether two languages belong to the same family, ought to be principally deduced from that alone; since the identity of words only proves a resemblance such as may be purely historical and accidental."

There are nine letters of the Arabic alphabet which never occur in pure Afghān words,—ث, ح, ذ, ص, ض, ط, ظ, ع, and ف; and therefore the language really contains but twenty-nine letters, including five peculiar ones, to which, after a careful comparison of six hundred alphabets, I find that there is no similarity as to form or sound, either in Arabic, Zend, or Sanskrit; but characters similar in sound are contained in most of the Semitic, and some Tārtārīan dialects. The Pushto letters with the corresponding ones in the languages referred to are as follow:—

څ *ts* or *tz*, pronounced *tse* or *tze*, has an equivalent in the Chaldaic צ *ts*, Hebrew צ *tsōde*, Samaritan ࠑ *tsādc*, Syriac ܨ *tsōde*, Ethiopic and Amharic ጸ *tza*, Armenian Ջ ջ *tsa*, Palmyren 𐡑 *ts*, Phœnician 𐤑 or 𐤑 *ts*, Punic 𐤑 *ts*, Kufic ص *ts*, Georgian ც *ts*, Mongolish ᠴ *ts*, Mandchu ᠴ *tsa*, Thibetan ཙ *ts*, Albanian. ʓ ʓ *ts*, Corean ㅈ ㅈ *ts*, and the Japanese ツ ス ミ *tse*.

ځ *dz* or *ds*, pronounced *dze* or *dse*, similar to the Hebrew ז *dsain*, Aramāic | *ds*, Palmyren ו *ds*, Phœnician Z *ds*, Kufic ز *ds*, Syriac ܙ *dzain*, the Assyrian cuneiform 𒍝 *dz* or *ds*, Armenian Ձ ձ *dza*, Greek ζ *zeta*, Georgian ძ *ds*, Mongolish ᠵ *ds*, Corean ㅊ ㅊ *ds*, Mandchu ᠵ *ds*, and Japanese ヅ *dz*.

ړ *urray*, or *rrey*, for which, with the exception, perhaps, of the harsh Ռ ռ *rh* of the Armenian, there is no equivalent in any of the known dialects of the old world. Some persons, and among them Major Leech, have considered the Sanskrit lingual ड as similar in sound;* but it is merely necessary to hear it pronounced by an Afghān mountaineer to convince any one of the total difference; indeed it is almost impossible to give a proper idea of its sound in writing.

ښ *khīn* or *shey*, bears some similarity to the כ *k'ch* of the Chaldaic, and with this exception, no sound like it is to be found amongst the letters of the six hundred alphabets before referred to.†

ڼ or ڼ *urrūn* or *rrūn*, is a combination of the sound of *urray* and ن *nūn*, the latter nasal. It is quite impossible to acquire the real pronunciation, except from an Afghān mouth when using such a word as بانړه *bārrnah*, the eye-lash, or کاڼړي *kārrnaey*, stone. The ڻ *rūn* of the Sindhian language is like it in sound.

Pushto also, like the Semitic dialects, of which family I am inclined to consider it, has the *t'h* with a strong aspiration, to which sound the Persians have an unconquerable antipathy; indeed, their mouths seem to be so formed as to be unable to utter it. Like the Jews and Egyptians, as well as the Arabs, the Afghāns uniformly give the hard sounds, *t'h*, *d'h*, *ds*, *dtz*, *dz*, etc., to those characters which the Persians have ever softened to *z* and *s*. The pronunciation too, is somewhat difficult on account of the use of several gutturals, and the combinations of such letters as ښپ, ګځ, خلک, etc., which are difficult to enunciate.

In harshness of pronunciation, and in the declensions of its nouns, it bears resemblance to the Zend and Pehlavī; and, like the former language, can be, and often is, written in old works, on which alone we can place dependence, by distinct letters in the body of each word, instead of introducing the short vowels. Of the affinity of the Zend and Sanskrit, at present there is no doubt; but the

* Pushto ړ is equivalent to Sanskrit ड

† See "DIE SCHRIFTZEICHEN DES GESAMMTEN ERDKREISES." Vienna. 1851. Also, "ALPHABETE ORIENTALISCHER UND OCCIDENTALISCHER," Sprachen zum Gebrauch für Schriftsetzer und Correctoren. Leipzig. 1850.

Pehlavī appears to have a greater affinity to the Arabic, and to differ little from the present language of Persia.*

In Arabic and Persian it is impossible to sound a consonant which may be the first letter of a word, without the aid of a vowel, whilst in Pus͟hto there are numbers of words beginning with a consonant immediately followed by another; as, شپه *s͟hpah*, 'night;' ورځ *rwadz*, 'day;' غلا *g͟hlā*, 'theft;' ښکته *k͟hkatah*, 'below.'

The vowels and consonants used in Pus͟hto have the same powers as those of the Arabic, Hebrew, and other Semitic dialects. Like them, it has but two genders,—the masculine and feminine; but the former have a dual form, which is wanting in Pus͟hto. In this respect the Afg͟hān also differs distinctly from the Zend and the Sanskrit, both of which have a neuter gender, but agrees with the Pehlavī, from which the modern Persian is derived. In common with the Hebrew, Arabic, and Persian, it has the peculiar separable and inseparable pronouns, the latter being invariably attached to some preceding word, whether a noun, verb, or particle. When attached to nouns they signify possession or propriety; with intransitive verbs in the course of conjugation, they are used in the place of personal pronouns; and, with transitives, point out the objective case.† This is also a peculiar feature of the Sindhīan language, which has several letters in common with Pus͟hto, besides its own peculiar ones. The inflections of the Afg͟hān verbs too, are formed according to the Arabic and Hebrew system, from two original tenses only—the *māzī* or past, and the *muẓāriʿ* or aorist, the past participle being used in the construction of the compound tenses, with the aid of the auxiliary, *to be.* Another peculiarity is, that the intransitive verbs agree in gender with the nominative, whilst the transitives are governed, both in gender and number, by the objective case. In many respects the Pus͟hto syntax agrees with that of the Hebrew; and I have no doubt but that much greater affinity will be found to exist between them, if compared by any one well versed in the latter language.

The Pus͟hto language is spoken with slight variation in orthography and pronunciation, from the valley of Pis͟hīn, south of Ḳandahār, to Kāfiristān, on the north; and from the banks of the Helmand, on the west, to the Aṭṭak, Sindhu, or Indus, on the east—throughout the Sama or plain of the Yūsufzo'es; the mountainous districts of Bājawṛṛ, Pānjkora‡ Suwāt, and Buner, to Astor, on the borders of Little Thibet—an immense tract of country, equal in extent to the entire Spanish peninsula.

The numerous convulsions to which the country of the children of Afg͟hānah

* Sir William Jones stated that "having compared a Pehlavī translation of the inscription in the Gulistān on the diadem of Cyrus, and from the Pāzend words in the Ferang-i Jehāngīri, he became convinced that the Pehlavī is a dialect of the Chaldaic."—Asiatic Researches.

† See "Hebrew Grammar," by Professor Lee, p. 80, Art. 153, p. 260, Art. 220. London. 1827.

‡ *Kor* is the Pus͟hto for 'house,' and *Pānj* the Persian for 'five.'

has been subjected for the last seventy or eighty years, have necessarily affected their language also; hence the great variation observable in the orthography and mode of writing of modern Pus͟hto works. On this account, no dependence whatever can be placed on any manuscript of later date than the reign of the founder of the Durānī empire,—Aḥmād S͟hāh, Abdālī (one of their poetical authors), or, at furthest, of his son, Tīmūr S͟hāh; for it is almost impossible to find two copies of an author, unless written by one person, agreeing on these essential points. I have in my possession a rare prose work, which was written in the reign of the Emperor Aurangzeb, which I picked up in a most out-of-way place—a pawn shop at Bombay. The mode of writing and orthography in it, I have generally adopted, together with that of the Mak͟hzan Afg͟hānī, one of the earliest works we know of, throughout the following pages.

The assistance which I have derived from a knowledge of the dialects of the neighbouring territories, to six of which I have devoted many years, has been very great, indeed more than I can well express. It has enabled me to trace words of Arabic, Persian, Tūrkī, Sanskrit, and Hindī origin, greatly garbled in orthography, and vitiated in pronunciation, which a person unacquainted with them in any way would, in all probability, set down as pure Pus͟hto.

As an example of this, I will mention one instance alone. M. Klaproth, in his apparent eagerness for classing the Belūc͟h language, which is a mixture of Persian, Sindhī, Panjābī, Hindī, and Sanskrit, amongst the Indū-Germanic family of tongues, commits an error, from, I fancy, ignorance of the Persian language. He gives the following table:—*

BELŪC͟H.	GERMAN.	LATIN.	GREEK.	ENGLISH.
S͟has͟h Hapt	Sechs	Sex Septem	Hepta	Six Seven

Now the Persian for six is شش *s͟has͟h*, and seven is هفت *haft*, which two words, to all appearance, have a greater affinity to the Belūc͟h words here mentioned, than to either German, Latin, Greek, or English; in fact, they are precisely the same words, for ف (*f*) is used for and pronounced پ (*p*) indiscriminately, and would be written exactly the same in both languages. If we consider that Belūc͟histān is merely separated from the Persian province of Kirmān by a range of mountains, the similarity is naturally accounted for, without leaving Asia for that purpose, as the learned Professor appears to have done,—"Ea sub oculis posita negligimus: proximorum incuriosi, longinqua sectamur."

I think it will be generally allowed that, at the present time, a knowledge of the language of Afg͟hānistān is a desideratum, holding as we do the Derājāt,

* I am indebted for this to Thornton's "Gazetteer."

Banū Tāk, Kohātt, Peshāwer, and the Samah, or Plain of the Yūsufzo'es, throughout which districts, with the exception of Derā Ghāzī Khān, nine-tenths of the people speak no other dialect. By being acquainted with this language, an officer can communicate personally with the people of the country, and give ear to their complaints, without the aid of moonshees and others as interpreters. In respect to police officers, they can thereby communicate their secret orders direct, without fear of betrayal by a third party. Much discontent and heart-burning is enkindled in the minds of the Afghāns, who are by nature a proud, fiery, and independent race, from having to come into contact with natives of Hindūstān, whom they hold in supreme contempt; and their former triumphs over whom, at Pānīput and other places, they do not appear to have forgotten.

We have also in Sindh and the Panjāb seven local infantry corps,* which contain at least a proportion of one half Afghāns or Rohilas, whose native tongue is Pushto, and many of whom understand Hindūstānī but imperfectly from the lips of a qualified interpreter. A translation of the Articles of War can be easily made, of which a specimen will be found in the appendix to this Grammar. At Courts Martial a colloquial knowledge is indispensable; and all officers in those corps, as well as others holding appointments, of whatever description, beyond the Indus, should be expected to qualify themselves in the Pushto language. The plea hitherto has been the want of books, but I trust that my humble efforts during the last nine years will have removed that excuse.

The Russians appear to have paid considerable attention to, and to have made some progress in, the study of Pushto, if we may judge from the work (although containing very numerous errors) published some time since by Professor Dorn, of St. Petersburg, who was the first to produce a work in the language.

The age of Dost Muhammad Khān is now so great, that in all probability a year or two more must terminate the earthly career of that extraordinary man. His death will be the signal for the commencement of civil dissensions, and doubtless many astonishing changes will take place in Afghānistān. Opportunities may offer themselves for the renewal of friendly intercourse between the two nations, which should not be allowed to pass; and trade and commerce should be encouraged by all and every legitimate means. This effected, there is not much fear of the Russians establishing themselves in Afghānistān; although, should they even succeed in debouching from the Khaiber Pass on the plain of Jamrūd, there is not much doubt but that they will merely add other heaps to the bones which have already whitened on that scene of numerous conflicts.

The object of Russia, however, does not appear to be Afghānistān alone:† for

* This force has been very largely increased within the last two years, and now amounts to some thirty regiments, or even more, many of which, consisting entirely of Afghāns, behaved nobly before Dehlī and other places during the late rebellion.

† "One of the principal objects he (Prince Gortschakoff, Governor-General of Siberia,) had in view, was the organization of a Russian settlement through the Kirghis Steppes, in the direct line to Thibet. The distance, as the crow flies, from Omsk

twelve years back we have heard of their having established a line of Cossack posts, provided with guns, and all the munitions of war, on nine of the twelve hundred *versts* of desert, which separates the city of Omsk, the capital of Western Siberia, from the Thibetan frontier.

Pes͟hāwer, some fifty or sixty years since, was one of the principal seats of Muḥammadan learning, and by many was considered a more learned city than even Bok͟hārā itself.

The custom is for boys and girls of from five to twelve years of age to go to the same school. After learning the letters, they immediately commence reading the Ḳurān in Arabic, but of course without understanding it. On its completion they begin to read some Pus͟hto work, usually a commentary on the Ḳurān, or an explanation of the rites and ceremonies of their faith, such as may be found in the simple little work entitled Ras͟hīd-ul-By'ān, or some such religious subject. After the twelfth year, the girls either attend a dame's school, or, if their parents can afford it, are taught at home. Sometimes boys under twelve years of age, go to a dame's school with grown up girls of fifteen and upwards; but this custom is only prevalent at a distance from towns, as in most large places there are separate schools for males and females. The scholars either pay a small sum monthly to their teacher, or make him a present after having completed the perusal of the Ḳurān, according to the position and means of their parents. Amongst some tribes a portion of land is allotted to the Mullā or Priest, who also acts as village schoolmaster.

to the frontier of Thibet, is twelve hundred *versts*: through a part of this desert the natives are on friendly terms with the Russians. So soon, therefore, as a permanent settlement is established through the whole distance, immense advantages will be gained to Russian commerce. At this moment this object is accomplished in nine hundred *versts*, or three quarters of the way. A line of Cossacks is permanently formed, provided with guns, ammunition, and all the necessaries for a fixed residence, which may be liable to hostile incursions from time to time. The Kirghis, however, stand in such awe of the Cossacks, and the benefits they derive from trading with Russia are so great, that the caravans now go as securely the whole nine hundred *versts*, as in any part of the empire. *Every summer sees some fresh point gained;* and there is no doubt, that in a few years, the Russian dominion will only end where that of Thibet begins. They were for some time stopped by a district more desert and inhospitable than the rest, which was supposed to reach to the Thibetan frontier; but it has been discovered by a Cossack, who was three years prisoner in the country, that it only extends about ninety *versts*, and he described the other side of it as being fertile, well watered, and altogether different from the other Steppes. There will, therefore, probably be no further obstacle to their progress, and a glance at the map will show that *they are much nearer to our Indian frontier here, than by any other road they can take.*

"Once established *as far* as the boundary of Thibet, the Russians will have no great difficulty in obtaining a footing *in it*, and a transit for their merchandize to India would be a matter of course.

"There is at Omsk a military school where five hundred boys are educated, who are to become soldiers, most of them being soldiers' children, some few Kirghis, and the sons of exiles. The establishment is admirably conducted: we went over it several times, and nothing could exceed the regularity and order which prevailed. There is another military school for Cossacks only, and the boys are destined for a different career in some respects from the others. We may safely defy any country in the world to produce an establishment in any way superior to this; our only doubt is, if it is not too good for those who are brought up in it, considering what their future destination is likely to be. The boys are taught drawing, algebra, languages, history, and fortification; the first class, who were all under seventeen years of age, studied principally the Oriental languages, and are intended for interpreters and agents in the East. We were told by General Schramm, who has the superintendence of the school, that most of those who composed the first class understood Mongolish, Arabic, and Persian, and have also native youths to teach them the *patois* of the nomadic tribes.

"We cannot, however, wonder, when these pains are taken in the wilds of Siberia to educate boys for the services they are to perform as men, that Russian diplomatic agents should be so superior to our own; and the habit of thinking such a preparation must have created, cannot fail to give them great advantages as negotiators and general agents."—RECOLLECTIONS OF SIBERIA IN THE YEARS 1840 AND 1841, by C. H. Cottrell, Esq. London: J. W. Parker.

Unlike most eastern nations, the Afghāns appear to regard women in a great measure on an equality with themselves, in this world at least; and the latter generally receive some sort of education.

Many of the Afghān females are famous for their knowledge of Pus̲h̲to, which they both read and write; indeed most of the works on religious subjects, and the rites and ceremonies of the Muḥammadan faith, appear to be perused by them more than by the men. The daughter of the late Dalīl K̲h̲ān, Arbāb, or chief of Torū,* is justly celebrated for her learning, and general proficiency in the Afghān language. Another young person dwelling in the Yūsuf-zī district, supports herself, and also assists her family, by copying Pus̲h̲to books. She writes a nice hand, and copies very correctly: the MS. copy from which my Text Book is printed is chiefly from her pen. The custom with all copyists is, to write their names, and the date on which they complete a work, on the last page; but it being considered a breach of delicacy for a female to sign her own name, she inserts that of her father instead.

The young woman to whom I now refer is unmarried, and declares her intention of leading a single life, and devoting herself to literature. Considering the abject state in which the Muḥammadan women are kept, I think this a very favourable feature in the Afghān character.

The Afghān language, taking all things into consideration, is very rich in literature. There have been numerous poets, of whom Æabd-ur-Raḥmān, who flourished in the reign of the Moghal Emperor, Aurangzeb, is, perhaps, the best known, and, consequently, most generally esteemed. He was a Mullā or Priest; and his writings, which are of a religious and moral character, are collected in the form of a Dīwān,—a Persian term, given to a certain number of odes ending with each letter of the alphabet, from *a* to *y*. The Dīwān is the mode in which most of the poetical works are arranged.

The next most popular poet, whose poems would be the more highly esteemed if better known, particularly in Europe, is K̲h̲ūs̲h̲ḥāl K̲h̲ān, the celebrated chief of the powerful clan of K̲h̲aṭṭak, in the reigns of S̲h̲ah Jehān and Aurangzeb. A warrior as well as a poet, he passed the greater portion of his life in struggling against the oppressive power of the latter Emperor; and defeated the Moghal troops in many an engagement, as he proudly mentions in his "Ode to Spring." Some of his odes, written during his exile in India, are very beautiful, and evince a spirit of patriotism and love of home and country not usual in the Oriental heart, but such as we might look for in the Scottish Highlander or the Swiss mountaineer. The following verse from a poem, written during his confinement in the fortress of Gwalior, by order of Aurangzeb, is characteristic of the man:—

Cheer up then heart! I have by me, A healing balm for every throe—
That K̲h̲ūs̲h̲ḥāl K̲h̲ān's an Afghān true, Aurangzeb's mortal foe.

* Torū, or Tolū, is a town or cluster of villages in the Yūsufzo'e country, about eleven miles north of Noh̲s̲h̲airah, and containing about 5,000 inhabitants.

Khushhāl was unfortunate with regard to some of his children, of whom he had no less than fifty-seven sons, besides a number of daughters. One of these sons, named Bahrām, several times attempted to obtain possession of his father's person to place him in confinement, and, on more than one occasion, even made attempts on his life, in order to get the chieftainship into his own hands.

Notwithstanding all these troubles, however, he was a most voluminous writer, and composed no less (it is said by his family) than three hundred and sixty works, both in the Afghān and the Persian language. The names even of most of these are now lost; but the following are a few which have come under my own observation:—1. A Dīwān, or collection of odes; 2. Kuliyāt, containing an immense number of poems and odes; 3. The Bāz Nāmah, a treatise on the diseases of hawks and falcons, with their cure; 4. Hadāyah, a work on religious jurisprudence, translated from the Arabic; 5. Æināyah, on the same subject, and from the same language; 6. Dastār Nāmah, a treatise on the turban, and the various modes of wrapping it round the head, and the prayers to be used on such occasions; 7. Ṣiḥhat-ud-dīn, a medical work; 8. Faẓal Nāmah, a dispute between the sword and the pen, with the peculiar excellencies of both; and 9. Rubāæiyāt, a collection of stanzas of four lines.

Khushhāl also invented a sort of short-hand, or cipher, which was known only to himself and family. It is termed *zanjīrī*, or 'chained.' I have several specimens in my possession, but the key has been lost for many years.

A History of the Afghāns has been erroneously attributed to Khushhāl Khān by Mr. Elphinstone, who is so generally correct; as also a translation into Pushto, of Pilpay's Fables—the Anwāri Suhailī of the Persian—and entitled Æayār Dānish, or 'Touchstone of Wisdom.' This is, however, incorrect. The author of the history in question, the only known copy of which I have now before me, is Afẓal Khān, the son of Ashraf Khān, who, on the death of his father in the Dakhan, where he had been confined as a state prisoner for the last ten years of his life, succeeded his grandfather, Khushhāl, in the chieftainship of the Khattak tribe. The work is very extensive, consisting of upwards of 1,600 pages in small folio, and is entitled, Tārīkh-i-Murraṣṣæ, or the 'Gold and Gem Studded History.' The translation of Pilpay's Fables is also by Afẓāl Khān, and was, as he states in the Preface, undertaken in his fifty-third year, from the abridgment of the Anwāri Suhailī, by the celebrated Ab-ul-Faẓal, minister of the Emperor Akbar, and made by direction of that monarch. It was entitled 'Kalīlah-wo-Damnah;' and is a great improvement on the bombastic and long-drawn style of the original. Afẓal Khān's work may have at first been named Æayār Dānish; but in the Preface he says, that on a second revision, he determined to give his work the title of Æilm Khānah-i-Dānish, or the 'Science-house of Knowledge;' or 'Kalīlah-wo-Damnah'—the names of the two wise jackals mentioned in the work. This book is rare.

Afẓal Khān wrote a few other works, and made a number of translations from Arabic and Persian, chiefly historical, viz.:—Aœsam-i-Kūfī, containing the principal incidents of the life of Muḥammad; Si'ar-i-Mullā Maœīn; and Tafsīr-i-Ḳur'ān, a commentary on the Ḳurān. He left four sons, one of whom Kāẓim, surnamed Shaidā, or 'The Lovelorn,' was the author of a Dīwān, the original and only known copy of which, most beautifully written, with the author's own revisional marks, is in my possession. His style is not so simple as that of the Afghan poets generally—the great charm of their writings—but his poems are of a superior order. He uses many Persian words; and the odes approach nearer than any others to the polish of the poetry of the Persians.

The literary talent, inherent, it would appear, in Khushhāl's family, is surprizing. Five of his sons are also the authors of many excellent works:—

Ashraf Khān, the eldest son, appears to have passed a considerable portion of his life as a state prisoner of Aurangzeb, who probably imagined that Khushhāl's patriotism would be restrained as long as his firstborn should remain in his power. The name assumed by Ashraf, according to the custom of eastern poets, is 'The Severed or Exiled;' and, as might well be imagined, his poems are most pathetic in their style, but at the same time contain many admirable sentiments. The place of Ashraf's exile was Bijāpūr, a strong fortress in the Dakhan, and where his poems were composed: here, too, it was that he died, severed from home and friends.

Æabd-ul-Ḳādir Khān, who wielded his sword as bravely as his pen, wrote a Dīwān, or collection of odes, and the love tale of Adam and Durkhāna'i, so celebrated throughout the Afghān country. He also translated into Pushto, Jāmī's poem of Yūsuf and Zulīkhā; and the Gulistān and Bostān of Shaykh Sāœdī; all three celebrated works in the Persian language; and a little work entitled Muœamma, or 'Enigmas and Rebuses.'

Ṣadr Khān—another son—was the author of a Dīwān, and a poem on the popular love tale of Adam and Durkhāna'ī, already referred to. He also translated into Afghānī the well-known Persian poem of Khusrau and Shīrīn of Nizāmī, the first of Persia's romantic poets.

Another son—Sikandar Khān—wrote the poem of Mihr-wo-Mushtarī; and a collection of odes.

A fifth son — Gohar Khān—also wrote a number of minor poems, together with numerous enigmas and chronograms.

Æabd-ur-Raḥīm, Nuṣrāt Khān, Shāhzādah Sikandar, Æajab Khān, Kāmgār Khān, and others of the family, were also gifted with the poetical genius, but their compositions are not to be met with in the present day.

Another still more singular circumstance regarding this family, and particularly when we consider the condition of females in Eastern countries, is the fact that numbers of the ladies of Khushhāl's family were also gifted with the *cacoëthes scribendi*, and composed numerous poems! One of Khushḥāl's own wives, the mother of Ashraf Khān, was a poetess of no mean powers; and although the mention of the females of their families is a most delicate matter with all Afghāns, I have been so fortunate in my researches, that, with the aid of a friendly chief, to whom I am under considerable obligations, I have been able to obtain some of the poetical effusions of the lady referred to, who, it must be remembered, wrote two hundred years since. These will appear in the TEXT-BOOK; and also in the translations of some of the choicest of the Afghān poems, a selection from which, together with the memoirs of the different authors, I hope, in the course of next year, to offer to the public in an English dress.

I have also been so fortunate as to discover, since the first edition of this Grammar was published three years since, a collection of poems of great merit, by Khwājah Muḥammad of the Bangash tribe, whose work has seldom been heard of, much less seen, in Afghānistan itself. The author lived in Aurangzeb's reign, and led the life of a recluse.

The poems of Aḥmad Shāh Abdālī, the great founder of the Durānī monarchy, and the conqueror of the Murāthī host at Pānīpat, are principally in an amorous and metaphysical strain. His poetry is much esteemed, more so, perhaps, than its merit demands.

The next author to be noticed is Mullā Æabd-ul-Ḥamīd, who flourished in the time of Timūr, the son and successor of Aḥmad Shāh, towards the latter part of the last century. His odes, which are mostly of an amorous or moral tendency, contain many admirable sentiments, which would be creditable to any European author. He is the cynical poet and Shaykh Sāædī of the Pushto; and I must say I prefer his poems to any of the others, except those of Khushḥāl, whose style, however, is very different. Up to the present day he has certainly never been, neither is he likely to be, surpassed; and the beauty of his compositions is even acknowledged amongst a nation so rich in poets as the Persians, by whom he is styled 'Ḥamīd, the hair-splitter.' The numerous extracts I have taken from his works, as examples in the Grammar, will give some idea of his poems. His odes are entitled, Dur-wo-Marjān—'Pearls and Corals.' He is also the author of a poem called Nairang-i-æishḳ, or 'Love's Fascination.' It appears to have been translated from a Persian work of the same name, the author of which was a native of the Panjāb.

The next poet in point of popularity is Mīrzā Khān, a descendant of the notorious Bāyizīd Anṣārī, the founder of the Roshānīān sect, presently to be referred to. His odes are highly metaphysical in their strain, and in accordance with the mystical tenets of the sect; but, at the same time, I must acknowledge that some of them are very sublime. He has been sometimes erroneously called Fat'ḥ Khān, Yūsufzī, which also led me astray in my remarks on the literature of the Afghāns, in the first edition of this work. His poems are somewhat rare.

Ḳāsim Æelī Khān, of the notorious tribe of Afrīdī, is the author of a Dīwān; but his odes bear the stamp of mysticism, and are of no particular merit. He was, however, a Hindūstānī Afghān, a very different style of being to the real. He was born at Farrukhābād, in Hindūstān, in the time of Nawwāb Muẓaffar Jang; and, according to the account given of himself in one of his odes, he was acquainted with Afghānī, Arabic, Tūrkī, Persian, Hindī, and a little English. He has devoted an entire ode to the abuse of the English, just arrived in India, whom—forestalling the first Napoleon—he denominates "A nation of shop-keepers, who, in Hindūstān, have turned soldiers."

There are other poetical works of great merit in the Pus̲hto language, now rarely to be met with; such as the Dīwān of Shāh Sharf, of Jelalābād, which is said to be superior to Hamid's; and that of Pīr Muḥammad of Kandahār; the Dīwān of Æelī Khān; the poems of Dawlat, said to have been a Hindū; and those of Miān Æabd-ur-Raḥīm; Meher Æelī; Arzānī; Ghulām Ḳādir; Latārr; Æelī Khān; Karīm Khān; Jān Muḥammad; Fāẓil; Mukhlis; Ṣāḥib Shāh; and Meher Shāh. Shāh Sharf also translated the Arabic poem, known as the Ḳasīdah Bardah, into Pus̲hto.

Mullā Dādīn, Khattak, who flourished in the reign of Aḥmad Shāh, Abdālī, also composed a collection of odes, as well as a little work on theology, entitled Muntakhab-ul-æaḳāyid, from the Arabic.

There are also a few living poets whose compositions are by no means deficient in merit, the chief of whom are Mī'ān Muḥammad Bāḳir, surnamed Æabd, and Mī'ān Muḥammad, surnamed Naghzī; but their works have not been published.

The romantic and interesting poems of Saif-ul-Mulūk and Badrī Jamāl, by Ghulām Muḥammad; and Bahrām Gūr, by Fy'āz, must not be overlooked. The authors were minstrels who sung their own compositions on festive occasions, much in the same manner as our bards of old. These effusions were frequently composed at the request of, or to be dedicated to, some chieftain who generally paid liberally for the honour. The other few works deserving of notice, are: The Tale of the Rose and the Pine; The Jang Nāmah of Amīr Hamzah; Shāh Gadā, 'The King of the Beggars'; and a few others.

There are some poetical works of less importance, pretty generally known, viz.: The Tale of Sulṭān Jumjumah, by Emām-ud-Dīn; Mærāj Nāmah, by Ghulām Muḥammad; Rashīd-ul-By'ān, by Akhūnd Rashīd, a sort of religious Text-book and Catechism for women and children; Mukhammas,* of Æabd-ul-Ḳādir; Majmūæāt-i-Ḳandahārī, and a few others of a similar character.

The works of many authors are little known, because all books have to be copied by the professional scribes chiefly, as was the case in the dark ages of

* A kind of verse containing five lines.

Europe before Guttenburg conferred his blessing on mankind; and the charge for transcribing is high. It follows, therefore, that only those in comparatively easy circumstances can afford to purchase such expensive luxuries as books.

The prose writings are also numerous, particularly on divinity.

The most ancient author amongst the Eastern Afghāns, that I am able to discover, is Shaykh Malī, a chief of the Yūsufzīs, who wrote a history of the conquest of Suwāt, and other mountain countries north of the Kābul river, by that powerful tribe, between the years 816 and 828 of the Hijrah—A.D. 1413 to 1424—and the account of the measurement by his orders of the conquered lands, and distribution of them amongst the different clans and families of Yūsuf and Mandarr, and the Kābulīs, Lamghānīs, and people of Nangrahār, who had accompanied them in their immigration into the Peshāwer valley. It was Shaykh Malī who instituted the *wesh*, or interchange of land every three or four years, peculiar to the Yūsufzīs and a few petty clans connected with them, referred to by Elphinstone in his "Account of Caubul,"* under the name of *waish*, and which is, as in days of yore, rigidly observed in the present day.

Some years subsequently, in the year of the Hijrah 900—A.D. 1494—Khān Kajū became chief of the Yūsufzīs; and during his rule the conquest of Buner and Panjkorah was completed. Of these events he wrote an account, and included in it the history of the Yūsufzī tribe, from the period of its departure from Kābul, during the reign of Mīrzā Ulugh Beg, grandson of Timūr, down to his own time.†

Both these works are extensive, but they are not procurable. They would be invaluable, as being likely to throw some light on the Suwātī dynasty of the Jehāngīrīān Sultāns, claiming descent from Alexander the Great, and who, up to the conquest by the Yūsufzīs, held all the hill countries north of the Kābul river, as far west as the Indus, together with the Alpine Punjāb as far east as the Jhīlum or Hydaspes.

The other more important prose writings are those of Bāzīd, or Bāyizīd Anṣārī, the founder of the Roshānīān sect, whose tenets caused such a sensation throughout the Afghān countries, and some parts of India, during the reign of the Emperor Akbar. Bāzīd took to himself the name of Pīr-i-Roshān, or the 'Saint of Light,' from the Persian word '*roshān*,' signifying 'light,' and hence the name given to the whole sect. One work is entitled Khair-ul-By'ān, or 'Exposition of Goodness,' written in four languages—Pushto or Afghānī, Arabic, Persian, and Hindī, to which Akhūnd Darwezah gave the title of Sharr-ul-By'ān, or 'Exposition of Depravity;' another, entitled Khurpān, the meaning of which word is not known at present, a burlesque on the word, "Furkān," as the Kurān is also called; and,

* Vol. ii., p. 20.

† This history is the one from which the Persian work, Tārīkh Ḥāfiz Raḥmat Khānī, now in the East India House, was composed, A.H. 1184.

like the others, is written in contempt of the Muḥammadan faith; together with several pamphlets on the same subject. Copies of his works are exceedingly scarce, all having been burnt on which the Mullās could lay their hands during his lifetime, and at his death, and the subsequent dispersion of the sect. There are no doubt copies existing in the possession of those who still secretly follow his doctrines, and they are not a few, but they fear to produce them.

Bāzīd or Pīr Roshān was principally assisted in his literary labours by Mullā Arzānī, whose pen was a very sharp one. The latter was also the author of a Diwān, and other poetical works, which have now entirely disappeared.

The Makhzan-ul-asrār, or Makhzan Afghānī, as it is more commonly called, was written, as well as other works, by Akhūnd Darwezah,* the venerated Saint of the Afghāns, in refutation of the opinions of Pīr Roshān, who found a bitter antagonist in the Ākhūnd, who conferred upon him the nick-name of Pīr-i-Tārīk, or the 'Saint of Darkness,' by which he is best known in Afghānistān up to the present day. Akhūnd Darwezah is said to have been the author of upwards of fifty works, the greater number pamphlets probably; but with the exception of the foregoing, and the Tazkirat-ul-abarār, in Persian, they are not known in the present day. His son Karīm Dād appears to have assisted his father in the composition of these works.

The other prose writings remaining to be noticed, are, the Fawā'īd-ush-Sharī'aa'h, or 'Advantages of the Laws Ecclesiastical,' a very valuable work, written in the year A.H. 1125, A.D. 1713, by Ākhūnd Ḳāsim, who was the chief prelate and the head of all the Muḥammadan ecclesiastics of Hasht-nagar and Peshāwer, which places, in those days, rivalled Bokhārā itself, in learning; the works of Bābū Jān, a converted Sī-āh-posh Kāfir, who, having acquired a great name amongst the Muḥammadans for his learning, again relapsed; the Jang Nāmah, containing the history of Ḥasan and Ḥusain, by Ghulām Muḥammad; another work on the same subject by Sayyid Ḥasan, written about a hundred years since; the Nūr Nāma'h, by Jān Muḥammad; Adam and Durkhāna'ī, by Fakhr-ud-Dīn, Ṣaḥibzādah; Gulistān-i-Raḥmat, by Nawwāb Muḥammad Mustajib Khān, in the year 1800 A.D.; Tafsīr, a commentary and paraphrase of the Ḳur'ān; Hazār Masā'īl; Ḥiyātu-l-Mumīnīn; Akhīr Nāma'h, and several others. Copious extracts from the choicest of the works mentioned in the foregoing pages, both poetical and prose, will be found in the TEXT BOOK, published at the same time as this work.

Besides the translations into Pushto from the Persian and Arabic authors

* Professor Dorn in his "Chrestomathy" states that Akhūnd Darwezah was the first author who composed in the Afghan language; but he neither states how he has arrived at this conclusion, nor his authority for such a statement. In the same manner he considers Khūshḥāl Khān to be the author of Adam Khān and Durkhāna'ī. Both conclusions are entirely incorrect. Shaykh Malī, as shown in the preceding page, wrote his history about a century-and-a-half before. In the same manner, it is proved that two of Khushḥāl's sons, each composed a poem on the love tale of Adam Khān and Durkhāna'ī. Another version, in prose, by one Fakhr-ud-Dīn, was written about a hundred years ago.

already enumerated, both poetical and prose, there are a few others which have come under my own observation:—the Gulistān of Sāædī, translated by Amīr Muḥammad, Anṣārī; Majnūn and Lailā of Jāmī, by Bai Khān, of Buner; the Kasīdah Surī'ānī; and the Kasīdah Bardah, by Akhūnd Darwezah.*

There are two valuable lexicographical works,—the Rī'āz-ul-Maḥabbat, or 'Gardens of Friendship,' by the Nawwāb Ḥāfiẓ Maḥabbat Khān, compiled at the request of Sir George Barlow in 1805–6. It is an extensive work, but is chiefly devoted to the conjugation of the Afghān verbs, which are exceedingly difficult from their irregularity. The author, however, was a native of Hindūstān; and many peculiarities regarding the verbs and tenses, of which he must have been ignorant, have been omitted. The vocabulary is valuable. The other work, entitled Æajā'ib-ul-Lughat, or 'Curiosities of Language,' was written about the year 1808, by Nawwāb Allāh Yār Khān of the Barech tribe, who was also a native of India, but it is very valuable.

There is a host of ballad writers, and some of their compositions, sung by the wandering minstrels, are very spirited, and put me in mind of those of our own land. During my residence at Peshāwer I had several of them written out. The following is a specimen of one which I have attempted to turn into English ballad style, retaining in some measure the metre of the original. The translation is almost literal.

THE FIGHT AT NOHSHAIRAH.†

In misery and grief I'm plung'd.
By ruthless Fate's decree;
Alas! that from its cruel laws
There's no escape for me.

What shall I say of Abbās Khān.
That Khaṭṭak chief so bold;
At his sad fate I'm sorely griev'd.
And that by me 'tis told.

He first did march to Wuzīr Bāgh,‡
Where cypresses do wave;
And there he muster'd all his clan—
They were like lions brave.

He from Peshāwer then did start,
For Æaẓīm Khān to fight;
And with five hundred Khaṭṭaks true,
He reached Nohshair that night.

* The so-called translation into Pushto of the New Testament, made by the Serampore Missionaries in 1818, bears a very slight resemblance to the Sacred Writings; in fact, it is quite painful to read. I will merely give one specimen—the well-known verse from the Sermon on the Mount—"*Judge not, that ye be not judged.*" The Pushto is in the following terms:—

انصاف مکوئي دَ پارد دَ ديه چه انصاف کړي شوي به نشيّ

"*Do not justice unto any one, lest justice shall be done unto you!!*" Is this Christian doctrine? Verily, if Infidels are to judge of our religion from such translations as this, it is not to be wondered at that they should scoff at it, hold our faith in ridicule, and call us kāfirs or blasphemers. It is quite evident that, in making this translation, the English has been merely transposed for the Pushto, without the slightest consideration as to difference of idiom, style, and arrangement of the languages. I trust the other translations of the Scriptures are better than the Pushto one, which is the most ridiculous thing I have ever met with.

† The battle of Nohshairah was fought in 1823, between the Afghāns under Sirdār Muḥammad Æaẓīm Khān, Bārakzo'e, brother of Dost Muḥammad Khān, and the Sikhs under Runjīt Singh, in which Abbās Khān, Khattak was slain, besides a host of Yūsufzo'es.

‡ The Wūzīr Bāgh, or Minister's Garden, lies outside the city of Peshāwer to the south. It contains a residence, and was remarkable on account of the number of cypress trees it formerly contained. The garden was laid out by Sirdār Fat'ḥ Khān, the celebrated Wūzīr of Muḥammad Shāh, and the brother of Dost Muḥammad Khān, Bārakzo'e, ruler of Kābul. The garden has since been chiefly occupied by the other brother, Sulṭān Muḥammad Khān, and his numerous Ḥaram.

When morning dawn'd, the Sikhs advanc'd
  The Afghān host to crush;
But Ghāzīs* they, on Nānak's sons†
  Did like a torrent rush.

On Khaibar's heights, when rains do pour,
  And wintry blasts do blow,
The little rills, to torrents swell'd,
  All Jamrūd's plain ‡ o'erflow.

That day they kill'd of Singhs enough
  Of heads to raise a dome;
But 'twas decree'd Nohshairah's plain
  To them should be a tomb.

At eventide, the chieftain's steed
  Fell midst a heap of slain;
By night, his band, oh! where were they?
  Dead on the bloody plain!

Night clos'd around him, still he fought,
  All faint and out of breath:
A Hourī's § hand the Sherbat gives;
  The Martyr meets his death.

To spare his life, the Sikhs they did
  Pledge every sacred word:
No Heav'n they dread—deceitful foes!
  They put him to the sword.

In Akorra‖ when this tale was told,
  The people were dismay'd;
And when night came, the hero's corse
  They from the field convey'd.

It seem'd the latter day was come,
  So sore aggriev'd were they;
And minstrels did their rebeks break,
  Deep sorrow to display.

Next morning from Akorra then
  Set out a mournful train;
And to Peshāwer bore the corpse,
  Of him so basely slain.

The people of Peshāwer wept,
  When they his fate did hear;
And then they laid the body in
  The grave-yard of Pānj Pīr. ¶

Hakīm! lament for Abbās Khān,
  That Khattak chief so bold;
Oh where! the like of him, oh where!
  Shall we again behold?

* Ghāzī—one who fights against infidels, a gallant soldier.

† Nānak—the name of the Saint of the Sikhs, and the founder of the sect.

‡ "Jamrūd's plain"—"After heavy rains in the mountains, the rivulets, swelled to torrents, rush from the hills with violence, and carry everything before them." See my Account of Peshāwer: On the rivers of the Province. "Bombay Geographical Transactions," 1851-52.

§ Hourī—a black-eyed nymph of the Muhammadan Paradise, of which every true believer is to have no less than seventy-two.

‖ Akorrā is a small town about ten miles west of the Indus or Attak: it is the chief town of the Khattak tribe.

¶ "The grave-yard of Pānj Pīr"—the Zī'ārat-i-Pānj Pīr, or the "Shrine of the Five Saints," is situated about a mile south-east of Peshāwer.

ERRATA.

INTRODUCTION.

PAGE	LINE	FOR	READ
11 (note)	24	Ismæīl,	Ismāæīl.

GRAMMAR.

PAGE	LINE	FOR	READ
2	25	ځ	ځي
9	30	pierceth,	piercest.
31	30	شوئِي	شوئي
39	31	behaveth,	behavest.
41	27	پوي ليږي	په ويليږي
76	20	ژړه مي	ژړوي or ژړدوي
96	13	وُروي	وُرو
99	9	رسيدلي	رسيدلۍ
103	4	كړيږي	كړئي
113	14	from,	for.
,,	33	brother's,	brothers'.
121	11	hisown,	his own.
122	28	found,	finds.
123	10	called,	calls.
,,	28	heard,	hears.
137	23	itcomes,	it comes.
151	33	have done,	have *or* has done.
152	8	have done,	have *or* has done.
154	35	شوِ شولِ	شوِ or شولِ
162	12	caused to fly, etc.	caused to fly.
164	14	را وړه	راوړد
177	15	*yai-i-nisbut*,	*yā-i-nisbut*.
193	25	my water-vessel,	MY water-vessel.

APPENDIX.

PAGE	LINE	FOR	READ
200	16	كه سپاهِي وي	كه سپاهۍ وي
204	18	خوشحلي	خوشحالي
,,	23	ځري	ځوي

A

GRAMMAR

OF THE

PUK͟HTO OR PUS͟HTO LANGUAGE.

" In languages which have both a *written* and a *spoken* form, the usages of the former rather than the latter are held to determine the rules of grammar. The *written* is always more perfect than the *spoken* form of a language. The latter exhibits *actual* usage; but the former exhibits also *national* and *reputable* usage."   J. M. M'CULLOCH, D.D.

CHAPTER I.

THE ALPHABET.

1.   THE Pus͟hto, or language of the Afghāns, is written in the ‎ﻧﺴﺦ *naskh* character of Arabic, which is of the same general use amongst the Arabs as the Roman in Europe.*   It succeeded the Kūfik in which the Ḳor'ān was first written; and is considered to have had a common origin with the Hebrew and Chaldaik, from the Semitic.†

2.   It was invented in the third century of the Hijrah by Ibn Moklah, who was successively *wazīr* or minister to the K͟hālifs, Al Moktadir, Al Ḳāhir, and Al Rādī, who occupied the throne of Bāghdād about three hundred years after the time of the Prophet—from 908 to 940 of our era; and was subsequently altered and improved by Nāzim and Tograi, who were respectively ministers to the K͟hālifs, Jelāl-ud-Dīn and Māsūd.   It was brought to great perfection by Alī Ibn Bowāb, who flourished in the following century, and other celebrated caligraphists, amongst whom was Yaḳūt-al-Mostāsimī, the Secretary of Al Mostāsim, the eighth of the Abbāsīdis, with whom the glory of his family and nation expired.‡

3.   The original Pus͟hto alphabet, before the introduction of foreign words into the language, consisted of twenty-nine different sounds only, as may be seen by comparison with old manuscripts; but, at present, the Afghāns also use the twenty-eight Arabian letters, with the addition of the extra four—‎پ, ‎چ, ‎ژ, and ‎ک—

---

* The Sindīān language is also written in the *naskh*.   † See Introduction, p 4.   ‡ Gibbon, vol. ii., p. 335.

adopted by the Persians, altogether making a total of forty characters, the whole of which are consonants.

4. Several letters assume different shapes according to their position at the commencement, middle, or end of a word; the names, order, and figures of which may be seen in the following table.

PUS'HTO LETTERS.

UNCON-NECTED.	MEDIAL.	INITIAL.	NAMES.	NAMES.	ROMAN.	EXAMPLES.
ا	ا	ا	الف	*alif*	a, ā, i, u,	As in English.
ب	ـبـ	بـ	بي	*bey*	b.	,, ,,
پ	ـپـ	پـ	پي	*pey*	p.	,, ,,
ت	ـتـ	تـ	تي	*tey*	t.	,, ,,
ټ	ـټـ	ټـ	ټي	*ttey*	tt.	By reverting the point of the tongue [to the palate.
ث	ـثـ	ثـ	ثي	*sey*	s.	As *th* in *thing*, or lisped *s*.
څ	ـڅـ	څـ	څي	*tzey*	ts *or* tz.	As *ts* or *tz*, in Hebrew צ *tsode*.
ج	ـجـ	جـ	جيم	*jīm*	j.	As *j* in *judge*.
چ	ـچـ	چـ	چي	*chey*	ch.	As in *church*.
ح	ـحـ	حـ	حي	*ḥey*	ḥ.	Strongly aspirated, as in double *h*.
خ	ـخـ	خـ	خي	*khey*	kh.	Guttural, as *ch* in Scotch *loch*.
د	ـد	د	دال	*dāl*	d.	As in *dear*.
ډ	ـډ	ډ	ډال	*ddāl*	dd.	Harsh, as double *d*, or Sanskrit ड.
ذ	ـذ	ذ	ذال	*zāl*	z.	As in *zeal;* by Arabs *dth*.
ر	ـر	ر	ري	*rey*	r.	As in *run*.
ړ	ـړ	ړ	ړي	*rrey*	rr.	As broad Northumbrian *r*.
ز	ـز	ز	زي	*zey*	z.	As in English.
ځ	ـځـ	ځـ	ځ	*dzey*	ds *or* dz.	As *ds* or *dz* would be in English, or [Hebrew ז *dsain*.
ژ	ـژ	ژ	ژي	*jzey*	jz.	As *s* in pleasure, or soft French *j*.
ږ	ـږ	ږ	ږي	*jzey*	jz.	By reverting the point of the tongue on the palate. It is a slight degree harsher than the Persian ژ.
س	ـسـ	سـ	سين	*sīn*	s.	As in *sense*.
ش	ـشـ	شـ	شين	*shīn*	sh.	As *sh* in *shell*.
ښ	ـښـ	ښـ	ښين	*khīn* *shey*	kh (E.) sh (W.)	Peculiar to Pushto. Pronounced by bringing the tip of the tongue to the roof of the mouth.

UNCONNECTED.	MEDIAL.	INITIAL.	NAMES.	NAMES.	ROMAN.	EXAMPLES.
ص	ـصـ	صـ	صاد	*ṣwād*	ṣ. *or* ss.	As *ss* in *dissolve*.
ض	ـضـ	ضـ	ضاد	*ẕwād*	ẕ.	As in English; by Arabs *dwd*.
ط	ـطـ	طـ	طوي	*ṯoey*	ṯ.	English *t* with slight aspiration.
ظ	ـظـ	ظـ	ظوي	*ẕoey*	ẕ.	,, ,, ,, [change of vowel points.
ع	ـعـ	عـ	عين	*aæin*	æ *or* â.	Guttural; becomes also *i*, *o*, *u*, by
غ	ـغـ	غـ	غين	*ghain*	gh.	Guttural.
ف	ـفـ	فـ	في	*fey*	f.	English *f*.
ق	ـقـ	قـ	قاف	*ḳāf*	ḳ *or* q.	Guttural.
ك	ـكـ ـک	كـ کـ	كاف	*kāf*	k.	As in *king*.
گ	ـگـ	گـ	گاف	*gāf*	g.	As in *give*.
ل	ـلـ	لـ	لام	*lām*	l.	As English *l*.
م	ـمـ	مـ	ميم	*mīm*	m.	,, ,,
ن	ـنـ	نـ	نون	*nūn*	n.	,, ,,
ڼ	ـڼـ ـڼ	ڼـ ڼ	نون	*rrnūn*	rrn.	{ Pronounced *rrūn*, a combination of the sounds of ړ and ن. Peculiar to Pushto and Sindhian.
و	ـو	و	واو	*wāo*	w, ū, o, ow.	According to the vowel points.
ه, ـه, ـهـ	ـهـ	هـ	هي	*hey*	h.	Slightly aspirated.
ي	ـيـ	يـ	يي	*yey*	{ y, e, ī, ai, aey, a'ī or ey }	According to the vowel points.
ء	ـئـ	ئـ	همزه	*hamza'h*		As another form of *alif*.

Books are occasionally to be met with in which the letters peculiar to Pushto are rejected for others, either through the ignorance or affectation of the copyist. Thus, ټ and ټ for ت; چ and څ for خ; ډ for د; ړ and ړ for ر; ږ for ژ; and کب for ك or ښ.*

5. The eastern Afghāns, such as the tribes of Peshāwer, the Ut-mān Khel, the Yūsufzīs of the Sama'h, of Suwāt, Panjkorah, and Buner, and many others, often change the خ occurring in Persian words, used in Pushto, into ښ, which they pronounce *khīn*, and use the letter گ instead of ږ. In the same manner the western Afghāns invariably give ښ the softer sound of *shey*, and use ږ in place of گ. The Dāmānīs and Ghalzīs substitute چ for څ; and the Khaiberīs alter the place of the letters so much that at first it is difficult to understand them.

* The system of orthography followed for the last three centuries or more, with these exceptions, was first arranged by Akhūnd Darwezah, the celebrated saint of the Afghāns, and the great antagonist of Pīr Roshān, the founder of the Roshanian sect.

6. Although the different tribes are widely dispersed, and often hold little or no intercourse with each other, no very considerable variation exists with regard to the pronunciation, beyond what has been noticed above. Where such cases occur, the ear will be found a sure, and at the same time, easy guide, together with the knowledge of the powers of the Arabian letters, with which the student is supposed to be already acquainted.

THE VOWELS.

حرکات *ḥarkāt.*

7. There are three vowels in Pus̲h̲to, as in Arabic and Persian; viz.: (ـَ) زبر *zabar*, or فتحه *fat'ḥa'h*; (ـِ) زير *zer*, or كسره *kasra'h*; and (ـُ) پيش *pes̲h̲*, or ضمه *ẕamma'h*.

8. The consonants ا, و, ي, are often found in old manuscript works, used instead of these vowel points; and, in this respect, the language bears a striking resemblance to the Zend and Sanskrit, which express all the long and short vowels by distinct marks. This will be more fully explained in another place.

9. The vowels, if not followed by the letters ا, و, ي, represent the short vowels *a*, *i*, *u*, respectively; thus بَ *ba*, بِ *bi*, and بُ *bu*; but the consonant must invariably begin the syllable.

10. Should the vowels be followed by ا, و, ي, respectively, then the syllable is long, as با *bā*, بِي *bī*, بُو *bū*; and these three letters ا, و, ي, are then called quiescent and homogeneous with their preceding vowels.

11. When (ـَ) *zabar* is followed by و or ي, the syllable then becomes a dipthong, as بَو *bau* or *bow*, بَي *bai*, or *baey*.

12. There are some cases in Persian in which و preceded by خ having the vowel *fat'ḥa'h* or *zabar*, and succeeded by ا, is very slightly, if at all, sounded. Thus خواب (sleep) is pronounced *k̲h̲'āb* not *k̲h̲wāb*, and خوان (a table) *k̲h̲'ān*, not *k̲h̲wān*. It must, however, be borne in mind that it is quite the *contrary in Pus̲h̲to*, and *all* the letters must be sounded; for example—خواري *k̲h̲wārī*, 'humility,' خواښي *k̲h̲wāk̲h̲ey* or *k̲h̲wās̲h̲ey*, 'a wife's mother.'

13. ْ or ^, جزم *jazm*, or جزمه *jazma'h*, placed over a consonant, shows that the letter is quiescent and the syllable ends there; as پَرْهَر *par-har*, 'a wound,' څَرْمَن *ts̲ar-man*, 'leather.'

14. ~, مدّه, or مدّ, *madda'h* or *madd*, is another form of ا (*alif*), and, placed over a letter, prolongs the sound; as آس *ās*, 'a horse,' آغزي *āg̲h̲zaey*, 'a thorn,' and آخښ *āk̲h̲k̲h̲*, 'alas!'

15. ّ, تشديد *tashdīd*, signifies that the consonant must be doubled; but this remark has a reference more to Arabic words used in Pushto than Pushto itself; thus, تولاّ *tawallā*, 'friendly.'

16. ٓ, وصل *waṣl*, serves to connect Arabic words, in which the Arabian article ال (*al*) is lost in the pronunciation, if the letters be either ت, ث, د, ذ, ر, ز, س, ش, ص, ض, ل or ن; as for example قال الرسول *ḳāl ār rasūlu*, 'The Prophet said;' قل الحق *ḳul-il ḥaḳḳu*, 'Speak the truth.'

17. ٔ, همزه *hamza'h*, is another form of *alif*, as أ or ء *a*, إ or ء *i*, أ or ء *u*. The Persians call it softened *hamza'h*.

18. As the Pushto writings, particularly those on Theology and the like, contain a number of Arabic words, it is as well to mention the تنوين *tanwīn*, signifying nunnation. It is formed by doubling the terminating vowel, and expressed by double *zabar*, *zer*, and *pesh* (ً, ٍ, ٌ) when they take the sound of *aṇ*, *iṇ*, and *uṇ* respectively; as رئيت رجلاً *ra'etu rajulaṇ*, 'I beheld a man;' مررت برجلٍ *marartu bi-rajuliṇ*, 'I went to a man; جاني رجلٌ *jā'anī rajuluṇ*, 'A man came to me.'

CHAPTER II.

THE PARTS OF SPEECH.

كلمه *Kalima'h.*

19. The Afghān language, like the Arabic model on which it is based, contains but three parts of speech—the اسم *ism* or noun, the فعل *fi'el* or verb, and the حرف *harf* or particle. Those who have studied the Persian language, and are in some measure acquainted with the Arabic terms of grammar, will require no explanation of the above; but as it may tend to puzzle Europeans unacquainted with the rules of Arabian grammarians, I shall subdivide these three parts of speech into those with which they are more familiar.

20. The Pushto language contains no article: the article is supposed to be inherent in the noun, or is expressed by the indefinite numeral يو *yow*, or the demonstrative pronouns, as in the following examples:—

چه ئي علم و عقل نه وي که په تخت د پاسه کښيني
يا يو شير دي يا ليوه دي يا ئي کاو خر شماره

"He who sitteth on A throne, and may neither possess capacity nor understanding,
Is either A LION, OR A WOLF, or otherwise account him AN OX OR AN ASS."

—*Khushḥāl Khān, Khaṭṭak.*

بیا له کومه را پیدا شه دا بهار چه په هر لورِ ئي ملک کړ یو ګلذار
ارغوان دي ضمیران سوسن ریحان دي یاسمن دي نسترن نرګس ګلنار

"From whence has THE SPRING again returned unto us,
Which has made THE whole COUNTRY round A GARDEN of flowers?
There is THE ANEMONE and sweet-basil; THE lily and sweet-herbs;
THE jasmine and white-rose; THE narcissus and pomegranate blossom."
—*Khushhāl Khān, Khattak.*

CHAPTER III.

THE NOUN.

اسم *Ism.*

21. A noun denotes simply the name of an object, as سړي *sarraey*, 'a man,' کور *kor*, 'a house.'

22. The term اسم (*ism*) includes nouns substantive, nouns adjective, numeral nouns, pronouns, and the past and present participles; but, for the reasons before stated, I have generally adopted the divisions and terms of grammar most convenient to Europeans, and therefore the pronouns will be treated of separately, and the participles with the verbs.

23. Nouns may be divided into substantive and adjective. The former are either primitive or derivative.

24. A primitive noun is that which proceeds from no other word in the language; as, هلک *halak*, 'a boy,' جینۍ *jīna'ī*, 'a girl,' آس *ās*, 'a horse,' کر *kar*, 'husbandry,' بډه *baḍḍa'h*, 'a bribe,' ویار *wiār*, 'jealousy.'

25. Derivative nouns are those which spring from other nouns, or from verbs; as, تیاره *tiāra'h*, 'blackness,' بیلتون *beltūn*, 'separation,' وینا *wainā*, 'speech,' ښیګړه *kheguṛṛa'h* or *sheguṛṛa'h*, 'goodness,' رڼړا *ranṛṛā*, 'brightness,' زړه سوي *z'ṛrah-s'waey*, 'sympathy.'

26. Nouns are of two numbers or اعداد *aadād*, as in Persian,—واحد *wāḥid* or singular, and جمع *jamaa* or plural; and of two genders or جنسان *jinsān*; viz., مذکر *muẕakkar* or masculine, and مونث *mūannaṡ* or feminine, the whole of which will be explained in their proper places.

27. There are seven اعرابات *iarābāt* or cases;—the nominative, or حالتِ فاعلي *ḥālat-i-fāailī*; the genitive, or حالتِ اضافت *ḥālat-i-iẓāfat*; the dative, or حالتِ مفعول *ḥālat-i-mafaaūl*; the accusative, or حالتِ مفعول بهٖ *ḥālat-i-mafaaūl bihi*; the

vocative, or حالتِ ندا *ḥālat-i-nidā*; the ablative, or حالتِ جرّي *ḥālat-i-jarrī*; and the فاعل *fāæil*, or actor; or, as it may be termed, the instrumental case.

28. To form the various cases besides the nominative, several particles called حروفِ جر *ḥurūf-i-jarr* are used with the nouns in the inflected state.

29. دَ *da** or sometimes دَه *dah*, the particle governing the genitive case, must always precede the noun, as will be seen from the following examples:—

ستا دَ حسن له تاراجَ زړه ژړا که لکَ بلبل دَ زړه ژړا که په خزان کښِ

"The heart lamenteth at the depredations OF thy beauty,
Like as the heart OF the nightingale bewaileth when the autumn is come."
—*Aḥmad Shāh, Abdālī.*

وه نيوَ مشه پدوستي دَ دنيا خلق دا بي شرمَ بي وفا بي حيا خلق

"Be not captivated by the friendship of the people OF the world!
This shameless, faithless, immodest world."—*Æabd-ul-Ḥamīd.*

ته چه گل دَ آشنائي لباغ غواړي خبر زده کړه دَ هجران لغارُ خندَ

"Thou who seekest in the parterre after the rose OF friendship,
Be aware of the stump and the thorn tree OF separation."—*Æabd-ur-Raḥmān.*

30. The particle is not subject to any change in prose more than in verse, as will be seen from the following extract. Ākhūnd Ḳāsim says:—

پوښتنَ دَ رنځور کول سنت دي په اسلام کښي چه پوښتنَ دَ رنځور کا پرحمت دَ خداي تعلي داخليږي

"To make enquiry AFTER the sick is also the law of the Prophet, and a regulation of the true orthodox faith; (and) whosoever enquireth AFTER the sick, entereth into the mercy OF the Almighty."—*Fawā'id-ush-Sharī'æ'ah.*

31. In this manner I shall continue to give quotations from the various Afghān authors as I proceed: such examples will not only serve, in some measure, as specimens of the style, and be more easily retained in the memory than simple prose, but they will also show that the Pushto has a grammatical system as regular as that of most languages.

32. There are four particles governing the dative case,—ته *tah*, or وته *watah*, and و ,وته *wa-watah*, one و of which is sometimes placed before the noun, and the ته after it; لره *larah*; and له *lah*. The latter is less often used, as a particle similar in form governs the ablative; but the meaning is unmistakable, as will be seen from the examples I shall give.

نور ئي توپک واخستل د غرد وَ اړخي تهَ شول رغ ئي پرؤ کړ چه هر څوک چه مردان ياستِي توري ته راشئي د خان ادب په هر چا غالب وه اګرچه که دغه بد بخت دا ويلي هم وه د چاوٌلاسه نه کيده

* Also دِ amongst the Khattaks and some other tribes.

"They then seized their fire-arms and ascended TO the crest of the mountain, and from that position called out; 'Whoever are men amongst you, come TO the sword;' but veneration for the Khān was so predominant with every one, that notwithstanding that wretch had given them directions (to seize him), yet no one could carry them out."—*Afẓal Khān; Tārīkh-i-Muraṣṣaæ.*

چه مدام دَ بل وَ عیب وته نظر کړِ خداي له خپل عیبَ ولي بیخبر کړِ

"He who ever scrutinizes (TO) the faults of others,
Why did the Almighty make him ignorant of his own."—*Æabd-ur-Raḥmān.*

دد لویو لوئي څه کم نشي که وَ هلک ته چري وائي دلي راشَ

"The greatness and dignity of the great becometh not a particle less,
Should they at any time say UNTO a child, 'Come here.'"—*Aḥmad Shāh, Abdālī.*

په دنیا مَین له ټولو احمقان دي لکه وړکي وَ سره اور ته کا هوس

"They who are in love with the world are the greatest of all fools;
Like the baby, they show great eagerness FOR the flaming fire."—*Æabd-ur-Raḥmān.*

چه دَ هند دَ ملکو فتح مي روزي شوه نور ایران لرَ پتوغ په نغاره ځم

"Since it was my good fortune to conquer Hind,
I now go TO Īrān both with banner and drum,"—*Aḥmad Shāh, Abdālī.*

The following prose examples are from the Fawā'id-ush-Sharī'æa'h, in which the various particles of the dative may be seen.

زکوة دِ مکاتب له ور کوینَ چه وَ څښتن ته يې ادا کا چه خپل گردن پر خلاصَ وینَ پنځم دي پورد وري بل زکوة دِ قرض دار له ور کوینَ چه پرِ قرض ادا کوینَ شپږم حاجیان غازیان فقیران دي بل زکوة دِ وَ حاجیانُ وَ غازیانُ وَ فقیرانُ له ور کوینَ چه پرِ دوي خپل غزا حج حاجت پورد کوین

"Fourth—alms also should be given TO the slave who wishes to manumit himself, that he may repay (TO) his proprietor, and by means of it release his neck from the yoke. The fifth is the debtor. Alms should also be given TO the debtor, that by their assistance he may pay off his debts. The sixth are Pilgrims, Champions or Soldiers of the Faith, and Devotees. Alms should also be given TO these, that by means of them they may perform their pilgrimage, fight for the faith, and carry out the object of their vows."

33. The particles of the dative case are often used to denote 'for,' 'for the sake of,' etc., and must be used or translated accordingly. Thus:—

که شاهباز لرَ سینه دد دَ چنجریو عنکبوت لرَ سینه دد دَ مکس

"If the breast of the partridge is FOR the falcon,
FOR the spider is the breast of the fly."—*Æabd-ur-Raḥmān.*

ندي حسي زیان من رنځ دَ عاشقي چه رنځور يې وَ علاج ته لري شوق

"The anguish of love hath no such injurious effect,
That the afflicted one desireth a remedy FOR it."—*Æabd-ul-Ḥamīd.*

34. According to the Arabic system, on which the Muḥammadan languages are based, the noun has but two variations from the nominative, (terming the latter فاعل *fāæil*, or *actor*); the إضافت *iẓāfat*, or *attribute*; and the مفعول *mafaæūl*, or *acted upon*, in which the dative, accusative, and ablative cases are included. Pushto has another or second form, as it may be termed, of the مفعول *mafaæūl*, or *dative*, similar to the objective case of our own language, in which the particles ته, لره, له, etc. are not expressed, but are understood. For example:

عمر دَ زيد آس وهي or عمر آس دَ زيد وهي

"ÆUMAR strikes Zeid's HORSE."

Here *Æumar*, as the فاعل or *actor*, is in the *nominative* case; *Zeid's*, as expressing the relation of the ownership, is in the إضافت *attribute*, or *genitive*; and *horse*, being the name of the object acted upon, is in the حالتِ مفعول or *dative*. In the preceding sentence, the actor *must* be placed at the commencement, or, in other words, the noun or pronoun at the commencement of the sentence is the *actor*. For instance, if we merely change the noun *Æumar* for *horse*, and vice versâ, the signification is, "*Zeid's horse strikes* ÆUMAR," or exactly contrary. As all verbs in the language agree with the object in the past tenses in gender and number, it can be easily distinguished; but this second form of the dative is one of the difficulties of Pushto, and is only to be got over by practice in the language. Examples of this case are contained in the following couplets:—

دوبوي تخپله ځان حاكمِ دَ عقل   چه دَ عشق دَ ملك خراج ته لريِ شوق

"The prince of prudence and reason himself sinketh his own LIFE,
When he entertaineth a desire towards the taxes of the country of love."
—*Æabd-ul-Ḥamid.*

وارِه جور دَ دي دور مي قبول دي   كه خداي ما له خپله يارِه جدا نكا

"All the injustice and oppression of the world is acceptable TO ME,
If God separateth ME not from the object of my love.—*Æabd-ur-Raḥmān.*

ليندي وروځي بانړه غشي   عاشق ولي پكنار كښي

"Eyebrows like bows, eyelashes like arrows—
Thou pierceth the LOVER in the heart."—*Aḥmad Shāh.*

35. The next case is the accusative,* which remains the same as the nominative, or assumes the dative form, as:

و تا ته ډيره پندونه وايم   ولي زه پرِ ولاړ نه يم

"I give thee much GOOD ADVICE, But I am not acting on it myself."—*Mīrzā Khān, Anṣārī.*

* In old books, nouns may be found in this case inflected; as, يو ورځ 'on a certain,' or 'on one day.'

چه نا اهلَ ته دَ اهلَ وينا وايم ‌ ‌ زه حميد به دَ منصُور په دود په دار شم

"If I speak to the unworthy the WORDS of the good,
I Ḥamīd shall become like Manṣūr,* on the stake."—*Æabd-ul-Ḥamīd.*

مدام ناست يم وُچ کوګل سترګې په نم کښې ‌ ‌ عشق را وُ ښو بحر وُ بر په خپل حرم کښې

"With heart dried up, I sit all day long in the moisture of my tears;
In my own cell, love showed to me both OCEAN and LAND."—*Æabd-ur-Raḥmān.*

36. The vocative case is denoted by the Arabic sign اي *ai*, sometimes pronounced *ay*, together with او *ao* and وُ *wo*; but the latter signs are rarely used in writing, and are peculiar to Afghānī. The vocative sign, when used, must precede the noun, which, with but few exceptions, takes (ـَ) *zabar* after the final letter, and sometimes adds ا or ه instead, as will be seen from the examples, and the declensions of nouns.†

اي رحمانَ دَ بلبلو لفظ زده کړه ‌ ‌ دَغه پس پصفت دَ ګل اندام شَ

"OH RAḤMĀN, first learn the song of the nightingales!
Then commence to praise the rosy-bodied."—*Æabd-ur-Raḥmān.*

احمد شاهَ و بل ته وعظ وائي ‌ ‌ ولي خپل نفس خبر نکري اي واعظَ

"AḤMAD SHĀH! thou preachest a sermon to others;
But why not, OH MONITOR! caution thine own soul?"

37. Sometimes the noun takes the final (ـَ) ا or ه without being preceded by any sign of the vocative, as:

دلبره خونخوارَ ‌ ‌ ولي نه ګوري يکبارَ

"RAVISHER OF HEARTS! OH, UNMERCIFUL ONE! Why not give one glance?"
—*Aḥmad Shāh, Abdālī.*

38. The ablative case is governed by the particles له *lah*, or له نه *lah nah*, the له preceding, and the نه following the noun. The noun in this case, in some instances takes (ـَ) or (ـِ) after the final letter, which will be seen on reference to the declensions. The other particles used in this case are تر *tar* and دَ *da* or دِ *di*. The latter form is not common except amongst the Khattak tribe, who do not appear to make much, if any, difference between it and the دَ of the genitive, but it may generally be known from being followed by نه. The following are examples of the ablative case:

* Al Manṣūr, a Ṣūfī who was put to death for making use of the words, انا الحق 'I am God.'

† It should be borne in mind that there is little or no difference made in Pushto between (ـَ), ا, and ه, and between (ـِ) and ي. For example, دلبره, محبوبا, خونخوارَ, etc., the whole of which are in the vocative case.

دَ يو ونې له شاخَ پيدا كيږي   په چمن كښې هم گلونَ هم خارونَ

"In the garden FROM the branch of the same tree,
Is produced both thorns and roses too."—*Æabd-ur-Raḥmān.*

نوم دَ بيلتون مه آخله خوشحال خانَ   له هجران ريز مريز يم پې هدو كښې

"Mention not the name of absence, O Khūshḥāl Khān!
THROUGH separation my very bones are broken in pieces." *

Khūshḥāl Khān, Khaṭṭak.

پري كوي تر خپلُ پښو لاندِ ښاخونه   چه بدي دَ عزيزانو په زړه نهال كا

"He cutteth away the branch FROM beneath his own feet,
Who nurtureth in his heart malice towards his friends."—*Æabd-ul-Ḥamīd.*

39. Examples of the ablative دِ *di* are contained in the following couplets: as previously stated, they are not often to be met with in the writings of standard authors.

له ناصحَ به ئي وُ انگيرم په قطعه   كه دِ صبرَ څه اوبال شه را ته پيښ

"I will consider the monitor the real cause of it,
Should I suffer any injury FROM patience and long-suffering."—*Æabd-ul-Ḥamīd.*

د آب سند دِ غاړي نه چه ئي كوچ وُ كړ ناگاه مزري پيدا شه آواز ئي وُ كړ زلزله په آسونه گډه شوه اور د لوره ئي په غشيو په تورو په نيزو وُ واهه بابر خود هم يو غشي وُ ويشت په سيند گډ شه له سينده ئي را وُ كيښ

"When they marched FROM the banks of the Āb-i-sind (the Indus), a panther suddenly made his appearance, which set up a roar and caused great confusion and perturbation amongst the horses. On this they assailed him on all sides with arrows, swords, and spears; and the Emperor Bābarr himself discharged an arrow at the animal, which plunged into the river, but he was drawn out."—*Afẓal Khān: Tārīkh-i-Muraṣṣaæ.*

40. The locative, which I shall include in this case, merely substitutes other particles in place of له, له نه, and تر. They are په *pah* or پَ *pa*, which precede the noun, and have various significations, such as 'in,' 'on,' 'with,' 'through,' 'by means of,' etc.; and كښې *kkhey* or *kshey*, or كښِ *kKhi* or *kshi*,† which usually follow a noun preceded by په and signify 'in' or 'within.' Other particles are also used in this case such as په ميان *pah-mī-ān*, په ميَنځ *pah-mi-yandz*, etc.; the whole of which will be found in their proper places. Examples:—

يو دَ بل په دردو غم خوښو خورم شي   دَ شبنم په ژړا گل په خندا خورك

"One man becometh merry and gay AT the afflictions of another.
THROUGH the weeping of the dew, the rose smileth and blooms."—*Bahrām Gūr.*

* Literally, 'I am in pieces *in* my bones.' † These words are often erroneously written كښي and كش in modern MSS

ستا دَ شوندو لَه رطبَ هسِ خوند دي   چه دا خوند نشي موندَ پَه نخلستان کښِ

"There is such deliciousness IN the ripeness of thy lips,
That it is impossible to find such sweetness even IN the date grove."
—*Aḥmad Shāh, Abdālī.*

څه به رنګ شما پَه ځاي وي اې دلبرَ   چه لګيا مي ږ پَه زړه هجر منګورک

"How can my understanding remain IN its proper place, Oh beloved one?
When thou appliest TO my heart the viper of separation."—*Æabd-ul-Ḥamīd.*

41. The whole of the particles governing the different cases just described, remain unchanged both before masculine and feminine nouns, and in the singular and plural number.

42. Before transitive verbs, in all past tenses of the active voice, the noun denoting the فاعل or 'agent,' takes the oblique form both singular and plural, if capable of inflection. Thus سړیَ *sar̤racy*, 'a man,' becomes سړي *sar̤rī*; and ښځه *khadza'h* or *shadza'h*, 'a woman,' ښځي *khadzey* or *shadzey*. When the noun is uninflected, the agent remains the *same* as the nominative. The following are examples:—سړي ښځه ؤ وهله *sar̤rī khadza'h wu-wāhala'h*, 'the *man* struck the woman;' ښځي سړيَ ؤ واهه *khadzey sar̤racy wu-wāhah*, 'the *woman* struck the man;' thus:—

چه دَ ګلو پريشاني شود ور څرګنده   غنچي سر په زانؤ کښيښو خندا نکا

"Since the dishevelled state of the roses became manifest unto it,
The BUD placed its head on its knees, and smileth not."—*Æabd-ur-Raḥmān.*

زماني دَ رحمان زړه دي کباب کړي   له احوالَ ئي څوک نه دي خبر دار

"CRUEL FATE hath scorched the heart of Raḥmān: Of its state no one hath any conception."

43. There are two genders in Pushto, مذکر *muzakkar*, or masculine, and مونث *mūannas*, or feminine; and they affect the terminations of nouns, adjectives, and verbs.

44. The genders of many nouns can be distinguished by attention to the different powers of the letters ه and ي, in which a great number of them terminate.

When the former occurs at the end of a word, it may be either هاي ظاهر (*hā-i-ẓā-hir*) apparent or perceptible *h*, as in ويښته *weshtah* or *wekhtah*, 'hair,' and قارغه *kār-ghah*, 'a crow;' or هاي خفي (*hā-i-khafī*) imperceptible, secret, or concealed *h*, as in ښځه *shadza'h* or *khadza'h*, 'a woman,' 'a female,' and وينه *wīna'h*, 'blood.' All words terminating in the former are masculine, and those ending in the latter are feminine.

45. Words having *yā-i-mā-ḳabl-i-maf-tūḥ*, that is ي preceded by (َ) *fat-ḥa'h* as the final letter, are all masculine, and take *yā-i-maæ-rūf*, or ي preceded by (ِ) *kas-ra'h* for the nominative plural; as, سړيَ *sar̤racy*, 'a man,' سړي *sar̤rī*, 'men.' The masculine forms of the active and past participles of verbs also come under these rules, and will be found explained in their proper place.

The above form of ي is also used as the Pushto *yā-i-nisbat*, to express relation or connexion; as, كابل *kā-bul*, 'the city of Kābul,' كابلي *kā-bulaey*, 'a man of Kābul,' كابلي *kā-bulī*, 'men of Kābul.'

Nouns terminating in *yā-i-maa-rūf mā-kabl-i-hamza'h-i-khafī-i-maksūr*, or ي preceded by (ـٔ) *hamza'h* and (ـِ) *kasra'h*, are all feminine, and are both singular and plural; as, جينئ *jīna'ī*, 'a girl or girls.' It is also used as the feminine *yā-i-nisbat*; as, پيښاور *peshāwer* or *pekhāwer*, 'the city of Peshāwer;' پيښاورئ *peshāwera'ī* or *pekhāwera'ī*, 'a female or females of Peshāwer.'

Many feminine nouns, amongst which will be found a great many Persian derivatives, terminate in *yā-i-maa-rūf mā-kabl-i-maksūr*, or ي preceded by (ـِ) *kasra'h*, which is changed to ئ preceded by (ـٔ) *hamza'h* and (ـِ) *kasra'h* (explained in the preceding paragraph) in the plural; as, ميرځي *mīr-tsī*, 'trouble,' 'distress;' ميرځئ *mīr-tsa'ī*, 'troubles,' 'distresses.'

Other nouns again, chiefly foreign words which have crept into the language, terminating in ي, may be either masculine or feminine, and form their plurals by affixing the terminations ان, گان or يان for the masculine, and انِ or انئ, گانِ or گانئ, and يانِ or يانئ for the feminine; as, هاتي *hā-tī*, 'an elephant,' دائي *dā'ī*, 'a nurse.'

Nouns terminating in *yā-i-mau-kūf*, or silent ي, are all masculine, and affix other terminations for the plural; as, ځوي *dzo'e*, 'a son,' سوي *so'e*, 'a hare,' the rules respecting which will be seen from the following declensions.

46. The gender of some nouns is distinguishable from the sex of those to whom they are applicable; as, ميړه *merrah* or ميړَ *merra*, 'a husband,' ماندينه *māndīna'h*, 'a wife.' In other instances they are expressed by words totally different from each other; as, پلار *plār*, 'a father,' مور *mor*, 'a mother,' ورور *w'ror*, 'a brother,' خور *khor*, 'a sister.'

47. Feminine nouns are formed from masculines by the addition of ه (*hā-i-khafī*); changing ي into ئ; and inserting ن before the final letter; as, اوښ *ūsh* or *ūkh*, 'a *male* camel,' اوښه *ūsha'h* or *ūkha'h*, 'a *female* camel;' مرغمي *murghumaey*, 'a *male* kid,' مرغمئ *murghuma'ī*, 'a *female* kid;' ميلمه *melmah*, 'a *male* guest,' ميلمنه *melmana'h*, 'a female guest.'

48. Pushto nouns have nine declensions, distinguished according to the various methods of inflection, and the formation of the nominative plural. Several declensions have two or more varieties.

1st Declension.

49. This comprehends all nouns which inflect the oblique cases of the singular and nominative plural. It has two varieties.

50. The first variety consists of nouns ending in ي (with *fat-ḥa'h* and *yā* quiescent) which take (ـَ) in the vocative, the whole of which are masculine; as, سړي *saṛṛaey*, 'a man,' مځري *m'dzaraey*, 'a tiger,' مريئي *m'rayaey*, 'a slave,' etc.

51. The oblique plural of *all* nouns in this language, with the exception of those of the 9th declension, is formed by substituting و or (ـُ) for the final letter of the nominative plural, and therefore requires no further explanation.

52. The masculine noun سړي *saṛṛaey*, 'a man,' is thus declined:

سړي *saṛṛaey*, 'a man.'

SINGULAR.

Nom.	سړي *saṛṛaey*,	a man.
Gen.	دَ سړي *da saṛṛī*,	a man's, *or* of a man.
Dat.	سړي ته, لره, or له *saṛṛī tah, larah,* or *lah*; or و سړي ته, لره, or له *wa saṛṛī tah, larah,* or *lah*; or و سړي وته etc. *wa saṛṛī watah*, etc.	to a man.
Acc.	سړي *saṛṛaey*.	a man, *or* to a man.
Voc.	اي سړي or وُ سړي or سړي *ai saṛṛaeya*, or *wo saṛṛaeya*; or *saṛṛaeya*,	O man!
Abl.	له سړي له سړي نه *lah saṛṛī*, or *lah saṛṛī nah*,	from a man.
Act.	سړي *saṛṛī*,	by a man.

PLURAL.

Nom.	سړي *saṛṛī*,	men.
Gen.	دَ سړو *da saṛṛo*,	men's, *or* of men.
Dat.	سړو ته, لره, or له *saṛṛo tah, larah,* or *lah*; or و سړو ته, لره, or له *wa saṛṛo tah, larah,* or *lah*; or و سړو وته etc. *wa saṛṛo watah*, etc.	to men.
Acc.	سړي *saṛṛī*.	men, *or* to men.
Voc.	اي سړو or وُ سړو or سړو *ai saṛṛo*, or *wo saṛṛo*; or *saṛṛo*,	O men!
Abl.	له سړو or له سړو نه *lah saṛṛo*, or *lah saṛṛo nah*,	from men.
Act.	سړو *saṛṛo*.	by men.

53. The second variety embraces nouns which take (ـِ) and occasionally ي (*yā-i-maj-hūl*) in all the oblique cases of the singular, and the vocative; as, لار *lār*, 'a road,' جل *jal*, 'a maiden,' and ستن *stan*, 'a needle.' They are all feminine, and generally inanimate.

لار *lār*, 'a road.'

	SINGULAR.	PLURAL.
Nom.	لار *lār*, a road.	لارِ *lāri*, roads.
Gen.	دَ لارِ *da lāri*, of a road, *or* a road's.	دَ لارُ *da lāro*, of roads, *or* roads'.
Dat.	لارِ ته, لره, or له *lāri tah, larah,* or *lah*, to a road.	لارُ ته لره or له *lāro tah, larah,* or *lah*, to roads.

Acc.	لار *lār*, a road, *or* to a road.	لارِ *lāri*, roads, *or* to roads.
Voc.	اي or وُ لارِ *ai* or *wo lāri*, O road!	اي or وُ لارُ *ai*, or *wo lāro*, O roads!
Abl.	له لارِ or له لارِ نه *lah lāri*, or *lah lāri nah*, from a road.	له لارُ or له لارُ نه *lah lāro*, or *lah lāro nah*, from roads.
Act.	لارِ *lāri*, by a road.	لارُ *lāro*, by roads.

2ND DECLENSION.

54. The nouns of this class which are distinguished by not inflecting the singular oblique, take (ـَ) in the vocative; affix two or more letters to form the nominative plural; and often reject the long vowel of the first syllable. They are of two varieties, and are all masculine.

55. The first variety are those which take وَن or ونه in the nominative plural; as, پلار *plār*, 'a father,' نيايه *niyāyah*, 'a maternal uncle,' آس *ās*, 'a horse,' مروند *maṟṟwand*, 'the wrist,' غاښ *ghākh* or *ghāsh*, 'a tooth,' شپول *shpol*, 'a hedge of thorns.'

پلار *plār*, 'a father.'

	SINGULAR.	PLURAL.
Nom.	پلار *plār*, a father.	پلارون or پلرونه *plārūna*, or *plarūnah*, fathers.
Obl.	دَ پلار *da plār*, of a father, etc.	دَ پلارونُ *da plārūno*, of fathers, etc.
Voc.	اي or وُ پلارَ *ai*, or *wo plāra*, O father!	اي or وُ پلارونُ *ai*, or *wo plārūno*, O fathers!
Act.	پلار *plār*, by a father.	پلارونُ *plārūno*, by fathers.

56. The second variety consists of those nouns which insert the two letters ان before the final letter; as, ميلمه *melmah*, 'a guest,' غوبه *ghobah*, 'a cowherd.'

ميلمه *melmah*, 'a guest.'

	SINGULAR.	PLURAL.
Nom.	ميلمه *melmah*, a guest.	ميلمانه *melmānah*, guests.
Obl.	دَ ميلمه *da melmah*, of a guest, etc.	دَ ميلمانو *da melmāno*, of guests, etc.
Voc.	اي or وُ ميلمه *ai*, or *wo melmah*, O guest!	اي or وُ ميلمانو *ai*, or *wo melmāno*, O guests!
Act.	ميلمه *melmah*, by a guest.	ميلمانو *melmāno*, by guests.

57. آه *āh*, 'a sigh,' which is feminine amongst some tribes, takes the above masculine form of the plural; but it is a Persian, not an Afghān word.

3RD DECLENSION.

58. This comprises all nouns ending in ه (*hā-i-khafī*, or imperceptible *h*) which is changed into ي (*yā-i-majhūl*) in the oblique singular, vocative, and nominative plural; as, ښځه *khadza'h* or *shadza'h*, 'a woman,' مچوغنه *machoghna'h*, 'a sling,' لينده *lenda'h*, 'a bow.' They are all feminine.

ښځه *khadzah* or *shadza'h*, 'a woman.'

	SINGULAR.	PLURAL.
Nom.	ښځه *khadza'h*, a woman.	ښځي *khadzey*, women.

Obl.	دَ ښځي	*da Khadzaey*, of a woman, etc.	دَ ښځو	*da Khadzo*, of women, etc.
Voc.	اي or وُ ښځي	*ai*, or *wo Khadzey*, O woman!	اي or وُ ښځو	*ai*, or *wo Khadzo*, O women!
Act.	ښځي	*Khadzey*, by a woman.	ښځو	*Khadzo*, by women.

59. There is another variety which may be included in this declension terminating in *yā-i-maarūf mā-kabl-i-maksūr*, or perceptible ي preceded by (ِ) *kasra'h* which is changed into what is called *yā-i-maarūf mā-kabl-i-hamza'h-i-khafī-i-maksūr*, or perceptible ي preceded by (ٔ) *hamza'h* and (ِ) *kasra'h*, for the singular oblique, and nominative plural; as, ميرځي *mīr-tsī*, 'distress,' ميرځئ *mīrtsa'ī*, 'distresses;' دښمني *dukhmanī* or *dushmanī*, 'enmity,' دښمنئ *dukhmana'ī* or *dushmana'ī*, 'enmities.'*
This form is rare with regard to pure Pushto words, but includes a number of Persian derivative nouns.

ميرځي *mīr-tsī*, 'distress.'

	SINGULAR.		PLURAL.	
Nom.	ميرځي	*mīr-tsī*, distress.	ميرځئ	*mīr-tsa'ī*, distresses.
Obl.	دَ ميرځئ	*da mīr-tsa'ī*, of distress, etc.	دَ ميرځيو	*da mīr-tsīo*, of distresses, etc.
Voc.	اي or وُ ميرځئ	*ai*, or *wo mīr-tsa'ī*, O distress!	اي or وُ ميرځيو	*ai*, or *wo mīr-tsīo*. O distresses!
Act.	ميرځئ	*mīr-tsa'ī*, by distress.	ميرځيو	*mīr-tsīo*, by distresses.

4th Declension.

60. In this declension are contained nouns which take (ٔ) in the oblique, and vocative singular, and the nominative plural. They are of two varieties, and generally masculine.

61. The first variety merely add the (ٔ) sometimes ۀ, for the singular oblique and nominative plural; as, غل *ghal*, 'a thief,' مل *mal*, 'a companion.'

غل *ghal*, 'a thief.'†

	SINGULAR.		PLURAL.	
Nom.	غل	*ghal*, a thief.	غلۀ or غلٔ	*gh'læ* or *gh'leh*, thieves.
Obl.	دَ غلٔ	*da gh'læ*, of a thief, etc.	دَ غلُ	*da gh'lo*, of thieves, etc.
Voc.	اي or وُ غلٔ	*ai*, or *wo gh'læ*, O thief!	اي or وُ غلُ	*ai*, or *wo gh'lo*, O thieves!
Act.	غلٔ	*gh'læ*, by a thief.	غلُ	*gh'lo*, by thieves.

62. The second variety consists of such nouns as نمونځ *n'mūndz*, 'prayer,' يون *yūn*, 'gait,' 'custom,' etc., كوګ *kog* or كوږ *kojz*, 'a hyena,' شكنر *shkurrn*, 'a porcupine,' which change the و or (ُ) of the nominative into ا and affix ه or (ٔ) in the oblique and vocative singular and the nominative plural.

* In the first edition of this work, this termination, as warranted by the system of some Pushto authors, was written with (ٔ) over the ي—thus, ميرځئ, but the above is the more correct mode of writing it.

† The feminine form of this word ends in *hā-i-khafī*—غله *ghla'h*. It belongs to the first variety of the third declension, and shows how the feminines of such nouns are obtained.

نمونځ *n'mūndz*, 'prayer.'

	SINGULAR.	PLURAL.
Nom.	نمونځ *n'mūndz*, prayer.	نمانځه or نمانځ *n'māndza* or *n'māndzah*, prayers.
Obl.	دَ نمانځ *da n'māndza*, of prayer, etc.	دَ نمانځ *da n'māndzo*, of prayers, etc.
Voc.	اي or وَ نمانځ *ai*, or *wo n'māndza*, O prayer!	اي or وَ نمانځ *ai*, or *wo n'māndzo*, O prayers!
Act.	نمانځ *n'māndza*, by prayer.	نمانځ *n'māndzo*, by prayers.

5TH DECLENSION.

63. The nouns of this declension are not subject to inflection except in the vocative singular, which, if masculine, take (ـَ) *fut-ha'h*, and if feminine, (ـِ) *kasra'h*, sometimes written with ه and ي instead. They may be divided into four classes—those which take ان, گان, or يان in the nominative plural, and those whose plurals are irregular. The nouns embraced in this declension are mostly names of human beings, or animals; and contain a number of exotic words which have crept into Pushto from the languages spoken in the countries bordering on Afghānistān, together with numerous primitive nouns. They are both masculine and feminine, but the former predominate.

64. The first variety includes nouns which take ان in the nominative plural; as توت *tūt*, 'a mulberry,' اوښ *ūkh* or *ūsh*, 'a camel,' هاتي *hātī*, 'an elephant.'

اوښ *ūkh* or *ūsh*, 'a male camel.'

	SINGULAR.	PLURAL.
Nom.	اوښ *ūkh*, or *ūsh*, a camel.	اوښان *ūkhān*, or *ūshān*, camels.
Obl.	دَ اوښ *da ūkh*, of a camel, etc.	دَ اوښانُ *da ūkhāno*, of camels, etc.
Voc.	اي or وَ اوښَ *ai*, or *wo ūkha*, O camel!	اي or وَ اوښانُ *ai*, or *wo ūkhāno*, O camels!
Act.	اوښ *ūkh*, by a camel.	اوښانُ *ūkhāno*, by camels.

65. Nouns of the second variety take گان in the nominative plural; as مندانړ *mandūrrnu*, 'a churning stick,' جولا *jolā*, 'a weaver,' کارغه *kārghah*, 'a crow,' ميلو *mīlū*, 'a bear.'

مندانړو *mandārrno*, or مندانړ *mandārrnu*, 'a churning stick.'

	SINGULAR.	PLURAL.
Nom.	مندانړ *mandārrnu*, a churning stick.	مندانړګان *mandārrnogān*, churning sticks.
Obl.	دَ مندانړ *da mandārrnu*, of a churning stick, etc.	دَ مندانړګانُ *da mandārrnogānu*, of churning sticks.
Voc.	اي or وَ مندانړ *ai*, or *wo mandārrnu*, O churning stick!	اي or وَ مندانړګانُ *ai*, or *wo mandārrnogānu*, O churning sticks!
Act.	مندانړ *mandārrnu*, by a churning stick.	مندانړګانُ *mandārrnogānu*, by churning sticks.

66. The third variety contains nouns which take يان in the nominative plural; as, ملا *mullā*, 'a priest,' چارپا *chārpā*, 'a quadruped.'

ملا *mullā*, 'a priest.'

	SINGULAR.	PLURAL.
Nom.	ملا *mullā*, a priest.	ملايان *mullā-yān*, priests.
Obl.	دَ ملا *da mullā*, of a priest, etc.	دَ ملايانُ *da mullā-yānu*, of priests, etc.
Voc.	اي or وَ ملا *ai*, or *wo mullā*, O priest!	اي or وَ ملايانُ *ai*, or *wo mullā-yānu*, O priests!
Act.	ملا *mullā*, by a priest.	ملايانُ *mullā-yānu*, by priests.

67. The fourth variety consists of nouns of consanguinity or connexion, whose plurals are irregular; as, مور *mor*, 'a mother,' ځوي *dzo'e*, 'a son,' وور *w'ror*, 'a brother,' يور *yor*, 'a husband's brother's wife;' and a few adjectives, used substantively; as, سور *sor*, 'a rider.'

مور *mor*, 'a mother.'

	SINGULAR.	PLURAL.
Nom.	مور *mor*, a mother.	ميندِ or ميندئ *mendi*, or *mendey*, mothers.
Obl.	دَ مور *da mor*, of a mother, etc.	دَ ميندُ *da mendu*, of mothers, etc.
Voc.	اي or وَ مور *ai*, or *wo mori*, O mother!	اي or وَ ميندُ *ai*, or *wo mendu*, O mothers!
Act.	مور *mor*, by a mother.	ميندُ *mendu*, by mothers.

ځوي *dzo'e*, 'a son.'

	SINGULAR.	PLURAL.
Nom.	ځوي *dzo'e*, a son.	ځامن *dzāman*, sons.
Obl.	د ځوي *da dzo'e*, of a son, etc.	دَ ځامنُ *da dzāmanu*, of sons, etc.
Voc.	اي or وَ ځويَ *ai*, or *wo dzo'ea*, O son!	اي or وَ ځامنُ *ai*, or *wo dzāmanu*, O sons!
Act.	ځوي *dzo'e*, by a son.	ځامنُ *dzāmanu*, by sons.

68. A fifth variety of this declension consists solely of nouns denoting sounds of whatever description, the whole of which take هار in the plural; as, هينګ *heng*, 'a groan,' هڼر *harrn*, 'a neigh,' ژرنګ *jz'rang*, 'clash,' 'ring,' غړنب *ghurrumb*, 'a roar.'

هينګ *heng*, 'a groan.'

	SINGULAR.	PLURAL.
Nom.	هينګ *heng*, a groan.	هينګهار *hengahār*, groans.
Obl.	دَ هينګ *da heng*, of a groan, etc.	دَ هينګهارو *da hengahāro*, of groans, etc.
Voc.	اي or وَ هينګَ *ai*, or *wo henga*, O groan!	اي or وَ هينګهارو *ai*, or *wo hengahāro*, O groans!
Act.	هينګ *heng*, by a groan.	هينګهارو *hengahāro*, by groans.

6TH DECLENSION.

69. This declension contains nouns which remain unchanged in all cases but the oblique plural, which as before stated at page 14, para. 51, never varies in Pus̲h̲to. They are of five different classes.

70. The first variety embraces all nouns terminating in ه (*hā-i-z̤āhir*, perceptible or apparent *h*), and which, in direct contrariety to those of the 3rd declension,

are all masculine; for example, واښه *wākhah* or *wāshah*, 'grass,' and ویښته *wekhtah* or *weshtah*, 'hair.' They chiefly apply to a class, genus, or species.

واښه *wākhah* or *wāshah*, 'grass.'

	SINGULAR.	PLURAL.
Nom.	واښه *wākhah*, grass.	واښه *wākhah*, grasses.
Obl.	دَ واښه *da wākhah*, of grass, etc.	دَ واښو *da wākho*, of grasses, etc.
Voc.	اي or وُ واښه *ai*, or *wo wākhah*, O grass!	اي or وُ واښو *ai*, or *wo wākho*, O grasses!
Act.	واښه *wākhah*, by grass.	واښو *wākho*, by grasses.

71. The second variety are those which terminate in ا and are all feminine; as, غوا *ghwā*, 'a cow,' امسا *amsā*, 'a crutch,' ملا *m'lā*, 'the waist,' رڼا *raṛṇā*, 'brightness.'

غوا *ghwā*, 'a cow.'

	SINGULAR.	PLURAL.
Nom.	غوا *ghwā*, a cow.	غوا *ghwā*; (W.) غواوي *ghwāwī*, cows.
Obl.	دَ غوا *da ghwā*, of a cow, etc.	دَ غواوُ *da ghwāwo*, of cows, etc.
Voc.	اي or وُ غوا *ai*, or *wo ghwā*, O cow!	اي or وُ غواوُ *ai*, or *wo ghwāwo*, O cows!
Act.	غوا *ghwā*, by a cow.	غواوُ *ghwāwo*, by cows.

72. The third variety terminate in *yā-i-maarūf mā ḳabl-i-hamza'h-i-khafī-i-maksūr*, or perceptible ي preceded by (ـٔ) *hamza'h* and (ـِ) *kasra'h*, and are, without exception, all feminine; and with the exception of the oblique plural, are both singular and plural; as, جینئي *jīna'ī*, 'a girl,' سیلئي *sīla'ī*, 'a slap,' مچئي *macha'ī*, 'a bee.' These words may also be written with ئ.*

جینئي *jīna'ī*, 'a girl.'

	SINGULAR.	PLURAL.
Nom.	جینئي *jīna'ī*, a girl.	جینئي *jīna'ī*, girls.
Obl.	دَ جینئي *da jīna'ī*, of a girl, etc.	دَ جینو *da jīno*, of girls, etc.
Voc.	اي or وُ جینئي *ai*, or *wo jīna'ī*, O girl!	اي or وُ جینو *ai*, or *wo jīno*, O girls!
Act.	جینئي *jīna'ī*, by a girl.	جینو *jīno*, by girls.

73. Nouns terminating in (—) are the fourth variety; as, بانړَ *bāṛṛna*, 'an eyelash,' خوارَّ *khwāṛṛa*, 'food,' ړانځَرَ *ṛrāndzara*, 'tar.' They may also be written with ه.†

بانړَ *bāṛṛna*, 'an eyelash.'‡

	SINGULAR.	PLURAL.
Nom.	بانړَ *bāṛṛna*, an eyelash.	بانړَ *bāṛṛna*, eyelashes.
Obl.	دَ بانړَ *da bāṛṛna*, of an eyelash, etc.	دَ بانړُ *da bāṛṛno*, of eyelashes, etc.
Voc.	اي or وُ بانړَ *ai*, or *wo bāṛṛna*, O eyelash!	اي or وُ بانړُ *ai*, or *wo bāṛṛno*, O eyelashes!
Act.	بانړَ *bāṛṛna*, by an eyelash.	بانړُ *bāṛṛno*, by eyelashes.

74. The fifth variety embraces all nouns terminating in any other consonant

* See note (†) page 16. † See note (‡) at page 10.

‡ By the Western Afghāns بانړو *bāṛṛno*, and conjugated as second variety of 5th declension.

than those mentioned for the three first varieties; as, ټيپر *ṯṯepar*, 'a turnip,' کور *kwar*, 'a wild grape,' سخوندَر *skhwandar*, 'a steer;' and which, in the plural, shorten the final vowel to (ـَ), a sound shorter than that of *fatḥah*, the nearest approach to which in English is *æ*.

سخوندَر *skhwandar*, 'a steer.' *

	SINGULAR.	PLURAL.
Nom.	سخوندَر *skhwandar*, a steer.	سخونډَر *skhwandær*, steers.
Obl.	دَ سخوندر *da skhwandar*, of a steer, etc.	دَ سخونډَرُ *da skhwandæru*, of steers, etc.
Voc.	اي or وُ سخوندَرَ *ai*, or *wo skhwandara*, O steer!	اي or وُ سخونډَرُ *ai*, or *wo skhwandæru*, O steers!
Act.	سخوندَر *skhwandar*, by a steer.	سخونډَرُ *skhwandæru*, by steers.

7th Declension.

75. This declension comprehends nouns which take (ـَ) in the oblique and vocative singular, and وُنَ or ونه in the nominative plural. With the exception of being capable of inflection, and being names of inanimate objects, and the first letter becoming silent or quiescent in the oblique cases and nominative plural, the nouns of this differ but slightly from the 2nd declension, which see. They are all masculine; as غر *ghar*, 'a mountain,' جغ *jagh*, 'a yoke for oxen,' آړ *ārr*, 'an obstacle,' and اوربل *aor-bal*, 'the forelock.'

غر *ghar*, 'a mountain.'

	SINGULAR.	PLURAL.
Nom.	غر *ghar*, a mountain.	غرُونَ *gh'rūna*, or غرُونه *gh'rūnah*, mountains.
Obl.	دَ غرَ *da gh'ra*, of a mountain, etc.	دَ غرُونُ *da gh'rūnu*, of mountains, etc.
Voc.	اي or وُ غرَ *ai*, or *wo gh'ra*, O mountain!	اي وُ غرُونُ *ai*, or *wo gh'rūnu*, O mountains!
Act.	غرَ *gh'ra*, by a mountain.	غرُونُ *gh'rūnu*, by mountains.

8th Declension.

76. The nouns of this declension are extremely rare. They terminate in ي and are not inflected in the singular, but take ئ in the nominative plural; as سيزني *sīz-nī*, 'a swaddling band.'

سيزني *sīz-nī*, 'a swaddling band.'

	SINGULAR.	PLURAL.
Nom.	سيزني *sīz-nī*, a swaddling band.	سيزنئ *sīz-na'ī*, swaddling bands.
Obl.	دَ سيزني *da sīz-nī*, of a swaddling band, etc.	دَ سيزنو *da sīz-no*, of swaddling bands, etc.
Voc.	اي or وُ سيزني *ai*, or *wo sīz-nī*, O swaddling band!	اي or وُ سيزنو *ai*, or *wo sīz-no*, O swaddling bands!
Act.	سيزني *sīz-nī*, by a swaddling band.	سيزنو *sīz-no*, by swaddling bands.

77. There are a few feminine nouns terminating in ي (*yā-i-maj-hūl*) or (ـِ) *kas-*

* The Western Afghāns decline this noun as the first variety of Class 5th.

rd'h, which may be entered as the second variety of this class; but as they are generally animate objects, small in size or of tender age, or the feminine forms of the active and past participles of verbs, they are, properly speaking, adjectives. The masculine form comes under the first variety of the 1st declension, and from which the feminines merely differ as regards the nominative and vocative singular; as, كچوټي *kuchūṭṭey*, or كچوټ *kuchūṭṭi*, 'a puny female child;' زيره گري *zerah-garey*, or زيره گر *zerah-gari*, 'a female who brings good news.'

كچوټ *kuchūṭṭi*, 'a puny female child.'

	SINGULAR.	PLURAL.
Nom.	كچوټ *kuchūṭṭi*, a female child.	كچوټي *kuchūṭṭī*, female children.
Obl.	دَ كچوټي *da kuchūṭṭī*, of a female child, etc.	دَ كچوټيو *da kuchūṭṭio*, of female children, etc.
Voc.	اي or وُ كچوټي *ai*, or *wo kuchūṭṭī*, O female child!	اي or وُ كچوټيو *ai*, or *wo kuchūṭṭio*, O female children!
Act.	كچوټي *kuchūṭṭī*, by a female child.	كچوټيو *kuchūṭṭio*, by female children.

9TH DECLENSION.

78. There are many nouns in Pushto, which neither change in the singular oblique, nor in the nominative or oblique plural or vocative, which I have included in this declension; thus, گيسو *gī-sū*, 'a ringlet,' ويار *wī-ār*, 'jealousy,' بارخو *bār-kho*, 'the cheek,' زانگو *zān-go*, 'a swing or cradle,' لانبو *lān-bo*, 'act of swimming.' There are many foreign words included in this form; and they are both masculine and feminine.

ويار *wī-ār* (masc.) 'jealousy.'

	SINGULAR.	PLURAL.
Nom.	ويار *wī-ār*, jealousy.	ويار *wī-ār*, jealousies.
Obl.	دَ ويار *da wī-ār*, of jealousy, etc.	دَ ويار *da wī-ār*, of jealousies, etc.
Voc.	اي or وُ ويار *ai*, or *wo wī-ār*, O jealousy!	اي or وُ ويار *ai*, or *wo wī-ār*, O jealousies!
Act.	ويار *wī-ār*, by jealousy.	ويار *wī-ār*, by jealousies.

CHAPTER IV.

THE ADJECTIVE.

اسم صفت *ism-i-sifat.*

79. The Adjective, called the اسم صفت *ism-i-sifat*, or noun of quality, denotes some property or attribute of the noun; as, تور *tor*, 'black,' سپين *spīn*, 'white,' ښه *khah* or *shah*, 'good,' ناكار *nākār*, 'bad,' لور *lūwarr*, 'tall.' مندري *mundaraey*, 'short.' Example:—

ندي هسي پوله کيف دَ عشق دَ ميو   چه وُرکيږي دَ پندوُنو په ترشو

"There is no such WEAK intoxication in the wine of love,
As becometh quenched by the sourness of admonitions."—*Yūsuf and Zulīkhā.*

80. The adjective should in all cases precede the noun, as:

ملک دَ سوات دَ ملوکانو دَ نشاط دي   په دوران دَ يوسفزيو وران رباط دي
و شمال وته ئې غر بلورستان دي   شرق کشمير غرب ئې کابل او بدخشان دي
هندوستان وته تور غر لري بد غاښي   پر خاته به دَ لښکرو په غوغا شي

"Suwāt is intended to give sovereigns gladness, and delight;
But now in the time of the Yūsufzīs, it is a desolate caravansary.
On the north it is bounded by the mountains of Bilaūristān; *
To the east lies Kashmīr; to the west is Kābul and Badakhshān.
Towards Hindūstān it has BLACK MOUNTAINS and FROWNING PASSES,
In the ascent of which, armies will get entangled, and confusion ensue."
—*Khushhāl Khān, Khattak.*

که دَ وادہ په ورځِ څوک سره جامه آغندي که هغه جامه له هسي رنګَ پنبه وي چه په اصل کښي
دا سره وَه دَ هغِه جامهِ آغستَ روا دي

"If on a marriage day a person dresseth himself in RED coloured clothes, if that dress be of cotton which was originally RED, then the wearing of such garments is RIGHT and LAWFUL."
—*Fawā'id-ush-Sharī'ica'h.*

81. The adjective admits of but three forms—the nominative, oblique, and vocative, in the same manner as the noun, although it has also seven cases. The actor is the same as the oblique, and the remainder are made up by the addition of the different particles.

82. Some adjectives are undeclinable,† and are not subject to change for number; with this exception, they assume the same terminations in gender, number, and case, as the nouns they qualify. The following are examples:

لکَ اور په وچ واښه باندِ څوک بل کا   هسي کار کاندِ په زهد و په تقويٰ عشق

"Like as by applying fire, one setteth DRY grass in a blaze,
So doeth love to devotion, and to piety."—*Æabd-ul-Hamīd.*

هغه سترګِ چه نرګس وي يا بادام وي   تيرِ تورِ شوِ خما په قتلولُ

"Those eyes, whether they be narcissuses or almonds,
Became SHARP swords for slaughtering me.—*Æabd-ur-Rahman.*

* The country of 'crystal,' from P. بلور, so called from containing mines of transparent quartz or rock-crystal, which is sometimes brought to Peshāwar for sale.

† Except in the oblique plural, which is always inflected. See 'Nouns,' Para. 51.

The following is the mode of declension :

مشر ورور *mashar w'ror*, 'an elder brother.'

SINGULAR.

Nom.	مشر ورور	*mashar w'ror,*	an elder brother.
Gen.	دَ مشر ورور	*da mashar w'ror,*	of an elder brother.
Dat.	مشر ورور ته ,لرد or له	*mashar w'ror tah, larah,* or *lah,*	to an elder brother.
Acc.	مشر ورور	*mashar w'ror,*	an elder brother.
Voc.	اي or وُ مشرَ رورَ	*ai,* or *wo mashara w'rora,*	O elder brother !
Abl.	له مشرَ رورَ or له مشرَ ورورَ نه	*lah mashara w'rora,* or *lah mashara w'rora nah,*	from an elder brother.
Act.	مشر ورور	*mashar w'ror,*	by an elder brother.

PLURAL.

Nom.	مشر ورونړَ or ورونړه	*mashar w'rūrrna,* or *w'rūrrnah,*	elder brothers.
Gen.	دَ مشرُ ورونړُ or ورونړو	*da masharo w'rūrrno,*	of elder brothers.
Dat.	مشرُ ورونړُ or ورونړو ته ,لرد or له	*masharo w'rūrrno tah, larah,* or *lah,*	to elder brothers.
Acc.	مشر ورونړَ or ورونړه	*mashar w'rūrrna,*	elder brothers.
Voc.	اي or وُ مشرُ ورونړُ or ورونړو	*ai,* or *wo masharo w'rūrrno,*	O elder brothers !
Abl.	له مشرُ ورونړُ or ورونړو or له مشرُ ورونړُ or ورونړو نه	*lah masharo w'rūrrno,* or *lah masharo w'rūrrno nah,*	from elder brothers.
Act.	مشرُ ورونړُ or ورونړو	*masharo w'rūrrno,*	by elder brothers.

83. Before feminine nouns adjectives take ه (*hā-i-khafī*), as will be perceived from the following couplet :

شاه احمده تنگسه توره بلا دة   په تنگسه گوره یار وفادار شه

" Aḥmad Shāh ! adversity is a BLACK calamity ;   Mind ! in misfortune be a faithful friend."

—*Aḥmad Shāh, Abdālī.*

Declension of an adjective governed by a feminine noun :

لويه جل *lo-e-a'h jæl,* 'a grown up girl.'

SINGULAR.

Nom.	لويه جل	*lo-e-a'h jæl,*	a grown up girl.
Obl.	دَ لويي جلِ	*da lo-e-ey jæli,*	of a grown up girl, etc.
Voc.	اي or وُ لويي جلِ	*ai,* or *wo lo-e-ey jæli,*	O grown up girl !
Act.	لويي جلِ	*lo-e-ey jæli,*	by a grown up girl.

PLURAL.

Nom.	لويي جلِ	*lo-e-ey jæli,*	grown up girls.
Obl.	دَ لويو جلُ	*da lo-eo jælo,*	of grown up girls, etc.
Voc.	اي or وُ لويو جلُ	*ai,* or *wo lo-eo jælo,*	O grown up girls !
Act.	لويو جلُ	*lo-eo jælo,*	by grown up girls.

84. Sometimes a noun is used instead of an adjective to qualify another noun; thus:

چه دَ اوسپنو چنړي شوي پرِ چيچلي   خداي زده بچ کړه هغه غاښ کومو ترشو

"That tooth by means of which IRON-LIKE pulse was masticated,
God alone knoweth what acids have blunted it."—*Æabd-ul-Ḥamīd.*

کاڼرئ زړه *kārrnaey z'rrah*, 'a hard (stone) heart.'

SINGULAR.

Nom.	کاڼري زړه *kārrnaey z'rrah,*	a hard heart.
Obl.	دَ کاڼري زړه *da kārrnī z'rrah,*	of a hard heart, etc.
Voc.	اي or وُ کاڼري زړه *ai,* or *wo kārrnī z'rrah,*	O hard heart!
Act.	کاڼري زړه *kārrnī z'rrah,*	by a hard heart.

PLURAL.

Nom.	کاڼري زړوُنَ or زړونه *kārrnī z'rrūna,* or *z'rrūnah,*	hard hearts.
Obl.	دَ کاڼرو زړوُنُ *da kārrno z'rrūno,*	of hard hearts, etc.
Voc.	اي or وُ کاڼرو زړوُنُ *ai,* or *wo kārrno z'rrūno,*	O hard hearts!
Act.	کاڼرو زړوُنُ *kārrno z'rrūno,*	by hard hearts.

85. Adjectives may be, and often are, used alone, the substantive being understood; thus:

نه قدم لري نه دم همدم دَ ښکليو   گوره شمعه پا بسته سر بريده

"Nor footstep nor breath hath the friend of the FAIR:
Behold the candle, foot-bound, and head severed!"—*Æabd-ul-Ḥamīd.*

زلف دَ دلدار دي چه هر څوک ئې طلبګار دي   لوي دي که هلک دي که ځوان دي که واړه

"The locks of the beloved are the desired objects of every one,
Whether OLD or YOUNG, whether GREAT or SMALL."—*Æabd-ur-Raḥmān.*

86. Adjectives are declined in the same manner as substantives, as explained at paragraph 82.

غټ *ghaṯṯ* (masc.) غټه *ghaṯṯa'h* (fem.) 'stout,' 'thick.'

SINGULAR.

	M.	F.	
Nom.	غټ *ghaṯṯ,* or	غټه *ghaṯṯa'h,*	stout or thick.
Obl.	دَ غټ *da ghaṯṯ,* or	دَ غټي *da ghaṯṯey,*	of stout, etc.
Voc.	اي or وُ غټَ *ai,* or *wo ghaṯṯa,* or	غټي *ghaṯṯey,*	O stout! etc.
Act.	غټ *ghaṯṯ,* or	غټي *ghaṯṯey,*	by stout, etc.

PLURAL.

	M.	F.	
Nom.	غټان *ghaṯṯān,* or	غټي *ghaṯṯey,*	stout, thick.
Obl.	دَ غټانُ *da ghaṯṯāno,* or	دَ غټو *da ghaṯṯo,*	of stout, etc.
Voc.	اي or وُ غټانُ *ai,* or *wo ghaṯṯāno,* or	غټو *ghaṯṯo,*	O stout! etc.
Act.	غټانُ *ghaṯṯāno,* or	غټو *ghaṯṯo,*	by stout, etc.

87. Adjectives having *wāw-i-maj-hūl* (concealed or unknown, as not occurring in Arabic) as one of its letters, and in sound like *o* in the English word *robe*, change the و to ا in the singular oblique and nominative plural, and affix *hā-i-zāhir* (or perceptible *h*), to the final letter, but the و is sometimes retained; as, وروست *wrost*, 'rotten,' pl. وراسته *wrāstah*; خوږ *khojz*, 'sweet,' pl. خواږه *khwājzah*; سوړ *sorr*, 'cold,' pl. ساړه *sārrah*; موړ *morr*, 'satiated,' pl. ماړه *mārrah*. For the feminine form the و is dropped, and ه (*hā-i-khafī*) affixed, which is changed to ې (*yā-i-maj-hūl*) or (ـِ) *kasra'h* in the singular oblique and nominative plural; but the plural oblique cases are the same, in the plural, for both genders.

سوړ *sorr*, 'cold.'

	SINGULAR.	PLURAL.
Nom.	سوړ *sorr*, سړه *sarra'h* (F.)	ساړه *sārrah*. سړې or سړِ *sarrey*, or *sarri* (F.)
Obl.	دَ ساړه *da sārrah*, دَ سړې or سړِ *da sarrey*, or *sarri* (F.)	دَ سړو *da sarro* (M. and F.)
Voc.	اي or وُ سړَ *ai*, or *wo sarra*, اي or وُ سړې or سړِ *ai*, or *wo sarrey*, or *sarri* (F.)	اي or وُ سړو *ai*, or *wo sarro* (M. and F.)
Act.	ساړه *sārrah*, سړې or سړِ *sarrey*, or *sarri* (F.)	سړو *sarro* (M. and F.)

88. There are a number of adjectives, principally the active and past participles of verbs, which in the masculine, terminate like the nouns of the first variety of the 1st declension in ئ (*yā-i-mā-kabl-i-maftūh*), and whose feminines take ې (*yā-i-maj-hūl*), or (ـِ) *kasra'h* in the singular; as ويونكَي *wa-yūnkaey*, 'a speaker;' ماتيدونكَي *mātedūnkaey*, 'brittle,' (*lit.* a breaker); نښتَي *n'khataey*, or *n'shataey*, 'entrapped;' ويروونكَي *werawūnkaey*, 'alarming,' 'terrific;' كچوټَي *kuchūttaey*, 'a little child,' etc. Both take ي (*yā-i-maarūf*) in the singular oblique and the nominative plural, and و (*wāw-i-maj-hūl*) in the oblique cases, and may be thus declined:

ويونكَي *wa-yūnkaey*, 'a speaker.'

	SINGULAR.	PLURAL.
Nom.	ويونكَي *wa-yūnkaey*, a speaker, ويونكِ or ويونكې *wa-yūnki*, or *wa-yūnkey* (F.)	ويونكي *wa-yūnkī*, speakers.
Obl.	دَ ويونكي *da wa-yūnkī*, of a speaker, etc.	دَ ويونكيو *da wa-yūnkīo*, of speakers.
Voc.	اي or وُ ويونكيَ or *ai*, or *wo wa-yūnkaeya*, اي or وُ ويونكِ *ai*, or *wo wa-yūnki*, or *wa-* ويونكې *yūnkey*, O speaker! (F.)	اي or وُ ويونكيو *ai*, or *wo wa-yūnkīo*, O speakers!
Act.	ويونكي *wa-yūnkī*, by a speaker.	ويونكيو *wa-yūnkīo*, by speakers.

89. The ordinal numbers اسماي عدد *asmā'e-æadad* are declinable, and subject to the same changes by inflection as other adjectives; thus, ړنبي خل *rrunbaey dzal*, 'the first time,' دويم كال *dweam kāl*, 'the second year,' دريمه مياشت *dreama'h mī-āsht*, 'the third month,' په څلورم كور كښي *pah tsaloram kor kkhey*, 'in the fourth house,' له پنځمي ښځي نه *lah pindzamey Khadzey nah*, 'from the fifth woman,' etc. Examples:

په سرپوښ محل كښي نورد آفتاب نوي   ښه دي زړه په يوه غم سره چاك چاك

"The sun's rays penetrate not through the roof of the covered building:
The heart rent and torn by ONE grief is good."—*Æabd-ul-Ḥamīd.*

پيغمبر دي فرمايلي زه مَيِن يم په درځيزه ړنبي دا چه زه عرب يم دويم قران په عربي دي دريم
په جنت چه به خبرِ عربي وي

"The Prophet of God hath said: I am overjoyed on account of three things; FIRST, that I am an Arab; SECOND, that the Kur'ān is in Arabic; and THIRD, that the language of Heaven will be the Arabian.—*Fawā'id-ush Sharī'æa'h.*

90. The adjunct of similitude شان *shān*, is also subject to change to agree with its governing noun in number and case, as will be seen from the following examples: تور شان آس *tor shān ās*, 'a blackish horse;' سپينه شان آسپه *spīnah shān āspa'h*, 'a whitish mare;' زما په شان ښه سړي *dzamā pah shān khah* or *shah sarraey*, 'a good man like me;' د هلك په شان جينۍ *da halak pah shān jīna'ī*, 'a rompish girl.' Examples:

لكه غم دَ بيلتانه چه په ما اوري   چا ليدلي كنږه اور دي پدا شان

"Like the grief of separation which raineth on me,
Think! hath any one ever seen SUCH fire as this?"—*Æabd-ur-Raḥmān.*

هسي شان په لږ لوږه مبدل شي   چه كونكټ آخلي په طمع دَ املوك

"Thou becometh so changed from slight hunger,
That thou seizeth a beetle in thy avidity instead of a sloe."*—*Æabd-ul-Ḥamīd.*

91. There are several words used in Pushto to denote similarity, but they are adverbs, and not declinable, viz.: غندِ *ghundi*, دود *dod*, څير *tser*, لكه *laka* or لكه *lakah* and هسي *hasey* or هس *hasi*, which generally go together, and may be translated, 'as,' 'so,' 'such,' etc., and the adjective مخي *makhaey* (masc.), or مخۍ *makha'ī* (fem.), but the latter are rare. Examples:

چه مجنون غندِ په مينه كښي كم نام شي   دَ هغو په جهان ږ خپږي نامون

"They who LIKE Majnūn through love lose their reputation,
Their names become renowned throughout the world."—*Æabd-ul-Ḥamīd.*

* The sloe and blackberry grow in the Khaiber mountains, and in the hills north of Peshāwer.

دَ خوشحال په دود به ستا په در پراته وي چه په پښو ئي ستا دَ زلفو زولاني کړ

"LIKE unto Khushḥāl, at thy door fallen, there will be others
Who have made thy tresses fetters on their feet."—*Khushḥāl Khān, Khaṭṭak.*

په ژړا مي دَ خپل يار ديدن حاصل کړ دَ شبنم په څير له گل سره يکتا يم

"By lamentation and weeping I obtained a sight of my beloved:
LIKE UNTO the dew, I am united to the queen of flowers."—*Æabd-ul-Ḥamīd.*

دَ هجران غمونو زه هسي په تنگ کړم لکه کښيني په چا رَوي ميلمانه

"The sorrows of absence reduced me to SUCH extremity,
As when a demon sitteth with one as a guest."—*Æabd-ul-Ḥamīd.*

لکه قند هسي دروغ ور ته خواږه شو لکه زهر هسي ترّ کړه رينښتيا خلق

"As sugar so is falsehood pleasant to the world:
LIKE poison so it spitteth out truth."—*Æabd-ul-Ḥamīd.*

ندي گل دَ ستا دَ مخ غوندي خوشرنگ گل جلوه کا په يوه رنگ ته په سل رنگ

"There is no rose of such a beautiful colour AS thy cheek:
The rose shineth with one colour—thou art resplendent with a hundred."
—*Æabd-ul-Ḥamīd.*

92. The اسماي تفضيل و مبالغه *asmā'e-tafẓīl wo mubālaghah*, comparative and superlative degrees, are not expressed by any peculiar form of adjective: the superiority of one thing over another being expressed by the addition of various particles and adjectives.

93. The positive is made comparative by the particles تر *tar*, له *lah*, له نه *lah nah*, etc., used with the object to which comparison is made; and such words as ډير *ḍer*, 'much,' زيات *zī-āt*, 'more,' لوي *lo'e*, 'great,' and many others; thus, ډير ښه *ḍer khah*, '*very* good,' ډير لوي *ḍer lo'e*, '*very* large,' ډير لنډ *ḍer lanḍ*, '*very* small,' تک سپين *tak spīn*, '*very* white.' Examples:

له ښو ښه غواړه احمد شاهَ بد سپک گڼره تر بنږ

"Look for excellence from the good, Aḥmad Shāh! Evil consider LIGHTER THAN A FEATHER."

بهرام حکم پشماس ؤ که ور دروم سرداسيا هم سهيلي ترده چاپيره
شبانه پوشاک دِ واغوندِ دوي واړَ ور سره روح افزا تر گل نامېره

"Bahrām said unto Shamās, go you to her:
All should dress themselves in royal robes;
Sardāsī'ā too with her hand-maidens around her.
And with them Rūḥ Afzā, MORE LOVELY THAN THE ROSE."—*Bahrām Gūr.*

94. A mere repetition of the positive is commonly used in forming the comparative; thus—

چه په شوي کار خه وائي پوچ پوچ وائي وهي جګ

"He who murmureth at that which hath happened,
Talketh GREAT NONSENSE: he beateth the froth bubbles on the water."
—*Æabd-ul-Hamīd.*

95. In forming the superlative, such words as تول *ttol*, 'all,' حد *hud*, 'boundary,' پهورته *pahor-tah* or پورته *por-tah*, 'over,' 'above,' are used in addition to the particles employed to express the comparative; as دغه له تولُ لوي دي *daghah lah ttolo lo'e daey*, 'this is the *biggest of all*,' or, 'this is the *greatest*;' له حدَ زيات *lah hada zī-āta*, 'beyond bounds;' دا سړي له تولُ نه ډير هوښيار دي *dā sarraey lah ttolo nah dder hosh-yār daey*, 'this man is the *cleverest of all*.' Examples:

ستا جفا ترحدَ پهورته شوه صنمَ تل مي اوښي موج وهي دَ زړه له يمَ

"Thy oppression, Oh beloved one! hath EXCEEDED ALL BOUNDS:
The waves of my tears are ever rolling from the ocean of my heart."
—*Æabd-ul-Hamīd.*

هماي مرغه په تولُ مرغانُ له دي سبب لوئي لري چه هډوکي خوري او نور مرغان نه آزاروي

"The Hūmā on this account enjoyeth the GREATEST RANK OF ALL birds,
That it consumeth bones, and injureth not the feathered race."—*Gulistān.*

له تولُ خلقو نه سړي په ليدُ کښي ډير ښه دي او ترواړُ خلقو نه سپي ډير ناکار دي ولي په صلاح دَ هوښيارانُ وفادار سپي غوره دي له بي وفا سړي نه

"Man to all appearances is the MOST EXCELLENT OF CREATED THINGS, and the dog THE MOST VILE; yet with the concurrence of the wise, a grateful dog IS FAR SUPERIOR to the man without gratitude."—*Gulistān.*

96. Many adjectives have a plural signification only; as, تول *ttol*, 'all,' 'the whole,' etc. They take ه (*hā-i-khafī*) with feminine nouns, in place of which (ـَ) *fat-hah* is commonly written. The following is the mode of conjugation:

(Masc.) تول *ttol*, 'all, 'the whole,' etc.

Nom.	تول	*ttol*,	all, the whole.
Gen.	دَ تولو or دَ تولُ	*da ttolo*, or *da ttolu*,	of all, etc.
Dat.	تولو or تولُ ته, لره or له or تولو or تولُ وته	*ttolo*, or *ttolu tah*, *larah* or *lah*; or *ttolo*, or *ttolu watah*, etc.	to all.
Acc.	تول	*ttol*,	all, *or* to all.
Voc.	اي or وُ تولو or تولُ	*ai*, or *wo ttolo*, or *ttollu*,	O all!
Abl.	له تولو or تولُ or له تولو or تولُ نه	*lah ttolo*, or *ttolu*: or *lah ttolo*, or *ttolu nah*,	from all.
Act.	تولو or تولُ	*ttolo*, or *ttolu*,	by all.

(Fem.) توله *ttola'h.*

Nom.	تولہ or تولَ	*ttola'h*, or *ttola.*	all, the whole.
Gen.	دَ تولو or دَ تولُ	*da ttolo*, or *da ttolu.*	of all, etc.
Dat.	تولو or تولُ ته, لره or له or تولو or تولُ وته etc.	*ttolo tah, larah* or *lah* ; or *ttolo watah*, etc.	to all.
Acc.	تولہ or تولَ	*ttola'h*, or *ttola*,	all, *or* to all.
Voc.	اي or وُ تولو or تولُ	*ai*, or *wu ttolo*,	O all !
Abl.	له تولو or تولُ له تولو or تولُ نه	*lah ttolo* ; or *lah ttolo nah*,	from all.
Act.	تولو or تولُ	*ttolo*,	by all.

97. The اسم تصغير *ism-i-tasghīr* used to lessen the importance of a word, or to convey contempt, is affixed to the noun. There are several of these particles in general use; viz. ړئ, کي, ګي, وټ, وړي, وکي, ګوټي, and the letters ک, ي, ئ, thus: کوزړئ *kūza'hrra'ī*, 'a small goglet;' جينکئ *jīnaka'ī*, 'a little girl;' بازارګي *bāzārguey*, 'a small market;' سړوټي *sarrotaey*, 'a mean fellow (here the particle وټ is inserted before the final letter); چرګوړي *chargorraey*, 'a young cock;' ډنډوکي *ddanddūkaey*, 'a small pond;' مږک *majzak* or مګک *magak*, 'a mouse' (*lit.* a small rat); بهادري *bahāduraey*, 'a coward' (*lit.* a small hero); and ملاګوټي *mullāguttaey*, 'an illiterate priest.' Examples:

يو سړوټي کم عقل مي وُ ليد چه عيب دَ لوي سړي وِ ور ته مي وُ وِ اي صاحبَ که ته خوارئ بختور سړي لره څه ګناه دي

"I once saw a MEAN SCOUNDREL of a fellow, who was speaking ill of a man of rank and respectability. I said to him: 'Oh master! if thou art unlucky, what fault is that of a more fortunate man?'"—*Gulistān.*

ووړکي نه بازي دا رنګ کاڼري کودري　　　　اکثَ زد بازم پتا دين و ايمان خپل

"The CHILD gambleth not in this manner with stones and shards,
Like I stake on thee both my religion and my faith."—*Æabd-ul-Hamīd.*

98. The particle of diminution affixed to a noun is also used to express endearment, as will be seen from the following extract.

دا مي نه مرګ دي نه ژوندون دي تر ځانَ حال دَ مړو ښه وينم له شوق وچ شوم له غمه وُ سوم ميروکي وروره درخو به وُ وينم

"To me this is not death, neither is it life—than existence, the condition of the dead I look upon as preferable—through love I am become dry—from anguish I am consumed. Oh DEAR BROTHER Mīrū! I must see Durkhāna'ī."—*Tale of Adam Khān and Durkhāna'ī.*

شاه زادہ چه دا خبره ؤد ویله بادشاه ؤه ژول زار زار درست خانه دان
بادشاه ؤه ویل چه اي ځما زرګيَ دا کوم وقت دي چه تا کره حسي بیان

"When the prince spoke these words, The king and his family wept a great deal.
The king said, 'Oh my DEAR BOY! What time is this that thou hast made this declaration?'"

—*Saif-ul-Mulūk and Badrī Jamāl.*

CHAPTER V.

THE PRONOUN.

ضمیر *ẓamīr*.

99. The Pus͟hto pronouns are of five different classes—the personal, demonstrative, reflective or reciprocal, interrogative, and indefinite.

100. The language contains no peculiar form of relative and co-relative pronouns, but other pronouns are used instead; the explanations of which, as also examples, will be found in their proper places.

101. As the pronouns in declension admit of considerable changes, they require to be exhibited separately.

102. The personal pronouns, or ضمایر منفصله *ẓamāʼīr-i-munfaṣilah*, are زه *zah*, ته *tah*, and دغه *hag͟hah*.

103. The 1st person is termed متکلم *mutakallim*, the 2nd مخاطب *muk͟hāṭab* or حاضر *ḥāẓir*, and the 3rd غایب *g͟hāyib*.

104. As it would far exceed the intended limits of the present work to give separate examples of each pronoun, both in the singular and plural number, I shall content myself by giving a specimen, either inflected or otherwise, as occasion may require; the whole of the changes for person and case, gender and number, can be seen at a glance from the following declensions.

105. The first personal pronoun زه *zah* is not subject to any change for gender, and is thus declined:

1st Person زه *zah*, 'I.'

SINGULAR.

Nom.	زه *zah*,	I.
Gen.	ځما *dz'mā*,	mine, of me.
Dat.	ما ته, لره, له or *mā tah, larah, lah;* or و ما ته or و ما وته etc. *wa mā tah*; or, *wa mā watah*, etc.	to me.
Acc.	ما *mā*,	me, *or* to me.
Abl.	له ما or له ما نه *lah mā*, or *lah mā nah*,	from me.
Act.	ما *mā*,	by me.

PLURAL.

Nom.	and منګئ or * منګه mungah, or munga; and مونږ and مونګئ or مونګه mūngah, or mūnga (E.), and mūjz (W.),		we.
Gen.	ځموږ or ځمنګه dz'mungah, or dz'mūjz,		our, of us.
Dat.	مونږ ته or منګه mungah, or mūjz tah; or و مونږ ته or و منګه wa mungah, or wa mūjz tah, etc.; or etc. و مونږ وته or و منګه wa mungah, or wa mūjz watah, etc.		to us.
Acc.	مونږ or منګه mungah, or mūjz,		us, *or* to us.
Abl.	or مونږه or له منګه lah mungah, or mūjza; or له مونږه نه or له منګه lah mungah, or mūjza nah,		from us.
Act.	مونږ or منګه mungah, or mūjz,		by us.

The following are examples of the preceding:

زه ياري غواړم له تا نه توفيق ته را كړه رحمانه كه توفيق م كړ په بخرد ما به خلاص كړه له نيرانه

"I seek assistance from thee oh God! grant unto me thy grace! If with my lot thou grantest me thy grace, thou wilt redeem me from the flames."—*Makhzan Afghānī.*

106. The uninflected form of this pronoun is sometimes used for the dative, the pronominal affix م (described at paragraph 135) with the verb, also marking the objective case. The following is an example:

زه د يار غمونو هسي هډ و پوست كړم — لكه ونه په خزان كښي شي بي بركه

"The care and anguish which I suffer on account of my beloved, hath reduced ME to skin and bone,
Like as the tree becometh in the autumn without leaves."—*Aabd-ul-Hamīd.*

ځمونږ پير چه پير صالح دي خبري كاندي چه دست گيري ام وكاند او كه دا كار و نكړ مونږ
د دد له موريدي ويزار يو

"Give you information to OUR spiritual guide, which is Pīr Sāleḥ, that he should assist us; and if he does not do this, WE are tired and disgusted with his discipleship."—*Adam Khān and Durkhāna'ī.*

The following quotation contains examples of several pronouns:

په شعبي كښي هسي دي راوري د جنت يود طفه به د دوزخ بو طني ته هسي وائي مونږ ستاس
په تعليم په نصيحت سره داخل شوو په جنت كښي څه سبب د بد بختي وه چه داخل شوي په
دوزخ كښي دوي به هسي ور ته وائي مونږ امر د نيكي كاوه عالم ته ولي مونږ پرو لا نوو له بدي به
مونږ نهي كړه د خلق ولي مونږ تر پرهيز نوو

* منګئ, or منګه as it is also written, is the Eastern or Peshāwerī form of the first person plural, and مونږ the Western dialect. I have already explained at page 3 that some tribes change the letters ج for ګ, and ګ for ږ and *vice versâ*.

In the Shaœbī it is thus stated: "A party of people in Paradise will thus say to another party in Hell—'Through YOUR instruction and exhortations WE have entered into Heaven. By what evil destiny was it that you entered into Hell?' These will thus answer them: 'WE gave good counsel to the world, but WE did not act up to it ourselves. WE interdicted others from evil, but WE did not abstain from it ourselves.'"—*Fawā'id-ush-Sharī'a'h.*

107. 2nd Person تهٔ *tah*, 'Thou.'

SINGULAR.

Nom.	تهٔ	*tah,*	thou
Gen.	ستا or د تا	*stā*, or *da tā*.	thine, of thee.
Dat.	تا ته، لره، or له و تا ته etc. or و تا وته etc.	*tā tah*, *larah*, or *lah*; or *wa tā tah*, etc.; or *wa tā watah*, etc.	to thee.
Acc.	تا	*tā,*	thee, *or* to thee.
Voc.	اي تا or وُ تا	*ai tā*, or *wo tā*,	O thou!
Abl.	له تا or له تا نه	*lah tā*, or *lah tā nah*,	from thee.
Act.	تا	*tā*.	by thee.

PLURAL.

Nom.	تاسو، تاسُ or تاسي or تاسِ	*tāsū*, *tāsu*, or *tāsey* or *tāsi*,	ye *or* you.
Gen.	ستاسو، ستاسُ or ستاسي or ستاسِ	*stāsū*, *stāsu*, or *stāsey*, or *stāsi*,	yours, of you.
Dat.	تاسو or تاسُ ته، لره، له or تاسي or تاسِ ته، لره، له or تاسو، تاسُ، تاسي، or تاسِ وته	*tāsū*, or *tāsu tah*, *larah*, *lah*; or *tāsey*, or *tāsi tah*, *larah*, *lah*; or *tāsū*, *tāsu*, *tāsey*, or *tāsi watah*, etc.	to you.
Acc.	تاسو or تاسُ and تاسي or تاسِ	*tāsū*, or *tāsu*; and *tāsey*, or *tāsi*,	you, *or* to you.
Voc.	اي or وُ تاسو، تاسي	*ai*, or *wo tāsū*, *tāsey*, etc.	O you!
Abl.	له تاسو or تاسي or له تاسو or تاسي نه	*lah tāsū*, or *tāsey*; or *lah tāsū*, or *tāsey nah*,	from you.
Act.	تاسو، تاسُ، تاسي، or تاس	*tāsū*, *tāsu*, *tāsey*, or *tāsi*,	by you.

اي اعرابي ويريږم چه کعبي ته به وُ نرسي دا لار چه تهٔ پرِ ځي ترکيستان ته ځي

"Oh Arab! I fear thou wilt not arrive at Mekka, for the road that THOU followest leadeth to Turkistān."—*Gulistān.*

108. In old writings, the dative particle is often written with an extra و thus: و وته, of which the following is an example.*

زه هر صبح شام و تا وته دعا کړم ته و ما وته کوِ دشنام په څه

"Every morning and evening I offer up a prayer for thee:
Wherefore treatest thou me with contempt and abuse?"—*Raḥmān.*

* This form of the dative is also used with nouns: and it may also be translated—'for,' 'for the sake of,' etc. See Chap. III.

تاسي وُ پوښتي بلبلَ　　چه څه وائي له گلَ

"You should make enquiry of the nightingale— 'What sayest thou to the rose?'"
—*Aḥmad Shāh, Abdālī.*

109. 3rd Person هغه *haghah*, 'He, she, or it.'

SINGULAR.

Nom.	هغه	*haghah*,	he, she, *or* it.
Gen.	دَ هغه	*da haghah*,	of him, *or* it.
	دَ هِغِه or دَ هِغي	*da highih*, or *da highey*,	of her, *or* it.
Dat.	هغه ته, لره, له or هغه وته	*haghah tah, larah, lah*; or *haghah watah*, etc.	to him, *or* it.
	هِغِه or هِغي ته, لره, له	*highih*, or *highey tah, larah, lah*; or	to her, *or* it.
	هِغِه or هِغي وته or و هِغِه وته	*highih*, or *highey watah*, etc.; or *wa highih watah*, etc.	
Acc.	هغه	*haghah*,	him, *or* to him, her, *or* it.
Abl.	له هغه or له هغه نه	*lah haghah*, or *lah haghah nah*,	from him, *or* it.
	له هِغِه or له هِغِه نه	*lah highih*, or *lah highih nah*,	from her, *or* it.
	له هِغي or له هِغي نه	*lah highey*, or *lah highey nah*,	
Act.	هغه or هِغِه or هِغي	*haghah*, or *highih*, or *highey*,	by him, her, *or* it.

PLURAL (USED FOR BOTH GENDERS).

Nom.	هغه	*haghah*,	they.
Gen.	دَ هُغو or دَ هُغوي	*da hugho*, or *da hughocy*,	of them.
Dat.	هُغو or هُغوي ته, لره, له	*hugho*, or *hughocy tah, larah, lah*; or	to them.
	و هُغو or و هُغوي ته	*wa hugho*, or *wa hughocy tah*, etc.; or	
	و هُغو or و هُغوي وته	*wa hugho*, or *wa hughocy watah*, etc.	
Acc.	هغه	*haghah*,	them, *or* to them.
Abl.	له هُغو or له هُغوي	*lah hugho*, or *lah hughocy*, or	from them.
	له هُغو or له هُغوي نه	*lah hugho*, or *lah hughocy nah*,	
Act.	هُغو or هُغوي	*hugho*, or *hughocy*,	by them.

په خوا تر پاك سروره دا په نام دَ عتيق بن عامر وَد يود لور ترِ پيدا شوه چه هنده دِ هِغِه نوم وُه

"Before the time of the Prophet, this (woman) was married to Ætiḳ bin Æāmir, and she had a daughter by him: HER name was Hinda'h.—*Fawā'īd-ush-Sharī'æa'h.*

110. The feminine form of this pronoun, of which the example just given is a specimen, is also written with a ي instead of (ـِ), thus:

بي‌بي هسي ور ته وُ وِ چه مرگ دير دير يادوه زړه نرمي به دِ حاصلَ شي دَ بيبي عايشي بند هِغي
شجي په ځاي كړ

"The mother of the Faithful said thus to her, 'Always remember death; by means of it meekness and gentleness of heart is produced.' The counsel of Lady Æā-Isha'h took effect on THAT woman, and she acted up to it."—*Fawā'īd-ush-Sharī'æa'h.*

111. The singular nominative is also used for the plural, but the inflected plural form is occasionally adopted; as,

حضرت هسي ور ته وه وِ خليفگان خما هغه دي چه طريق سنت خما به دوي کوين

"The Prophet said thus unto him—'THEY are my vicars who act up to the rules and institutions of my orthodox faith.'"—*Fawā'īd-ush-Sharī'æa'h.*

پس هغه هلته د کټ د لاندِ چپ کښيناست او ساه يې نه نښکله تر هغه وقت پوري چه هغو له عيش
خلاص شوُ او نښان د تورِ شپي سر ښکته شه

"After that he sat down beneath the couch, and did not draw his breath until such time as THEY had consummated their pleasure, and the black flag of night became inverted."
—*Kalīlah wo Damnah.*

112. This pronoun is also used as the remote demonstrative, or اسم اشاره *ism-i-ishāra'h*, and is declined in a similar manner, as will be seen from the following examples:

هر رنګ تخم چه کرِ هغه به آخلي خپله خپله ميوه نسي هرِ ونِ

"Whatever kind of seed thou sowest, THAT wilt thou reap:
Every tree beareth each its own peculiar fruit."—*Æabd-ur-Raḥmān.*

بخپل عمر به هيچا ليدلي نه وي هغه چارِ چه يار هر ساعت په ما کا

"No one in the whole course of his lifetime will have experienced
THOSE sorrows which my beloved every hour inflicts upon me."
—*Æabd-ur-Raḥmān.*

113. The demonstrative pronouns are of two kinds, the proximate and the remote. The proximate demonstratives are دغه *daghah* and دا *dā*, which, when uninflected, are both masculine and feminine; but in the oblique cases دغه becomes دِغه *dighih*, or دغي *dighey*, for the feminine gender; and the final letter of دا is changed for ي (*yā-i-majhūl*) or ِ (*kasrah*) in the oblique cases, but is used for both genders; as in the following declension:

دغه *daghah*, or دا *dā*, 'this' (person or thing).

SINGULAR.

Nom.		دا or دغه *daghah*, or *dā*,	this.
Gen.	M.	دَ دِ or دَ دي ,دَ دغه *da daghah, da dey*, or *da di*,	of this.
	F.	دَ دي or دَ دِغي ,دَ دِغه *da dighih, da dighey*, or *da dey*,	

Dat.	M.	دغه or دي ته, لره or له *daghah*, or *dey tah*, *larah*, or *lah*; or		to this.
		و دغه ته or و دغه وته *wah daghah tah*, etc., or *wah daghah watah*, etc.		
	F.	دِغِه, دِغي or دي ته, لره or له *dighih*, *dighey*, or *dey tah*, *larah*, or *lah*; or		
		و دِغِه ته or و دِغِه وته *wa dighih tah*, etc.; or *wa dighih watah*, etc.		
Acc.		دغه or دا *daghah*, or *dā*,		this, *or* to this.
Abl.	M.	له دغه, دي or دِ *lah daghah*, *dey*, or *di*; or		from this.
		له دغه, دي or دِ نه *lah daghah*, *dey*, or *di nah*,		
	F.	له دِغِه, دِغي or دي *lah dighih*, *dighey*, or *dey*; or		
		له دِغِه, دِغي or دي نه *lah dighih*, *dighey*, or *dey nah*,		
Act.	M.	دغه, دي or دِ *daghah*, *dey*, or *di*,		by this.
	F.	دِغِه, دِغي or دي *dighih*, *dighey*, or *dey*,		

PLURAL (USED FOR BOTH GENDERS).

Nom.	دغه *daghah*,	these.
Gen.	دَ دغو or دَ ديوو or ديوُ *da dagho*, or *da dewo*,	of these.
Dat.	دغو, ديوو or ديوُ ته, لره, له *dagho*, or *dewo tah*, *larah*, or *lah*; or	to these.
	و دغو ته or و دغو وته *wa dagho tah*, etc.; or *wa dagho watah*, etc.	
Acc.	دغه *daghah*,	these, *or* to these.
Abl.	له دغو, ديوو or ديوُ *lah dagho*, or *dewo*,	from these.
	له دغو, ديوو or ديوُ نه *lah dagho*, or *dewo nah*,	
Act.	دغو ديوو or ديوُ *dagho*, or *dewo*,	by these.

EXAMPLES.

د رنځور علاج ترخه دارو دي   دغه دارو دي چه هم درد شه هم درمان شي

"The remedy of the sick is bitter bitter medicine:
THIS is a physic which becometh not only the disease, but also its cure."
—*Æabd-ur-Rahmān.*

تل دَ اوښو په اوبو کښي لرد تر مخ   په دغو اوبو کښي ليده شي دَ گوهر مخ

"Keep thy cheek ever moist with the waters of thy tears:
In THESE waters can be seen the face of the gem."—*Æabd-ul-Hamīd.*

دا سور گل به هم دِ تا په وينو سور کا   چه دِ ايښي زماني دي په دستار کښي

"Destiny will ensanguine THIS red flower in thy blood,
Which itself hath placed in thy turban."—*Æabd-ul-Hamīd.*

په لښکر کښي دَ بيزاد څه شور و شر وُو   نيمي شپي وي چه فرياد او وا ويلا شوه
شهزاده وُ و دَ قلا و سر وته خيژئي   چه تر دِ وقتهٔ جنگ نشته څه بلا شوه

"What noise and confusion was there in the army of Bihizād!
It was about midnight that a tumult and cries for help arose:—

'Mount,' said the prince, 'to the summit of the fortress :
What calamity has happened that up to THIS time no battle has ensued?'"
—*Bahrām Gūr.*

114. هايه *hāyah*, هايَ *hā-ya*, is another, although less common, form of the proximate demonstrative pronoun, and more emphatic in its signification than the former; but it is more generally used by the Western than the Eastern Afghāns. It is not subject to change for gender or number, but rejects the final letter in the oblique cases. The following is the mode of declension :

هايه *hā-yah*, 'this.'

Nom.	هايه *hāyah.*
Gen.	دَ هي *da ha-ey.*
Dat.	هي ته or هي وته *ha-ey tah*, etc.; or *ha-ey watah*, etc.
Acc.	هايه *hāyah.*
Abl.	له هي or له هي نه *lah ha-ey*, or *lah ha-ey nah.*
Act.	هي *ha-ey.*

هر چا ور ته وُ ويل اي ناداني كم عقلي اوښ له تا سره څه مناسبت لري او ته له اوښه سره څه مشابهت لري هغي ور ته وُ ويل چه چپ شئي كه حاسدان خپل غرض دپاره وُ وائي چه يو اوښ هايه دي اوگرفتاره شم چا لره څما دَ خلاصولو غم دي

"Everyone said unto her, 'Oh thou foolish one of little wisdom! what resemblance beareth a camel to thee? and what similitude existeth between thee and a camel?' She said unto them, 'Be silent! for if the envious, for their own designs, should say, "THIS is a camel," and I should in consequence be seized, to whom is the concern and trouble for my release?'"—*Gulistān.*

115. The remote demonstratives are دي *daey* for the masculine, and دا *dā* for the feminine. The latter, it will be noticed, is the same as one of the proximate demonstratives before described; but the difference is that the former is used for both genders, whilst the remote form is used only for the feminine gender. The personal pronouns of the third person, as already noticed at paragraph 112, are also used as remote demonstrative pronouns,* and *vice versâ.*

دي *daey*, or دا *dā*, 'that' (persons or things).

SINGULAR.

Nom.	دي or دا *daey*, or *dā*,	that.
Gen.	دَ ده or دَ دي *da dah*, or *da dey*,	of that.
Dat.	ده or دي ته, لره or له *dah*, or *dey tah*, *larah*, or *lah*; or و ده or دي ته or و ده وته *wa dah*, or *dey tah*, etc.; or *wa dah watah*, etc.	to that.

* These forms of the demonstrative—دي, دا, and دِ, are apt to be used indiscriminately in conversation, particularly by the Eastern Afghāns. Those of the West conform more to the written form of the language in this particular.

Acc.	دي or دا	*dacy*, or *dā*,	those, *or* to those.
Abl.	له ده or دي له ده or دي نه	*lah dah*, or *dey* ; or *lah dah*, or *dey nah*,	from that.
Act.	ده or دي	*dah*, or *dey*,	by that.

PLURAL.

Nom.	دوي	*dū-ī*,	those.
Gen.	دَ دوي or دَ دويو	*da dū-ī*, or *da dū-īo*,	of those.
Dat.	دوي or دويو ته, لرد or له و دوي ته or و دوي وته	*dū-ī*, or *dū-īo tah*, *larah*, or *lah* ; or *wa dū-ī tah*, etc. ; or *wa dū-ī watah*, etc.	to those.
Acc.	دوي	*dū-ī*,	those, *or* to those.
Abl.	له دوي or دويو له دوي or دويو نه	*lah dū-ī*, or *dū-īo* ; or *lah dū-ī*, or *dū-īo nah*,	from those.
Act.	دوي or دويو	*dū-ī*, or *dū-īo*,	by those.

دَ خلاصي لوريه مي نشته دي اي ځوانَ زيست روزگار مي هميشه دَ غم په خونه
دي ځما ديدن كوي نور په امان يم ولي عالم را باندِ كاندِ گمانونَ

"Alas, brave youth! there is no road of escape for me:
The employment of this life of mine is in the house of grief.
THAT (demon) merely looks at me—in other respects I am safe;
But the world entertaineth suspicions against me."—*Bahrām Gūr*.

خوشحال خټک چه بياموند لذت دَ يار د شوندو دَه وته نور واړد دَ جهان خوارِه گندهير دي

"Since Khūshhal Khattak has drunk nectar from the lips of the beloved,
All the other sweets of the world are TO HIM as nauseous poison."

دوي وائي دا عورتي دي گلونَ گل هم هر څوک بويوينَ دغه قوم دَ عبدالله شمراخي دي په ظاهر
دوي مسلمان دي په باطن دوي كافران دِينَ

"THEY say that these women are roses, and every person smelleth a rose. This is the sect of Æabd-ullah Shamrākhī. Outwardly they are Musalmāns, but inwardly are infidels."—*Makhzan Afghānī*.

116. The first letter of the demonstrative هغه is sometimes lost by elision, thus:

دَ ناسوت په وهم ورک شو عندليب زد غه گل يم چه دَ ميني په بهار ځي

"The nightingale became lost in the imagination of humanity:
I am THAT rose which roameth about in the spring time of love."
—*Ahmad Shāh, Abdālī*.

117. The reflective or reciprocal pronoun ضمير مشترك (*zamīr-i-mushtarak*) خپل *khpul* is applicable to all three persons. It is placed before the verb in the

sentence, and must refer to the agent or nominative case either expressed or understood, whatever it may be. The changes to which it is subject for gender and by inflection will be seen in the following declension:

(M.) خپل *khpul,* or (F.) خپله *khpula'h,* 'myself, thyself, my own,' etc.

SINGULAR.

Nom.	خپل or خپله	*khpul,* or *khpula'h,*	myself, self, etc.
Gen.	دَ خپل or دَ خپلي	*da khpul,* or *da khpuley,*	of myself, etc.
Dat.	خپل or خپلي ته, لره, له etc. خپل or خپلي وته	*khpul,* or *khpuley tah, larah, lah;* or *khpul,* or *khpuley watah,* etc.	to myself, etc.
Acc.	خپل or خپله	*khpul,* or *khpula'h,*	myself, *or* to myself, etc.
Abl.	له خپلَ or له خپلي نه له خپلَ نه or له خپلي نه	*lah khpula,* or *lah khpuley nah,* *lah khpula nah,* or *lah khpuley nah,*	from myself, etc.
Act.	خپل or خپلي	*khpul,* or *khpuley,*	by myself, etc.

PLURAL.

Nom	خپل or خپلي	*khpul,* or *khpuley,*	ourselves, etc.
Gen.	دَ خپلو	*da khpulo,*	of ourselves, etc.
Dat.	خپلو ته, لره, له etc. خپلو وته	*khpulo tah, larah,* or *lah;* or *khpulo watah,* etc.	to ourselves.
Acc.	خپل or خپلو	*khpul,* or *khpulo,*	ourselves, *or* to ourselves.
Abl.	له خپلو or له خپلو نه	*lah khpulo,* or *lah khpulo nah,*	from ourselves, etc.
Act.	خپلو	*khpulo,*	by ourselves.

118. The following are examples of this pronoun:

په تاريخ دَ زر څلويښت وايم دا خبر　　چه ليدد شي دَ دکهن دَ گجرات په عالم جبر
په خپل عمر څو و نيک و بد خبر شوم　　په دا دود مي قتل نليدد په دبر

"In the year one thousand and forty I relate, this occurrence.
That on the people of Dakhan and Gujerāt such tyranny and oppression is seen.
In the whole of MY life, since I could distinguish good from evil;
I never beheld after this fashion massacre with stones."—*Mīrzā Khān, Anṣārī.*

The inflected form of the feminine may be written خپلِ *khpuli.*

حق دَ ښځي دا دي پر څښتن باندِ چه له وروڼو له مورَ پلارَ دَ خپلِ ښځي دِ دي ښه اخلاص کوينَ

"The just claim which a wife has over her husband is this, that he should show proper love and affection towards HIS wife's brothers, her mother and father."

—*Fawā'id-ush-Sharī'aa'h.*

پس له هغه درخانۍ ورته وُ وِ چه يو عرض مي دي را ته غوږ کړه آدم خان وِ چه څه حکم وي
په سترګو مي قبول دي دِ ور ته خپل غمونه په دا مضمون وُ وِ

"Afterwards Durkhāna'ī said to him, 'I have a request to make: pray give ear to it.' Adam Khān answered, 'Whatever the command may be I agree to it with all my heart.'* She then related to him HER OWN sorrows in the following manner."

—*Adam Khān and Durkhāna'ī.*

119. When no agent is expressed this pronoun denotes individuality and reciprocity, or may refer to either of the three persons, which is only discoverable by something that has preceded it, or comes after; as it would be in the sentence دا خپل مال دي.

چه و قبر ته سجده کا يا حاجت له مړده غواړي حصليدد دَ خپل مقصود هم دَ مړده له لوري ګنړينَ
په کښي ويره وي دَ کفر

"Whoever maketh a prostration before a tomb, or wisheth for anything from the defunct; and he considereth the fulfilment of HIS wish to have been accomplished by means of the deceased, there is danger of blasphemy."—*Fawā'id-ush Sharī'aa'h.*

له دِ خپلي بدي بخري   چا ته ژاړم په چا داد کړم

"Concerning this my own hard fate,
To whom shall I tell my sorrows? from whom seek redress?"

—*Laylā and Majnūn.*

هرچه تا سره ياري کا نه ياران دي   همګي واړه لړم دي يا ماران دي
زوي واړه رنج دل دَ خپل بابا دي   لونړه ګل واړه ژوري دَ ماما دي
که دِ خويښ دي که دِ ورور دي   دَ خپل ځان دي دَ خپل سود دي دَ خپل کور دي

"Those who show friendliness towards thee are not thy friends:
The whole set of them are scorpions or serpents!
The whole of the sons are the plague and chagrin of THEIR OWN father!
The daughters are all leeches—blood-suckers of their mother's brother!
Whether are they thy kinsfolk, or whether thy brother,
They are all for THEIR OWN selves, their OWN profit, their OWN house."

—*Khūshhāl Khān, Khattak.*

لکه ته چه ئي پخپله پخپل ځان کړي   دښمن نه کا په دښمن دا بيدادي

"Like as thou of THINE OWN ACCORD behaveth towards THINE OWNSELF;
No one ever acteth towards an enemy with such iniquity and injustice."

—*Æabd-ul-Hamīd.*

120. The interrogative pronouns, اسماي استفهام (*asmā'e-i-istifhām*), are څوک *tsok*, کوم *kom*, and کم *kam* or کمه *kuma'h*.

* Literally, 'on my eyes.'

څوک is applied to persons and rarely to inanimate objects. It is used both for the singular and plural, and masculine and feminine, and is thus declined :

څوک *tsok*, 'who? which? what?'

Nom.	څوک	*tsok*,	who? which? what?
Gen.	دَ چا	*da chā*,	of whom? which? what?
Dat.	چا ته, لرہ, له or وِ چا ته etc. or وِ چا وته etc.	*chā tah, larah, lah*, or *wa chā tah*, etc., or *wa chā watah*, etc.	to whom? which? what?
Acc.	څوک	*tsok*,	whom? which? what?
Abl.	له چا or له چا نه	*lah cha*, or *lah chā nah*,	from whom? which? what?
Act.	چا	*chā*,	by whom? which? what?

EXAMPLES.

را ته وايه چه ته څوک ئي نوم دِ څه دي   چه دا عشق دِ په خاطر زره دِ غم زده دي

"Tell me WHO art thou? and what is thy name,
That this love of thine affects thy mind so much."—*Bahrām Gūr*.

تير شه درست عمر څما په دا هوس   که مي وُ پوښتي چه څوک ئي يا څه کس

"The whole of my lifetime has passed in this vain hope,
That thou wouldst ask me, WHO art thou? and what?—*Æabd-ur-Raḥmān*.

121. This pronoun is also in common use as an indefinite, and is for the most part applied to persons, but in some instances to things also. Examples of its use with respect to persons are contained in the following extracts :

که څوک مت په نيکي وُ که بيا په مينه محبت پسِ روان شه

"If any one taketh courage in acting with uprightness, he will follow after it with affection and love."—*Makhzan Afghānī*.

چا ويل چه يوسفزي دي لوي مړونَ خوراك خوري په تالو کښي اوبه څکي په جامونَ

"Some persons say that the Yūsufzīs are a great people—they (certainly) eat victuals out of platters, and drink water from bowls."—*Adam Khān and Durkhāna'ī*.

122. The following couplet contains an example of its use with reference to things.

يو اصل دَ ابو دي يو دَ زمکي   او ميوه ذني ترخه دد څوک شيرين.

"There is one element of water, and one element of earth ;
And SOME fruits are bitter, and some pleasant and sweet."
—*Mīrzā Khān, Anṣārī*.

123. The interrogative pronouns كوم *kom* and كم *kam* are both singular and plural, but they take the addition of ه (*hā-i-khafī*) or (ـَ) *fat-ḥa'h* for the feminine gender, and may be thus declined :

كوم *kom* or كم *kam* (M.), كومه *koma'h* or كمه *kama'h* (Fem.), 'what ?'

SINGULAR AND PLURAL.

Nom.	كوم or كم or كومه or كمه	*kom*, or *kam* ; or *koma'h*, or *kama'h*,	what ?
Gen.	دَ كوم or دَ كم or دَ كومي or دَ كمي	*da kom*, or *da kam* ; or *da komey*, or *da kamey*,	of what ?
Dat.	كوم or كم ته, لره, له or و كوم or و كم وته etc. كومي or كمي ته, لره, له or و كومي or وكمي وته etc.	*kom*, or *kam tah, larah, lah* ; or *wa kom*, or *wa kam watah*, etc. ; or *komey*, or *kamey tah, larah, lah* ; or *wa komey*, or *wa kamey watah*, etc.,	to what ?
Acc.	كوم or كم or كومه or كمي	*kom*, or *kam* ; or *koma'h*, or *kamey*,	what? or to what ?
Abl.	له كومَ or كمَ or له كومي or كمي or له كومَ or كمَ نه or له كومي or كمي نه	*lah koma*, or *kama* ; or *lah komey*, or *kamey* ; or *lah koma*, or *kama nah* ; or *lah komey*, or *kamey nah*,	from what ?
Act.	كوم or كم or كومي or كمي	*kom*, or *kam* ; or *komey*, or *kamey*,	by what ?

EXAMPLES.

كوم وادہ كومه كوزدہ دہ په دنيا كښي   چه فلك ئې و آخر وته وير نكا

"WHAT wedding—WHAT betrothal is there in the world,
That cruel fate at last turneth not into wailing and lamentation ?"
—*Æabd-ur-Raḥmān.*

دغه كم ساعت چه زړه پوي ليري   غه ساعت وي چه په زړه شي رخسارون

"WHAT hour is it that the heart palpitates and beats ?
It will be that hour when the shadow of beloved faces falls on the heart."
—*Aḥmad Shāh. Abdālī.*

124. The pronoun څه *tsah* is used both in an interrogative as well as in an indefinite sense. Its conjugation is as follows :

(Masc. and Fem.) څه *tsah*, 'What ?' or 'a, an, any,' etc.

SINGULAR AND PLURAL.

Nom.	څه *tsah*,	what ?—a, an, any, some, etc.
Gen.	دَ څه *da tsah*,	of what ?—of a, an, any, some, etc.

Dat.	or له, لره, څه ته *tsah tah, larah, lah*; or or etc. و څه ته *wa tsah tah*, etc. or etc. و څه وته *wa tsah watah*, etc.	to what?—to a, an, any, some, etc.
Acc.	څه *tsah*,	what?—a, an, any, some, etc.
Abl.	له څه نه or له څه *lah tsah*, or *lah tsah nah*,	from what?—from a, an, any, etc.
Act.	څه *tsah*,	by what?—by a, an, any, some, etc.

EXAMPLES.

پير صالح هلته معركي تنګ كړي ؤ چه څه كوي وقت دي موږ ستړي شؤ

"The party had reduced Pīr Ṣāleḥ to great extremity, saying—'WHAT art thou doing?—it is now time! we are tired of waiting!'"—*Adam Khān and Durkhāna'ī.*

Example as the Indefinite, اسم مبهم *ism-i-mubham*:

كه په ما دي څه اثر كولي وعظ   تا ناصح را ته هله ويلي وعظ

"If there was ANY chance of thy admonition taking effect on me,
Thou, oh monitor! wouldst then have given me advice.—*Æabd-ul-Ḥamīd.*

125. څنِ *dzini*, څني *dzinī*, or ذنِ *zini* or ذني *zinī*, as it is sometimes written, is another form of the indefinite. It is applicable to things both animate and inanimate; it is not subject to any change in termination for gender; and is both singular and plural. It is declined as follows:

څني *dzinī* or څنِ *dzini*, 'Some, any, a few,' etc.

SINGULAR AND PLURAL.

Nom.	څنِ or څني *dzinī*, or *dzini*,	some, any, a few, etc.
Gen.	دَ څنُ or دَ څنو *da dzino*,	of some, any, a few, etc.
Dat.	له, لره, څنُ ته or څنو *dzino tah, larah, lah*; or etc. و څنُ ته or و څنو *wa dzino tah*, etc.; or etc. و څنُ وته or و څنو *wa dzino watah*, etc.	to some, any, etc.
Acc.	څنِ or څني *dzinī*, or *dzini*,	some, or to some, etc.
Abl.	له څنُ or له څنو *lah dzino*, or له څنُ نه or له څنو نه *lah dzino nah*,	from some, any, etc.
Act.	څنُ or څنو *dzino*,	by some, any, a few, etc.

EXAMPLES.

كه څوك ښكنځل كا و هغه ته چه نامه ئې محمد وي يا احمد ابوالقاسم وي څنِ وائي چه كفر نشته
څنِ وائي كه په وقت دَ ښكنځلو دَ ده فهم و نبي صاحب ته ؤ شي كافر كيږي

"If a person abuseth him who may bear the name of Muḥammad, or Aḥmad-abul-Ḳāsim. SOME say that it is not blasphemy. OTHERS again state, that at the time of giving abuse, if his thoughts should be directed towards the Prophet, he is a blasphemer."—*Fawā'īd-ush-Sharī'æa'h.*

و هر چا و ته پخپل قسمت رسيږي   له ازل ئې سور سور دي پلي پلي
او آدم په اصل واړه سره وصل   ذنِ ذنِ بادشاهي که څوک نتلي

"The decree of destiny reacheth unto every one—
From its beginning the horseman is mounted, the footman on foot;
And man himself originally is of one race and origin;
Yet SOME rule empires, and some beg from door to door."—*Mīrzā Khān, Anṣārī.*

126. Several pronouns admit of composition; thus, هرڅوک *har-tsok*, 'whoever,' هرڅه *har-tsah*, 'whatever,' هريو *har-yow*, 'every one,' کميو *kam-yow*, 'which one,' or 'whichever,' etc. They are subject to the same rules of inflection and change in termination for gender as the pronouns from which they are derived. کميو *kam-yow* is declined in the following manner:

کم يو *kam-yow* (Masc.), or کمه يوه *kama'h-yowa'h* (Fem.), 'Which one?'

SINGULAR AND PLURAL.

Nom.	کم يو or کمه يوه *kam-yow*, or *kama'h-yowa'h*,	which one.
Gen.	دَ کم يوَ or دَ کمي يوي *da kam-yowa*; *da kamey-yowey*,	of which one.
Dat.	کم يوَ ته, لره, له or *kam-yowa tah, larah, lah*; or کمي يوي ته, لره, له etc. *kamey-yowey tah, larah, lah*; etc.	to which one.
Acc.	کم يو or کمه يوه *kam-yow*, or *kama'h-yowa'h*,	which one, etc.
Abl.	له کم يوَ or له کم يوَ نه *lah kam-yowa*, or *lah kam-yowa nah*, له کمي يوي or له کمي يوي نه *lah kamey-yowey*, or *lah kamey-yowey nah*,	from which one.
Act.	کم يوَ or کمي يوي *kam-yowa*, or *kamey-yowey*.	by which one.

EXAMPLES OF کميو AND هرڅوک.

هغه عالم په تلواري وخپل کور ته را ؤ بالَ اوګله ئې ور ته ؤ کړد چه لور ته مي ولي په شا ئې لور مي
هرګورد دَ علم عاشقه دَد چه عزيزانُ ته ئې سبق وائې کميو له دي فايق دي

"He quickly called the learned man to his house, and upbraided him, saying—'Why turnest thou thy back on my daughter? she is at all times a seeker after knowledge: since thou teachest her companions, WHICH ONE of them is superior to her?'"—*Adam Khān and Durkhāna'ī.*

په دا خداي چه دَ هرچا دي نه ګروهيږي   واړوم له رقيبانو په کوم خداي دوست

"Since she feareth not that God, who is the God of all,
By the assistance of what Deity shall I divert my friend from the keepers?"
—*Æabd-ul-Hamīd.*

127. The only relative pronoun, اسم موصول *ism-i-mawṣūl*, which the Pushto language contains is چه *chih*,* which must not be confounded with the interrogative

* This particle has a great similarity to the Persian چه.

څه *tsah* already explained, there being no connection between them. The co-relative, جواب موصول *jawāb-i-mawṣūl*, is supplied by the demonstrative pronouns, as will be seen from the examples.

128. چه may either precede or follow after its substantive:

چه ايري دَ بي قدرۍ شي پوري مښوي   آئينه دَ هغو زړونو وي رڼړه

"THEY WHO have been well anointed with the ashes of humility,
The mirror of THEIR hearts becometh clear and bright."—*Æabd-ul-Ḥamīd.*

په خرپوسو صبر زهد څني تښتي   چه په ګرت کا تيره غشي دَ مږګانو

"Patience and continence fly from her on all fours,
WHEN SHE taketh between her finger and thumb the arrows of her eye-lashes."
—*Æabd-ul-Ḥamīd.*

په يوي بوسي به څه صبوري کړم   چه آخست شي له جهانَ نصيب ورو ورو

"With one kiss merely, how shall I be contented?
SINCE from the world, good fortune is only to be obtained by degrees."
—*Æabd-ul-Ḥamīd.*

129. In addition to the regular form of the personal pronouns already explained and illustrated, there are three other forms which require a lengthened explanation.

The first form of these pronouns is used with all past tenses of the active voice, to denote the agent in a sentence; but they have no meanings separate from the verbs. With any other than active or transitive verbs they point out the object, or the possessive case, and have but these two inflections from the nominative. They are not affected by gender, and may be prefixed or inserted.

FIRST FORM.

SINGULAR. PLURAL.

1st person, مِ or مي *mī* or *mi*, I, mine, to me. مو or مُه, أم *ūm*, *muh* or *mū*, we, ours, to us.
2nd ,, دِ or دي *dī* or *di*, thou, thine, to thee. مو or مه *mah* or *mo*, you, yours, to you.
3rd ,, يه or ئي *yey* or *yah* (W.), he, she, it, his, hers, etc.; and them, theirs, to them.

130. In the following examples, the first shows the actor, and the second the inflected form respectively:

سل توبي مي ماتِ کړِ وا نه وُ بيتم له عشقَ   ساد ويساد مي نوره پاتو نشوه په توبو کښِ

"*I* broke a hundred vows, yet did not abandon love;
Therefore my faith remaineth no longer on pledges."—*Æabd-ur-Raḥmān.*

هله ګل وُم چه هيچري مي سيال نوُ   ولي اوس دَ آشنائۍ په زړه خار څم

"I was a rose when there were no equals TO ME.
But now I become a thorn in the heart of friendship."—*Æabd-ul-Ḥamīd.*

چه دِ رنګ دَ ميو ور کړ و لبانو — اور دِ پوري کړ په کور دَ ميخوارانو

"When THOU didst give the colour of wine to thy lips,
THOU didst set all on fire the houses of the wine drinkers."—*Æabd-ur-Raḥmān.*

چه ئي ؤ ليده ستا دَ جمال عکس په خپل ځان کښي — هم په دا دَ آئيني په څير حيران دي ځما روح

"Since IT saw the reflection of thy beauty in its own heart,
On this account also, my soul like the mirror is filled with amazement."
—*Æabd-ur-Raḥmān.*

درخانۍ ور روانه شوه لاس ګرفته ئي را وست پس درخانۍ اول په پهلنګ ؤ خته او آدم خان ورسټي کړ

"Durkhāna'ī went to him, and having taken HIS hand led him in. She first sat down on the bed, and then seated Adam Khān on the floor."—*Adam Khān and Durkhāna'ī.*

که هرڅو موؤ سره راز کړ — بي له عشقَ خبر نه وَد بلَ

"Whatever secrets WE mentioned to each other,
There were no words spoken but those of love."—*Aḥmad Shāh, Abdālī.*

په تفسير حسيني کښي دي راوري چه شيطان ستاسِ لوي غليم دي مومنانُ او په رنګ رنګ به موَ غلوينَ

"It is stated in the Tafsīr Ḥusainī, that the devil is your great enemy, oh true believers! and will deceive YOU in manifold ways."—*Fawā'īd-ush-Sharī'æa'h.*

ځمونږ سرور دي فرمايلي دير سړي په ظاهر نمونځونَ کاندِ ولِ زړونَ ئي غافل دي

"Our Prophet has said—'There are many persons who to all outward appearances say their prayers, but THEIR hearts are remiss.'"—*Fawā'īd-ush-Sharī'æa'h.*

نقل دي له آخوند درويزه نه چه زه هم د يوسفزويو سره په سر درو دَ سوات لاړم په هغه ځاي را
باند په شپه هسي ږلي او باران ؤ وريده چه تر صباح پورِ مُه اميد دَ زندګانۍ نه ود

"Ākhūnd Darwezah relates—'I was also going in company with the Yūsufzīs towards the head of the Suwāt valley; and in the same place, on the night in question, such quantities of hail and rain fell, that up to the dawn of morning WE entertained no hope of our lives.'"—*Afẓal Khān; Tārīkh-i-Muraṣṣaæ.*

آخوند درويزه وائي چه ما ور ته ؤ وي چه دا کتاب په تاسو کښي برکت وه دا مه دير بد ؤ کړل
چه له دي عالمَ مه غصب کړ ور مه ستاود په دا شومي به تاسو خراب شئي

"Ākhūnd Darwezah states, 'I said unto them, this book was a blessing unto you, and YOU have acted very improperly in this, inasmuch that YOU have taken it from those people forcibly, and YOU have sent it unto him: by this unfortunate mishap you will become ruined.'"—*Afẓal Khān.*

131. These affixes and prefixes being one of the difficulties of Pushto, the examples of each person given above were necessary, and will be required for those which follow.

132. The second form of pronoun, or pronominal dative prefix, as it may be termed, is alone used to point out the object in a sentence. It is used with all verbs; but, like the preceding, has no independent meaning, and is not subject to change in termination for gender: it is both singular and plural.

SECOND FORM.

PERSON.	SINGULAR AND PLURAL.		
1st	را، را ته، را لره or را له	*rā, rā tah, rā larah,* or *rā lah,*	to me, *or* to us.
2nd	در، در ته، در لره or در له	*dar, dar tah, dar larah,* or *dar lah,*	to thee *or* you.
3rd	ور، ور ته، ور لره or ور له	*war, war tah, war larah,* or *war lah,*	to him, her, it, *or* them.

EXAMPLES.

که لږ سترګې پرې بله کېږدم را ته وائي   په ياري کښې عالم نه کوي خوبونه

"If I close my eye ever so little, she says UNTO ME,—
'When really in love, people neither slumber nor sleep.'"—*Æabd-ul-Ḥamīd.*

رښتيا ترخه دروغ خواږه دي   اي نادانه تر بېه در ته بده شوه بديع

"Truth is bitter, but falsehood is sweet:
It is marvellous, oh fool! that evil is pleasant TO THEE."
—*Aḥmad Shāh, Abdālī.*

آدم خان په اندرپايه ور ؤ خوت په بياسته ور خوړند شه او ميرو ور ته ولاړ ؤ په اوږو ئي کوز کړ

"Adam Khān ascended the ladder, swung himself off by the rope TOWARDS HIM, and Mīrū who was standing near (TO HIM), received him on his shoulders and lowered him down."
—*Adam Khān and Durkhāna'ī.*

133. These particles, particularly را *rā* and ور *war*, are also used in the formation of verbs, thus: را *rā*, 'to me,' and وړل *w'ṛṛal*, 'to carry,' becomes را وړل *rā-w'ṛṛal*, 'to bring;' and ور *war*, 'to him,' and کول *kawul*, 'to do,' etc.—ور کول *war-kawul*, 'to give.'

134. These same forms undergo other changes in writing and conversation, but particularly in the latter. The cause appears to be merely greater facility in enunciation. Thus, for را لره *rā larah* they use لا لره *lā larah*; دَ له *da lah* or دَ لره *da larah*, for در لره *dar larah*; and و لره *wa larah* for ور لره *war larah*. The following are examples:

ته خپل حال په کاغذ لا لره را کړه   ستا مطلب به شي که خداي کاندِ ترسره

"Give UNTO ME an account of thy circumstances on paper,
And if God so wills it, thy wishes will be fulfilled."—*Bahrām Gūr.*

وقت د مرګ چه د لره راشي   روح به ور کړي بي عذابه

"When the angel of death cometh UNTO THEE,
Thou wilt give up thy soul without pain."—*Aḥmad Shāh, Abdālī.*

نغفور ډير گوهر جوهر وَ لره ور کړل   څلويښت سَوه سوهيلۍ ملک بيار شه

"Fag̲hfūr gave UNTO HER numerous gems and precious stones:
Forty hundred handmaids: the country became as spring (from the bloom of their beauty)."
—*Bahrām Gūr.*

135. The affixed personal pronouns,* ضماير متصله *ẓamā'ir-i-muttaṣila'h*, are used in forming the tenses of intransitive and substantive verbs, and, with the exception of the six past tenses, for those of verbs transitive also. They are inseparable from the verbs, and have no independent signification. The regular personal pronouns may also be prefixed to the verbs with which they are used, but are not absolutely required, and not generally adopted. On reference to the conjugations, the manner in which these affixes are used with the different tenses and persons will be seen at a glance. They are as follow:

THIRD FORM.

	SINGULAR.		PLURAL.	
1st person,	مَ *am*,	I.	وُ *ū*,	we.
2nd ,,	ي *ey*,	thou.	ئي *a'aī*,	ye or you.
3rd ,,	ي *ī*,	he, she, it, *or*		they.

The following are examples:

وينمَ واړه تلوني هيڅوک ندي پاتو شوني   يون دي په دا لاِرهم دَ ځوان هم دَ زاړه

"*I* see all departing, no one whatever is to remain behind—
On this road both young and old must travel."—*Æabd-ur-Raḥmān.*

که دَ عشق تر کمرَ پريوزيَ غاښ به بايليَ   ته چه ما تهَ غاښ چيچيَ په نصيحت کښې

"If THOU fallest from the precipice of love, THOU wilt lose thy teeth,
Oh THOU who gnashest thy teeth at me by way of admonition!"
—*Æabd-ur-Raḥmān.*

چه ئي وُ وهيَ تور ديو دَ عاشقۍ   هيڅ صحت ئي دَ جهان په افسون نشي

"For him whom the black DEMON of love strikes,
There is no health or cure through the charms or incantations of the world."
—*Æabd-ul-Ḥamīd.*

زد و يار چه سره خپل غمونه شمار کړو   يار و ما ته حيرانيږي زه و يار تهَ

"When I and my beloved together make a computation of OUR sorrows,
She is astonished with her lover, and I am filled with amazement at mine."
—*Æabd-ur-Raḥmān.*

نور ميرماميي له هغه سورو سره شه او چه څخو لاړ شه ور ته وِ تلوار کړئي چه لښکر ته زر وُ رسئي

* There is great similarity between these pronouns and those of the Arabic and Persian languages. In Sindhī also there is scarcely a sentence spoken in which they are not used with verbs, nouns, and prepositions.

"On this Mīr Māmī set out in company with those horsemen; and when he had gone a short distance, he said to them—'Make YOU haste that YOU may reach the Force quickly.'"—*Adam Khān and Durkhāna'ī.*

چه زبیخيَ مَي گوني شونډِ دَ خوبانو   دَ مُغو به كله مينه په مَي كيږي

"When will THEY who taste of the wine-coloured lips of the fair,
Set their hearts on the juice of the grape?"—*Æabd-ul-Ḥamīd.*

136. There are three prepositions used in Pushto requiring explanation here, which are used as demonstrative pronouns. They are تر *tar* and پر *par*, which affix a *zer* (ـِ); and نا *nā* or نه *nah*, which prefix تي *tey* or تِ *ti* in the oblique cases. They are used both for things animate and inanimate, are both singular and plural, and are not subject to any change for gender. The following are examples:

په هر عاقل بالغ مُؤمن دد روږه فرض پرِلازمه ده لکه قرض له روږي که څوک منکر شي کل عمل حبطه پرِ به کافر شي

"On every sensible adult believer, to fast is a divine command and a duty. Like the repayment of a debt it is necessary and incumbent ON HIM. If any one repudiates fasting, all acts FROM HIM are entirely vain, and HE will become an infidel."—*Fawā'īd-ush-Sharī'æa'h.*

گل نازي وُ وِ چه دا هغه آدم خان دي چه درخانۍ ترِ بيولِ ده

"Gūl Nāzey said, 'This is that same Adam Khān FROM WHOM Durkhāna'ī has been carried off."—*Adam Khān and Durkhāna'ī.*

تاسُ واروئي مؤمنانُ اوس څمورِ په زمانه کښي دَ ږبِ آفت ډير شه چه الفاظ دَ کفر ترِ پيدا کيږي

"Listen, oh true believers—In our day the calamities produced by the tongue are manifold, since blasphemous words are uttered FROM IT."—*Makhzan Afghānī.*

اي مرغه دَ سحر له پتنگ‌َ په عشق پوه شه   خان دَ غه سوي لاړ آواز تِنا را نه غي

"Oh bird of the dawn! learn thou love from the moth!
That consumed one's life went, but no sound escaped FROM HIM."
—*Æabd-ul-Ḥamīd.*

په زړه کښي مي وُه وِ هر كله دَ گلو په وني به وُ رسم دَ يارانو پيبس كبس دپارد خپله لمن به تِنا ډکه کرم

"I said in my mind, when I reach the rose tree, I will fill my skirt with roses FROM IT, as a present for those whom I love."—*Gulistān.*

CHAPTER VI.

THE VERB.

فعل *Fiœl.*

137. A verb is a word which affirms or asserts; as وائي 'speaks,' خوري 'eats.' It may also of itself constitute a sentence, and unless it be expressed or understood, no sentence is complete.*

138. Verbs are of two kinds—primitive and derivative—which may again be divided into six classes, the رابط الزماني, or substantive; لازمي, neuter or intransitive; متعدي, active or transitive, in which also are comprised causals; the derivative, or فعل مشتق; and the passive, or مجهول.

139. Some verbs have both an active and a neuter signification; as سول 'to burn.'

نور بهرام وي سرداسيا خوري ور دروم   گل اندام که خبر خما له نوم
ور ته وايه ستا دَ ميني په اور سَوي   شهزاده بهرام راغلي دي له روم

"Then Bahrām said, 'Oh sister Sardāsīā! go unto Gūl Andām;
Give unto her information respecting my name.
Say, that CONSUMED in the fire of thy love,
Prince Bahrām hath again returned from Rūm.—*Bahrām Gūr.*

مجنون ملک دَ عاشقي دله بيا موند   چه په اور باندِ سه خان و مان خپل

"Majnūn at that time acquired the dominion of love,
When in the fire of affection he CONSUMED all his worldly wealth."
—*Æabd-ur-Raḥmān.*

140. The active voice may be obtained from some intransitives, by changing the ل and the يدل of the infinitive into ول; as بليدل 'to take fire,' بلول 'to set on fire;' سړيدل 'to become cool,' سړول 'to make cool;' ستونيدل 'to revolve,' ستونول 'to make revolve;' زنگيدل 'to swing,' زنگول 'to make swing.' Example:

خو توانيکي زړه دَ چا مه آزاروه   چه په دي لارِ کښي ډير آزغي وي
کارِ دَ فقير او محتاج وُ کړه   چه تا لره هم کارونَ وي

"As much as thou art able, PAIN not the heart of any one;
Since there may be very many thorns in this path.

* As the student, now that we have advanced so far, may be supposed to have thoroughly mastered the sounds of the letters, vowels, and orthographical marks, there will be no necessity for giving the pronunciation of every word in the Roman character, and, in case of doubt, the Dictionary can be easily referred to.

Give assistance unto the poor and indigent in their affairs;
Since thou hast many matters in this world to be brought to conclusion."
—*Gulistān.*

141. The causal verb, also termed متعدي *mutaʿaddī*, may be formed from intransitives and transitives, by adding ول in place of ل or يدل; thus زغليدل 'to run,' زغلول 'to cause to run;' خندل 'to laugh,' خنددول or خندول 'to cause to laugh;' ژړل 'to lament,' *ژړدول or ژړول 'to cause to lament.' Example:

وارہ ته يِ خنددول که ژړدول کړِ　　زه بخپله نه خندا کړم نه ژړا کړم

"If thou CAUSE one TO LAUGH, or CAUSE one TO LAMENT, thou art the cause of all:
Of my own accord I do not make merry, neither do I mourn nor bewail."
—*Æabd-ur-Raḥmān.*

142. The derivative verb, or فعل مشتق *fiʿl-i-mushtakk*, may be formed from nouns, adjectives, or pronouns, either by alone adding the sign of the infinitive, as پوهه 'understanding,' پوهيدل 'to understand;' وچ 'dry,' وچيدل 'to become dry,' وچول 'to make dry;' or by shortening the long vowel of the word, as رڼرا 'bright,' رڼول 'to make bright;' غاړه 'a brink *or* side,' غړول 'to put aside;' خپل 'self, myself;' خپلول 'to make one's own,' 'to gain the affections of.' The following is an example:

په هر سانګ چه يار خوښيږي کړي بوي　　خپلول دَ صاحبانو په پيښو دي

"It is necessary to practice every disguise to please the beloved:
To GAIN THE AFFECTIONS of the fair, dependeth on art and skill."
—*Æabd-ur-Raḥmān.*

143. Pus͟hto also contains a sort of compound verb, which may be divided into two classes—nominals and intensives. The former are formed by the mere subjoining of a verb regularly conjugated to a noun or adjective; as اودد 'sleep,' اوده کيدل 'to sleep;' وږي 'hunger,' وږي کيدل 'to become hungry;' جنګ 'battle,' جنګ کول 'to fight.' These verbs being very commonly used, need no example, there being scarcely a sentence without one.

144. Intensitives are obtained by adding or prefixing to a regularly conjugated verb two adjectives or an adverb; thus:

غرخ مي ستا دَ بڼُ غشي پر سينه دي　　پورِ اورمي وتلي تر اينه دي

"The arrows of thy eyelashes have pierced me in the breast:
Verily they HAVE PASSED RIGHT THROUGH unto my heart."
—*Æabd-ur-Raḥmān.*

* This method of using a letter instead of a vowel point, in خنددول for خندول, is in accordance with the orthographical system of the Zend language. See Introduction, page 22.

گاد سړي خوښ و خورم وي گاد له غمه وي هک پک

"Sometimes a man may be cheerful and happy;
At times, through grief, TROUBLED and DISTRESSED."—ʻAbd-ul-Ḥamīd.

145. The passive voice is formed by the addition of the different tenses of the substantive or auxiliary verbs کيدل and شول 'to be *or* become,' to the past participle or imperfect tense of a transitive verb, both of which are subject to the same changes in termination for gender as other verbs, to agree with the governing noun in the sentence. Examples:

گل چه بي دَ يار له مخ ليده کيږي جورِ دَ سترگو نظر وي په خارستان گډ

"When the rose-tree IS VIEWED without the beloved being at one's side,
The eye-sight merely falleth on a place of thorns and brambles."—ʻAbd-ul-Ḥamīd.

څو ترياق له عراق راوړې شي مار خوړلي مړ دي

"By the time the treacle IS BROUGHT from Irāḳ,* the snake-bitten person is dead."—*Gulistān.*

146. It will be necessary now to show the inflections of the different auxiliaries, which are the models for the variations of the persons, and in forming the definite tenses of the verbs.

147. The following auxiliary or substantive verb, called the رابط الزماني *rābiṭ-uz-zamānī*) is ناقص (*nāḳiṣ*) or imperfect, and has no known infinitive. It is very easy, and should be carefully committed to memory. Want of space will compel me to content myself with a single example of each tense in the conjugations of the verbs, unless some peculiarity requires to be more fully explained.

'To be *or* become.'—Infinitive unknown.

صيغهٔ حال PRESENT TENSE.

SINGULAR.	PLURAL.
زه يم I am.	مونگ يو we are.
ته ئي thou art.	تاسُ ئي or ياستي you are.
دَغه دي or شته he *or* it is.	دَغه دي or شته they are.
دغه دَه or شته she is.	

EXAMPLES.

ساقي جام د ميو راوړه غرق دَ اوښيو په درياب يم

"Cupbearer! bring the bowl of wine: I AM overwhelmed in the ocean of grief."
Aḥmad Shāh, Abdālī.

* The treacle of Irāḳ is a celebrated antidote for venomous snake-bites.

چه مي شته دَ عشق خواري همېره بهادي دَه   كه مي وركه دا خواري شوه نور به خوار شم

"Since to me love's anguish IS equal to its rapture,
If this distress of mine be lost, I shall again become wretched."
—*Æabd-ul-Ḥamīd.*

چه دَ دور دا كږي كيڼي پيري شته   كوهِ قاف دِ نه نازيږي په خپل تول

"Since these crooked and left-handed revolutions ARE occasioned by fate;
Mount Caucasus itself should not coquet about its own weight."—*Æabd-ul-Ḥamīd.*

The following form of the 2nd person plural is to be found in ancient writings, but it is not commonly used. It, as well as شته, is in all probability derived from an obsolete infinitive ستل or شتل.

تاسُ بندگان دَ پاك الله ياستي مؤمنانُ الله حي لا يَمُوت دي مرگ ئي نشته خپل ايمان عقيدد جوړ لرئي بندگانُ

"You, oh faithful! ARE the servants of the Most High. God liveth! death affects him not! keep firmly the tenets of your faith, oh people of God!"—*Fawā'id-ush-Sharī'æa'h.*

شته and دي are sometimes used together, but the latter seems to be merely added by way of emphasis. The following is an example:

هسي رنگ سحر جادوكا په نظر دَ شالا سترگو   نه ئي سيال په هند كښي شته دي نه ثاني په بنگاله كښي

"With the glance of her dark-grey eye she enchants and charms in this manner—
There IS no one eye equal to it in Hind, not another in Bengāla'h.—*Æabd-ul-Ḥamīd.*

ماضي مطلق PAST TENSE.

SINGULAR.		PLURAL.
زه وُم I was.		مُوږ or مُنكا وُو we were.
ته وې thou wast.		تاسو or تاسُ وئي you were.
هَغه وُ or وَه he *or* it was.	M.	هَغه وُو they were.
هَغه وَه she was.	F.	هَغه وِ they were.

This tense with the prefix كه is often used as the Conditional or Optative tense, of which examples will be found in their proper places.

The following example shows both the masculine and feminine form of this tense, and both methods of writing the third person masculine, as above given.

يو سردار دَ يوسفزيو په دولت كښي لكه طهمورث وُ په اسم طاووس خان نوماندي وَد دَ ده يوه لور وَه درخان نوماندي او دَ حسن سيال ئي نه وَه

"There was a chief of the Yūsufzīs'—a Ṭahmūraṣ* in wealth—who WAS yeleped Ṭā'ous

* The third Persian King of the Pishdādiān dynasty, said to have been the founder of Babylon, Nineveh, etc., and the discoverer of fire. He reigned about 830 B.C., although some carry him centuries beyond.

K̲h̲ān. There WAS also a daughter of this chieftain, named Durk̲h̲ān,* and there WAS no equal to her in beauty."—*Story of Adam K̲h̲ān and Durk̲h̲āna'ī.*

يو عالم وَه چه خلورسوه صندوق ئي دَ علم وارَه ياد وُ

"There WAS a learned man who WAS proficient in all the sciences contained in as many books as required four hundred chests to hold them.—*Fawā'id-ush-Sharī'ææ'h.*

The future tense of this auxiliary shows the very irregular and imperfect nature of many of the Afg̲h̲ān verbs. The 1st and 2nd persons are formed by prefixing the particle به to the present, and the 3rd person by prefixing it to the aorist or future indefinite, which again has no 1st or 2nd persons. In the conjugations of all other verbs, the 2nd future tense is formed from the aorist.

مستقبل FUTURE TENSE.

SINGULAR.		PLURAL.	
زه به يم	I shall *or* will be.	مُونږ or مُنگا به يو	we shall *or* will be.
ته به ئي	thou shalt *or* wilt be.	تاسو or تاسِ به ئي or تاسُ به ياست (W.)†	you shall *or* will be.
دَغه به وي or به وِينَ	he, she, it, shall *or* will be.	دَغه به وي or به وِينَ	they shall *or* will be.

EXAMPLES.

په راستي مي دَ خپل آه هسي باور دي چه همدم به يم له ښکليو پس له مرگَ

"I have such confidence in the truth of my own sighs,
That after death even, I SHALL still BE a companion of the fair."

—*Æabd-ul-Ḥamīd.*

شهزاده بهرام به وي په هغه ځاي کښِ چه باد بوي و له راوړي دَ يار له دره

"Prince Bahrām WILL certainly BE present at that place,
That the breeze may bring him perfume from the door of his beloved."

—*Bahrām Gūr.*

په ديرش کال به قراري شي نه سړي به چرِ وِينَ نه ميږي چه دانه وُ خوري

"In the space of thirty years there will be stability, (during this time) there WILL not BE a man—not even an ant to eat up the grain."—*Makhzan Afg̲h̲ānī.*

The aorist or future indefinite tense of this auxiliary, as previously stated, has but one form for all three persons. It is also used in forming the doubtful past tenses of other verbs, as will be seen from the different conjugations.

مضارع AORIST, OR FUTURE INDEFINITE.

SINGULAR.		PLURAL.	
زه, ته or دَغه وي or وِينَ	I, thou, he, she, *or* it may be.	مُنگه, تاسُ or دَغه وي or وِينَ	we, ye, *or* they, may be.

* The chieftain's pearl. † (W.) refers to any peculiarity of the language as in use in Western Afg̲h̲ānistān.

EXAMPLE.

خو مي لاس وي يا مي توان وي　　ژوند به صدقه دَ دلبر کړم

"As long as I MAY HAVE hands, or as long as I MAY BE possessed of strength,
I will devote my life and my existence to my beloved."—*Aḥmad Shāh, Abdālī.*

ماضي استمرار The Imperfect Tense, as the Conditional or Optative.

SINGULAR.		PLURAL.	
زه وي, واي or به وم	were I.	موږ or مُنږ وي, واي or به وو	were we.
ته وې, واي or به وې	wert thou.	تاسو or تاسِ وئي, واي or به وئي or تاسُ واست or به واست (W.)	were you.
هَغه وي, واي or به وه	were he, *or* it.	M. هَغه وي or واي or به وو	were they.
هَغه وي, واي or به وَه	were she, *or* it.	F. هَغه وي, واي or به وِ	were they.

This tense implies continuity, and, with a conditional conjunction or adverb of wishing, expressed or understood, is used as the Conditional or Optative, which is its most general form. Examples:

نفع دَ درياب ښه وَه که ويره دَ موج نه وي　　ياري دَ ګل ښه وَه که نه وي تشويش دَ خار

"The utility of the ocean would be great, WERE there no apprehension of the waves;
The intimacy of the rose would be considerable, WERE there no fear of the thorn."
—*Gulistān.*

It is also frequently used after interjections, as in the following couplet:

کاشکي مه واي په دنيا غم دَ فراق　　چه ډوب نه واي زړه په دا يم دَ فراق

"Alas! that there WERE no such thing in the world as anxiety on account of absence—
That the heart WERE not overwhelmed in the ocean of separation."
—*Aḥmad Shāh, Abdālī.*

The following is an example of the simple past tense, with the prefixed particle به used in a hypothetical sense,* as referred to at page 53.

اي دَ پلار دَ زړه سَخه که ته هم ویده شَوي وي له دِ نه ډیر ښه به وو چه دَ وګړي په عیب جوئي
کښي پرِوتي

"Oh joy of thy father's heart; if thou hadst been asleep, IT WOULD BE far better, than that thou hadst commenced searching after the defects of others."—*Gulistān.*

There is no imperative mood of this auxiliary, and that of اوسيدل 'to remain,' etc., is used for it.

148. The following, as well as the preceding verb, is also used generally to

* This should not be confounded with the 1st Future, which see.

denote mere existence. It is like all auxiliary verbs in this language—ناقص or imperfect. Its conjugation is as follows:

مصدر INFINITIVE.

اوسيدل *aosedal*, 'to be, exist, continue,' etc.

اسم لياقت NOUN OF FITNESS.

SINGULAR AND PLURAL.

دَ اوسيدلُ or دَ اوسيدُ of, *or* for being, existing, etc.

اسم فاعل ACTIVE PARTICIPLE.

SINGULAR.

M. اوسيدونَي or اوسيدونكَي F. اوسيدونِ or اوسيدونكِ ; or اوسيدوني or اوسيدونكي exister.

PLURAL.

M. and F. اوسيدوني or اوسيدونكي existers, etc.

صيغهٔ حال PRESENT TENSE.

SINGULAR.		PLURAL.	
زه اوسم	I exist.	مُونږ or مُنكا اوسؤ	we exist.
ته اوسې	thou existeth.	تاسو or تاسِ اوسئِ	ye, *or* you exist.
دَغه اوسي	he, she, *or* it exists.	دَغه اوسي	they exist.

EXAMPLE.

هسي يم په درد و غم کښي دَ دلبر خوَښ — لکهٔ اوسي په سره اور کښي سمندر خوَښ

"I am so pleased with the pain and grief inflicted on me by my beloved,
Like as the Salamander EXISTETH contented in the red fire."—*Æabd-ul-Hamīd.*

The following tense is used with a conjunction, as the Conditional or Optative tense. It implies continuity, and may also be understood as the simple imperfect.

ماضي استمراري CONDITIONAL OR OPTATIVE TENSE.

SINGULAR.			PLURAL.		
زه اوسيدم	were I	existing.	مُونږ اوسيدؤ	were we	existing.
ته اوسيدې	wert thou		(W.) اوسيداست or تاسُ اوسيدئِ	were you	
دَغه اوسيدَ or اوسيده	were he, *or* it		M. دَغه اوسيدل	were they	
دَغه اوسيده or اوسيدله	were she		F.* دَغه اوسيدِ or اوسيدې ,اوسيدلِ or اوسيدلې	were they	

EXAMPLE.

كه دلِ اوسيدم دا مانړئي به جوړه کړم

"WERE I REMAINING (or going to remain here), I would repair this house."

* Instead of giving both forms of feminine words ending in ې (*yā-i-majhūl*) or (ِ) (*kasra'h*), I have generally adopted the latter throughout this work by way of distinction, and as it is—as I have already noticed at paragraph 63 and note † page 10—most generally used.

مستقبل FUTURE TENSE.

SINGULAR.	PLURAL.
به اوسم or زه به وُ اوسم I will exist.	به اوسو or مُوږ به وُ اوسو we will exist.
به اوسې or ته به وُ اوسې thou wilt exist.	به اوسئ or تاسُ به وُ اوسئ you will exist.
به اوسي or هَغه به وُ اوسي he, she, *or* it will exist.	به اوسي or هَغه به وُ اوسي they will exist.

EXAMPLE.

جام دَ مېو چه غمخور دَ درست جهان شه   زه به اوسم په دا غم كښې تا بكې

"Since the goblet of wine has become the comforter of the whole world,
How long SHALL I CONTINUE in this distress and sorrow?"—*Æabd-ur-Raḥmān.*

مضارع SUBJUNCTIVE, OR AORIST TENSE.

SINGULAR.	PLURAL.
اوسم or زه وُ اوسم I may, shall, etc. exist.	اوسو or مُوږ وُ اوسو we may, shall, etc. exist.
اوسې or ته وُ اوسې thou mayest, etc. exist.	اوسئ or تاسُ وُ اوسئ you may, etc. exist.
اوسي or هَغه وُ اوسي he, she, *or* it may, etc. exist.	اوسي or هَغه وُ اوسي they may, etc. exist.

EXAMPLE.

دا ژوندون په هر نفس دي   هر نفس اوسئ تايب

"Existence dependeth on the drawing of a breath,
Therefore you SHOULD BE repentant on each respiration."—*Æabd-ul-Ḥamīd.*

امر حاضر PRECATIVE, OR 1ST FUTURE TENSE.

SINGULAR.	PLURAL.
اوسم or زه وُ اوسم I should exist.	اوسو or مُوږ وُ اوسو we should exist.
اوسې or ته وُ اوسې thou shouldst exist.	اوسئ or تاسُ وُ اوسئ you should exist.
دِ اوسي or هَغه دِ وُ اوسي he, she, *or* it should exist.	دِ اوسي or هَغه دِ وُ اوسي they should exist.

EXAMPLE.

چه امام قرأة لوړلي مقتدي دِ خله پټ ولاړ اوسي قرأة دَ امام آرويده واجب دي

"When the priest reads with a solemn voice, the congregation, being silent, SHOULD REMAIN standing. To listen to the reading of the priest is necessary and correct."
Fawā'id-ush-Sharī'æa'h.

امر IMPERATIVE MOOD.

SINGULAR.	PLURAL.
ته اوسه exist thou.	تاسُ اوسئ exist you.
هَغه دِ اوسي let him, her, *or* it exist.	هَغه دِ اوسي let them exist.

EXAMPLE.

كه سختي كړي يار احمده   په سختي اوسه سرباز

"If thy mistress treat thee with asperity, Aḥmad!
BE THOU resolute in adversity and affliction.—*Aḥmad Shāh, Abdālī.*

The verbs كېدل and شول, used in forming the passive voice, are conjugated as follow. The first is ناقص or imperfect, and has but three tenses.

كېدل 'To be *or* become.'

Noun of Fitness.

دَ كېدلُ or دَ كېدٔ of *or* for, being *or* becoming.

صيغهٔ حال Present Tense.

Singular.		Plural.	
زه کېږم or کېږم	I become.	مُنگا کېږوُ or کېږوُ	we become.
ته کېږيْ or کېږيْ	thou becomest.	تاسُ کېږئي or کېږئي	you become.
هَغه کېږي or کېږي	he, she, *or* it, becomes.	هَغه کېږي or کېږي	they become.

EXAMPLE.

په ديدن لګئَ باران پر تازه کېږم جدائي په مثال اور پر ما لګين

" A pleasant interview is like rain, by it I BECOME refreshed ;
But separation like fire overtakes me."—*Mīrzā Khān, Anṣārī.*

ماضي استمرار Imperfect Tense.

Singular.			Plural.	
زه کېدم or به کېدم	I was becoming.		مُنگا کېدوُ or به کېدوُ	we were becoming.
ته کېديْ or به کېديْ	thou wast becoming.		تاسُ کېدئي or به کېدئي	you were becoming.
هَغه کېدَ or کېده or هَغه به کېدَ or به کېده	he, *or* it was becoming.	M.	هَغه کېدل or به کېدل	they were becoming.
هَغه کېده or کېدله or هَغه به کېده or به کېدله	she was becoming.	F.	هَغه کېدِ or به کېدِ هَغه کېدلِ or به کېدلِ	they were becoming.

EXAMPLES.

ځاي پځاي ځلي کېدَ په ځو ځو قسمَ ميلمانه دَ سرداس وڔُ له هجومَ

" In every place there WERE different kinds of food BEING cooked,
For the guests of Sardās were a numerous crowd."—*Bahrām Gūr.*

پس له هَغه هرد جرګه چه به کېده درخانۍ و نرمۍ ته وِ چه خبرۍ را لرد راوړه

"After that time, every Jirga'h* that WAS IN THE HABIT OF MEETING, Durkhāna'ī used to say to Narma'ī, 'bring me news from it.'"—*Story of Adam Khān and Durkhāna'ī.*

مستقبل 2nd Future Tense.

Singular.		Plural.	
زه به کېږم or به کېږم	I will become.	مُوږ به کېږوُ or به کېږوُ	we will become.
ته به کېږيْ or به کېږيْ	thou wilt become.	تاسُ به کېږئي or به کېږئي	you will become.
هَغه به کېږي or به کېږي	he, she, *or* it will become.	هَغه به کېږي or به کېږي	they will become.

* An assembly of the heads of the different *ulūses* or divisions of tribes amongst the Afghāns, particularly the Yūsufzīs.

EXAMPLE.

جوهر دَ خوبي له ښه خدايْ ؤ موندلي له ديچا به ويشه نه شه نه بَ کېږي

"The jewel of excellence he acquired from the good God. Such never before fell to the lot of any one, and WILL never BECOME so."—*Makhzan Afghānī.*

149. The conjugation of the following verb, as well as کېدل which precedes it, imports transition from one state to another, whilst the auxiliary, 'to be,' which is also a substantive verb, generally denotes mere existence.

مصدر INFINITIVE.

شوَل *sh'wal*, 'to be *or* become.'

اسم لياقت NOUN OF FITNESS.

دَ شوَو or دَ شوَلُ of *or* for, being *or* becoming.

اسم فاعل ACTIVE PARTICIPLE.

	SINGULAR.			PLURAL.	
M.	شوونکَي or شوونَي	the becomer.	M. and F.	شوونکي or شووني	the becomers.
F.	شوونکِ or شوونِ				

اسم مفعول PASSIVE PARTICIPLE.

SINGULAR.		PLURAL.	
M. and F. شوَلَي or شوَي ; شوَلِ or شوِ	become.	M. and F. شوَلي or شوَي	become.

صيغهٔ حال PRESENT TENSE.

SINGULAR.		PLURAL.	
شَم	I become.	شُو	we become.
شي	thou becomest.	شيُ	you become.
دَغه شي	he, she, *or* it becomes.	دَغه شي	they become.

EXAMPLE.

که هر څو په صبر زړه تولوم نه شي   بي اختيارد لکَ مُوم ويلي په نار شَم

"Notwithstanding I endeavour to calm my heart, IT IS not soothed :
Spontaneously I BECOME melted like wax before the fire."—*Æabd-ur-Raḥmān.*

ماضي استمرار IMPERFECT TENSE.

SINGULAR.		PLURAL.	
شوَم or به شوَم or شوَلم	I was becoming.	شوَوْ or به شوَوْ or شوَلوْ	we were becoming.
شوَي or به شوي or شوَلي	thou wast becoming.	شوَئي or به شوَئي or شوَلئي	you were becoming.
دَغه شه or به شه	he, *or* it was becoming.	M. دَغه شوُ or به شوُ or شوَل	they were becoming.
دَغه شوَه or به شوَه or شوَله	she was becoming.	F. دَغه شوِ or به شوِ or شولِ	they were becoming.

EXAMPLE.

چه دَ سرور له اصحابُ نمونځ په جماعت چرِ قضا شه اود ورځ به عالم عذر خواهي ورتَ کوله
تکبير اؤلي چه به قضا شه درِ ورځِ به عالم عذر خواهي ورتَ کوله

"When any one of the companions of the Prophet USED to omit TO BE present with the congregation for divine worship, the people condoled with him for a period of seven days; and, if HE USED to fail TO BE present at the first Takbīr (the commencement of the service), the people condoled with him for three days."—*Fawā'īd-ush-Sharī'æa'h.*

ماضي مطلق PAST TENSE.

SINGULAR.	PLURAL.
وُ شوم or شوم ; وُ شولم or شولم I became.	وُ شوو or شوو ; وُ شولو or شولو we became.
وُ شوې or شوې ; وُ شولې or شولې thou becamest.	وُ شوئي or شوئي ; وُ شولئي or شولئي you became.
وُ شه or شه he, *or* it became.	M. وُ شوُ or شوُ ; وُ شول or شول they became.
وُ شوه or شوه ; وُ شوله or شوله she, *or* it became.	F. وُ شوِ or شوِ ; وُ شولِ or شولِ they became.

EXAMPLES.

چه مشغول دَ ستا دَ مخ په خال و خط شوم   مشغولا را څخه پاتي دَ كتاب شوه

"Since I BECAME dedicated to thy mole and ringlets,
My employment with the book BECAME entirely relinquished."—*Æabd-ul-Ḥamīd.*

دويم زده كړه چه وجود دَ حق دانا دي هرڅه وُ شوو يا به شيني له كل زره حبَ آگاه دي چه هيڅ خبر نه نوي نوي زده كوي نه وهيروينَ

"Secondly:—Know thou that the Almighty is all-wise, and knoweth all things that have HAPPENED or will happen. He is cognizant of every jot and tittle, every atom and iota, for He learneth nothing new, and He forgetteth nothing."—*Makhzan Afghānī.*

ماضي قريب PERFECT TENSE.

SINGULAR.	PLURAL.
شوَې يم I have become.	شوي يو we have become.
شوَې ئې thou hast become.	شوي ئي or شوي ياست (W.) you have become.
شوَې دي or شوِ ده .F he, she, *or* it has become.	شوي دي they have become.

EXAMPLES.

ولي هسي شوَې ئې له غمَ خما دِله   عمر هوا غند چليږي دريغَ دريغَ

"Why hast thou BECOME thus affected by grief, oh heart of mine?
Since, alas! life passeth away like the wind."—*Aḥmad Shāh, Abdālī.*

حضرت هسي ورته وُ وِ چه په اوه لكه نيكئ حساب شوِ دَ حرم يوه نيكي دَه

"The Prophet said thus unto him, 'One good work performed at Ḥaram,* HAS BEEN accounted equal to seven hundred thousand performed at any other place."—*Fawā'īd-ush-Sharī'æa'h.*

ماضي بعيد PLUPERFECT TENSE.

SINGULAR.	PLURAL.
شوَې وُم I had become.	شوي وُو we had become.
شوَې وې thou hadst become.	شوي وئي you had become.
شوَې وُه or شوِ وَه .F he, she, *or* it, had become.	شوي وُو or شوي وِ .F they had become.

* Ḥaram, the sacred plain of Makka, with the sanctuary.

EXAMPLE.

دَ مُوږ دَ ځوانانُ آسونه هم زخمي شَوي وو ځوانان هم ستړي وو له ديره تردده جلو ئي وُ نيوه اوبو لره وُ رغي اوبه ئي وُ څښي نورکور ته روان شول

"The horses of our young men HAD BEEN also wounded, and the youths themselves were tired out from exertion. They seized the bridles of the horses and went to the water, and, having drank some, they set out for their own homes."—*Afẓul Khān.*

امرحاضر 1ST FUTURE TENSE.

SINGULAR.	PLURAL.
وُ شَم or شَم I should become.	وُ شُو or شُو we should become.
وُ شي or شي thou shouldst become.	وُ شئي or شئي you should become.
دِ وُ شي or ځغه دِ شي he, she, *or* it, should become.	دِ وُ شي or ځغه دِ شي they should become.

EXAMPLE.

که منصور غندِ په دار و په سنکسار شَم — نشته دا چه ستا له ميني توبه ګار شَم

"SHOULD I BE raised to the gibbet like Manṣūr, or be stoned to death;
It is not this, that SHOULD make me forswear thy love and affection."
—*Æabd-ul-Ḥamīd.*

مستقبل 2ND FUTURE TENSE.

SINGULAR.	PLURAL.
زه به وُ شَم or وُ به شم I will become.	مُنګا به وُ شُو or وُ به شُو we will become.
ته به وُ شي or وُ به شي thou wilt become.	تاسُ به وُ شئي or وُ به شئي you will become.
ځغه به وُ شي or وُ به شي he, she, *or* it, will become.	ځغه به وُ شي or وُ به شي they will become.

EXAMPLES.

څه له کا دَ حسن لاف صاحب جمال — خود به وُ شي انګشت نماي لکَ هلال

"Wherefore do the possessors of beauty boast of (their) good looks?
THEY WILL BECOME celebrated of their own accord, like the new moon."
—*Æabd-ul-Ḥamīd.*

موړ به نه شي هيڅ سړي بي قناعتَ — که ئي خونه وي په سيم و په زر ډکَ

"No man WILL BECOME satiated without contentment,
Even though his house be full of silver and gold."—*Æabd-ur-Raḥmān.*

مضارع SUBJUNCTIVE, OR AORIST TENSE.

SINGULAR.	PLURAL.
شَم or وُ شَم I may, shall, will, etc. become.	شُو or وُ شُو we may, shall, will, etc. become.
شي or وُ شي thou mayest, etc. become.	شئي or وُ شئي you may, etc. become.
شي or ځغه وُ شي he, she, it may, etc. become.	شي or ځغه وُ شي they may, etc. become.

EXAMPLES.

يو بادشاد لره يو مهم را پيښ شه وُ ئي ويل كه انجام دَ دِ كار څما دَ زړه په مراد وُ شي دا قدر درهمونه زاهدانو لره به ور كړم

"A certain king had a difficult matter to perform. He said, if the upshot of this SHOULD TURN OUT according to my wishes, I will give so many dirhams to devotees and holy men."—*Gulistān*.

دَ ليوانو زو ذات ليوه شي كه دي لوي دَ سړي په ليمه شي

"The offspring of wolves WILL still BE wolves,
Even though they MAY BE grand and powerful in the sight of men."—*Gulistān*.

شرطيه CONDITIONAL, OR OPTATIVE TENSE.

SINGULAR.	PLURAL.
كه زه شواي if I became.	كه مُنگا شواي if we became.
كه ته شواي if thou becamest.	كه تاسُ شواي if you became.
كه هَغه شواي if he, she, *or* it, became.	كه هَغه شواي if they became.

EXAMPLE.

اي رحمانَ دَ خداي نوم به چا وا نه خست كه دَ خداي چارِ په پلار شواي يا په ورور

"No one, oh Rahmān! would take the name of the Almighty,
If his works BECAME accomplished by either father or brother."

—*Æabd-ur-Raḥmān*.

ماضي شرطيه PAST CONDITIONAL TENSE.

SINGULAR. F.	M.		PLURAL. M. AND F.	
شَوِ وي or	كه زه شَوَي وي	if I had become.	كه مُنگا شَوِي وي	if we had become.
شَوِ وي or	كه ته شَوَي وي	if thou hadst become.	كه تاسُ شَوِي وي	if you had become.
شَوِ وي or	كه هَغه شَوَي وي	if he, she, *or* it, had become.	كه هَغه شَوِي وي	if they had become.

EXAMPLE.

اول مه وي مَين شَوَي چه مَين شَوم اوس دا پيښه هر چه شوه نسه په خويښ

"Alas that I HAD not BECOME enamoured when I fell in love!
Whatever has happened endure with cheerfulness, for now it is face to face."

—*Æabd-ul-Ḥamīd*.

ماضي نشكيك PAST FUTURE TENSE.*

SINGULAR. F.	M.		PLURAL. M. AND F.	
شَوِ به يَم or	شَوَي	I shall, *or* will have become.	شَوِي به يوُ	we shall, *or* will have become.
شَوِ به ئِي or	شَوَي	thou shalt, *or* wilt have become.	شَوِي به ئِي	you shall, *or* will have become.
شَوِ به وي or	هغه شَوَي	he, she, it, shall, *or* will have become.	هَغه شَوِي به وي	they shall, *or* will have become.

* Also called the Doubtful Past Tense.

EXAMPLES.

ښائي هنر ځما سبب دَ نا کارتیا دَ هَغه به شَوي وي چه ګرندي آس لره ګرندي توب ئي سبب دَ ستومانئ شي

"Perhaps my cleverness MAY HAVE BEEN the cause of his aversion, since the swiftness of the swift horse becometh the cause of his fatigue."—*Kalīlah wo Damnah.*

The به of this tense is sometimes omitted, as in the following example:

آب و تاب دَ نا سره مُهروي هُمېره   څو نظر پري شَوَي نه وي دَ صراف

"The lustre and polish of the false muhar* may doubtless continue,
Until the glance of the money-changer SHALL not HAVE FALLEN on it."
—*Æabd-ur-Raḥmān.*

امر IMPERATIVE MOOD.

SINGULAR.	PLURAL.
وُ شه or شه become thou.	وُ شئي or شئي become you.
هَغه دِ وُ شي or دِ شي let him, her, *or* it, become.	هَغه دِ وُ شي or دِ شي let them become.

EXAMPLE.

که په توره تاریکي کښِ رڼرا غواړي   تندارچي دَ یار دَ زلف و دَ رخسار شه

"In the blackest darkness, if thou desirest light,
BECOME a spectator of the curls and countenance of the beloved."
—*Æabd-ul-Ḥamīd.*

The prefixed وُ of this mood, like the ب of the Persian imperative, is often omitted as redundant, as in the example above given.

TRANSITIVE AND INTRANSITIVE VERBS.

افعال لازمي و متعدي *afæaāl-i-lāzimī wo mutaæaddī.*

مصدر INFINITIVE.

150. All infinitives in the Pus͟hto language end in ل *l*, يدَل *edal*, or وُل *wul*; as, شاربل *s͟hārbal*, 'to churn,' ګډيدل *gaḏḏedal*, 'to mix,' آرويدل *ārwedal*, 'to hear,' ډکيدل *ḏḏakedal*, 'to fill,' تودول *tawdawul*, 'to make hot,' etc.

Verbs which merely take ل in forming the infinitive are both transitive and intransitive; those which take يدَل are, without exception, intransitives;† and those ending in وُل are all transitives.

* An Indian gold coin.

† The يد of some verbs are radical letters, and therefore should not be confounded with the affixed يدَل of some intransitives; as, for example, آرويدل 'to hear,' in which the ل only is the sign of the infinitive, and واوريدَ its past tense, or root of the verb. Again, in پوښتيدل 'to ask,' in which وُ پښتيدَ is the past tense; whilst the sign of the infinitive in ډکيدل 'to fill,' is يدل and ډک شه the past tense; and in ماتيدل 'to break, *or* become broken,' the past tense is مات شه.

The infinitive of verbs is also used as the حاصل مصدر (*ḥāṣil-i-maṣdar*) or verbal noun; as in the following examples:

لکۀ گل څو خپه کېږي بوي ئي لا پسي زياتيږي   هسي رنګ لا غلبه شي په زغمل دَ مينې دوک

"Like the rose, as much as thou concealest it, so much its perfume increaseth;
In the same manner, the anguish of love from ENDURANCE, becometh overpowering."
—*Æabd-ul-Ḥamīd.*

پادشاه لره ويل دَ دَغه دير ښورد راغلل او دَ شپې و دَغه ځاي ته وُ رغي

"This SPEECH was exceedingly acceptable to the king, and that night he came to his house."—*Gulistān.*

اول زړه زهيرول مينه په يار څه   بيا له مينې جاروتل په لږ چار څه

"In the first place, what use is it PAINING the heart with love?
Again, of what advantage is TURNING BACK from it at a slight obstacle?"
—*Æabd-ur-Raḥmān.*

151. There are in the Pushto language no less than thirty-seven classes of verbs, the whole of which vary in some way or other in the formation of the different inflections.* Of this number thirteen are intransitive, and twenty-four transitive.

Five of the thirteen classes of intransitives are imperfect; and, of the transitives, nineteen classes contain perfect and imperfect verbs; and the remaining classes are entirely imperfect.

INTRANSITIVES.

CLASS I.

152. Changes the last radical letter, after dropping the ل of the infinitive, for another letter, in the present tenses and the imperative mood, but retains it in the past tenses and the past participle; as, پوهيدل *poh-edal*, 'to know,' آلوتل *ālwatal*, 'to fly,' نښتل *n'k̲h̲atal*, or *n's̲h̲atal*, 'to be entrapped,' لويدل *l'wedal*, 'to fall.'

Infinitive.	Present.	Aorist.	Imperative.	Imperfect.	Past.	Past Part.
پوهيدل	پوهيږي	وُ پوهيږي	وُ پوهيږه	پوهيده	وُ پوهيده †	پوهيدلَي
آلوتل	آلوزي	والوزي	والوزه	آلوت	والوت	آلوتلَي
نښتل	نښلي	وُ نښلي	وُ نښله	نښت	وُ نښت	نښتَي
لويدل	لويږي	وُ لويږي	وُ لويږه	لويده	وُ لويده	لويدلَي

* There appear to be two eras, if I may so term it, in the Pus̲h̲to language. The first, of words which are evidently pure Afg̲h̲ān, and probably those used by the Afg̲h̲ānah, when they first settled in their present country. The second, when Arabic, Persian, and Sanscrit became engrafted on the original stock. This is particularly apparent with regard to the conjugations of the verbs.

† The past and imperfect tenses of some verbs, as above, may be written with (ے) instead of ه (*hā-i-ẓāhir*), particularly in poetry. The feminine termination is ۀ (*hā-i-k̲h̲afī*), which is generally affixed to the infinitive itself; as وُ پوهيدله *wu-po-hedala'h*, 'she knew.' See conjugations.

CLASS II.

153. Rejects the two last radical letters in the present and future tenses and the imperative mood, and retains them in the past tenses and past participle; as, زغليدل *z'ghaledal*, 'to run,' څاڅيدل *tsātsedal*, 'to leak *or* drop.'

Infinitive.	Present.	Aorist.	Imperative.	Imperfect.	Past.	Past Part.
زغليدل	زغلي	وُ زغلي	وُ زغله	زغليده	وُ زغليده	زغليدلَي
څاڅيدل	څاڅي	وُ څاڅي	وُ څاڅه	څاڅيدَ	وُ څاڅيدَ	څاڅيدلَي

CLASS III.

154. Rejects the sign of the infinitive and the three last radical letters in the present and future tenses and imperative, but retains them in the past tenses and past participle; as کښيناستل *k'khenāstal*, or *k'shenāstal*, 'to sit.'

Infinitive.	Present.	Aorist.	Imperative.	Imperfect.	Past.	Past Part.
کښيناستل	کښيني	کښيني	کښينه	کښيناست	کښيناست	کښيناستلَي

CLASS IV.

155. Drops the last radical letter and loses the long vowel by elision, in the present, future, and imperative, but retains it in the past; as چاودل *chāw-dal*, 'to split.'

Infinitive.	Present	Aorist.	Imperative.	Imperfect.	Past.	Past Part.
چاودل	چوي	وُ چوي	وُ چوه	چاود	وُ چاود	چاودلَي

CLASS V.

156. Changes the last radical letter for two others in the present, future, and imperative, similar to Class XIX of transitives; and merely rejects the ل of the infinitive for the past; as ختل *khatal*, 'to ascend.'

Infinitive.	Present.	Aorist.	Imperative.	Imperfect.	Past.	Past Part.
ختل	خېژي	وُ خېژي	وُ خېژه	خوت	وُ خوت	ختلَي

CLASS VI.

157. Merely rejects the ل of the infinitive throughout; as مړل *m'rral*, 'to die.'* The past participle is shortened. In the present, aorist, and imperative, the ړ of this verb is changed to ر.

Infinitive.	Present.	Aorist.	Imperative.	Imperfect.	Past.	Past Part.
مړل	مري	وُ مري	وُ مره	مړ	وُ مړ	مړ

* This, as well as many other verbs, often retains the ل of the infinitive in all the inflections, merely affixing, inserting, or prefixing the necessary pronouns and particles to form the various tenses. The past participle may be considered an adjective.

CLASS VII.

158. The verbs of this class take a letter after the last radical letter in the present, future, and imperative, and reject both of them in the past; as سوَل *swal*, 'to burn.'

Infinitive.	Present.	Aorist.	Imperative.	Imperfect.	Past.	Past Part.
سوَل	سوځي	وُ سوځي	وُ سوځه	سه (W.) سوُ	وُ سه (W.) وُ سوُ	سوَيَ

CLASS VIII.

159. The verbs of this and the following classes of the intransitives are imperfect. They change the last radical letter for another, like Class I., in the present tense, and retain it in the imperfect and the past. The auxiliary شوَل *s̲h̲wal*, 'to become,' is required in forming the other tenses of the verb with which the adjective, or shortened past participle is used; as ماتيدل *mātedal*, 'to break,' پاتيدل *pātedal*, 'to remain,' etc.

Infinitive.	Present.	Aorist.	Imperative.	Imperfect.	Past.	Past Part.
ماتيدل	ماتيکي	مات شي	مات شه	ماتيده	مات شه	مات or مات شوَيَ

CLASS IX.

160. The infinitive زغاښتل *z'g̲h̲ūk̲h̲tal*, or زغاستل *z'g̲h̲ūstal*, 'to run,' which is a specimen of this class of verbs, has no present, aorist, or future tense; but the past and imperfect tenses and past participle are formed in the same manner as those of other verbs, by merely rejecting the ل of the infinitive, and affixing and prefixing the different pronouns and particles. The other tenses appear to belong to another infinitive, at present obsolete.

Infinitive.	Present.	Aorist.	Imperative.	Imperfect.	Past.	Past Part.
زغاښتل	زغلي	وُ زغلي	وُ زغله	زغاښت	وُ زغاښت	زغاښتلَيَ or زغاښتيَ

CLASS X.

161. This class, of which دروُمل *drūmal*, 'to go,' is an example, is similar to Class VI. as far as it goes; but it is just the reverse of the preceding, having a present, future, and imperative, but no past tenses or past participle, which are taken from other imperfect infinitives.

Infinitive.	Present.	Aorist.	Imperative.	Imperfect.	Past.	Past Part.
دروُمل	دروُمي	وُ دروُمي	وُ دروُمه	ته	لاړ	تللَيَ or تليَ

CLASS XI.

162. لاړل *lārral*, 'to go *or* depart,' is another of the imperfect verbs. It has merely an infinitive mood and a past tense. By using the aorist and imperfect

of the auxiliary شول shwal, 'to become,' with its past tense, the aorist and imperative are formed. The other tenses are wanting.

Infinitive.	Present.	Aorist.	Imperative.	Imperfect.	Past.	Past Part.
لاړل	ځي	لاړ شي	لاړ شه	ته	لاړ	ټللي or ټلي

CLASS XII.

163. ټلل t'lal, 'to go,' is the only verb of this class, and has only an infinitive, and an imperfect tense, formed by rejecting the ل of the infinitive; as ټله, or by rejecting the radical ل altogether, as ته. The pronouns را, در, and ور, are also used with it. It has a regular past participle.

Infinitive.	Present.	Aorist.	Imperative.	Imperfect.	Past.	Past Part.
ټلل	ځي	لاړ شي	ځه	ته or تله	لاړ	ټللي or ټلي

CLASS XIII.

164. راغلل rāghlal, 'to come,' is the only verb of this class, and has merely a past tense and past participle. The pure infinitive was doubtless غلل, to which the pronouns referred to in the former class have been added, but without them it conveys no meaning. It differs from the preceding inasmuch as it adds را to the imperfect tense of ټلل to form its own imperfect tense, and has a regular past. In other respects it is similar.

Infinitive.	Present.	Aorist.	Imperative.	Imperfect.	Past.	Past Part.
راغلل	راځي	راشي	راځه	راته	راغي	راغللي or راغلي

The whole of these imperfect verbs use the tenses of others to supply the want of their own, as will be seen from the conjugations. The latter have been marked by a dash over them.

TRANSITIVES.

CLASS I.

165. The verbs of this class are the most numerous in the language. They reject the ل of the infinitive for the present, future, and imperative, and lengthen the first vowel from (ـَ) to ا for the past tenses. The past participle is regular; as تړل tarral, 'to bind,' وهل wahal, 'to strike,' ګرزول garzawul, 'to turn.'

Infinitive.	Present.	Aorist.	Imperative.	Imperfect.	Past.	Past Part.
تړل	تړي	ؤ تړي	ؤ تړه	تاړ	ؤ تاړ	تړلي
وهل	وهي	ؤ وهي	ؤ وهه	واهه	ؤ واهه	وهلي
ګرزول	ګرزوي	ؤ ګرزوي	ؤ ګرزوه	ګرزاوه	ؤ ګرزاوه	ګرزولي

CLASS II.

166. The verbs of this class are also very numerous, but are irregular. In forming the present tense and imperative mood, they reject the ل of the infinitive, and sometimes form the latter by affixing the imperative of کړل *krral*, 'to do,' to the shortened past participle. The aorist, future, and past tenses are alone formed by the aid of the shortened past participle prefixed to the same tenses of کړل respectively. The middle vowel of the root is lengthened from (َ) to ا for the imperfect tense; as خښول *khakhawul*, or *khashawul*, 'to bury.'

Infinitive.	Present.	Aorist.	Imperative.	Imperfect.	Past.	Past Part.
خښول	خښوي	خښ کړي	خښ کړه	خښاوُه	خښ کړ	خښ کړَي

CLASS III.

167. Changes the two last radical letters of the root for two others in the present, future, and imperative; as ښت for ار in غوښتل *ghokhtal*, or *ghoshtal*, 'to desire;' ست for ند in آغوستل *āghūstal*, 'to clothe;' ښت for نړ in سکښتل *skakhtal*, or *skashtal*, 'to clip;' ښو for ږد or ګد in پريښول *pre-khowul*, or *pre-showul*, 'to abandon,' etc.

Infinitive.	Present.	Aorist.	Imperative.	Imperfect.	Past.	Past Part.
غوښتل	غواړي	وُ غواړي	وُ غواړه	غوښت	وُ غوښت	غوښتلَي
آغوستل	آغوندي	واغوندي	واغونده	آغوست	واغوست	آغوستلَي
سکښتل	سکنړي	وُ سکنړي	وُ سکنړه	سکښت	وُ سکښت	سکښتلَي

CLASS IV.

168. The verbs of this class, after dropping the ل of the infinitive, reject the two last radical letters for another letter, in the present, future, and imperative; as ند for م in موندل *mūndal*, 'to find;' ست for ل in لوستل *l'wastal*, 'to read;' and آخستل *ākhistal*, 'to seize;' and retain them in the past tenses.

Infinitive.	Present.	Aorist.	Imperative.	Imperfect.	Past.	Past Part.
مُوندل	مُومي	وُ مُومي	وُ مُومه	مُوند	وُ مُوند	مُوندلَي
لّوستل	لّولي	وُ لّولي	وُ لّوله	لّوست	وُ لّوست	لّوستلَي

CLASS V.

169. These verbs do not take the prefixed وُ, and form all the tenses and the imperative by the mere rejection of the ل of the infinitive, the present tenses taking the affixed, and the past the prefixed pronouns; as بايلل *bā'e-lal*, 'to lose at play.'

Infinitive.	Present.	Aorist.	Imperative.	Imperfect.	Past.	Past Part.
بايلل	بايلي	بايلي	بايله	بايله	بايلو or بايله	بايللي

CLASS VI.

170. Lengthens the first vowel from (َ) into ا in all the inflexions except the past participle; as ويل *wa-yal*, 'to speak.'

Infinitive.	Present.	Aorist.	Imperative.	Imperfect.	Past.	Past Part.
وَيل	وائي	وُ وائي	وُ وايه	وايه	وُ وايه	وَيلي

CLASS VII.

171. Lengthens the first syllable in all the inflexions in the same manner as the preceding, but with this exception, that it changes (َ) into و for the present and future tenses and the imperative mood, and (َ) into ا for the past; as بلل *balal*, 'to call.'

Infinitive.	Present.	Aorist.	Imperative.	Imperfect.	Past.	Past Part.
بلل	بولي	وُ بولي	وُ بوله	باله	وُ باله	بَللي

CLASS VIII.

172. After dropping the ل of the infinitive, changes the last radical letter for another in the present, future, and imperative; as ل for ن in وژلل *wajz-lal* or وجلل *waj-lal*, 'to kill.' The radical letter is retained in the past tenses, and the first vowel lengthened from (َ) to ا.

Infinitive.	Present.	Aorist.	Imperative.	Imperfect.	Past.	Past Part.
وژلل	وژني	وُ وژني	وُ وژنه	واژه	وُ واژه	وژلي

CLASS IX.

173. The verbs of this class are irregular, as are all the infinitives ending in ت, which reject the prefixed وُ, the sign of the past tense. They change the last radical letter for another in the present, future, and imperative; as ت for خ in پرانتل *prā-natal*, 'to unloose;' but retain it in the past. By rejecting the prefixed وُ there is no difference between the past and the imperfect in the mode of writing. See page 87, para. 220.

Infinitive.	Present.	Aorist.	Imperative.	Imperfect.	Past.	Past Part.
پرانتل	پرانځي	پرانځي	پرانځه	پرانت	پرانت	پرانتي

CLASS X.

174. After dropping the sign of the infinitive, rejects the three last letters of the root for another, in the formation of the present, future, and imperative, and retains them in the past tenses; as وِيشتل *wishtal*, 'to discharge.'

Infinitive.	Present.	Aorist.	Imperative.	Imperfect.	Past.	Past Part.
وِيشتل	وُلي	وُ وُلي	وُ وُله	وِيشت	وُ وِيشت	وِيشتلي

CLASS XI.

175. The verbs of this class reject the two last radical letters in the present and imperative, but retain them in the past and past participle; as پوښتيدل *pū<u>kh</u>t-edal* or *pū<u>sh</u>t-edal*, 'to ask,' پيروّدل *pīraw-dal*, 'to purchase,' آرويدل *ār-wedal*, 'to hear.'

Infinitive.	Present.	Aorist.	Imperative.	Imperfect.	Past.	Past Part.
پُوښتيدل	پُوښتي	وُ پُوښتي	وُ پُوښته	پُوښتيده	وُ پُوښتيده	پُوښتيدلي
پيروّدل	پيري	وُ پيري	وُ پيره	پيروّد	وُ پيروّد	پيروّدلي
آرويدل	آروي	واروي	واروه	آرويدَ	وارويدَ	آرويدلي

CLASS XII.

176. Rejects the last radical letter of the root in the present, future, and imperative, but retains it in the past. The middle vowel is also lengthened from (ـَـ) to ا for the past tenses: the past participle is regular; as پيژندل *pejzandal*, 'to know.'

Infinitive.	Present.	Aorist.	Imperative.	Imperfect.	Past.	Past Part.
پيژندل	پيژني	وُ پيژني	وُ پيژنه	پيژاند	وُ پيژاند	پيژندلي

CLASS XIII.

177. Lengthens the first vowel from (ـَـ) to ا for the present, future, and imperative, and uses the simple infinitive of the verb for all the inflexions of the imperfect and the past, with the addition of the prefixed وُ in all three persons, singular and plural; as خندل *<u>kh</u>andal*, 'to laugh.' The past participle is regular.

Infinitive.	Present.	Aorist.	Imperative.	Imperfect.	Past.	Past Part.
خندل	خاندي	وُ خاندي	وُ خانده	خندل	وُ خندل	خندلي

CLASS XIV.

178. The verbs of this class exchange the last radical letter for another in the present, future, and imperative, and retain it in the past; as ښ into ر in مُښل *mu<u>kh</u>al*, 'to rub.'

Infinitive.	Present.	Aorist.	Imperative.	Imperfect.	Past.	Past Part.
مُښل	مُري	وُ مُري	وُ مُره	مُښَ or مُښه	وُ مُښَ or وُ مُښه	مُښلي

CLASS XV.

179. The verbs of this and the following classes are all imperfect.

The infinitive ييښل *yekhal* or *yeshal*, 'to place,' is an example. It has no present, future, or imperative, but the imperfect tense is regularly formed. It is generally used with the two following infinitives, which are of the same meaning, and have no past tenses.

Infinitive.	Present.	Aorist.	Imperative.	Imperfect.	Past.	Past Part.
ييښل	ږدي	ږدي	ږده	ييښه	كيښو	ييښې

CLASS XVI.

180. كيښول *kekhwal*, 'to place,' is a specimen of this class. It has but one tense, which is used both for the imperfect and the past. كيږدل *kejz-dal*, which again has no past tenses or past participle, is used with it to supply the tenses which the former infinitive requires.

Infinitive.	Present.	Aorist.	Imperative.	Imperfect.	Past.	Past Part.
كيښول	كيږدي	كيږدي	كيږده	كيښو	كيښو	ييښې

CLASS XVII.

181. ږدل *jz'dal*, 'to place,' the example of this class, has no past tenses or past participle, and, as before mentioned, is used to supply the wants of ييښل, which has no present, future, or imperative. The present tense is formed by merely rejecting the ل of the infinitive, and affixing the necessary pronouns. The imperative is formed in the same manner, but the past tenses are taken from كيښول and the past participle from ييښل.

Infinitive.	Present.	Aorist.	Imperative.	Imperfect.	Past.	Past Part.
ږدل	ږدي	ږدي	ږده	كيښو	كيښو	ييښې

CLASS XVIII.

182. وړل *w'rral*, 'to take *or* carry,' which is an example, and about the only one of this class, is merely imperfect as regards the aorist and future tenses, which are taken from يوسل *yo-sal* when required. The imperative is formed by merely rejecting the ل of the infinitive, and the present by affixing the necessary pronouns. The past is formed by prefixing يو to the root, which is obtained from يوړل, an infinitive nearly obsolete.

Infinitive.	Present.	Aorist.	Imperative.	Imperfect.	Past.	Past Part.
وړل	وړي	يوسي	وړه	وړ	يووړ	وړې

CLASS XIX.

183. بیول *bī-wul*, 'to take *or* bear away,' and آښل *ā**kh**al*, or *ā**s**hal*, 'to knead,' are specimens of this class. They change the last radical letter for two others in the present tenses, and imperative mood, and retain it in the imperfect: the other tenses are wanting, but the past participle is regular.

Infinitive.	Present.	Aorist.	Imperative.	Imperfect.	Past.	Past Part.
بیول	بیائي	بوزي	بیایه	بیوّه	بوت	بیولیَ
آښل	آغگي	واغگي	واغگه	آښه	واښه	آښليَ

CLASS XX.

184. The infinitives of this class which prefix the postposition کښي *k**kh**ey* or *k**s**hey*, 'in,' etc., to another verb, reject the ل of the infinitive in the present tenses and imperative mood, and lengthen the short vowel preceding the last characteristic letter from (ــَ) to ا for the past; as کښینول *k**kh**enawul*, or *k**s**henawul*, 'to cause *or* make to sit.' The past participle is regular.

Infinitive.	Present.	Aorist.	Imperative.	Imperfect.	Past.	Past Part.
کښینول	کښینوي	کښینوي	کښینوه	کښیناوّه or کښیناوو	کښیناوّه or کښیناوو	کښینوليَ

CLASS XXI.

185. These infinitives are the most regular in the language, merely rejecting the ل of the infinitive, and affixing the different pronouns for the present tense, taking the root for the imperfect, and prefixing وُ to it for the past; as ساتل *sā-tul*, 'to nourish,' پیایل *pī-ā-yal*, 'to graze.'

Infinitive.	Present.	Aorist.	Imperative.	Imperfect.	Past.	Past Part.
ساتل	ساتي	وُ ساتي	وُ ساته	ساته	وُ ساته	ساتليَ

CLASS XXII.

186. Rejects the last radical letter, and the sign of the infinitive for the present and imperative, and retains it in the past. The past participle is regular; as نغردل *n'**gh**a**rr**dal*, 'to swallow,' سپردل *spa**rr**dal*, 'to undo *or* unravel.'

Infinitive.	Present.	Aorist.	Imperative.	Imperfect.	Past.	Past Part.
ںْغردل	ںْغري	وُ ںْغري	وُ ںْغره	ںْغرد	وُ ںْغرد	ںْغرديَ

CLASS XXIII.

187. The infinitive سْول *swal*, 'to burn,' which is a specimen of this class, is used both as a transitive and intransitive. The sign of the infinitive is dropped and

an extra letter taken for the present tenses and imperative. The past tenses reject the extra letter, and are regular in their formation.

Infinitive.	Present.	Aorist.	Imperative.	Imperfect.	Past.	Past Part.
سٙول	سٙوځي	وُ سٙوځي	وُ سٙوځه	سه or سوُ	وُ سه or وُ سوُ	سَوَيَ

CLASS XXIV.

188. The infinitive كول *kawul*, 'to perform,' which comes under this class, is exceedingly irregular in the formation of the different tenses. The most regular form of the present is obtained by rejecting the ل and the last radical letter (of which there are but two) for the masculine singular. It is also written كا and كاندِ for the third person, but the radical letter, lost in the third, is retained in the first and second. The past tenses are also irregular, and there is no change in termination for gender.

Infinitive.	Present.	Aorist.	Imperative.	Imperfect.	Past.	Past Part.
كول	كوي	وُ كي	كوه	كاوُه or كاوو	وُ كه	كَرِيَ

THE PARTICIPLES.

اسماي حاليه و مفعول *asmā'ī ḥālīah wo mafœūl.*

189. Pus̲h̲to verbs admit of inflexion to form the participles, which may be termed imperfect or present, and perfect or past, as they notify whether the action of the verb be unfinished or complete.

These participles partake of the properties of the verb, the adjective, and the noun; and are intransitive or transitive according to the verbs from which they are derived.

The participles of intransitive and transitive verbs are formed according to the same rules.

190. The present or imperfect participle is formed from the infinitive in six different ways.

I.—First by dropping the ل of the infinitive, and adding ن for the masculine, and نه for the feminine; as جاروتل 'to turn away,' جاروتنه 'turning away;' كتل 'to see, to behold,' كتنه 'seeing;' زغاستل 'to run,' زغاستن 'running;' لوَستل 'to read,' لوَستن or لوَستنه 'reading.' Examples:

بيارته نه كيږي عاشق په هيڅ يو شان　　كه ئې كور به شي تاراج يا خانومان

كه څوك ور كه سلطنت دَ اين و آن　　وا به نخلي محبوبا دد ديره گران

نه جاروزي جاروتنه دَ نادان دي

> "The lover is not to be separated in any way whatsoever from the beloved,
> Whether his dwelling be sacked and pillaged, or filled with wealth and goods.
> Though one would give him the sovereignty of this world and the next,
> He would not accept it, for the beloved one is of great price:
> Therefore he turneth not away, for TURNING BACK is the act of a fool."
> —*Kāsim A'alī, Afrīdī.*

بل لوستل پر تا واجب دي په ورنبي دواړو رکعت او که لولي په ورستي کښې ورنبي پريږدي خالي
نه يې له پساتَ

"Again: REPEATING is incumbent on thee in both of the first genuflexions; and shouldest thou repeat in the last, and neglect the first, thou art not devoid of sin."—*Makhzan Afghānī.*

191. II.—In the second form the ل of the infinitive is dropped and replaced by ه (*hā-i-ẓāhir*) or (ـَ) (*fat'ha'h*), if masculine, and ه (*hā-i-khafī*) if feminine; as وِلل 'to wash,' وِله or وِلَ 'washing;' ناستل 'to sit,' ناسته or ناستَ 'sitting.'

The following are examples:—

اول مخ وِلَه په وضو کښې فرض دي دَ وچولي له سرَ تر دلاندِ څنِ پورِ له يوه غوږه تر بله دَغه سپين
ځاي چه دَ غوږ او دَ مخ ترميان دي وِلَه دَ دَغه فرض دي

"First: WASHING the face from the top of the forehead as far down as the bottom of the chin, is a precept in ablution; also washing that clear space which is between the ears and the cheek, is a duty."—*Fawā'īd-ush-Sharī'aa'h.*

هسي شان دي ستا دَ ناستي اي دلبره   لکه ناسته دَ شهباز په کوهستان کښې

> "Thy mode of SITTING, oh sweetheart,
> Is like the PERCHING of the falcon on the mountain top."—*Ahmad Shāh, Abdālī.*

چه څوک حاضر شي په مسجد کښې په هرگام به دوه لس نيکئي کښې شي هم په تله هم په راتله

"Whenever one attends in a place of worship, for each footstep, both in COMING and in GOING, twelve good actions will be written."—*Fawā'īd-ush-Sharī'aa'h.*

192. III.—To form the third division, it is necessary to insert an ا before the final consonant of the root, which in this class is generally ت, and add the same terminations, as in the preceding form; thus آلوتل 'to fly,' آلواته 'flying;' جاروتل 'to change' or 'turn round,' جارواته 'changing' or 'turning round;' وتل 'to come out,' واته 'coming out.' Examples:

نه گورَ مچ و مچۍ په يوه خير دي آلواته يې په بل فير دي مچ به دروميي و گندگئي ته دَ مچۍ له
خوږ دير طالبان سير دي

"Behold! the fly and the bee are of one species, but their mode of FLYING is different;

for the fly will fly to filthiness and impurity, whilst many seekers are satiated with the honey of the bee."—*Makhzan Afghānī.*

دَ دغه درُ دیوار خضر دربان شه   چه پري کیږي ستا واته نن واته

"Let Khiẓr* become the gatekeeper of that gate and wall,
Through which thy COMING IN and GOING OUT may be."†—*Æabd-ul-Ḥamīd.*

ستا له محبت جاړواته خما دروغ دي   ولي خاورِ نه شي په دا لار بشر خما

"My CHANGING from thy love and affection is false indeed:
Why should not my body become dust on this road?"—*Æabd-ur-Raḥmān.*

خانَ زه چه ستا و لورِ ته کاته کړم مرګ را ته ګړنګ دي دا صورت به و ګړنګ ته پرېواته کړم

"Alas, oh chief! when I look towards thee, death to me is an abyss, and this form I make a PRECIPITATION of into it."—*Adam Khān and Durkhāna'ī.*

193. IV.—The fourth class is obtained by lengthening the vowel of the first letter from (ـَ) to ا after cutting off the ل of the infinitive as usual, and affixing (ـَ) or ه to the final consonant of the root; as يستل 'to draw forth' or 'eject,' یاستَ or یاسته 'drawing forth' or 'ejecting;' جاریستل 'to change,' 'alter,' or 'turn round,' جاریاستَ and جاریاسته 'changing,' 'altering,' 'turning round.' Example:

پر وقت دَ سلام په ښي او په کینړ لوري مخ جاریاستَ مستحب دي

"At the time of making salutation (at prayer), TURNING the head to the right side and the left is desirable."—*Fawā'id-ush-Sharī'æa'h.*

لسم پیژاندہ دَ محمد فرض دي پر دا رنګ چه رسول دَ خداي دي چه موږ ایمان په دا راوړي

"Tenth: KNOWING Muḥammad is a divine command, in this manner; that he is the Prophet of God, on whom we have placed our faith."—*Fawā'id-ush-Sharī'æa'h.*

194. V.—The present participles of the fifth class are obtained from intransitive infinitives, formed from adjectives by dropping the يدل of the infinitive and adding وُن; as ګډیدل 'to mix,' ګډون 'mixing;' ډکیدل 'to fill,' ډکون 'filling.' They may also be obtained from pure transitives having ل as the sign of the infinitive; thus تړل 'to bind,' تړون 'binding.' They can also be formed from the intransitives above referred to, by merely rejecting the ل and adding the وُن; as ډکیدل 'to fill,' ډکیدون 'filling.' These forms are rare, the former particularly so.

* The name of a prophet who, according to Oriental tradition, was Wuzīr to Kaikobād, king of Persia. He is said to have discovered and drank of the water of life, and that in consequence he will not die until the Day of Judgment.

† واته and نن واته may also be translated, *exit* and *entrance*. See Chapter VII., On the Derivation of Words.

له اغيار سره گډون دي دَ يار هسي لکَ څوک کا سره گډ پاك و ناپاك

"The ASSOCIATING (mixing) of the beloved with a rival is,
As if a person were to mix together purity and defilement."—*Æabd-ul-Ḥamīd.*

195. VI.—The sixth class, which consists of transitive and causal verbs, is formed by dropping the ل of the infinitive and inserting ا before the final letter of the root, to which ن or نه is affixed; as ماتول 'to break' or 'rend,' ماتاوُن 'breaking' or 'rending;' ښکلول 'to kiss,' ښکلاوُن 'kissing.' Example:

يو ورځ په صحرا سپي ؤ ليد مجنون ترِ قربان شه هزار ځله گونا گون
رنگا رنگ ئي ښکلاوه په دوؤ چشمانو حق حيران ور ته خلق شه په ښکلاوُن

"Majnūn one day beheld a dog in the desert, and caressed him a thousand times.
He kissed him on both eyes in various ways, and people became astonished with him for KISSING."—*Adam Khān and Durkhāna'ī.*

196. The whole of these participles are capable of inflexion, in the same manner as nouns, in three different ways:

197. Those of the first form, ending in ه (*hā-i-khafī*), such as جاروتنه 'turning away,' and ناستنه 'sitting,' which are all feminine, come under the first variety of nouns of the 3rd Declension; those of the second, third, and fourth forms, terminating in ه (*hā-i-ẓā-hir*), such as ؤله 'washing,' and آلوانه 'flying,' being masculine, are declined as nouns of the first variety of the 6th Declension; and those of the first, fifth, and sixth forms, ending in ون, such as گډون 'mixing,' and ترون 'binding,' which are also masculine, as nouns of the 9th Declension.

198. The present participle is also used as a noun; thus آلوانه signifies 'flight,' as well as 'fleeing;' پرېوانه 'falling,' also 'a fall;' and پيراندء 'knowledge,' as well as 'knowing:' this will be more fully noticed under the head of حاصل مصدر *ḥāṣil-i-maṣdar*, or Verbal Noun.

THE PERFECT OR PAST PARTICIPLE.

اسم مفعول *ism-i-mafæūl.*

199. The perfect or past participle denotes that the action of the verb is complete, and is obtained in three different ways both from transitives and intransitives.

200. I.—The first method is by adding ي (*yā-i-mā-ḳabl-i-maftūḥ*)* to the infinitive for the masculine, and ي (*yā-i-majhūl*) or (ـِ) (*kasrah*) for the feminine singular; as کيښول 'to place,' کيښولي 'placed;' ليدل 'to see,' ليدلي 'seen;' غلول 'to cheat,' غلولِ 'cheated,' etc. The following are examples:

* For explanation regarding the letter ي, see paragraphs 44 and 45.

چه دَ عشق له بحرَ روغ سلامت وُ وزي   زد ئې نن گنړم له مورَ زیږیدلئ

"Whoever emergeth in safety from the sea of love,
I consider this very day BORN of his mother."—*Æabd-ur-Raḥmān.*

که یو شخص و بل ته وائِي چه څموږ بابا آدم کرباس وودلي هغه هسي ور ته وائِي بارِ مورِ جولا بچه
یوُ که غرض ئې سپکاوي وي کافر کیږي

"If one person sayeth to another that our father Adam WOVE linen, and he sayeth unto him, 'Yes, and we are weaver's children,' and his (the latter's) intention be to lower the estimation of father Adam, he becometh a blasphemer."—*Fawā'id-ush-Sharī'æa'h.*

Examples of the feminine singular, Intransitives and Transitives.

دوَیم گروه ور ته ښکارد شه په دوزخ کښې آتشي طوق ئې په غاړه پښې تړلِ

"A second party of people appeared to him in hell, each with a fiery collar round the neck, and foot BOUND."—*Miærāj Nāma'h.*

هغې وِیشتلِ شهزادئې له ډیره شوقَ   دا آبیات ئې غزل وِ په خپل زبان

"That STRICKEN princess through excess of love,
Was singing these verses in her own language."—*Saif-ul-Mulūk.*

The plural form for both masculine and feminine is the same; and is obtained by substituting ي (*yā-i-maærūf*), in the same manner as for the nouns of the first variety of the 1st declension, and the form of adjectives described at paragraph 88.

ښځ خندا مي له دې خلق سره نه شي   ژړه وي مي هغه تللي تللي خلق

"I cannot laugh and make merry with the people of the world,
For those DEPARTED ones make me weep and lament."—*Æabd-ur-Raḥmān.*

دواړه سترګي ئې دَ یار په لورِ نیولي   مُبتلا ناست وُ دَ عشق په مي خمار

"With both eyes DRAWN TOWARDS the path of the adored one,
He was sitting distressed, in the intoxication of the wine of love."—*Saif-ul-Mulūk.*

201. II.—The second form of this participle is obtained in a similar manner to the first, the only difference being that the ل of the infinitive is dropped, and the ئ, ئې, or (ـَ) affixed to the root for the masculine and feminine singular, and ي for both plurals, as in the first class. They are sometimes formed from the same verbs and used indiscriminately; thus آغوستل 'to be dressed,' آغوستلئ or آغوستئ 'dressed;' ناستل 'to sit,' ناستلئ or ناستئ 'seated;' آوښتل 'to turn back,' آوښتئ or آوښتلئ 'turned back.' Examples:

ته ځ خوره اي نيک خصلته او کړه ښوانه   چه غه آوښتي بخت ټول کړي ځ نه خوړ بي ګمانه

"Consume and enjoy, oh! thou of good disposition, and true man,
What that one of INVERTED fortune collected together, but did not expend."—*Gulistān.*

آهو چشم وړي زړه که هر څو بولم   نه مني لکه آهو بلل ځما

"Notwithstanding I summon back this stag-eye CAPTURED heart,
Yet like the deer it heedeth not my calling."—*Æabd-ul-Ḥamīd.*

دا سټي چه په اور سوځي مُراد يې دا دي   چه په اور کښي سَوِ ښه يم نه بي پتَ

"This Sata'ī,* who consumeth herself, her intention is this—
That CONSUMED in the fire I am content; but not without honour."
—*Æabd-ur-Raḥmān.*

په ظاهر جامه فقير په خُله بخيل   لکَ نغښتِ په ايرو تازه سکروټَ

"In outward dress a beggar, in words a niggard—
Like a bright spark of fire ENVELOPED in dust and ashes."—*Mīrzā Khān, Anṣārī.*

Examples of the plural masculine and feminine.

تمام جهان لمن را ښخه نغاړي   سپين زړوکي آغوستي تور کودي شوم

"The whole world pluck away their vestments from near me:
I am become like a smoke-blackened pot, though clothed in white garments."
—*Æabd-ur-Raḥmān.*

بل سړي ور ته ښکاره شه په دوزخ کښِ چه فرياد يې له ژړا سره يکسان کا سر ته پاي يې دَ اور نَوري
آغوستي پر عذاب رګو بي هر اُستخوان کا

"Another man appeared to him in hell, who was alike weeping and wailing. CLOTHED in garments of fire from head to foot, they tormented his every vein and artery—every nerve and bone."—*Majmūæat-i-Ḳandahārī.*

عاقبت به لکَ تش بادام خجل شي   ډيرو دَ إسلام جامي آغوستي کافران دي

"At the Last Day they will, like an empty almond, become ashamed and confounded;
For many DRESSED OUT in the garments of the True Faith are infidels and blasphemers."
—*Æabd-ur-Raḥmān.*

دَ يار سترګي خمار دي   را آوښتي نن پرِ يار دي
جوړي ګولۍ دَ ګذار دي   ګوره دَ چا په تاتار دي

"The eyes of the beloved are intoxicators, TURNED ROUND upon the lover to-day:
They are balls ready prepared for striking; observe for whose spoil and plunder they are."
—*Aḥmad Shāh, Abdālī.*

* Sata'ī—a woman who burns on her husband's funeral pyre.

202. III.—The third class of past participles is formed from the irregular and defective verbs, such as پريوتل 'to fall,' and ورستيدل 'to rot,' and those similar to ولاړل 'to stand,' and ناستل or كښيناستل 'to sit,' which have no regular past tense of their own. The past tense of the auxiliary شول 'to become,' is sometimes used in forming it. They appear to have originally been adjectives from which these infinitives have been formed, particularly those ending in يدل. The terminations for the masculine and feminine are also different to the other participles,* being subject to the same changes for gender and number as the classes of adjectives described at paragraphs 86 and 87.

The masculine singular is formed by dropping the يدل of the infinitive; as ولاړيدل 'to stand,' ولاړ 'stood;' پريوتل 'to fall,' پروت 'fallen;' ناستل 'to sit,' ناست 'seated;' ورستيدل 'to rot,' وروست 'rotten.' Examples:

وږي تږي پروت په خپلې بوزيې ښه يې   نه په تخت دَ پَاسه ناست دَ بل كره

"Hungry and thirsty, on thy own mat FALLEN thou art well off;
But not so, SEATED on the dais in the house of another."—*Æabd-ul-Ḥamīd.*

پروت په وينو كښي لت پت ښه يم په پت كښي   نه دَ سرو زرو په تخت باندِ بي پتَ

"Fallen over and over in red blood with fame, I am fortunate;
But not so without honour, even seated on the throne of red gold."—*Æabd-ul-Ḥamīd.*

At times, some of the participles of this class assume the form of the first class, by adding ي to the infinitive, as in the following:

اي خما دوؤ سترګو وداع ؤ كړئ اي دَ لاسُ ورغوو او دَ ووږو ليچو تاسؤ همه رخصت دَ يكڅ دګر را ؤ كړئ په خوار عاجز پريوتليَ باندِ آخر اي دوستانو ګذر ؤ كړئ

"Oh mine eyes, you should bid farewell! you, oh palms of my hands, and arms of my shoulders, too, should take leave of each other! Finally, you, oh my friends, should pass over (the grave) of this poor and humble FALLEN one!"—*Gulistān.*

To form the feminine singular, ه (*hā-i-khafī*) or (ـَ) (*fat'ḥa'h*) is affixed to the masculine. Examples:

كه دَ اوسپنِ قلا ترخانَ چاپير كړِ   خلاص به نشي دَ مرګي خيمه پر هر غولي ولاړه

"Though thou environ thyself with a fortress of iron,
Thou wilt not escape from the tent of death ERECT in every court."
—*Mīrzā Khān, Anṣārī.*

ماتَ ملا په مشقت په محنت ښه ده   نه حرامَ هميانيِ دَ چا ترملا

* Strictly speaking, the participles are not parts of the verb, as they do not apply affirmation, but are merely adjectives, particularly this form.

"A waist BROKEN through the toil of industry and labour is good;
But not a purse of the money of unlawfulness round a man's waist."—*Æabd-ur-Raḥmān.*

The plural masculine form of the third class of these past or perfect participles is the same as the singular, but the feminine plural changes the ه and (ـے) of the singular into ي (*yā-i-majhūl*) or (ـِ) (*kasrah*). Examples:

نن په خپل عمر غره يو   صباح به مؤ تير خلق بولين

"To-day we are proud of our existence:
To-morrow the world will count us amongst the DEPARTED."—*Aḥmad S̲h̲āh, Abdālī.*

واړه مشق دَ خونريزئ کړي در پوهيږم   دا چه ناست يې پټي سترګي لکه باز

"I know that thou merely perfectest thyself in bloodshed,
Seated in this manner like the falcon, with eyes VEILED."—*Æabd-ul-Ḥamīd.*

203. The past participles are capable of inflexion, and are subject to the same general laws as nouns; as in the following extracts:

که هر خو په صحرا سر شوم هم په کليو   بيا مي نه مُوند هيڅ خبر دَ هغو تلليو

"Notwithstanding I searched both in deserts and in hamlets,
I did not again obtain any information of those DEPARTED ones."—*Æabd-ur-Raḥmān.*

خبر نه يم چه په باب مي کښلي څه دي   زه رحمان په انديښنه يم دَ دِ کښلو

"I know not what is WRITTEN on my account:
I, Raḥmān, am in anxiety concerning these WRITTEN things."—*Æabd-ur-Raḥmān.*

THE ACTOR OR NOUN OF ACTION.

اسم فاعل *ism-i-fāœ'il.*

204. The active participle, agent, or noun of action, denotes the performer of any action, and is an inflection of the verb, as in Arabic and Persian. It is transitive or intransitive, according to the verb from which it is derived; is both singular and plural; masculine and feminine; and is capable of inflection in the same manner as described at paragraph 88.

205. There are two methods of forming it—by dropping the ل of the infinitive and adding ونکي *ūnkaey* or وني *ūnaey* for the masculine, and ونکِ *ūnki* or ونکي *ūnkey*, or ونِ *ūni* or وني *ūney*, for the feminine singular. Examples:

ضرر نفع نيکي بدي له خدايه چه ور کړونکي دَ ملکونو آخستونکي دَ ملکونو واړه خداي دي

"Detriment and advantage, good and evil, are from God, who is the GIVER of kingdoms, and the TAKER of dominions: all is from God."—*Fawā'īd-us̲h̲-S̲h̲arī'æa'h.*

زه به تلوُني له دنيا يم هسي تيز لكه توپ چه خلاص كاندِ انكريز

"I shall be a DEPARTER from this world,
As rapidly as the English discharge a cannon."—*Ḳāsim Æalī, Afrīdī.*

په هغه ورځ هيڅ كار مه كوه ته يا دَ ستا ځوي يا دَ ستا لور يا ستا مرئي يا وينځه يا دَ ستا چار پاي يا
ستا په دروازِ كښي اوسيدوُنيَ مسافر

"In it thou shalt not do any work, thou, nor thy son, nor thy daughter, nor thy man-servant, nor thy maid-servant, nor thy cattle, nor the stranger A DWELLER within thy gates."
—*Translation of the Pentateuch.*

دَ قيامت ورځ هم دد راتلوُنِ شك ئِي مه كانږئ يارانو څو هولونه به نازل شي څو هيبت په آدميانٌ

"The day of judgment is also A COMER; doubt this not, oh my friends! On that day, what terrors and what fears will descend upon men!"—*Fawā'id-ush-Sharī'æa'h.*

په جامع صغير كښي هسي وائِي چه سجدد غم دَ شيطان دد بل پوره كړوُنِ دَ نقصان دد بل رضا
دَ پاك رحمان دد

"In the '*Jāmiæ-i-Ṣaghīr*' it is thus stated: 'Prostration (in prayer) is the cause of grief and affliction to the devil; is also the CORRECTOR of any error or inadvertency (in prayer); and, moreover, is the will of Almighty God."—*Fawā'id-ush-Sharī'æa'h.*

The plural form of this participle is both masculine and feminine. It is obtained, in the same manner as the plural form of the past participles of the first and second classes, by rejecting the final يَ, ئِ, or (ـَ) of the singular for ي (*yā-i-maærūf*); as لوستونيَ or لوستونكيَ 'a reader,' لوستوني or لوستونكي 'readers.' Examples:

وينم وارد تلوُني هيڅ څوك نه دي پاتوشوُني يوُن دي پدا لارِ هم دَ ځوان هم دَ زارد

"I perceive all are TRAVELLERS, there are no TARRIERS behind:
The journeying on this road is both for young and for old."—*Æabd-ur-Raḥmān.*

The following extract contains examples of the plural, both masculine and feminine:

بينځه څيزد ماتوُونكي دَ نمانځه دي وارد عام دي اول خبرِ ماتوُونكي دَ نمانځه دي په اودد وي
كه په وينه په قصد وي كه په سهود كړوي كه ديرِ

"Five things are BREAKERS of prayer, and all are common. First, words are BREAKERS of prayer, whether they may be in sleep or in waking moments, whether intentionally or inadvertently, whether few or many."—*Fawā'id-ush-Sharī'æa'h.*

Noun of Fitness.

اسم لياقت *ism-i-liyāḳat.*

206. The noun of fitness is merely the infinitive in the genitive case; as,

دروازه چا ؤد وهله بي‌بي عايشي وِ چه څوک ئي مه راځي دا وقت دَ راتلو نه دي

"Some one knocked at the door, on which lady Æā'eshā said: 'Who art thou? do not come in; for this is not a fit time FOR COMING.'"—*Farā'id-ush-Sharī'at'h.*

چه بي وقتَ ارمان که په وقت اُودد شي   دَ ځغو عالمُ ږيري دَ وُ کښو دي

"They who lament out of season, slumber at the proper time:
The beards of those persons are only FIT TO BE PULLED."—*Æabd-ur-Raḥmān.*

There is an active participle or noun of action of intransitive verbs, but it is alone used as a noun of fitness. The following is an example:

مه ضايع کود دم و دوا په ما طبيب   نه يم رغيدونيَ يم دَ عشق له رنځه مړونيَ

"Waste not uselessly on me thy breath and thy medicine, oh physician!
For I am not ONE TO RECOVER, but ONE TO DIE from the pangs of love."
—*Æabd-ul-Ḥamīd.*

صيغ Of the Tenses.

207. As there is considerable difference in the formation of the inflections of the verbs intransitive and transitive, they will require to be separately explained.

According to the system of the Arabian grammarians, on which the grammatical rules of Pushto, as well as other Muḥammadan languages are based, verbs have properly but one conjugation, and two changes of tense—the preterite or simple past, and the aorist; the other tenses being formed by the help of several particles, and the auxiliary verbs, 'to be,' 'to become,' 'to exist,' etc., already explained and illustrated.

With the exception of the infinitive, the verbs have two numbers,—the singular and the plural. There are also three persons, as in other languages; but the third person precedes the second, and the second the first person.

Verbs are also divided into perfect and imperfect, regular and irregular; the latter, and the imperfect verbs, being exceedingly numerous.

Much variation occurs in the formation of the different tenses of the last mentioned verbs, and there is also a change in termination for the feminine gender.

208. The paradigm of a regular intransitive verb in the active and passive voices, according to the Arabic system just referred to, given at paragraphs 405, 407, 408, and 409, shows the original tenses from which all the others can be formed. The active participle denotes the agent, and the passive participle the object acted on.

INTRANSITIVE VERBS.

افعال لازمي *afaʿāl-i-lāzimī.*

ماضي مطلق PAST TENSE.

209. The past being antecedent to the present, according to the Oriental grammarians, must be first noticed.

The past tenses of intransitives are tolerably regular in comparison with transitives; still there are seven methods or rules regarding them which require some explanation.

I.—Most intransitives form the past tense by merely rejecting the ل of the infinitive and prefixing the particle ؤ, the peculiar sign of the past, which is also written ده and sometimes ور; but the ؤ of this tense, like the ب of the past in Persian, is often omitted as redundant. The last radical letter is moveable; that is to say, it takes (َـ) (*fat'ha'h*), or ه (*hā-i-zāhir*) after the final letter, for the masculine; as پوهيدل 'to know,' ؤ پوهيدَ or ؤ پوهيده 'he knew.' From the third person five other inflections are formed, by the application of the affixed personal pronouns (ضماير متصله) which have been already described.

II.—Are infinitives which form the past after the same manner as the preceding, but whose final characteristic letter is quiescent; as چاودل 'to split,' ؤ چاود 'it split;' زغاستل 'to run,' ؤ زغاست 'he ran.'

III.—Some infinitives ending in a quiescent consonant insert a و for the third person masculine singular, which is changed into ا for the plural; as ختل 'to ascend,' ؤ خوت 'he ascended.' The other persons are regular; as ؤ ختم 'I ascended,' etc.

IV.—A few infinitives reject the last radical letter as well as the sign of the infinitive in the past; as سوّل 'to burn,' ؤ سه 'it burnt.' This verb is used both as a transitive and an intransitive.

V.—Intransitives formed from adjectives or nouns by affixing يدل reject it again in the past, and the past tense of the auxiliaries شوّل or کيدل is required to complete it; as ماتيدل 'to break,' مات شه 'it broke.'

VI.—Some infinitives ending in a silent consonant, which is generally ت, do not take the prefixed ؤ, and therefore their imperfect tenses are the same as the past; thus کښيناستل 'to sit,' کښيناست 'he sat,' and 'was sitting.'

VII.—Infinitives having a ل as the final characteristic letter, reject it in the third person masculine singular; as راتلل 'to come,' راغي 'he came.'

Examples will be found in the following extracts:

حاصل دَ خبرِ هلك په زور او په هنر كښي انتها ته وُ رسيدَ او هيچا لره مجال دَ برابرۍ او دَ سيالۍ ور سرد نه وُه

"In short, the youth ATTAINED the summit of strength and skill, and no one had the power of vying or competing with him."—*Gulistān.*

په څو ورځِ دِ بندي كړم | په وصل دِ دَ تندي كړم
وُ وتم له نام و ننگ | تل مي سر واهه له سنگ

"For some time thou madest a captive of me: Thou didst plunge me into inexpressible grief:
I ABANDONED for thee both name and fame. I constantly beat my head against the stones."
—*Yūsuf and Zulīkhā.*

210. There is an exception to the above general rule in the formation of the inflexions of this tense; for the ل of the infinitive is sometimes retained, and the affixed pronouns (except for the third person plural) added to it, as may be seen in the following couplet:

زد هرڅو چه دَ عادت په رسم تللم | دَ تحقيق و فهم ته نه وُ رسيدلم

"Notwithstanding that I went according to the precepts of custom and usage,
I ATTAINED not to the knowledge of certainty and truth."—*Mīrzā Khān, Anṣārī.*

211. To form the feminine singular of this tense, ه (*hā-i-khafī*) must be affixed to the final ل of the infinitive; but sometimes the *hā-i-khafī* is substituted for the د of the masculine. The former is the most generally used. Examples:

دا دَ مينې نتيجه دَه چه ژاړيږي | چه ليمه مي په ژړا وُ پړسيده

"It is the consequent result of love that the eye weeps:
And also, that from weeping, my eye BECAME SWOLLEN."—*ʿAbd-ul-Ḥamīd.*

يو خوان دې په لاس كښ واخِست شُود روان | په شتاب وُ رسيدله تر زندان

"She took a tray in her hand and set out;
And with great expedition REACHED the prison."—*Saif-ul-Mulūk.*

212. The third person singular and plural of the past tenses of intransitive verbs *is alone* subject to change in termination for gender, and the first and second persons merely take the plural form of the affixed personal pronouns for the plural number; as وُ رسيد-وُ 'we arrived,' وُ رسيد-ئِي 'you arrived.'

The following is an example:

هم د تقدير لاس وراندِ د سترگو د عقل څما پردد دَ غفلت آچول او لري كتون هوښياري څما په توري پردي دَ ناپوهي او نادانې كښي وُ لاړ او مُنگا تول په يو ځلَ په منگلي دَ بلا او دَ ارمان كښ وُ نښتوُ

"The hand of destiny lowered the veil of imprudence before the eye of my judgment, and detained behind the obscure curtain of ignorance and incapacity my far-seeing prudence; and suddenly we all became ENTRAPPED in the talon of misfortune and sorrow."—*Kalīlah wo Damnah.*

The following extract contains an example of the plural form of the past tense, in which, as explained in a preceding paragraph, the pronoun is affixed to the infinitive.

يو عابد په سبيل دَ حال دَ درويشانُ منكر او د دوي په درد بي خبرَ وُد هسي كجورد بني هلال ته وُ رسيدلوُ

"A holy man repudiated the feigned manner of the Darweshes, and was entirely unacquainted with their sorrows and afflictions. In this manner WE ARRIVED at the palm-grove of Banī Hillāl."—*Gulistān.*

213. The third person masculine plural of verbs which do or do not take the prefixed وُ in the past tense, whether the tense be formed by rejecting or retaining the ل of the infinitive or otherwise, is generally the simple infinitive with the وُ prefixed for the former, and the infinitive unchanged for the latter; thus ريږديدل 'to tremble,' وُ ريږديدل 'they trembled;' راغلل 'to come,' راغلل 'they came.' The plural form of those which reject the وُ or drop it as redundant, will be explained in its proper place. The following is an example of the regular verbs:

علي اكبر او قاسم چه دوارِه وُ لويدل اهلِ بيت وارِه ولاړ وُ نوليدد دَ ازل په ارادد كښي كښلي دا وُد

"When Æalī Akbar and Ḳāsim FELL, their families were standing by, and were melting with grief; for such had been written from all eternity."—*Muḥammad Hanīfah.*

214. There is another form of the past tense for the masculine plural of the third person, which may be easily mistaken for the third person feminine singular, as it is written with the same consonants as the latter. There is, however, a difference in the pronunciation; yet it is difficult to describe it in writing, and even when uttered by an Afghān tongue, it is almost imperceptible, and requires an Afghān ear to distinguish it. The nearest approach is by writing (ـَـٗ) over the final ه, which vowel points give a sound equivalent to the diphthong *ai*, and similar to that which occurs in the plural form of the nouns of the fifth variety of the 6th declension. It is sometimes written with (ـَـ) only. This form of termination is used both for transitive as well as intransitive verbs.* The following is an example:

* The author of the "Æjaib-ul-Lughat," in the preface to that work, remarks on this very subject in the following manner:—"I have adopted the lexicographical system of the Persian to express the Afghānī in this work, in order that it may be more easy to those acquainted with the former language; yet, notwithstanding this, the perfectness of sound and completeness of enunciation is alone to be acquired by oral practice. The word راغله is an example of this. When written with simple *r*, *ā*, quiescent *gh*, *l* with the short vowel *a*, and unaspirated *h*, or *hā-i-khafī*, it is the third person feminine singular 'she goes;' and when written with simple *r*, *ā*, quiescent *gh*, *l* with a short vowel approaching to *a* and *i* slightly sounded, and unaspirated *h*, it is the third person masculine plural."

د اِمام سر شه دَ صالح په غولي پاتِ یزیدان گوره په تشه وُ غلیده صالح سر پر لمن پُټ ور سرِ یووړ
او په روضه کښ دَ حسن دفنیده

"The Imām's head remained in Ṣāleḥ's court. Behold the YAZĪDIS completely DECEIVED! Ṣāleḥ, having hidden the head under his skirt, carried it away and buried it in Ḥasan's tomb." —*Ḥasan and Ḥusain of Muḥammad Hanīfah.*

215. نه or نَ is sometimes affixed to the third person singular and plural of this as well as other tenses, for the sake of euphony, and as a respectful form in religious works. Examples:

نور ځما چه وُ خوځاوه خپل وجود په زورَ یو لکه څلیر ویشت زره څاڅکي دَ خولو تر پریواتنه

"When the light of my glory shook itself with force, a hundred and twenty-four thousand drops of perspiration FELL from it."—*Nūr Nāma'h.*

لس څاڅکي خولي ځما له کینر لاس نه توي شوُ له اولَ څاڅکي لس زره دَ پاك شرابُ دریابونَ له
دوهمَ دریاب دَ شهدُ له دریمَ زر دریاب په بهښت کښي دیر خواږه واړه سیل وُ بهیدنَ

"Ten drops of sweat were diffused from my left hand. From the first drop, ten thousand rivers of pure wine FLOWED like torrents through Paradise; from the second, a river of honey; and from the third, a thousand sweet streams."—*Makhzan Afghānī.*

To form the third person feminine plural of this tense the ه or (ـَـ) of the singular is changed to ي or (ـِـ), as will be seen in the following extracts:

یو پیر مرد به سري نیک نهاد موچي ته لور ئي ورکړه دا ود په بغداد
مردک سنگ دل شونډي ئي وُ چیچلي چه سرِ وینې زر تر وُ بهیدلي

"An old and respectable man who dwelt at Baghdād, gave his daughter in marriage to a shoemaker. The hard-hearted rascal bit her lips so, that the blood immediately FLOWED from them."—*Gulistān.*

شیطانانُ ور ته وُ وِیل چه په څه سرد غمگین شوي اي صاحبَ چه دَ غم نارِ دِ لاړِ په ملکونُ

"The other devils said unto him, 'Oh, master! wherefore art thou become so sorrowful, that the cries of thy grief have GONE OUT into different lands?'"—*Fawā'id-ush-Sharī'a'h.*

216. I have already observed at paragraph 209, that a great many verbs at times reject as redundant the prefixed وُ, the sign of the past tense of regular verbs, both transitive as well as intransitive, without any apparent reason; thus:

بشر وُ وِ سوگند ځما په خداي دي څغه نوړئ چه مي په خله کړه پوهیدلم په زهر

"Bishr said, 'It is my solemn oath, by God! that the mouthful which I put into my mouth I KNEW was poisoned.'"—*Fawā'id-ush-Sharī'a'h.*

In the following extract, which is an example of the same infinitive as the preceding one—پوهيدل ‘to know,’ etc.—the ژ of the past is retained.

اهلِ بيت واړه ډيره په هَغه ځاي شوُ او پر مقام دَ شهادت ۋ پوهيدل

“The family encamped on the very place, and they RECOGNIZED the spot of martyrdom.” —*Muhammad Hanīfah.*

217. There are also a number of defective as well as irregular verbs which entirely reject the ژ: in fact, to add that particle would render the word meaningless. In other respects these verbs are subject to the same changes for inflection as the others already described, as will be perceived from the following examples:

صحابه حضرت ته راغلل عرض ئي ۋ كړ چه اوبه مُوږ څخه نشته چه ئي ۋ څښوُ يا اودس كړوُ

“The companions of the Prophet CAME to him and represented: ‘We have no water that we may drink, neither that we may perform our ablutions.’”—*Fawā'īd-ush-Sharī'æa'h.*

هر كله چه عاشقي او معشوقي په مينځ كښي راغلله مالكي او مملوكي پاځيدله

“When love-making and love-accepting CAME between, authority and dependence arose and departed.”—*Gulistān.*

218. When the verb has a radical ل, as well as the ل of the infinitive, as in راغلل, تلل, etc., one is generally rejected as redundant in the inflections for the different tenses, with the exception of the third person feminine singular and plural of a few, in which both are retained. In the third person masculine singular both are dropped. Example:

بلبلاں كاندِ چغار په باغ كښِ — دَ بهار گل په چمن مُصطفي راغي

“The nightingales sing both in garden and in meadow—
‘The flower of the spring, the Chosen One,* HAS COME into the parterre.’”
—*Kāsim Æalī, Afrīdī.*

Sometimes both ل's are retained in this, as well as in other tenses of the verb. Example:

يو نكيروُه بل منكروُه — عذاب څما په سروُه
آخر راغلهلي حاضري — را ته ۋ دريدي ناظري

“One was Nakīr, the other Munkir—the whole torment was on my devoted head.
At length THEY CAME forth—they stood before me, lookers-on.”
—*Story of Jumjumah.*

* A name of Muhammad.

219. The third persons of the past tense of some verbs, in which the letter ت precedes the sign of the infinitive, are somewhat irregular. In the third person singular they take و before the ت; thus, ختل 'to ascend,' instead of becoming ؤ خت, becomes ؤ خوت:

شهزاده په لوړه ؤ خوت نندارې ته   دو رخ سپاهیان لویدهٔ* دَ آس له شانَ

"The prince ASCENDED to a rising ground to obtain a view.
On both sides the warriors were falling from their steeds."—*Bahrām Gūr.*

For the plural, the ؤ is changed into ا; thus ؤ خوت becomes ؤ خاتهٔ. Sometimes, however, the past masculine plural is written ؤ ختل. An example of the former is contained in the following extract: †

په دا دیدن کښې آدم خان ځان ؤ ناته ناموس او ننګ له خاطره ؤ واته

"At this sight Adam Khān laid waste his heart; and all solicitude for name and fame WENT OUT of it."—*Story of Adam Khān and Durkhāna'ī.*

220. There are several compound ‡ verbs, both intransitive, as well as transitive, such as پریوتل 'to fall,' کښیوتل 'to fall into,' کښیناستل 'to sit down,' etc., which are obtained by prefixing a preposition or a post-position to a simple infinitive, the formation of the past tenses of which is difficult, and requires some explanation. Instead of placing the ؤ of the past tense, when expressed, before the word in its compound state, it is inserted after the preposition. Thus the past tense of the infinitive پریوتل, instead of becoming ؤ پریوت, is written پرې ؤ وت; and کښیوتل. کښې ؤ وت. In many recent manuscript works, and in some of older date also, one و is omitted in writing; and in conversation the sound of the second letter is scarcely perceptible. From this a difficulty arises, if the past tense be written or spoken without the second و; for then there is no difference between the past and the imperfect, and consequently there would be, in some instances, a doubt regarding the meaning. Mīrzā Khān, Anṣārī, who is one of the oldest Pushto authors we know of, always makes the difference between the past and the imperfect form, in which I have followed him; thus:—

په اختیار دَ محبت پر لنبه پریووت   دا نیم کړي ځان ور وُړ و تمام ته

'Of its own free will IT FELL into the flame of love—
This crude and imperfect one transported its soul to perfection."—*Mīrzā Khān, Anṣārī.*

* This is another example of the masculine plural described at page 84.

† In this case the final letter is no longer quiescent, but takes ه or (ـَـ) as in the example referred to.

‡ These verbs show in what manner some of the compound words in Pushto are formed. وتل means 'to go out,' and with پرې 'on' *or* 'from him,' etc., becomes پریوتل 'to fall.' Again, the same infinitive with the post-position کښې 'in,' 'inside,' etc., produces کښیوتل 'to become entangled,' 'to fall into,' etc.

Some of the best prose authors also make use of the second و to distinguish the past, as in this example:

چه خبر پرنجاشي شه له تخت َ ؤ لويدَ واشي شه ابرهه له آسَ پريووت دَ مرغونو په خُله کيووت

"When this news reached Najāshī, HE FELL from his throne; and Abrahah FELL DOWN from his horse into the birds' mouths."—*Babā Jān.**

Khūshḥāl, Ḥamīd, Raḥmān, Shaidā, Ḳāsim Æalī, and others, write the past tense of this class of verbs with one و, but with (ــٰ) over it; their meanings are, however, not to be mistaken. The following are examples:

محبت نه وُه يو تندر آسماني وُه چه ناګاه خما په سر او په مال پريوُت

"It was not love, it was a thunderbolt from the heavens,
That suddenly FELL on my head and my possessions."—*Æabd-ul-Ḥamīd.*

کښيوُتم دَ عشق په آدم خورو ګردابونو نه په وړاندي تلي شم نه په بيارته ګريزان

"I FELL right into the man-devouring whirlpools of love:
Neither can I advance, nor am I able to run back."—*Æabd-ur-Raḥmān.*

221. Another form of the past tense of intransitive verbs remains to be noticed. Infinitives, formed chiefly from adjectives, such as ماتيدل 'to break,' پټيدل 'to conceal,' تيريدل 'to pass,' etc., require the past tense of the auxiliary شول 'to become,' to be added after dropping the يدل of the infinitive. Thus مات شه 'broken,' پټ شه 'concealed,' تير شه 'passed.' The auxiliary, as well as the adjective, is subject to change in termination for gender and number. Examples:

نه ئي په آواز دَ جدائي لاړم بي هوښَ نه په غوږو کونړ شوم لکه وُم هسي لا بيا يم

"Neither did I go distracted at the rumour of being separated from her,
Nor did I BECOME DEAF: as I was, so indeed I now am."—*Æabd-ul-Ḥamīd.*

څو کالونَ په ما تير شوٓ چه بندي وُم تا خبر خما وا نخِست په هيڅ شان

"From the time I became a captive many years PASSED over me,
And thou didst not seek for any information regarding me."—*Saif-ul-Mulūk.*

222. In all the inflexions of intransitive verbs, the regular personal pronouns, 'I,' 'thou,' etc., may also be prefixed as in Persian. It is equally as correct to say زه راغلم as راغلم, or ته ؤ لويدي as ؤ لويدي; but the affixed pronouns are indis-

* This writer is said to have been a Sī'ah Posh Kāfir, who, after having been converted to Islāmism, again relapsed. For specimen of his writings, see 'Text Book.'

pensable, as in the language just referred to, as well as in Arabic and Hebrew, to which, in this particular, Pus̱hto bears a remarkable similarity.*

ماضي استمرار Imperfect Tense.

223. This tense denotes some incomplete past action, either near or remote; and is obtained by dropping the prefixed ۈ of the past; as,—

ده سرو دم هسي په ميرو شرونو ښتيدم   چه بي له خداي په بل څه مي نه وي مشغوليدل
قياس ۈ کړه څه حال مي به وي په دِ ساعت   چه دَ نا مردانو په طويلي کښي را بويه زغمل

"I USED TO FLY to deserts and mountains from the society of men, that I might not be occupied save in the worship of God.
Only imagine then what my state must be at this hour, that, in a tether with brutes, I must endure their society."—*Gulistān.*

224. The plural is formed, as in the past tense, by changing the different affixed personal pronouns to the plural form; and the third person masculine plural is the same as the simple infinitive. The following are examples:

پهلوان ځغو کاروانيان ۈ ليدل چه همه واړه سره په خان لرزيدل او زړونه په هلاکت ئي ايښي وۈ

"The wrestler saw that the whole of the caravan WERE TREMBLING for their lives, and had resigned their hearts to destruction."—*Gulistān.*

225. The same observation regarding the personal pronouns being sometimes affixed to the infinitive without dropping the ل, as in the past tense, described at paragraph 212, is equally applicable to the imperfect, except for the third person masculine plural, which, as mentioned in the preceding paragraph, remains unchanged. For the feminine plural, the ه or (ـَـ) of the singular is changed to ې or (ـےـ), and affixed to the simple infinitive. Examples:

شاد صفوان په نا اميدي شه   درد غمونَ پرِ دو بارد راغله چندان
بيا ئي وُ ډ وِ له اوّله نه پوهيدلم   چه به شي دا اور ښما په کور روښان

"Through excess of sorrow King Ṣaf'wān fell into despair,
And grief and affliction returned to him with increased force.
Again he said, 'In the first place I WAS NOT CONCEIVING for a moment,
That this fire would blaze up in my dwelling.'"—*Saif-ul-Mulūk.*

* The custom of affixing this class of pronouns probably sprung from the Semitic languages. In Sindhī they are also much used; for a Sindhian can scarcely utter a sentence without prefixing them to nouns as well as verbs. They are also used in Pehlavī, the mother of modern Persian.

څکه شوه تر زنګانه په وینو غرق چه يې زرکه سمیدله په یانَ

"The Chikor* for this reason is sunk up to the knee in blood,
That SHE WAS WONT TO VIE with her in walking."—*Æabd-ul-Ḥamīd.*

226. As I have already remarked at paragraph 220, the imperfect tenses of those verbs which do not take the prefixed و in the past, or drop it at times as redundant, are, in nine cases out of ten, written precisely the same as the past; and the signification in many instances is only to be discovered from the context. In conversation, too, the difference is scarcely perceptible; and it is only by practice in the language that the difficulty is to be overcome. Examples:

قول چه دِ له ما سره کړيَ ؤه اوس دِ رضا دَه چه مات يې کړِ زه پوهیدم چه په نن زمانه وفا څغه دارو دَه چه په دوکان کښِ دَ عطارِ روزګار موندہ نشي

"The agreement that thou hadst made with me, thou now desirest to break. I WAS THINKING, that in the present day, fidelity is a medicine which is not to be found in the shop of the druggist of the world."—*Kalīlah wo Damnah.*

څه صورت چه په نظر کښِ دَ چا کښیوت† په کاته به يې مبتلا شوه مجذوبان

"When this picture USED TO FALL under people's observation,
They were wont to be drawn towards it, on viewing it, as if fascinated."
—*Saif-ul-Mulūk.*

227. The third person singular and plural of this, as well as of the other past tenses, is alone subject to change in termination to agree with a feminine governing noun, whatever be the class of verb, regular, irregular, or defective, and will not require a separate explanation, as it has already been referred to at paragraph 210. I shall, however, give a few extracts as examples.

په ژړا راغله تر کوره پسي ؤه وته سر توره سرګردانه ګرزیدله له فراقَ زنګیدله

"In tears she came to the house, and went out after him with her head bare. SHE WAS WONT TO WANDER about in great distress; and, on account of separation, USED TO REEL and STAGGER."—*Tawallud Nāma'h.*

وزیر ؤه وِ دوي کوتري په یوه جاله کښي آستیدلي دَ یوِ نوم بازنده ؤه دَ بلي نوازنده

"The Wuzīr said, 'Two pigeons WERE DWELLING in the same nest. The name of one was Bāzindah,‡ the other Nawāzindah.'"§—*Kalīlah wo Damnah.*

* The Bartavelle or Greek partridge (Perdix chukar). It is found in great numbers in the hills north of Peshāwer. It has red legs, and is much larger than the common bird.

† See کښیوتم in the couplet at paragraph 220, which is written in the same manner as the above word, although the first person singular of the past tense of the same verb.

‡ Player. § Flatterer.

چه ئي سترګي دَ دنيا په خزانو نه مړيدلِ اوس په سترګو كښي سرِ ويني روانِ لكه بارانِ شوِ

"From the eyes of those which USED not TO BECOME SATIATED with the treasuries of the world, the red tears of blood have now flowed like rain."—*Babū Jān.*

228. The following extract contains an example of the masculine plural of the imperfect tense, formed according to the rules I have already explained for the past at paragraph 214, as being similar in mode of writing to the third person feminine singular, without the vowel points.

په بري دَ يزيدانو خداي راضي شه دَ فلك دورونَ كږ ؤ تاويده خيلخانه ئي په ژړا شوله رنځوره له
چشمانو ئي رودونَ بهيدهٌ

"God became pleased at the victory of the Yezīdis, and distorted the revolutions of destiny. His (Ḥusain's) family were becoming sadly afflicted through anguish, and rivers of tears WERE FLOWING from their eyes."—*History of Ḥasan and Ḥusain.*

229. Although the class of imperfect verbs, such as تيريدل, ماتيدل, دكيدل, پاتكيدل, etc., have no regular past tense, and require the past of شول 'to become,' to form it; yet they have a regular imperfect, as other verbs. Examples:

شهزاده كه ډال ترسر لاندِ نور ځملاست   نور په زړه ئي دا خطره تيريدله

"The prince placed his shield under his head and then stretched himself on the ground;
After which, the thought of this danger WAS PASSING in his mind."—*Bahrām Gūr.*

پهم و هوښياري زيات له حدَ كَغه لړل هم دا شان دَ هلكَ والي په وقت نښاني دَ لويئ دَ كَغه په
وچولي ځرګنديدي

"Understanding and intelligence he possessed beyond bounds. In the same manner in his childhood, the signs of his future greatness, USED TO BE APPARENT on his forehead."—*Gulistān.*

230. Another form of this tense is obtained by prefixing the particle به to the past. It implies continuity and habitude, as will be seen from the examples:

كَغه غم چه مي دَ يار وړه   كه هر څو را باندِ بار وړه
ايوني كه چا بللم   زه به خوښه ګرزيدلم

"That grief which I bore on account of my beloved, although it was a load upon me;
And, notwithstanding, some used to call me mad, yet I WAS WONT TO ROAM in happiness."
—*Yūsuf and Zulīkhā.*

دوي به وائي عملونَ څموږ دا وؤ چه آذان مؤ به ترغوږ شه نور به پاڅيدؤ و اودس ته په نور څه به
مشغول نه وؤ

"They will say, 'These were our practices, that when the summons to prayer reached our ears, we USED TO ARISE to perform our ablutions, and USED not TO BE occupied in any other matters.'"—*Fawā'īd-ush-Sharī'ea'h.*

دَ مجنون په خير وحشي به گرزيدلي   دَ ليلي طلب مدام په بيابان كري

" Like unto Majnūn THOU WERT USED TO WANDER about wildly,
Ever making inquiries after Laylā, both in deserts and in wilds."—*Kāsim Æalī, Afrīdī.*

231. It will be necessary here to notice the great imperfection and irregularity of some Pushto verbs, of which راغلل is a specimen. The real infinitive appears to be غلل, to which the class of pronouns described at paragraphs 132—134 are prefixed. Thus راغلل literally means 'to come to me *or* us;' درغلل 'to come to thee *or* you;' and ورغلل 'to come to him, her, it, *or* them. راغلل, however, appears to be the common form of the verb 'to come;' for در and ور are also used with it; as, در ته راغلم 'I came to thee *or* you;' ور ته راغلو 'we came to him *or* them;' but را cannot be used with درغلل or ورغلل

232. راتلل 'to come,' is another infinitive similar to the preceding, but its principal use is to form the actor, imperfect, and conditional tenses of راغلل, in which the latter is deficient. What is most surprising, and I imagine not to be found in the grammatical structure of any other language, is, that the proper past tense of راتلل conveys no preterite signification, and is only used as the imperfect of راغلل ; درتلل of درغلل ; and ورتلل of ورغلل. Several tenses in which both infinitives are defective, are obtained by prefixing را, در, and ور, to some of the inflections of the auxiliary شول 'to become,' and will be found in the conjugations. An example is contained in the following:

جبرائيل وِ يا رسول الله څما دَ زمكي دا وروستي ديدن شه چه څما مقصود خو ته وي چه راتلم
اوس چه ته له دنيا درومي نور مي نيست دَ راتلو نه دي

" Jabrā'īl said, 'O prophet of God! my last sight of the earth is taken, because thou wert the object of my desire when I USED TO COME. Now that thou departest from this world, I have no intention of coming again.'"—*Fawā'īd-ush-Sharī'ea'h.*

233. تلل, when used without the pronominal affixes, signifies 'to go;' but it is also imperfect, and has merely a past participle, agent, and imperfect tense. Examples of the masculine and feminine form of the imperfect tense of this verb are contained in the following extracts:

يك تنها په لارِ تهٔ څوك ئي مل نه ؤد   صد رحمت شه په دا شان څوان سنكين

" All alone he WAS GOING along the road—no one was with him:
A hundred praises on such a brave and bold-hearted youth."—*Bahrām Gūr.*

اما شرم ئي مانع شه   په تش آه ئي نور قانع شوه
راز ئي پټ ساته دَ ميني   كه ئي تلي له سترگوويني

"Nevertheless modesty became an obstacle, and with empty sighs she contented herself.
The secret of love she was wont to keep concealed, although from her eyes bloody tears USED TO FLOW."—*Yūsuf and Zulikhā.*

COMPOUND PAST TENSES.

234. The principal use of the past or perfect participle is in the formation of the compound tenses; and, as I have already given such a lengthened explanation of the former, little remains to be noticed regarding the latter, which are obtained from them by the addition of the auxiliary verbs, or روابط الزماني *rawābiṭ-uz-zamānī*, as they are termed by the Arabian grammarians. It will be necessary, however, to treat of them separately.

ماضي قريب. PERFECT TENSE.

235. The perfect tenses are formed by the addition of the present tense of the auxiliary 'to be,' to the past or perfect participles, described at page 75; and, like the latter, are of three different classes.

236. There is such a slight difference between the two first classes—the retention or rejection of the ل of the infinitive—that I shall give examples of them indiscriminately, as both end in ي, and the terminating letter is alone subject to change for gender and number. Examples of the masculine singular and plural will be found in the following extracts:

څو دَ مرگ په تمانچه آوښتي نه دي   آوښتوني له تا مه كړه خما مخ

"Until by the stroke of death it IS not TURNED ASIDE,
Make not my countenance a turner away from thee."—*Æabd-ur-Raḥmān.*

چه وقت دَ صبحدم شه په پرواز راغي متردد په مصلحت كښې چه څه كړم بيارته څم كه په عزم جزم چه وتلي يم طريق دَ سيل دَ تماشا واخلم

"When the morning dawned, and it was time to take wing, perplexed and irresolute in counsel, he began saying, 'What shall I do? shall I return, or with the purposed intention for which I HAVE COME OUT, should I take the road of amusement and recreation?"—*Kalīlah wo Damnah.*

237. The participle must agree with the auxiliary in gender in the formation of the feminine form of this tense. Example:

هره چار چه تر وقتَ تيره شي عنقا شي　　عنقا نه دهٔ په دام نښتي دَ هيچا

"That thing, the time for acquiring which may have passed away, becometh the Phœnix of one's desires;
But the immortal bird, as yet, HATH not BEEN CAUGHT in any one's net."—*Æabd-ur-Raḥmān.*

دَ ده دَ ښو خبرو آوازه په ملكونو تلِ دهٔ او دَ ده دَ اِنشا رقعه لكَ دَ قبالي يا دَ تمسك په دود هر څوك سره ئي عزيز گڼري

"The sound of his charming words HATH GONE OUT into every land; and a piece of his composition is held as precious as a bond; as valuable as a note of hand."—*Preface to the Gulistān.*

238. The plural form of the past participle being the same for both genders, the only difference in the masculine and feminine form of the tense is in the auxiliaries; thus:

تاسو لره ننوات راغلي يو يو سبب ساز كړئ چه درخانئ مخ را ته څرگند كړي

"WE HAVE COME to you for assistance, therefore, make some such excuse, that Durkhāna'ī may show her face to us."—*Adam Khān and Durkhāna'ī.*

ستا په سترگو دي پردي دَ غفلت پريوتي　　كنه يار په مخ نيولي پلو نه دي

"The CURTAINS of carelessness and inadvertency must HAVE FALLEN on thy eyes:
If not so, the beloved has not drawn the veil over her face."—*Æabd-ul-Ḥamīd.*

239. Properly speaking the auxiliary should immediately follow the participle, but it often precedes it, or follows after several intervening words, as in the following examples:

چه دَ ده دَ عدل نمر دي پريوتلي　　توره شپه دَ ظلم وُ خته ملك تور شه

"Since the bright luminary of his equity and justice HATH SET,
The black night of oppression has set in, and filled the land with darkness."
—*Æabd-ul-Ḥamīd.*

دَ دي مستِ ښها زلفِ تار پتار دي　　غوړيدلي لكَ سيوري پر رخسار دي

"The curls of this wanton sweetheart are hanging all dishevelled;
Like a shadow they have OVERSPREAD her lovely cheek."—*Mīrzā Khān, Anṣārī.*

240. Like their Persian neighbours, some of the best Afghān authors are fond of using the past participle for the perfect and pluperfect tenses, the auxiliary being understood, to connect the members of the sentence, and suspend the sense, both in prose as well as in poetry. Example:—

چه ستما بندگانُ ته وُ گوري له هوا دي گرد وهلي پريشان حال په خواريُ ستما كور لره راغلي طلبدار م دَ رضا دي اميدوارِ م دَ رحمت دي خاصه ما لره راغلي

"Shouldst thou look towards my servants, THEY (have) COME to my house in a state of affliction and distress, covered with dust from the blowing of the winds; searchers after my will; seekers of my mercy: THEY (have) COME solely on my account."—*Fawā'id-ush Sharī'æa'h.*

241. The following are examples, both masculine and feminine, of the perfect tense obtained from the third class of the past participles of verbs, which are either imperfect, irregular, or have a preposition or postposition prefixed. Examples:

که دِ مخ په زلفو پټ دي باك ئي نشته   دَ حيات اوبه هم پټ په تور تم دي

"If thy face IS CONCEALED with curls, there is no cause of apprehension;
For the waters of immortality, too, ARE CONCEALED in total darkness."
—*Æabd-ur-Rahmān.*

چا به وي چه دا پيريان دي   ناست دَ دي په ښکلي ځان دي
چه پيري په هر چا کښيني   نور له خلقه تنها کښيني

"Some were saying, 'This is caused by demons who HAVE SEATED themselves on this fair one's spirit:
When a fiend takes possession of any one, he then sits alone, and apart from others.'"
—*Yūsuf and Zulīkhā.*

دوبه زه په انديښنه يم   چه يم ويښه که اوده يم
دا په خوب کښي وصال وينم   دَ يار کښلي جمال وينم

"I AM SUNK into doubt and perplexity as to whether I AM AWAKE or whether I AM ASLEEP.
Do I see the fulfilment of my desires, and the exceeding beauty of my beloved, merely in a dream?"—*Yūsuf and Zulīkhā.*

ماضي بعيد PLUPERFECT TENSE.

242. The pluperfect tense is formed in the same manner as the perfect, from the three classes of the past participles, to which is affixed the past tense of the auxiliary 'to be.' It is subject to the same changes in termination for gender and number as the preceding tense.

243. Examples of the singular masculine and feminine:

يحيي خان له کشرانو ورونو سره چه هيڅ يو لا بلاغت ته رسيدلي نه وه په قصاص ئي د پلار ملا وتړله په مدد د ألس ئي رڼا ورځ په دښمنانو تورد شپه کړه انتقام ئي د پلار واخست دښمنان ئي نيست نابود کړه

"Yaḥyā Khān, together with his younger brothers, not one of whom HAD, as yet, REACHED man's estate, girded up their loins to avenge their father. With the assistance of the clan, they changed the bright day of the enemy into darksome night, and wreaked vengeance for his death upon the foe, whom they ruined and annihilated."—*Afẓal Khān: Tārīkh-i-Murassaæ.*

حليمه وَه چرته تلِ په دوست نه وَه پوهيدلِ چا خبره کړه له حضرتَ په نارو شوه له هيبتَ

" Halīma'h* HAD GONE OUT somewhere, and had not been apprised concerning the Prophet. Some one gave her information concerning him; and, through dread on his account, she uttered loud cries."—*Tawallud Nāma'h.*

يوه ورځ په تخت دَ پاسَ   خوشحال ناست وُم بي وسواسَ
تبي لاندِ کړم تب جن شوم   سُست اندام کاهل تن شوم

" One day I HAD SAT down on the throne quite happy, and without the least apprehension:
The heat wholly overpowered me, and I became feverish, my body weak and languid."
—*Story of King Jumjumah.*

زه تنها په تخت پرته وُم   دَ فراغت په خوب اوده وُم
چه ناگاه دي غلام   نا سپاس نمک حرام
کيښو لاس ځما په ځان   لب ځما په زنخدان
بيا ئي وُروي ځما په بند   گتي کيښوي نا پسند

" Alone I HAD LAIN DOWN on the couch; I HAD FALLEN ASLEEP in tranquillity and repose;
When suddenly this vile slave—the faithless, treacherous ingrate—
Laid his hand upon my person; and put his lips unto my chin:
Then on the fastening of my dress he placed his odious fingers."—*Yūsuf and Zulīkhā.*

244. Examples of the plural:

لس ايلچيان دَ هر ديار وُو   چه راغلي وار په وار وُو
پلار ئي واړه سرفراز کړه   ميلمانه ئي په آعزاز کړه

" There were ten envoys from each country, who HAD ARRIVED from time to time.
Her father treated them with distinction; he feasted them with magnificence."
—*Yūsuf and Zulīkhā.*

هَغه چه په مينز کښي ځاي نيولَي وُه پښي دَ ګَبو په شهتُ کښي نښتي وِ او چه ئي وُ غوښت چه والوزي وزرونَ ئي په شهتُ کښي ککړ شوُ په دام دَ مرګ کښي پريوتل

" The feet of those who had taken up a place in the midst, HAD STUCK FAST in the honey; and when they wanted to fly away, their wings also became smeared with it, and they fell into the net of destruction and perdition."—*Kalīlah wo Damnah.*

دَغه سراي په ديوالونُ ريښمين پري   باندِ پرتي ښي جورِ وِ شان در شان

" Around the walls of the palace there were silken lines fastened;
And splendid dresses of all sorts and kinds HAD DROPPED on them."—*Saif-ul-Mulūk.*

* The name of Muḥammad's nurse.

245. As I have already remarked respecting the use of the past participle for the perfect tense by some writers, they are in the same manner partial to the use of the participle for the pluperfect, the auxiliary being understood. Example:

ن نور دَ محمد دي ځليدلئ   پر کلي جهان دي غوړيدلئ
دَ عدم يوه توره شپه وَه   دي لکه نمر پرِ را ختلئ

" N. is the splendour of Muḥammad, which has shone and which has been diffused on the whole world.
It was the dark night of chaos and inexistence when he like a sun HAD ARISEN in it."
—*Aḥmad Shāh, Abdālī.*

ماضي تشکيک DOUBTFUL PAST TENSE

246. This tense is also formed from the different past participles by the addition of the aorist tense of the auxiliary 'to be,' which may precede or follow the participle, and is not subject to change in termination for gender and number, the participle being alone affected.

چه له غرونو پريوتلئ وي   بيا پاڅي   پاڅيدي نه شي له زړونو پريوتلئ

" He who MAY HAVE FALLEN from mountains again ariseth;
But he cannot arise again who may have dropped from hearts."—*Æabd-ur-Raḥmān.*

اتم دا سړي چه مرتبه ئي دښمن لټولِ او په دد باندِ وړاندِ شَوي ځغه مرتبي ته رسيدئ وي او بادشاد هم ور سره جوړ شَوي خبره ئي آوري

"The eighth is that man whose rank and employment an enemy may have sought; and having outstripped him, MAY HAVE ATTAINED that office, and gained the confidence of the sovereign who giveth ear to his tales."—*Kalīlah wo Damnah.*

په مردد چه لا ومړئي شپه تيره نه وي دا سنت دي چه خيرات دِ پسي وُ کا

" Before the first night as yet MAY HAVE PASSED over a dead person, it is a regulated institution that alms should be given on his account."—*Fawā'id-ush-Sharī'æa'h.*

247. Examples of the plural:

دغه چار پاي چه اکثر کال په خپل کور کښي وي ساتلي او په صحرا څريدلي نه وي په دغه کښي زکوة نشته

"The cattle which for the most part of the year may have been kept in thine own house, and MAY not HAVE GRAZED in the wilds, there is no portion of alms to be given on their account."—*Fawā'id-ush-Sharī'æa'h.*

دَ ځغو په لوري سترګي وي ختلئ   چه په لاس ئي سر سايه وي يا زکوة

" Their eyes WILL HAVE BECOME RAISED towards the road of those
Who may have in their hands charitable gifts and alms."—*Æabd-ur-Raḥmān.*

248. There is another form of this tense obtained by adding the 2nd future tense of the auxiliary 'to be,' to the different past participles. The following are examples:

په قېقه به خنديدلې وي که نه وي ‌‌ دَ زړه غم به ئې غليدلې وي که نه وي
فراغت به پسندلې وي که نه وي ‌‌ چا به حال تر پښتيدلې وي که نه وي

"He MAY HAVE LAUGHED heartily, or MAY not.
His heart's grief MAY HAVE BECOME BEGUILED, or MAY not.
He MAY HAVE CHOSEN tranquillity and ease, or MAY not.
Some one MAY HAVE INQUIRED about the matter, or MAY not."—*Æabd-ul-Ḥamīd.*

ګوره ناست به وي خپه په ښينو خرو کښي ‌‌ که به پروت وي لکَ لعل په ايرو کښي

"See! he MAY HAVE BECOME SEATED, aggrieved, amongst some asses,
Or MAY HAVE FALLEN like a ruby amongst dust and ashes."—*Æabd-ul-Ḥamīd.*

خداي دِ ورک کړه دَ ناسوت مچَ ‌‌ خوله به پاتِ نه وي ستا له مچَ

"May God confound thee, thou fly of human nature;
For no mouth MAY HAVE BEEN LEFT free of thy kiss."—*Aḥmad Shāh, Abdālī.*

ماضي شرطيه PAST CONDITIONAL TENSE.

249. The past conditional or optative tense of the Puṡhto verbs is obtained by subjoining the imperfect or conditional tense of the auxiliary 'to be,' to the past participle, with which a conditional conjunction or adverb of wishing must either be expressed or understood in the same sentence.

250. The auxiliary remains unchanged in all three persons; and the past participle is alone subject to change in termination for gender and number, therefore, a few examples will suffice.

کشکي زه زوولِ نه واي ‌‌ په جهان راغلِ نه واي
چه مي نه ليدلي غمونه ‌‌ هنمبرد ظلم و ستمونَ

"Would that I had never been born! that I HAD NEVER COME into this world!
That I had never seen grief, nor experienced this amount of tyranny and oppression!"
—*Yūsuf and Zulīkhā.*

دي په ژړا شه هم له خلقُ ئې ګله کړد چه کَه زوي خما مړ وي نيم اهلِ بلخ به خما عذر خواهي کړد

"He burst into tears; and he also complained against the folks, saying, 'IF my son HAD DIED, half the people of Balkh would have condoled with me."—*Fawā'id-ush-Sharī'æa'h.*

251. With a conditional conjunction or adverb of wishing, either expressed or understood, the second person singular of the imperfect tense of verbs also

conveys a conditional or optative signification similar to the preceding, but it is alone used for all six inflexions. The following are examples:

نادان لره بيتر له خاموشي نشته كه په دِ مصلحت پوهيدلي نادان به نه وُه

"For a fool there is nothing better than silence: WERE HE AWARE of this counsel he would not be a fool."—*Gulistān.*

زه به نه وَم ڈنبره ډوب په غم كښي تللَي   كه مي لږ و ډير و زړه ته تللَي وعظ

"I HAD NOT SUNK to this degree in grief and affliction,
IF admonition HAD GONE more or less into my heart."—*Æabd-ul-Ḥamīd.*

كه ئي لاس دَ خداي په چارِ رسيدلَي   بي مقصودَ به په يوَ دم نه سهيدل څوك

"COULD the hand of any one ACCOMPLISH the works of the Almighty,
No one would suffer a moment to pass without obtaining his own desires."
—*Æabd-ur-Raḥmān.*

252. The second form of the imperfect tense, obtained from the simple past by prefixing the particle به, as already described at paragraph 230, is also much used in the construction of the past conditional tense, as will be seen from the following example:

په هر لوري چه تښتيدد كاڼري پرِ ووريده كه به وُ خاته پرغرونَ پرِ پسي به ووُ مرغونَ

"By whatever road they were fleeing, the stones were raining on them: if THEY ASCENDED the mountains, the dread birds followed them."—*Tawallud Nāma'h.*

253. Sometimes the condition is expressed by the simple imperfect, and the consequence by the second form of the imperfect above alluded to. Example:

دَ تن كورمي به لرِڅون وَه ميني سَوَي   كه مي نه راتلَي ژړا په حمايت

"Ere this, love WOULD HAVE BURNT down the house of my body,
If tears HAD not COME to my assistance."—*Æabd-ul-Ḥamīd.*

254. The simple past tense is also often used in a hypothetical sense, and the consequence by the second future tense; as,

كافران به دَ كټار مسلمانان شي   كه رقيب مى په ژړا وُ ترسيدَ

"The Kattār Kāfirs WILL BECOME converts to Islām,
IF the guardian (of the beloved) IS SOFTENED by my tears."—*Æabd-ul-Ḥamīd.*

دَ همت تورد به واخلم   كه امان راغي له پټَ

"I WILL SEIZE the sword of courage and resolution,
IF grace and mercy COME from that which is hidden."—*Aḥmad S̱hāh, Abdālī.*

255. Of the two forms of the conditional just explained, that obtained from the imperfect, which is formed from the past tense of the auxiliary 'to be,' with the particle به prefixed, is alone subject to change in termination for gender and number.

صيغه حال PRESENT TENSE.

256. There being thirteen classes of intransitive verbs, including perfect and imperfect, the present tense of each is formed in a different manner, by altering, rejecting, or adding other letters after dropping the ل of the infinitive, and affixing the necessary pronouns.

257. The present tense of verbs of Class I. is formed by rejecting the ل of the infinitive, and changing the last radical letter for another; as رغيدل 'to recover' (health), رغيږي 'he recovers;' آلوتل 'to fly,' آلوزي 'he flies;' نښتل 'to become ensnared,' نښلي 'he becomes ensnared;' پوهيدل 'to know,' etc., پوهيږي 'he knows.'

نه سري ورځيني مري نه ترِ رغيږي　　　خداي دِ څوک دَ عشق په رنځ مبتلا نه که

"Man neither dies on account of it, nor RECOVERS from it:
Let not the Almighty afflict any one with the pain of love!"
—*Æabd-ul-Ḥamīd.*

بلبل نه دي دا چه آلوزي په ګلو　　　ستا په لور دي آلوتلې ځما رُوح

"This is not the nightingale which FLIETH around the roses:
It is my soul which hath flown towards thee."—*Æabd-ur-Raḥmān.*

څوک پيران څوک مريدان شوُ ولِ خُلق ئې کړ لومه خَلق ئې کړ ګمراد عامي خَلق لکه مرغي په کښي نښلي

"Some became prophets, and some became disciples; but they made a gentle disposition and good qualities a net; they led particular persons astray; and the public BECOME entangled in the net like birds."—*Makhzan Afghānī.*

په بندګي په دريا خولي بهيږي　　　تر غرمې نه ستړيږم په قلبه

"In the worship of God, the sweat FLOWS like a river;
But I TIRE not at mid-day from ploughing the land."—*Ḳāsim Æalī, Afrīdī.*

سرور هسي را ته وُه وِ څه پوهيږئ چه دا ګنده بوي دَ څه دي اصحاب ور ته وُه وِ نه پوهيږوُ چه دا ګنده بوي دَ څه دي

"The Prophet said to us, 'Do YOU KNOW what this stinking smell is occasioned by?' The companions of the Prophet said unto him, 'WE do not KNOW what this impure smell is produced from.'"—*Fawā'id-ush-Sharī'æa'h.*

258. The present tense of the verbs of Class II. is formed by dropping the ل of the infinitive, and rejecting the two last radical letters; as in زغليدل 'to run,' and اوريدل or ووريدل 'to rain,' زانگيدل 'to hang.' Examples:

دَ معني قوّت مي دسي مدد بيا مُند په يوه نفس له قاف تر قافـ زغلم

"I obtained such assistance from the potentiality of the spirit,
That in one breath I RUN from Ḳāf to Ḳāf—from one end of the world to the other."
—*Mirzā Khān, Anṣārī.*

كه دمه عمر باران ور باندِ اوري خس به گل دَ پيغمبر نه شي هرگز

"Though rain FALLETH on it for an age,
The thistle will never a violet become."*—*Æabd-ur-Raḥmān.*

سره په وينو د سرو گلو په څير زانگي هزار زړونَ ستا دَ زلفو په هر خم کښي

"Red with blood like unto red roses SWING
A thousand hearts in every bend and twist of thy ringlets."—*Æabd-ur-Raḥmān.*

259. The ا of infinitives of some of the verbs of this class, similar to those of which this last example is a specimen, is rejected; but chiefly by the Western Afghāns; as, زنگيدل for زانگيدل

260. The verbs of Class III. reject the ل of the infinitive and the three last letters in forming the present tense; as كښيناستل 'to sit.'

باز وُد وِ چه يو آواز وُد كا په پرواز راشم په لاس ئي كښينم چرگ وُد وِ رښتيا وائي

"The hawk said, 'When he calls out to me, I return from my flight, and I SIT on his hand.' The cock answered, 'Thou speakest truly.'"—*Kalīlah wo Damnah.*

261. The verbs which constitute Class IV. are few in number. They reject the ل of the infinitive and the last radical letter, altogether, in forming the present tense; and the first vowel, which is long, is lost by elision; as in چاودل 'to crack or split.' Example:

دَ ښايست سخى ئي نشته ور ته چوي مَين زړونَ

"She has no equal in loveliness, On her account, loving hearts BREAK."
—*Aḥmad Shāh, Abdālī.*

262. Class V. drops the ل of the infinitive and the last radical letter for two others in forming the present; as ختل 'to ascend' in the following example:

له خامي جوش و خروش خيژي له ديگه لي دَ زرد په مرگ گواهي عياند ژبه

* The violet is known as the Gul-i-Paighambar, or the Prophet's flower.

"Through crudity and rawness, ebullition and agitation ARISETH from the pot:
Of the heart's death, the manifest tongue giveth evidence."—*Æabd-ul-Ḥamīd.*

263. The verbs of Class VI. merely reject the ل of the infinitive, without altering the other letters more than substituting ړ for ر; as مړل 'to die.'

دَ وصال په چشمه مړم وچي شونډِ دَ هجران دَ انديښنو له تابَ تبَ

"At the fountain of attainment of desire, I DIE with lips parched,
From the burning inflammation of the anxiety of separation."—*Æabd-ul-Ḥamīd.*

264. Class VII. adds another letter after dropping the ل of the infinitive, for the present tense, as in سوّل 'to burn.' Example:

چه ملوک دَ محبت په اور سوزي دو باره په ښه ثنا شه ور ته گويان

"On becoming aware that Mulūk BURNETH in the fire of love,
He again began to speak his thanks and congratulations to him."—*Saif-ul-Mulūk.*

265. The verbs of the remaining six classes are all imperfect, and only two—Classes VIII. and X.—have any present tense; the remainder take the present of other verbs to supply the deficiency.

266. The present tense of verbs of Class VIII. is formed in a similar manner to that of the verbs of Class I., by dropping the ل of the infinitive and substituting another letter for the last radical one; as in ماتيدل 'to break,' پاتيدل 'to remain,' تيريدل 'to pass away,' etc. Example:

شيرين عمر چه تيريږي دريغَ دريغَ لکه اوبه هسي بهيږي دريغَ دريغَ

"Alas for pleasant life that PASSETH thus away!
Like a stream it floweth swiftly past, alas! alas!"—*Aḥmad Shāh, Abdālī.*

زغاستل 'to run,' which is of Class IX., has no present tense, but uses the present of زغليدل, which bears the same signification, and has been already described under Class II., to which it belongs.

267. Verbs of Class X. form the present tense in a similar manner to those of Class VI., by the mere rejection of the ل of the infinitive, and adding the different affixed pronouns; as in درومل 'to go.' Example:

هيڅ په ځان نه پوهيدد چه چرته درومو نه يې زدد وو چه کوم ملک دي کوم مکان

"We used not to know, at all, ourselves, as to where WE GO;
Neither did we (then) understand what country it is or what place."—*Saif-ul-Mulūk.*

268. لاړل 'to go,' which comes under Class XI., has no present tense, and uses that of تلل 'to go *or* depart,' which belongs to the following class.

269. The infinitive تلل 'to go *or* depart,' which constitutes Class XII. is one of the most irregular verbs in the Pushto language, and uses ځه or ځ as the present tense, which belongs to some unknown root. Example:

شهزاده وِ آس نيزه را ته حاضر کړئ يارانو   چين ته ځم را ته ډير دي منزلونَ

"The Prince said, 'Make ready my horse and spear, oh friends!
For I go to China: I have very many stages before me.'"—*Bahrām Gūr.*

270. راتلل 'to come,' constitutes Class XIII. of the intransitive verbs, and is similar to the preceding. The prefixed را is changed, according to the person referred to, for در and ور, the significations of which have been given in Chapter V. It has no present tense of its own, and uses that of تلل, with the prefixed pronouns already referred to. The following is an example:

بيا آواز شه چه ابراهيم خليل راځينَ   دَ امام حسين په مرګ پزړه غمګينَ
هم بي بي سائره راځي آخته له ويره   د امام حسين په مرګ په زړه زهيره

"Again a sound came, that Ibrāhīm the friend of God COMETH,
Aggrieved in heart on account of Imām Ḥusain's death.
The lady Sā'ira'h, too, approacheth afflicted and sorrowful;
Disconsolate on account of Imām Ḥusain's death."—*Muḥammad Hānīfah.*

271. In works on divinity and other religious writings, نَ or نه is very generally affixed to the third person singular and plural, masculine and feminine, of the present tense, as in the first line of the example just given. It is also added to the aorist, future, imperative, and the past; and will be found explained under those heads.

مضارع. AORIST TENSE.

272. Properly speaking, the present tense is formed from the aorist by rejecting the prefixed وَ of the latter, which constitutes the only difference between them; therefore, it will not be necessary to give separate examples of each of the thirteen classes of the intransitive verbs, but merely to point out any peculiarities that may exist, and exceptions to general rules. Examples:

که وَ نښلي مرغي په سست دام دَ سلو لومو   هسي رنګ پريشان زلفو کيښتم په کشاله کښي

"Like as a fowl MAY BECOME ENTANGLED in a loose snare of a hundred nooses,
So (her) dishevelled locks entangled me in embarrassment and perplexity."
—*'Abd-ul-Ḥamīd.*

چه ور ته یادَ شوه چه قعده مي کړِ نه دَه که و ناستِ ته نږدي وي و بیارته ؤ جاروزي او قعده دِ
پرِ ځاي کا

"When it comes to his recollection that 'I have not made the first *ḳaæda'h*,'* and he be about to arise from his sitting posture, HE SHOULD RETURN to the same position and perform the *ḳaæda'h*."—*Fawā'īd-ush-Sharī'æa'h.*

که په ځاي ؤ درېږم کارګه مي آخلي څه کړي بویه ؤ ئي وِ چه اسباب دَ عقل د دي ورطي دپاره
پیدا دي

"If I SHOULD STAND here, the crow will seize me: what is it necessary to do? He said—'The appliances of genius and prudence are invented as a remedy for difficulty and perplexity.'"—*Kalīlah wo Damnah.*

چه څوک ؤ مړي او توبه ګار وي له غیبتَ تر همه خلقُ ورستي به په جنت کښي داخلیږي او که
ؤ مړي او له غیبتَ توبه ګار نه وي تر همه خلقُ ورنبي به په دوزخ کښي داخلیږي

"If a person SHOULD DIE, and may have repented of calumny, he will enter into Paradise before all the rest of the creation; but if HE SHOULD DIE, and may not have repented of slander and evil-speaking, he will enter Hell long before the rest of the world."—*Fawā'īd-ush-Sharī'æa'h.*

273. The prefixed ؤ of this tense, like the ب of the Persian, is often rejected as redundant, but the proper signification can seldom be mistaken. Examples:

څه عجب دي که هما ئي په دام نښلي   هر صیاد څخه چه دام دي دَ اِخلاص

"What cause for astonishment is it, though the Phœnix SHOULD BECOME ENTANGLED in the net,
(By means) of every bird-catcher who possesseth the net of sincerity and love."
—*Æabd-ul-Ḥamīd.*

خردمندي هم دا تقاضا کا چه ګرد دَ بیوفايي په لمن دَ احوال دَ هیچا کښیننيِ† چرګ ځواب ور کړ
چه له ما کومَ بیوفائي او کومَ بد عهدي شوي دَه

"Wisdom also maketh this demand, that the dust of unfaithfulness SHOULD NOT REST on the skirt of any one's circumstances or affairs. The cock answered him—'What ingratitude, or what bad faith has been found in me?'"—*Kalīlah wo Damnah.*

څموږ خداي و مؤمنانو توفیق ور کړي چه په لارِ دَ مصطفي ځي

"Our God hath bestowed grace on the Faithful, that THEY SHOULD WALK in the ways of Muḥammad, the Chosen One."—*Fawā'īd-ush-Sharī'æa'h.*

274. An example of the نَ or نه prefixed to the third persons of the aorist, as

* A form of sitting at prayer.   † This is an example of the particle of negation inserted. See paragraph 422.

well as other tenses in religious writings, for the sake of euphony, referred to at paragraph 215, is contained in the following extract:

که سړي په اوبو ډوب شي يا په اور کښي وُ سوځينه يا ليوګان ئي وُ خورينَ دَ دِ وارو سوال هم حق دي دي عالم قادر مطلق دي

"Whether a man may sink in the water and be drowned, or MAY BECOME CONSUMED in fire, or may be devoured by wolves; under all these circumstances the interrogation (at the last day) is certain and beyond a doubt; for He is Omniscient, and Omnipotent."—*Fawā'id-ush-Sharī'æa'h.*

امرِ حاضر 1st Future or Precative Tense.

275. The first future or precative tense is precisely the same as the aorist with the exception that it adds the particle دِ to the third person singular and plural, whether masculine or feminine, and by which it is always distinguishable.

276. As the aorist merely differs from the present by the prefixed وُ, and the 1st future from the aorist by prefixing the دِ to the third persons, consequently it will be unnecessary to give examples of each of the intransitives, which have already been given for the present, as by prefixing the particles referred to, these tenses can be formed. Examples:

دَ سر په برابر دَ روضي په لورِ مخ په قبله دِ وُ دريږي درِ ګز يا څلور ګزَ دِ بيارته وُ دريږي

"He should stand parallel to the head of the mausoleum, with his face towards Makka'h, and he should stand about three or four yards distant."—*Fawā'id-ush-Sharī'æa'h.*

که سړي په سهود سورت ترک کا په ورنبي دواړه رکعتَ په رکوع کښي ور ته ياد شه دي دِ وُ جارووزي په ځَغه ځاي دِ سورت لولي

"If a man by inadvertency should omit the appointed section of the Kur'ān (in prayer) in either of the first two inclinations of the body, and, at the time of making the inclination, it cometh to his recollection; he should return to the bending position, and on that very place repeat the section required."—*Fawā'id-ush-Sharī'æa'h.*

277. Like the preceding tense, the prefixed وُ of this also is often rejected altogether, and sometimes understood; as in the following extract:

آرويدونيَ دَ غيبت لَه ګناه هله به خلاص شي چه پرِ ژبه دِ انکار دَ ځَغه وُ کا او پرهيز شي يا خبره دِ ترميان کا چه غيبت څنِ وران کا يا دِ پاځي له ځَغه ځايه دَ غيبت له آرويدو دِ ځان خلاص کا

"A listener to slander will become liberated from that sin, when he shall deny it with his tongue, and shall refrain from it, or shall put in a word, so that the calumny be refuted; or he should rise up from the place and release himself from hearing backbiting."—*Fawā'id-ush-Sharī'æa'h.*

278. When a personal pronoun is used with the third person of this tense, the دِ precedes the prefixed وُ, but when the third personal pronoun is not used, the وُ precedes the دِ; as in the following example:

وُ دِ نه لګيږي اور دَ چا په خونه   که رڼا ئي وي دَ شمس يا دَ قمر

"LET not fire REACH the house of any one,
Though its brightness be the sun's or the moon's."—*Æabd-ur-Raḥmān.*

مستقبل 2ND FUTURE TENSE.

279. The second future tense is formed from the aorist by the addition of the particle بهٔ, and is subject to exactly the same rules and variations as that tense. Examples are contained in the following extracts:

تله حقَ دَد يارانو پهٔ صراط به وُ خوږيږئ په هيبت بهٔ نيک و بد ور ته حضريږي عملونَ به دواړ
جوکل شي هر بنده بهٔ په خپل حال بهه وُ پوهيږي

"Passing over the bridge of Ṣarāṭ is true my friends, and YOU WILL BE PERTURBED through awe. Both good and bad WILL ASSEMBLE on it; all actions will be weighed; and every one WILL KNOW the state of his case."—*Fawā'id-ush-Sharī'æa'h.*

که زړه سوي را باندِ نه کړِ زه به وُ مرم بهه به نه کړِ خون به وُ کړِ دَ خورځي خله کړِ خبرِ تګئِي

"If thou dost not take pity on me, I SHALL DIE. Thou wilt not act rightly: thou wilt murder thy sister! Why dost thou speak, oh deceiver!"—*Adam Khān and Durkhāna'ī.*

دَ دوږخ ښي لړم دي که غر په لاشه وُ وهي به وُ سوځي ايري شي

"There are some scorpions of Hell, that if they strike a mountain with their sting, IT WILL BURN, and become ashes."—*Bābā Jān.*

280. As in the two preceding tenses, the prefixed وُ of this tense also, is rejected as redundant; but invariably so for those verbs which do not take وُ in the past tense, previously explained.

آدم خان په زړه نتلئ په صورت کوتلي و ميرو بلو ته ئي وُ وي که دا کار مي له لاسَ وُ نه شي زد
به له دي ملکَ ورکيګم تاسي بهٔ را سره ځئ که بهٔ نهٔ ځئ

"Depressed in mind, and altered in countenance, Adam Khān said unto Mīro and Balo: 'If this affair is not completed by my hand, I will disappear from this country. WILL YOU GO with me, or WILL YOU not?'"—*Adam Khān and Durkhāna'ī.*

281. When a regular personal pronoun (ضمير منفصل), as well as the affixed personal pronoun (ضمير متصل), is used in this tense, the به precedes the particle وُ, but when no separate pronoun is used, the به follows the وُ. Examples:

دَ گلونو يم مشتاقَ　　　دل سوخته يم له فراقَ
اوکه ته وِ ترنماښامَ　　　زه به وُ سوزم تمامَ

"I am a longer after roses: I am burnt to the heart by separation.
Shouldst thou put off the time to evening even, I SHALL BECOME entirely CONSUMED."
—*Yūsuf and Zulīkhā.*

وُ به خيږي سحر دَ شپي دَ غم　　　وُ به رسي په آخرغم دَ بيلتون

"The morning of the dark night of sorrow WILL DAWN at last!"
The grief of separation WILL at length REACH ITS TERMINATION!"—*Yūsuf and Zulīkhā.*

282. In poetry some license is taken with respect to the به: it is often inserted between the syllables of a word, and also, in the case of a compound verb, formed by prefixing a preposition or postposition to a simple infinitive.

په دِ شک دَ قوم په لوري　　　په گوښه دَ سترگي گوري
که دوي کښيني کښي به نم　　　که دوي پاڅي پا به څم

"When in this doubt, he should look from the corner of his eye towards the congregation, and determine
That 'if they sit, I WILL ALSO SIT, and if they rise, I WILL also RISE.'"—*Rashīd-ul-By'ān.*

Several words may also intervene between the particle and the verb—one may be at the commencement, the other at the termination of the sentence; as in this extract:

اوس به کفر ته دَ تورو زلفو وُ وزم　　　کنږه مه کود دَ پند خبرِ نورِ

"Utter not any more words of counsel or admonition unto me,
Otherwise I WILL now GO OUT to the paganism of black curls."—*Æabd-ul-Hamīd.*

امر IMPERATIVE.

283. The imperative mood is always formed in a similar manner to the 1st future tense, with these exceptions, that it has no first person singular or plural, and that it drops the affixed personal pronoun for the second persons, and is not liable to change in termination for gender; but in other respects it is subject to the same rules and exceptions as the preceding tenses of the aorist and first future. The following are examples:

ته دَ شام په لوري مه څه اوس په برته وُ جاروزه اوس قرار پر ځاي کښينه که پر حب دَ حضرت ئينه

"Go not towards Syria! TURN BACK now! Remain stationary in some place, if thou hast any affection for the Prophet."—*Tawallud Nāma'h.*

دَ ريا په زُهد مه غليږه زاهدَ　　　په کار نه راځي دَ وينځي زوي لور

"BE not DECEIVED, oh hermit, with the asceticism of hypocrisy!
For the slave-girl's son and daughter will be held in no estimation."—*Æabd-ul-Hamīd.*

رايشه دلبرد چري په گور باندِ ښما   مه سيځه په هجر زړه په اور باندِ ښما

"COME sometimes to my tomb, oh my beloved one!
Burn not my heart (even there) with the fire of separation."—*Ḳāsim Æalī, Afrīdī.*

TRANSITIVE VERBS.

افعال متعدي *afaæāl-i-mutaæaddī.*

ماضي مطلق PAST TENSE.

284. Under this head are included primitive and causal verbs, which form their past tenses somewhat differently from intransitives, by rejecting the ل, the sign of the infinitive mood, and prefixing to this base or root the particle, the sign of the past, which is written وُ, وُډ, and occasionally وو; as ښندل 'to shake,' وُ ښانڈ or وُ ښانډه 'he shook'; آلوزول 'to cause to fly,' والوزاوو or والوزاوُه 'he caused to fly.' When the first letter of the infinitive is آ, the و of the past tense is used without the (ـُ), and thus becomes united to the آ.

285. Derivative verbs formed from adjectives by the addition of وَل reject this termination in forming the past tenses, thus returning to their primitive state, and the past tense of the verbs کړل or کول 'to do,' must be used in forming them; as تيټ 'bent,' تيټول 'to bend,' تيټ که or تيټ کړ 'he bent;' کلک 'hard,' کلکول 'to harden,' کلک کړ 'he hardened.'

286. A few verbs derived from nouns and pronouns by the addition of وَل are subject to the same rules; as جار 'a sacrifice,' جارول 'to sacrifice,' جار کړ 'he sacrificed;' خپل 'self,' خپلول 'to make one's own,' خپل کړ 'he gained over.' There is, however, an exception to this, as in all other rules, in ويرول 'to frighten,' from ويره 'fright,' which becomes وُ ويراوو or وُ ويراوُه 'he frightened,' thus lengthening the vowel preceding the final letter from (ـَ) to ا, which is also the rule with regard to most primitive infinitives terminating in ل.

287. Primitive intransitives are made transitive by changing the ل of the infinitive into وَل, as رژيدل 'to shed,' 'to scatter,' رژول 'to strew,' 'to dispel;' زنګيدل 'to swing,' زنګول 'to make to swing;' and derivative intransitives obtained from adjectives are made transitive by changing the يدل of the infinitive into ول; as بليدل 'to burn,' بلول 'to consume;' and which are subject to the rules laid down in paragraph 285.

288. Transitive verbs must agree with their objects in gender and number, in all the inflections of the past; and the object must be in the nominative, and sometimes in the dative, and the agent in the instrumental case.

بادشاه مور او پلار دَ هغه هلک را وُ بلل او په دير نعمت ئي رضا کړل

"The king CALLED the boy's MOTHER and FATHER, and DISMISSED THEM with many gifts."—*Gulistān.*

289. The affixed personal pronouns (ضماير متصله) are not used with transitive verbs in the past tense, and the regular prefixed personal pronouns in the instrumental case must be used instead.

The other form of personal pronoun used with verbs to denote the agent, described at paragraphs 129–131, is used with transitive verbs to denote the agent, and may precede or follow the ؤ the sign of the past.

When, as in the following example, an affixed personal pronoun may be used with a transitive verb, it points out the objective case; as—

دا درست أُلس مداد او مدد ته ټول شه چه تاسي موږ له علم غيبَ خبر کانږي چه دَ أُلس به څه حال شي او تاسو له دي واقعي چه تيرد شوه ولي موږ خبر نه کړوُ چه فکر او سرانجام مُه دَ خپل کار کړي وي چه موږ ته دا هونبره زيان پيښ مه وي

"The whole of this tribe assembled before Midād and Madad, saying, 'Give us information with regard to the future, as to what will be the condition of the tribe; and why did you not INFORM US respecting the events which have passed, that we might have taken counsel in the accomplishment of our affairs, so that we had not sustained such detriment and injury?'"—*Afẓal Khān.*

290. The twenty-four classes of transitives, perfect and imperfect, have ten methods of forming the past tense, which I shall divide into as many forms.

291. Form I. The verbs of Classes I., VI., VII., VIII., and XII. form their past tenses by rejecting the ل of the infinitive, and lengthening the first vowel from (ـَ) to ا in the singular; as in the following examples:

زد و شرم ننګ ته په کم ننګ شرم ګورم واچاوُه په ګل پسي غنچي دَ سر پروني

"With what modesty and diffidence shall I behold bashfulness and chasteness?
The bud HATH THROWN BACK the veil from its head for the sake of the rose."
—*Æabd-ul-Ḥamīd.*

ملا کرمالي ترخانَ په خوا واستاوو چه ور شه په درخانۍ خبر ؤُ کړه چه سر خوړلَي چيني لرد له خلقو سره راغي

"Mullā Karmālī SENT SOME ONE on before, saying, 'Go and give information to Durkhāna'ī, that The Unfortunate, with people along with him, hath come to the spring.'"—*Adam Khān and Durkhāna'ī.*

292. The long vowel ا is again rejected in the plural for (ـَ); as

زين زينه هَغه کړي پسي واستول سري مطلب ؤُ باله کور ته ميله دار ؤُه لکَ ورور ته

"That very hour Zen Zenah SENT MEN after Muttalib and called him; and he entertained him like a brother."—*Tawallud Nāma'h.*

دائِکانَ ور ته وُ ویل اي لورِ   حال دِ څه دي خپل احوال کړه را بیان

"The NURSES SAID to her, 'Oh daughter!
What is thy condition? relate thy affairs unto us.'"—*Saif-ul-Mulūk.*

293. The first and second persons plural are the same as the third person masculine singular, with the plural form of pronouns prefixed; but the third person masculine plural is formed by merely prefixing the وُ to the simple infinitive, as in the two examples just given.

294. Another form of the third person plural, applicable to all classes of verbs, is written with the same letters as the feminine singular, and is also the case with regard to intransitive verbs;* but the final letter is preceded by the vowel (ـَ), which conveys a shorter sound than that of the feminine ه, and is equivalent to the diphthong *a*. The following extract is an example:—

زر خپل نوري دَ شاه و دختر ور کړَه   دَ شاهِيِ نوري دِ واغوستهٔ په ځان

"Quickly she GAVE her own CLOTHES to the king's daughter,
And CLOTHED herself in the ROYAL ROBES.—*Saif-ul-Mulūk.*

295. The feminine form of the past tense of transitive verbs is obtained in the same manner as that of intransitives, by affixing ه (*hā-i-khafī*) to the infinitive itself, which is changed to ې or (ـِ) in the plural.

296. Some verbs also drop the ل of the infinitive in the feminine singular, and substitute ه (*hā-i-khafī*) for the ه (*hā-i-ẓā-hir*) of the masculine; but not the verbs of this form. Examples of the feminine:

دَ کوچ نقاره لاس دَ اجل را وُ وهله اي څما دوو سترګو وداع دَ سر را وُ کړئ

"The HAND of destiny and death STRUCK the drum of departure, therefore, oh my eyes, you should bid adieu to the head."—*Gulistān.*

دا خبره پر موسي وَه سخته ترد چه دا واچوله مار شُود دا په قبردَ قهار شُود

"This matter was exceedingly difficult for Moses; nevertheless when HE CAST IT (his staff) down, it became a serpent. This happened by the power of the All Powerful."—*Bābā Jān.*

حکیم حکم وُ کا چه مرئي سیند ته واچود څو غوټي چه وُ خوړي تر وینهتو ئي وُ نیود بیرئي ته ئي را
واچاوه په لاس ئي بیرئي کلکه وُ نیوه

"The sage directed them to throw the slave into the river. After he had sunk several times, they caught him by the hair and cast him back into the boat, which HE SEIZED firmly with his hand."—*Gulistān.*

* See paragraph 214 and note.

297. Example of the plural:

روز روشن نیمه ورځ وَه چه کوټ وته نیژدي شوۇ ځوانانو په کوټ منګلي وُ لګولي په سر سواري په

یوه پهر کښي فتح شه

"It was in the middle of the day that they arrived near the fort. The brave fellows LAID their hands on it by the way, and in the short space of three hours they gained the victory."—*Afzal Khān.*

298. Some infinitives have more than one method of forming the past tense, and applicable both to masculine and feminine; as in ویل 'to speak' or 'to say.' Examples:

دَه چه درخانۍ ور کوله هلته یو سړي دَ ګوجر خان خادم ولاړ وَه حال ئې ګوجر خان ته وُ وایه ګوجر

خان په میرمامي دَ غشي ګذار وُ کړ غوځ نه شه

"When he (Mīrmāmī) delivered up Durkhāna'ī to him, a man who was a servant of Gūjar Khān's was standing by, to whom HE RELATED the circumstance, on which Gūjar Khān discharged an arrow at Mīrmāmī, but it did not take effect.—*Adam Khān and Durkhāna'ī.*

ملیکي و خپلي مور و ته وُد وِ   په دا حال ئې بدري هم کړه خبرَ

"The Queen SPOKE to her mother clandestinely;
And with this circumstance, also, she acquainted Badrī.'—*Saif-ul-Mulūk.*

نوشادد وِ* اي دَ روي زمین بادشاهَ   له کتابَ را معلومیږي پدا شان

"Nohshādah SAID—'Oh, King of the Universe!
In this manner I discover from the books.'"—*Saif-ul-Mulūk.*

299. Form II. consists of the infinitives of Classes III., IV., and X., which form the past tense by merely rejecting the ل of the infinitive and prefixing the particle وُ, as exemplified by the following extracts:

په ژوندون دِ دسي وُ یستم له یادو   لکه هیر کا څوک دَ سلو کالو مړي

"In my life-time thou didst thus PUT ME OUT of thy remembrance,
Like as one forgetteth a deceased person of a hundred years."—*Æabd-ul-Hamīd.*

ابوبکر چه پند وُ وِ پند ئې واخِست همه واړه پرِ عمل کړَ مستقیم شوُ

"When Abū Bakr made an exhortation, they all TOOK his ADVICE, acted up to it, and became resolute in it."—*Fawā'id-ush-Sharī'æa'h.*

300. The plural of Form II. of the past is derived in the same manner as Form I. Examples:

پس ځلوینښت ورځې حاضر شوُل و بادشاد ته   عرض ئې وُ کړ په طریق دَ عرض ګویان

په کوښښ اود اقلیمَ وُ ښوښتل مُوږ   اوه پښتَ دَ هر چا شوُ ناظران

شي پیدا به دَ شبهال دَ شاد رخ لور   نوم ئې دي بدري جمال شاه پریان

* This latter form is more properly speaking the imperfect tense, but used for the past. See paragraph 323.

"After forty days they came into the presence of the King,
And made their statement to him in a humble manner—
'We have SEARCHED through SEVEN REGIONS with great care,
And seven generations of every person has been inspected.
There will be a daughter born to Shahbāl, son of Shāh Rukh:
Her name is Badrī Jamāl—the Sovereign of the Fair.'"—*Saif-ul-Mulūk.*

301. Some of the infinitives of Classes III. and X. ending in ت, which are contained in Form II. of the past tenses, insert a و before the final letter for the third person masculine singular, which is changed to ا for the plural, the ت then taking an affixed (ـَ) or ه; as کتل 'to behold,' وُ کوت 'he beheld,' وُ کاته 'they beheld.' Examples:

ساعد وُ کوت شاهزاده په تخت ناست نه وُه — په خاطر ئي وُ کړه دا دليل گذران

"Sāæid SAW that the prince was not seated on the throne;
And in his mind this matter he passed over."—*Saif-ul-Mulūk.*

زرگر وُ کاته چه يار خما را دروميي — استقبال ته ئي روان شه خوش شادان

"The Goldsmith SAW that his sweetheart cometh, and
He went out to receive her, delighted and overjoyed."—*Saif-ul-Mulūk.*

302. The infinitives which constitute Form II. of the past use ه for the feminine singular termination, affixed to the masculine or to the ل of the infinitive indiscriminately, which is changed to ي or (ـِ) in the plural.

په شتاب ئي دعا وُ لوَسته هله ته — دم ئي پوُ کړه په سپين مخ دَ محبوبان

"With all speed HE there REPEATED the INVOCATION,
And he breathed on the fair face of the beloved."—*Saif-ul-Mulūk.*

مور مي را ته وُ وِ ستا نيکه دَ صدقِ خرما ويشي هورِ ور شه، ځکه راغلم او خرما مي واخسته

"My mother said unto me—'Thy grandfather divides the propitiatory offering of dates; go there:' therefore I came and TOOK UP A DATE.—*Faœā'id-ush-Sharī'œa'h.*

لس لس زر ئي په هر سردار پسي کړه — بيا ئي وُ غوښتي کښتئي له ملاحان

"He placed ten thousand men under each commander,
And then he DEMANDED BOATS from the boatmen.—*Saif-ul-Mulūk.*

303. Form III. The infinitives of Classes XI. and XIV. form the past tense by rejecting the ل of the infinitive and prefixing the particle و as in the preceding Form, with the exception that the last letter of the root is accented or moveable in this, whilst it is quiescent in the former.

دا جواب چه درخو واوريدَ په غوږو بي طاقتَ آهومنه کور و کر شوه

"When Durkhāna'ī HEARD THIS REPLY with her ears, she became faint and powerless; she sighed, and became (as it were) blind and deaf.—*Adam Khān and Durkhāna'ī.*

وُ ئي ويل دَ بادشاهي دولت دَ سيوري لاندِ همه واړه راضي مي وُ ساتل مگر حاسد چه راضي نه شه

"He said—'beneath the shadow of the wealth of royalty I KEPT ALL but the envious, pleased and contented, but they did not become satisfied.'"—*Gulistān.*

304. The feminine terminations of the infinitives of this Form are ه or (ـَـ) for the singular, and ې or (ـٍـ) for the plural. Examples:

صباح دَ وخته چه دغه پلار وُ ليده   زوم ته وُ رغي خبره وُ پوښتيده

چه اي کمينه دا دِ څه تيره دندان دي   شوندي ئي څو کاږي دا نه انبان دي

"In the morning, when her father beheld her, he came to his son-in-law, and ASKED him about it, saying:

'Oh rascal! how sharp are those teeth of thine? To what extent wilt thou stretch her lips? they are not leather!'"—*Gulistān.*

چه دائي تِرِدا خبره واوريدله   عاقبت شوِ دوي وُ کور وته روان

"When the nurse HEARD THIS SPEECH from him,
They at length departed from their own house."—*Saif-ul-Mulūk.*

چه دائي له دي خبري   واوريدي هسي نادري

شود حيرانَ په دا کار کښي   دَ علاج په کار وُ بار کښي

"When the nurse HEARD from her such singular and uncommon WORDS,
She became amazed at the circumstance, and perplexed as to its remedy."—*Yūsuf and Zulīkhā.*

305. By far the greater number of infinitives in the language form their past tenses according to one of the three Forms already explained, for which reason I have given pretty numerous examples of them. The infinitives of the remaining Forms, being few in number comparatively, will not require so many examples to illustrate them.

306. Form IV. These obtain their past tenses in a similar manner to the verbs of Form II. by rejecting the ل of the infinitive, the last characteristic letter being immovable or quiescent, but with this difference, that they altogether reject the وُ of the past, by which there is no difference in the mode of writing between the past and the imperfect; thus پرانتل 'to unloose,' پرانست 'he unloosed;' بوتلل 'to take away,'* بوت 'he took away.'

لاس په نامه ورته ولاړ شه په ادب کښي   په ثنا ئي دَ بادشاه پرانست زبان

"With hands folded on navel he stood before him in a respectful manner,
And in commendation of the king his TONGUE he UNLOOSED.—*Saif-ul-Mulūk.*

سرداسيا دَ رونړو پرانته بندونَ   چه بيرام په ډېر حکمت تړلي وونَ

"Sardāsī'ā UNLOOSED her brother's bonds, which Bahrām with much skill had fastened."
—*Bahrām Gūr.*

* This infinitive is used for animate objects, and وړل for objects inanimate.

په خواري زاري بوتلوٌ تر زندانَ   نا کردي چاري کړي څموږ په ځان

"With much distress and suffering they TOOK US AWAY to the prison,
And treated us with much impropriety and disrespect."—*Saif-ul-Mulūk.*

307. The feminine is obtained in the same manner as that of the infinitives of the preceding Form.

308. Form V. drops the ل of the infinitive in forming the past, the final characteristic letter being movable, and merely differs from Form I. (which see), inasmuch as it altogether rejects the prefixed ۇ; as کښېنول 'to seat,' or 'make sit.'

هِغي جلِ شاهزاده ترلاسَ وُ نيوٌه   پاس په تخت ئي کښيناوٌه په عز و شان

"The young woman took the prince by the hand,
And with much pomp and grandeur SEATED HIM on the throne."—*Saif-ul-Mulūk.*

309. The simple infinitive of this as well as other classes of verbs is often used for the past tense, but, in such cases, an affixed personal pronoun in the objective case is used with it, as in the following:

په ټَغه مجلس ئي واړه وُ بلل دوي   په ډېره مهر ئي له ځانَ کښېنول دوي

"He called the whole of them into the assembly,
And with much kindness SEATED THEM near himself."—*Saif-ul-Mulāk.*

310. The feminine termination for this class of infinitives in the past is the same as for the preceding Forms. Example:

چه ناګاه ټَغه خوبَ دَ تمام عالم مرغوبَ   پلارئي حضور ته وُ بلله ترخپل څنګَ ئي کښېنوله

"When suddenly that BEAUTIFUL ONE, the beloved of the whole world,
Was summoned to her father's presence, and SEATED by him at his side."
—*Yūsuf and Zulīkhā.*

311. Form VI. consists of the infinitives which wholly reject the sign of the infinitive and last or final letter in the past, as سول 'to burn' or 'consume,' وُ سه 'he burnt.' Example:

نه پوهېږم چه سړي وٌه که يا نور څه   زه ئي درست دَ عشق په اور وُ سوم بريان

"I know not whether it was a man, or some other thing,
Which entirely CONSUMED ME in the fire of love."—*Saif-ul-Mulāk.*

312. Form VII. rejects the ل of the infinitive and prefixes a syllable to the root, the final letter of which is quiescent. These infinitives also reject the prefixed ۇ and are not common; as وړل 'to remove' or 'take away,' يوړ 'he removed.' Example:

عاقبت را څخه يوړ دَ ستا سترګو   که هرڅو مي زړه په صبر کښېني ساته

"At last thine eyes CARRIED AWAY my HEART from me,
Notwithstanding I guarded it with patience and endurance."—*Æabd-ul-Ḥamīd.*

313. Form VIII. The past is formed by rejecting the sign of the infinitive and the prefixed وُ, as بايلل 'to play away' or 'lose at play,' بايله 'he played' or 'lost.' Example:

هرچا چه په خوښي توب سره عمر بايله   هيڅ ئي را وُ نه پيرودل زرئي بايله

"He who hath LOST his LIFE in pleasure, hath not bought anything, but hath LOST his GOLD."—*Gulistān.*

314. The past tense of the causal infinitive بايلول is often used for the past tense of بايلل, as in the following*:

چه غليمي کاندِ دَ خداي له ښو دوستانو دينَ ئي بايلو حساب شوُ له کافرانُ

"They who show enmity to the good friends of the Almighty, have LOST their FAITH and RELIGION, and have become accounted infidels."—*Fawā'id-ush-Sharī'aa'h.*

315. Form IX. The verbs of this class are formed from adjectives generally, and obtain the past tense by rejecting the وَل used in their formation, as also the prefixed وُ of the past, and, to complete it, the past tense of کول or کړل 'to do,' is required; as خښول 'to inter,' خښ کړ 'he interred.' Example:

بيا نبي وِ جهنم را ته ښکاره کړ خما زړه دِ را ته ډک په ډير ارمان که

"Then the Prophet said, 'Show unto me hell, for thou hast FILLED my HEART with much desire.'"—*Majmuaāt-i-Kandahārī.*

316. The whole of the infinitives of this, as well as Forms VI., VII., and VIII., obtain the plural in the same manner as those before described, and take ه or (ـے) for the feminine in the singular, and (ـې) or ئي in the plural.

317. Form X. The infinitives of this class use the simple infinitive with the prefixed وُ for all three persons, both singular and plural; as خندل 'to laugh,' وُ خندل 'he laughed,' etc. Example:

پر سينه ئي لعنتي داغ ور ښکاره شه اِمام وُ خندل دَ داغ په ننداره شه شمرؤ وِدا خندا دِ اوس په څه دَه څه دانه دِ له ژوندونَ پاتِ نه دَه

"The accursed mark was visible on his breast, and on beholding it the IMĀM LAUGHED. On this, Shimr said—'What is thy laughter at present occasioned by, now that not one grain of thy existence remaineth?'"—*Ḥasan and Ḥusain.*

The above form of the past is also used for the feminine singular and plural.

318. Form XI. کول 'to do' or 'perform,' which is imperfect, and used as

* See page 67, Class V.

an auxiliary, rejects the ل of the infinitive and the last radical letter in the past, and takes the prefixed وُ; as وُ کا or وُ کړه 'he did.' The following is an example:

حضرت هسي ځواب وُ کا و بي بي ته دَ نکير منکر آواز به دَ مؤمن پر غوږ هسي ښه لګيږي لکه رانجه
دَ چا په سترګو پورِ کيږي

"The Prophet MADE this REPLY to the lady Æā'esha'h, 'The sound of Nakīr and Munkir will fall as pleasantly on the ear of the Faithful as the application of a collyrium to one's eyes.'" —*Farā'id-ush-Sharī'æa'h.*

319. The prefixed particle of the past is sometimes omitted, as in the following extract:

که ئي هرڅو دَ إمام په لاس زور کړه ازاربند ئي له إمام حسينَ خلاص نه کا

"Notwithstanding all the FORCE HE USED to remove the Imām's hand, yet he did not undo the fastening of Imām Ḥusain's drawers."—*Ḥasan and Ḥusain.*

This verb does not undergo change in termination for gender or number.

320. نَ or نه is often affixed to the third person singular and plural of the past tense of verbs, particularly in religious writings, or at the termination of a line in poetry, for the sake of euphony; thus—

دَغه پس عمر بن سعد پهلوان وُد په سپاهيانُ کښې شمارد دَ يزيدانُ وُد په غصه ئي په ګرز باند
وُ وادَنَ دغه ځوان سر ئي له تنَ جدا کَنَ

"After that Æumar bin Saæd, who was a champion, and computed amongst the army of the Yezīdīs, with great wrath STRUCK HIM with a mace, and SEPARATED the head of that youth from his body."—*Ḥasan and Ḥusain.*

ماضي استمرار IMPERFECT TENSE.

321. After having explained the past tense so fully, the imperfect is easily described.

The different methods of obtaining the imperfect may be divided into six classes.

322. I. Out of the twenty-four classes of transitive verbs, fifteen form the past by prefixing the وُ, and the imperfect tenses of the whole of these are obtained by merely rejecting that prefix; as تړل 'to bind,' وُ تاړه or وُ تاړَ 'he bound,' تاړه or تاړَ 'he was binding.' The following extracts are examples:

لور په لور ئي لټاوُد ترڅَغه پوري   څو ئي بيا موند شاهزاده بي خود له ځانَ

"He WAS SEARCHING about for him every here and there,
Until at last he found the prince quite beside himself."—*Saif-ul-Mulūk.*

يو له پخوانو بادشاهانو په کار دَ بادشاهي کښې ډيرد سستي کوله او لښکر ئي تل تش په سختي لاړَ

"One of the kings of old was extremely negligent in affairs of state, and USED TO KEEP his army in arrears."—*Gulistān.*

323. ويل 'to say,' which is of the above class, has a second form of the imperfect, which is also obtained by rejecting the prefix.

درچا دا وِ چه بي شكه حورُ العين ده   په دنيا كښي له جنتَ را يستلي

"All WERE SAYING, 'This is a very virgin of paradise indeed,
Sent out of heaven into this world!'"—*Bahrām Gūr.*

324. The plural is formed according to the same rules as the past tenses already described. Example:

دَ آسمان په پلوونُ ئي دَ اور لنبي ليدلي چه له ستورو بليدلي دم بتان ئي نكون سار وؤ پريوتلي

"All round the heavens HE WAS VIEWING flames which were taking fire from the stars, and his idols too had fallen, and were turned upside down."—*Tawallud Nāma'h.*

325. The feminine termination is formed in the same manner as for the past tense. Examples:

اي خما نا پوهه دله   نصيحت له مَرد آخله
چه دنيا ئي تولهؤله   لار له دي دا ئي پريښوله
نن ديدن كاندِ بيلتؤن دي

"Oh thou ignorant heart of mine! take example from the dead!
For they that USED TO AMASS wealth, went from this world, and left it behind.
To-day is conjunction: to-morrow is separation."—*Mukhammas-i-Æabd-ul-Kādir.*

پريواته دَ رقيبانو په سر كانړي   ما چه خاورِ ستا دَ در په تندي لوَستِ

"Stones were falling on the heads of my rivals,
When I WAS SPRINKLING the dust of thy door on my forehead."—*Æabd-ul-Hamīd.*

326. II. The imperfect tenses of the four classes of infinitives which do not take the prefixed وُ are the same as the past in every way. Examples:

بادشاد وُد وِ چه په دي حكم كښِي له ما نه خطا وُ شوه او خبره په حال دَ قهر كښِ خما له خولي وُ ختله ولي بايده دي چه تا په هغِه چارِ كښي دَته رنگ تامل په ځاي راوړ چه لايق دَ حال دَ ناصحانُ وي

"The king said, 'By this command an error has been committed by me, and in a moment of anger an expression has escaped me; but under such circumstances it is necessary that thou WOULDST BRING* into play such reflection as may be suitable to the condition of a wise counsellor.'"—*Kalīlah wo Damnah.*

هيڅ آرزؤ ئي دَ خورو دَ ابو نه ود   نه ئي ستركي پرانه تي په هڅه عنوان

"He had no inclination for eating or for drinking,
Neither DID he OPEN his eyes in any manner."—*Saif-ul-Mulūk.*

327. III. Two classes of verbs, III. and XXIV., lengthen the short vowel (ـَ) preceding the last characteristic letter of the past for ا in the imperfect; as

* The imperfect tense is often used in a potential as well as an habitual sense, as in this example.

خښول 'to bury,' خښ کړ 'he buried,' خښاوُ or خښاوُه 'he was burying;' کول 'to do,' کړ 'he did,' کاوه 'he was doing.' Examples:

چه ئې غم لره دَ ترکو لويولم   مور و پلار ويې په هلکت را باندِ بور

"Since they WERE BRINGING ME up to suffer the pangs of love for the Fair,
Would that in my childhood my father and mother had been childless!"—*Æabd-ul-Ḥamīd.*

فرعون چه دِ بادشاه کړ چه په مصر ئې خدائي کړله اظهارد رودِ نيل ئې په فرمان شه تا دوستان
زهيرول دَ هغه دپاره

"When thou didst make Fir'æawn* a ruler, who in Miṣr† laid claim to divinity; the river Nīl‡ became obedient unto him, and thou for his sake DIDST AFFLICT thy chosen people."§
—*Babū Jān.*

328. IV. The imperfect tense of وړل 'to take away' or 'remove,' which forms its past by prefixing يو, and which differs from all the other infinitives in the language in this respect, is formed by rejecting يو in the same manner as the ؤ in the first form.

يو دانش مند مي وُ ليد چه په چا باندِ مبتلا شه او راز ئې له پردي نه را څرګند شه جور و جفا
به ئې زيات له حده وړد او دير تحمل وُد به کړ

"I saw a learned man who had become enamoured of a person, and his secret became known. Indeed he USED TO ENDURE no end of injustice and cruelty, and show great forbearance and resignation."—*Gulistān.*

329. V. Another form of the imperfect, used in a continuative sense, is obtained by prefixing the particle به to the past tense, as exemplified by the following extracts:

چه ژړا کړم تل ته تله   بل رفيق مي نموند بي بلبله
ما به حال وُ وايه له ياره   دد به ژړا کړلـه له ګـله

"Notwithstanding I constantly weep and wail, I found no other partner in my grief than the nightingale.
I WOULD SPEAK of the circumstances of my beloved, and he WOULD LAMENT on account of the rose."—*Aḥmad Shāh, Abdālī.*

القصه چميار خدمت دَ شاهزاده قبول کړ او بي وسواسه ئې به خپل کور ته را وست او بيا به ئې
دَ بادشاه کره بيوُ

"In short, the shoemaker accepted the young prince's service, and without apprehension he USED TO BRING HIM to his own house, and TAKE HIM BACK to the palace."—*Kalīlah wo Damnah.*

330. This prefixed به appears to be used indiscriminately with both the im-

* Pharoah. † Egypt. ‡ The Nile. § The Israelites.

perfect and past, as in the following extract, in which it is prefixed to the simple imperfect of one verb, and to the past of another, both forms conveying a continuative meaning.

که به هر څو سخت رنځور وُد یا ئې رنځ طاوون یا ناسور وُه له هَغه رنځ به فارغ شه چه همسا به ئې

په څان وُ مښله وچه به شوه تاندہ هم میوه پرِ آویزانده چه موسي به دا پر ونو وهله

"Howmuchsoever a person was diseased, or his sickness were even the plague or ulcers, yet he would become cured of that malady when Mūsā WOULD TOUCH HIM with the rod; and when he WOULD STRIKE dried up trees with it, they would become fresh, and fruit would hang from them."—*Babā Jān.*

331. A few imperfect verbs, which have no past tense, form the imperfect, when they have one, in a similar manner to those which take ؤ in the past.

332. The terminations for the feminine gender already explained are the same for all classes of verbs.

THE COMPOUND TENSES.

ماضي قريب PERFECT TENSE.

333. The compound tenses of transitive verbs are obtained in the same manner as intransitives, by adding the different tenses of the auxiliary, 'to be,' according to the gender and number of the governing noun, to the past participle of the verb conjugated.

334. Transitive verbs have but two forms of the past participle, which differ but slightly from each other—one affixing يَ with its variations for gender and number to the infinitive, whilst the other rejects the ل of the infinitive and affixes it to the root; thus پوښتیدل 'to ask,' پوښتیدلَيَ 'asked;' سول 'to burn,' سوَيَ 'burnt.'

335. There are consequently but two forms of the perfect tense formed by adding the present tense of the auxiliary 'to be,' to the past participles, and therefore a few examples will serve to illustrate it.

لړم وُد وِ اي ورورد آندیښنه مي دَ زړه له تیریدو له دي اوبو په گرداب کښي دَ حیرت آچولي یم

"The scorpion said, Oh brother! the fear produced in my heart from crossing this water. HATH THROWN ME into the whirlpool of perturbation.'"—*Kalīlah wo Damnah.*

دا ساده آسمان په نقش و نګار جوړ شه   دَ قدرت په الماسونُ دي کندلي

"This unembellished firmament became adorned with ornaments and embellishments;
Which the diamonds of omnipotence and power HAVE CARVED."—*Mīrzā Khān, Anṣārī.*

ما دَ صبر کتابونه دي سل لوَستي   ولي څه کړم شوم بي صبره زړه پریشان

"I HAVE PERUSED a hundred volumes on patience, and endurance,
But what shall I do? I am out of patience, and distracted in heart."—*Saif-ul-Mulūk.*

336. The participle and auxiliary assume the feminine form and number to agree with a governing noun of that gender; as—

چه مجنون ځني په قبر کښِ هيبت خوړ　　ګمارلِ دَه په ما هسي بلا عشق

"That from which even Majnūn was appalled in the grave,
Love HATH ASSIGNED such a grievous calamity unto me."—*Æubd-ul-Ḥamīd.*

ما قضا رضا سپارلِي دِي و تا ته　　په هر شان به کمترين عاشق ستا يم

"I HAVE ENTRUSTED unto thee both my destiny and inclination;
In every way I will be the most humble of thy lovers."—*Ḳāsim Æalī, Afrīdī.*

337. The auxiliary is often rejected in this tense, as in the following extract:*

ته څما دَ سترګو تورئِي دغه اوښ چه ته پرِ سورئِي له اسبابَ سره ليږملي ما و تا ته بخلي

"Thou art the apple of my eyes, and that camel on which thou art mounted, together with the goods loaded on it, I HAVE GIVEN unto thee."—*Tawallud Nāma'h.*

ماضي بعيد PLUPERFECT TENSE.

338. This tense is formed in the same manner as the preceding, from the past or perfect participle, to which it adds the past tense of the auxiliary 'to be.' Examples:

ما لا نوم دَ آشنايِي آخستي نه وَه　　جدايِي را ته جمع کړ لښکر بيا

"I HAD not as yet TAKEN the name of friendship
When separation again assembled an army against me."—*Æabd-ur-Raḥmān.*

په هيڅ وقت نبي چرِ سحرونَ کړِي نه وُ دوي هرګز چرِ دروغ ويلِي نه وُ

"At any time whatsoever, the Prophet HAD never PERFORMED any acts of enchantment, neither HAD he ever SPOKEN falsehoods in his life-time."—*Fawā'īd-ush-Sharī'æa'h.*

339. Examples of the feminine:

دمنه وَه وِ دَ شمشتي دَ يوه لړم سره دوستي وَه او يو دَ بله ئِي سره دم دَ يکانکِي واهه طرح ئِي دَ اخلاص غوړولِ وَه

"Damnah said, 'A certain tortoise had acquaintance with a scorpion, and one with another used to breathe the breath of unity and concord; and they HAD moreover LAID the foundation of friendship and affection.'"—*Kalīlah wo Damnah.*

په دا هسي ګفتګو کښ مطلب شه په هاي هوي کښ ښيي توري وِ وېکلِي لور په لور پرِ بريښيدلي

"At this dialogue Muttalib became much terrified, for by unseen hands swords HAD BEEN DRAWN, and were gleaming all around him."—*Tawallud Nāma'h.*

ماضي تشکيک DOUBTFUL PAST TENSE.

340. This tense is also obtained from the past participles and the aorist tense

* Also see paragraph 240.

of the auxiliary, 'to be,' for which there is but one form, which remains unchanged, in all six inflections, for both genders. Examples:

دَ درخو دَ آدم خان پښتنه څه کړي　　آغوستي چا په ژوند دَ مرګ کفن وي

"What inquiry makest thou respecting Durkho and Adam Khān!
A person in his life-time MAY HAVE CLAD himself in a shroud.—*Ḳāsim Æalī, Afrīdī.*

چې ئي نال دَ ليونتوب نه وي وهلي　　هر سمند دَ عشق پر زمکه شي سوده

"Until he MAY not HAVE BEEN SHOD with the shoe of madness,
The foot of every noble steed becometh rubbed on the ground of love."—*Æabd-ul-Ḥamīd.*

خما غم به دَ هغه سري په شمار وي　　چه شميرلي ئي ويښته وي دَ خپل ځان

"The amount of my sorrows will be within the computation of that man,
Who MAY HAVE COUNTED OVER every hair of hisown body."—*Æabd-ur-Raḥmān.*

341. Another form of this tense is obtained by using the 2nd future tense of the auxiliary, 'to be,' affixed to the past participle, as in the following examples:

په خپل عمر به هيچا ليدلي نه وي　　هغه چاري چه يار هر ساعت په ما که

"No one in the whole course of his life WILL HAVE BEHELD
The trials imposed upon me every hour by my beloved."—*Æabd-ur-Raḥmān.*

عالم ورته جواب از روي عذر خواهي وُ کړ چه خما فهم هرګز په درخانه شوي نه دي که به ما په
قصد بي التفاتي کړي وي خداي مي دِ په سترګو روند کا

"The learned man by way of apology gave answer unto him, saying, 'My notice has never been drawn towards Durkhāna'ī. If I knowingly MAY HAVE ACTED unkindly towards her, may the Almighty make my eyes sightless.'"—*Adam Khān and Durkhāna'ī.*

ماضي شرطيه PAST CONDITIONAL TENSE.

342. The inflections of the conditional tense of the auxiliary 'to be,' with the past participle and a conditional conjunction or adverb of wishing, gives the past conditional or optative tense. The auxiliary is not subject to change in termination for either gender or number, but the participle is liable to both. Examples:

که تا هم ليدلي وَي لکه ما ليدلي دي شايد چه صحرا دِ هم دَ ديوُ له غمَ پريښي وي

"IF thou also HADST SEEN in the same manner what I have beheld, perhaps thou too wouldst have fled from their oppression into the desert."—*Kalīlah wo Damnah.*

که دِ زړه آرام موندلي په اخلاص وَي　　تا به نه کړه چا ته ژبَ دَ لباس

"IF thy heart HAD FOUND any quiet in truth and sincerity,
Thou wouldst not have bestowed adulation or flattery on any one."—*Æabd-ul-Ḥamīd.*

که مي زده واي له دي هسي رنګ خوارئي　　ما به نوم آخستي نه وُه دَ يارئي

"HAD my heart but BEEN AWARE of such sorrows as these,
I would never have taken even the name of friendship."—*Æabd-ul-Ḥamīd.*

جدائي مي به يو دم قبوله نه كړه   كه چا مرګ و بيلتون ږدي واي په خوږ

"I would not for a moment have selected absence,
HAD any one PLACED death and separation for me to choose between."—*Æabd-ur-Raḥmān.*

صيغه حال PRESENT TENSE.

343. The twenty-four classes of transitive verbs have twelve methods of forming the present tense, the whole of which differ materially from each other.

344. Form I. This consists of the infinitives of Classes I., II., V., XVII., XVIII., XX., XXI., and XXIV., and constitutes the greatest number of verbs in the language, which obtain the present by merely rejecting the ل of the infinitive and affixing the necessary personal pronouns. Examples:

نازولئ زوي نه آخلي ادب   او دَ سيوري نخل نه نسي رطب

"A pampered son taketh not to discipline and morality,
And a shaded palm GIVETH not ripe dates."—*Æabd-ul-Ḥamīd.*

بار په سر ږدم عبث دَ نفس دپاره   كله نه كيږي و نمونځ ته تيته ملا

"I profitlessly PLACE a load on my head for the sake of carnal desires,
But my waist never becometh bent for devotion or for prayer."—*Ḳāsim Æalī, Afrīdī.*

345. Form II. comprises the infinitives of Class III., in which the two last radical letters are rejected and two others taken in lieu of them; as غوښتل 'to demand' or 'desire,' غواړي 'he, she, it demands;' سكښتل 'to rive' or 'cleave,' سكڼري 'he, she, it cleaves.' Example:

له سهمَ كتي نه شم د حسن په لښكر ئي   وروځي ئي اندي دي بانړه ئي سكڼري زغري

"Through dread I am unable to look on the host of her beauty—
Her eyebrows are bows! her eyelashes RIVE coats of mail!"—*Aḥmad Shāh, Abdālī.*

346. Form III. In forming the present tense of the verbs of this division, which includes Class IV. of infinitives, the two last characteristic letters are rejected and another taken in place of them; as موندل 'to find,' مومي 'he, she, it found.' Examples:

پلار ته ئي سوال وُ كړ چه همزولي مي واړه لوَلي حكم را كړه چه زه هم لوَلم

"She made this request to her father, saying, 'All those of my own age LEARN TO READ, give directions that I may learn to read also."—*Adam Khān and Durkhāna'ī.*

صورتي همدمان دير دي په جهان كښي   ولي نه مومي رحمان همدم دَ زړه

"There are many extrinsic friends in the world,
But Raḥmān FINDETH not a friend of the heart."—*Æabd-ur-Raḥmān.*

347. Form IV. includes the infinitives of Classes VI. and XIII., which lengthen the first short vowel (ـَ) into ا for the present; as ويل 'to speak,' وائي 'he, she, it, etc. speaks;' ژړل 'to weep,' ژاړي 'he, she, it, etc. weeps;' خندل 'to laugh,' خاندي 'he, she, it laughs.' Example:

که څوک پښتي څشکله تير شؤ ليوني افريدي   خاندم ژاړم نه وايم حال پريشان خپل

"If any one asks, 'What hath happened to thee, O! mad Afrīdī?'
I LAUGH and WEEP, but I DO not TELL my perplexed state to any one."—*Kāsim Ælī, Afrīdī.*

348. Form V. This includes the infinitives of Class VII., and is something similar to the one immediately preceding. It changes the short vowel (ـَ) for و in the present; as بلل 'to call' or 'name,' بولي 'he, she, it, etc. called.' Example:

خداي رازق بولي او رزق ګڼري له کسبَ   په دا شناخت وخان ته وائي حق شناس

"Thou CALLEST God the giver of daily bread, nevertheless consider it acquired by employment;
Yet with all this knowledge, thou termest thyself grateful."—*Æabd-ur-Raḥmān.*

349. Form VI. comprises Classes VIII. and IX. of infinitives, which reject the last radical letter and take another in place of it; as وژلل 'to kill,' وژني 'he, she, it kills;' پرانتل 'to unloose,' پرانځي 'he, she, it unlooses.' Example:

ستا دَ سترګو دَ بڼرو تر مينځ حيران يم   يو مي وژني په سره اور بل په غمزو

"What between thy eyes and thy eyelashes, I am perplexed and bewildered;
For one KILLS me with red fire, the other with sparkling glances."—*Æabd-ul-Ḥamīd.*

350. Form VII. The infinitives of Class X. form the present by rejecting the three last radical letters and taking another in their place; as ويشتل 'to discharge,' وژلي 'he, she, it, etc. discharges.' Example:

هسي رنګ دَ بڼرو غشي رسا وژلي   چه هيڅ څوک ئي سلامت نه ځي له جنګَ

"So true doth she DISCHARGE the arrows of her eyelashes,
That no one escapeth with safety from the battle with her."—*Æabd-ur-Raḥmān.*

351. Form VIII. The present tense of Class XI. of infinitives is obtained by rejecting altogether the two last characteristic letters of the root, and the ل of the infinitive; as آرويدل 'to hear,' آروي 'he, she, it, etc. heard.' Example:

چه دَ سپي آواز ئي آروم هسي خوښ يم   لکه څوک په نغمه خوښ وي دَ رباب

"When I HEAR the sound of her dog's voice, I become as delighted,
As one becometh merry and glad at the melody of the rebeck."—*Æabd-ur-Raḥmān.*

352. Form IX. The verbs of Class XII. contained in this form of the present reject the last radical letter and the ل of the infinitive; as پيژندل 'to recognize.' پيژني 'he, she, it, etc. recognizes.' Example:

هغه بل هسي ورته وائي چه زه حکم دَ مولي نه پيژنم يا په دا ځاي حکم دَ خداي نه چليږي يا
دَ خداي حکم دلِ نشته کافر کيږي

"And if the other sayeth unto him, 'I DO not RECOGNIZE the will of the Almighty;' or, 'In this place the will of God availeth not;' or, 'The influence and power of God extendeth not here;' he becometh a blasphemer."—*Fawā'id-ush-Sharī'æa'h.*

353. **Form X.** The infinitives constituting Class XIV. of transitive verbs change the final letter for another in forming the present tense, similar to those of Form VI., but so far differ inasmuch as the former contain but two letters in the root and the latter three. Example:

هيځ گياه له ځايه نه خوځي نم موميي　　ته دَ رزق په طلب مڼي جهان ولِ

"The grass which moveth not from its proper place acquireth moisture;
Then wherefore SCOUREST thou the world in search of thy daily bread?"—*Æabd-ur-Raḥmān.*

354. **Form XI.** Class XIX. of infinitives form the present tense by rejecting the last radical letter of the root for two others; as آهيل 'to knead,' اغڼي 'he, she, it, etc. kneads;' بيول 'to take' or 'bear away,' بيائي 'he, she, it, etc. takes.' Example:

که خنگ دَ زړه دَ هوس پر لار بيايم　　قدم نه ځي خما دَ زړه فکر وُ کړ لنگ

"If I TAKE the steed of the heart on the road of carnal desire,
He goeth not along, for my heart's reflection made him lame."—*Aḥmad Shāh, Abdālī.*

355. **Form XII.** The verbs of Class XXIII. form the present tense by affixing an extra letter to the root, after rejecting the sign of the infinitive; as سول 'to burn,' سوځي 'he, she, it burns.' Example:

هر چه آچوي و اور ته واړه سوځي　　موړ به نه شي طلبکار دَ دِ دنيا

"Fire BURNS whatever may be cast into it;
In the same manner, a seeker after this world will not become satiated."
—*Æabd-ur-Raḥmān.*

356. It is here necessary to mention that the infinitive کول 'to do,' included in the above, has two other forms of the third person, besides the regular one, viz. کاندِ and کا or که, examples of which are contained in the following extracts:

نصارا په هندوستان حکومت کاندِ　　چرته وُ لاړ هغه ځوانان شمشيرنگي
بقالان به سپاهي په هندوستان شوُ　　درويزه کاندِ اشراف چنگي چنگي

"Alas! Christians EXERCISE dominion over Hindūstān!
Oh! where are those valorous swordsmen gone?
Shopkeepers are now becoming soldiers in India,
And the great and noble of the land ASK for alms."—*Kāsim Æalī, Afrīdī.**

* The Afrīdīs of the present day do not seem to have a more favourable opinion of the "shopkeepers" than our friend Kāsim Æalī in the last century.

چه امید په عمارت د دِ دنیا کا   دَ کاغذ په کېښتۍ سیر دَ دریا کا

"Whosoever PLACETH his hopes on the fabric of this world,
VOYAGETH on the ocean in a paper boat."—*Æabd-ur-Raḥmān.*

357. The above form is often written with کَ, thus—

که په گنج دَ شاهي فخر شهریار کَ   عاشقان ئې دَ دلبرو په رخسار کَ

"If the monarch MAKETH a boast of the imperial treasure,
Lovers will make a boast of the cheeks of their beloved."—*Æabd-ur-Raḥmān.*

358. The affixed نَ or نه, already described as being occasionally added, by way of euphony at the end of a line for the other tenses, is also used with the present. Example:

چه دي وائي هغه مه کانږئ دَ ده پند واړه غلت دي گناهونَ دَ ده لومه دي ښکاري دَ مومنانْ
په رنگ رنگ ئې ښوهوينَ

"Act not as he says, for the whole of his advice and counsel is delusive and wrong. Sin is his snare—the fowler of the Faithful—and MAKETH them SLIP and slide in many ways."—*Fawā'id-ush-Sharī'æa'h.*

مضارع AORIST TENSE.

359. The aorist or future indefinite tense of transitive verbs is formed in a similar manner to that of the intransitives already described, but they have also some peculiarities of their own.

360. I have before remarked respecting the intransitive verbs, that, properly speaking, this tense is an original one, and that the present is formed from it by rejecting the prefixed وَ, whilst the present tense of those which reject this particle is the same as the aorist itself.

361. There are four different forms of the aorist, which I shall describe separately.

362. I. Thirteen out of the twenty-four classes of transitives—I., III., IV., VI., VII., VIII., XI., XII., XIII., XIV., XIX., XXI., XXII., and XXIII., merely differ from the present by taking the prefixed وَ, as will be seen from the following examples:

هر زاهد چه زهد واخلي بي مرشدَ   د خوشحال خټک په پوهه تش پلي دي

"Every recluse who MAY BEGIN a life of devotion without a guide or director,
In the imagination of Khūshḥāl Khaṭ'ak, is but an empty pod."—*Khūshḥāl Khān.*

سل جفا که وُ وینم په سترگو ستا له لاسَ   ستا په جفا نه کیږي هرگز باور څما

"Though I MAY BEHOLD with mine eyes an hundred wrongs at thy hand,
Yet I shall never become convinced of thy injustice and cruelty."—*Æabd-ur-Raḥmān.*

دنيا ځاي دي دَ ګندګۍ ئي له دِ ځايه ځان له لرِ ؤ ساتئ ئي چرِ نه وي سرنګون په کښې پريوزئ ئي*

"The world is a place of filthiness and impurity. YOU SHOULD KEEP your minds at a distance from it, that you may never fall head downwards into it."—*Fawā'id-ush-Sharī'æa'h.*

363. The prefixed ؤ of this class of infinitives is often rejected as redundant, like the ب of the Persian. The following is an example:

اميدوار يؤ چه په برکت دَ راستۍ دواړه له منګلې دَ اندوه خلاصي بيامومؤ

"We are hopeful that, through the blessing of veracity and candour, both of us MAY OBTAIN redemption from the talon of grief and anxiety."—*Kalīlah wo Damnah.*

364. II. Six classes of infinitives—V., IX., X., XVI., XVII., and XX., entirely reject the prefixed ؤ in the aorist, and therefore this form of the verb does not differ from the simple present in mode of writing. Examples:

که سر په مينه بايلم بيا څه ګيله ځما دَ چه سر ستا په ننګه بايلي دَ څغو ولي ژړا دَ

"If I SHOULD stake and LOSE my head on love, then what blame is it of mine?
If THEY SHOULD STAKE their heads on thy esteem, what cause of grief is it to them?"
—*Aḥmad Shāh, Abdālī.*

اوس راځه چه غم اندوه دَ دنيا پريږدؤ دا صحبت دَ شراب ګرم کړؤ به شان

"Come now, that WE MAY ABANDON the sorrow and trouble of the world!
That after a good fashion we may warm this companionship with wine!"
—*Saif-ul-Mulūk.*

365. III. The transitive infinitives of Class II., which are formed from adjectives by the addition of وَل,† require the aorist tense of کول and کړل 'to do,' 'to perform,' to complete them; as in the following examples of ډکول 'to fill,' and زبادول 'to prove:'

دَ سپوږمۍ په دود ئي ماتت صبا په سر کا که نن ډک کاندِ فلک کچکول دَ چا

"Like the moon, fate breaketh on the head to-morrow,
The wallet of any one which IT MAY FILL to-day."—*Æabd-ul-Ḥamīd.*

دَغه يار آشنا مې نه شته چه پرې حق دَ يارۍ زباد کړم

"That friend and companion of mine, alas! is now no more,
That by him I MIGHT PROVE the sincerity and truth of friendship."
—*Æabd-ul-Ḥamīd.*

366. The verb کول 'to do,' as before mentioned, besides the regular form, has two other forms of the present for the third persons singular and plural. One of these, written کَه, کَـ, or کا, is also used with the addition of the necessary affixed

* The second person plural in some works is written as above, instead of with simple ئ
† See paragraphs 166 and 285.

pronouns and the prefixed ۇ in all the inflections of the aorist, both singular and plural, as well as the regular form of the tense. Example:

که په ژبه اقرار ۇ کړه　　هم په زړه اعتبار ۇ که
چه خداي يو دي ما منليَ　　پاك رسول دي راستوليَ
دي بي شکه مسلمان شي　　مسلمان اهلِ ايمان شي

"He who MAY CONFESS with his tongue, and MAY truly VENERATE in his heart,
Saying, 'I have acknowledged the One God, and the holy Prophet has been sent'—
Verily, he becometh a Musalmān, and the Musalmān is an orthodox man."
—*Rashīd-ul-By'ān.*

367. کاندِ, the other form of the third person present, is also used for the aorist, but merely in the third persons, and with or without the prefixed ۇ. Examples:

معتزلهٔ دي ويلي مسلمان چه کبيره گناه ۇ کاندِ له ايمان به دي ۇ وزي ولي په کفر داخل نه وي
نه کافر نه مسلمان ور ته وايه شي

"The Mu'ætazilas* have said, that Musalmāns who MAY COMMIT an enormous sin, will doubtless depart from their faith, but it will not constitute blasphemy, and they cannot be termed either Infidels or Believers." —*Fawā'īd-ush-Sharī'æa'h.*

آب و تاب ئي عالم گير لکہ آفتاب شي　　هر جبين چه تابنده کاندِ إخلاص

"The brightness and lustre, will become world-conquering like the sun,
Of every brow, which candour and probity MAY ILLUMINE."—*Æabd-ul-Hamīd.*

امر حاضر 1st Future or Precative Tense.

368. This tense, like the corresponding one for the intransitives, merely differs from the aorist in the mode of writing the third persons singular and plural, which take the prefixed دِ, the peculiar sign of the 1st future, and the third persons of the imperative mood.

369. There are three forms of this tense, which differ slightly from each other.

370. I. The regular verbs which take the prefixed ۇ in the aorist, merely prefix the دِ to it for the 1st future. Example:

تازه اودس دِ ۇ کا ولِ غسل بهتر دي دود دِ پاك چادر واخلي چه وي نوي يا وي ۇلِلي يو دِ لنگ
کا بل دِ په اوږو کا

"He should perform the ablutions anew; still, washing the whole body is much better. HE SHOULD also TAKE two clean cloths, which may be either quite new or washed, one of which he should wrap round the loins, and the other he should throw over his shoulders."—*Fawā'īd-ush-Sharī'æa'h.*

371. II. Those verbs formed from nouns and adjectives by adding ۇل as already described,† which require the assistance of کول or کړل 'to do,' in forming

* A sect of Muhammadan schismatics.　　† See paragraphs 166 and 285.

their different tenses, do not generally take the prefixed و in this tense, as in the following example:

ولي لازم په هر مؤمن دي چه دا څو خبري دِ دي زده کا چه ايمان خپل پر قوي کا

"Moreover, it is incumbent on every believer, that HE SHOULD LEARN by heart these few words, that he may thereby strengthen his faith."—*Makhzan Afghānī.*

372. III. The different forms of the aorist of کول 'to do,' are used with the prefixed دِ of the third persons, for the 1st future also, either with or without the prefixed و; as—

شپه و ورځ دِ عبادت کا ترک دِ واړه معصيت کا
ځان دِ جوړ په شريعت کا تل دِ زړه ته نصيحت کا
نن ديدن کاندِ بيلتون دي

"Day and night HE SHOULD worship and adore; HE SHOULD abandon all sin and disobedience;
HE SHOULD ever give good counsel to his heart; and SHOULD keep himself according to the law.
He should make observation to-day, for to-morrow is separation."
—*Mukhammas of Ȝabd-ul-Kādir.*

که نمازي سړي رنځور شي ودريده باندِ ضرور شي
حکم دا دي په دد باندِ چه دِ نمونځ په ناستي کاندِ

"If a man in the constant habit of praying may become afflicted with sickness, and it may be difficult for him to stand up,
This is the order unto him, that HE SHOULD SAY his prayers sitting."—*Rashīd-ul-By'ān.*

373. The second person of the imperative is sometimes used with the دِ prefixed for the 1st future, as in the following extract:

په څه خوبنس په څواني کښي فراغت ئي خداي دِ واخله اي دَ پنجاب نادانَ جټَ

"In the hope of what pleasant thing art thou in the time of youth free from care?
MAY the Almighty REMOVE THEE! oh thou ignorant Panjābī Jatt."—*Mīrzā Khān, Anṣārī.*

374. The termination نَ or نه, previously described, is added to this as well as the other tenses of verbs for the third person, for the sake of euphony. Example:

په شرح تنبيه کښي دي راوړي پر عزيزانُ گاونديانُ دَ مړدد مستحب دي چه طعام دِ دوي دَ مړدد و قبيلي ته ور واستوين

"It is stated in the Sharah Tanbīh, that it is right on the part of the relations and neighbours of the defunct person, that THEY SHOULD SEND victuals to his family."—*Fawā'id-ush-Sharī'ca'h.*

مستقبل 2ND FUTURE TENSE.

375. The 2nd future tense of transitive verbs, of which there are four classes, is obtained from the different forms of the aorist by the addition of the prefixed به, and are as follow:—

376. I. Regular infinitives which take the prefixed وُ for the aorist; as—

تاسي ورونړه به په ښکار شئ — په خپل ښکار به گرفتار شئ
دي به وُ باسئ له دله — تر به وارد شئ غافله
زوړ ليوه به غاښ پر تيز کا — نازک تن به ئي ريز ريز کا

"You brothers will go in search of game, and will be so much taken up with your sport,
That YOU WILL PUT him altogether OUT of your minds, and will become incautious regarding him.
Then some old wolf will whet his fangs on him, and will tear his tender limbs asunder."
—*Yūsuf and Zulīkhā.*

377. The regular infinitives in this as well as in the aorist sometimes reject the prefixed وُ; as—

دائي وَد ويل اي لوُرِ خداي دِ نکا — چه وچا و ته به وايم دا شان راز نهان

"The nurse said, 'Oh, daughter! now God forbid
That I SHOULD MENTION such a secret matter to any one.'"—*Saif-ul-Mulūk.*

378. The به of this tense sometimes precedes the وُ, and *vice versâ*, and depends on whether a regular personal pronoun (ضميرِ منفصل) as well as an affixed pronoun (ضميرِ متصل) be used, or the regular personal pronoun omitted at the beginning of a sentence. If the former, the به should immediately precede the وُ, and, when no regular personal pronoun is used, the وُ should precede the به.

دا ئي وَد وِ که په اويه ورځ دَ حشر — پرسش وُ کاندِ په عدل پاك رحمان
زه به وُ پښتم صالح دَ حميد زويَ — دَ تمام خلق له عدل له احسانَ

"He said thus unto him, 'On the great day of resurrection, when the Almighty shall make inquiry concerning justice;
I WILL INQUIRE of thee, oh! Ṣāleḥ, son of Ḥamīd, regarding the equity and beneficence shown to the whole nation.'"—*Saif-ul-Mulūk.*

څو په خپلو وينو گل غندي غرق نه وي — وُ به نه وينيِ رخسار گلفام دَ ستا

"Until he may not have become immersed like the rose in his own blood,
HE WILL not BEHOLD thy blooming rose-coloured cheek."—*'Abd-ur-Raḥmān.*

379. II. Infinitives, in other respects perfect, which reject the prefixed وُ in the past tense, also reject it in the aorist, and consequently in the 2nd future also. Example:

اول غم څما دَغه دي چه په وقت دَ څنکندن بَ ايمان يوسم که بَ بايلم

"In the first place, my concern is, as to whether at the time of death I SHALL BEAR AWAY my faith, or whether I SHALL LOSE it."—*Fawā'id-ush-Sharī'a'h.*

380. Compound infinitives formed by prefixing a preposition or postposition to a simple verb, such as پريښول 'to place,' کښېښتل 'to seize,' etc., also reject the وُ and

insert the به, the peculiar sign of the tense, between the preposition or postposition and the verb, as in the following:

زه خو ستا په خبره حد دَ شرعِي پرِ به نږدم دَغه وُ ويل رښتيا دِ وُ فرمايل ولي هر څوک چه دَ
وقف له مالَ څه خيز په غلا يوسي لاس پريکول ئي نه شته

"'I certainly WILL NOT RELINQUISH the punishment agreeable to the laws.' The Darweṣẖ said, 'You command truly, nevertheless, he who stealeth part of any property devoted to pious uses, it is not lawful to cut off his hand.'"—*Gulistān*.

381. III. Infinitives formed from adjectives, nouns, or pronouns, by adding ول, require the aid of کول or کړل 'to do,' in this as well as the other tenses, and consequently are subject to the same rules as those verbs in forming the 2nd future tense; thus—

دِغي جلي وِ ځلمي چرته راغلي   دا کافر دي ستا به ماتِ کاندِ هدونَ

"The young maiden said, 'Oh, youth! wherefore hast thou come here?
This is an infidel, and HE WILL BREAK all thy bones!'"—*Bahrām Gūr*.

څو غم خورم دَ دِ چارِ پيدا نه شي   زه به ځوځه کړم مرئي په تيغ بران

"How long shall I endure sorrow? There is no remedy found for this!
And therefore I WILL CUT my throat with a sharp sword."—*Saif-ul-Mulūk*.

382. IV. The infinitive کول 'to do,' chiefly used as an auxiliary to other verbs, particularly those of Form III. just described, prefixes the به to its different forms of the aorist for the 2nd future. Examples:

زه رحمان به څه ځواب کوم و يار ته   و ژونديو ته دَ مړيو څه ځواب دي

"What answer SHALL I, Raḥmān, GIVE unto my beloved?
What reply is there from the dead unto the living?"—*Æabd-ur-Raḥmān*.

ګرزي په چمن کښي شنه طوطيان بلبلان ګډوډ   اوس به خزان راشي پرِ به کاندِ بوستان ګډوډ

"Green parrots and nightingales fly about the parterre in disorder and tumult,
But the autumn will now soon arrive, and WILL DISORDER the garden for them."
—*Æabd-ul-Ḳādir*.

امر IMPERATIVE MOOD.

383. The imperative of transitive verbs like that of the intransitives is not subject to change in termination for gender, and has no first person singular or plural. It merely differs from the aorist and 1st future as regards the pronominal affixes and the prefixed دِ, which is also the sign of the third person of the latter tense.

384. There are four descriptions of the imperative, which may be thus defined—

I. Regular infinitives which take the prefixed وُ in the past and aorist tenses, also use it in the imperative; thus—

نور اورنگ ؤ وِ غوږ ږ باسه و ما تَه   دَ جنگ حال واوره له ما نه څما مهمانَ

"Then Aurang said, 'GIVE EAR unto me!
HEAR the account of the battle from me, oh my guest!'"—*Bahrām Gūr.*

Like the ب of the Persian imperative, the regular infinitives in Pushto *often* reject the prefixed وُ, as in the following example:

که څوک واٸي هوښيار کوم دي وايه دا دي   چه بي خدايه نوره مينه په چا نه کا

"If a person enquireth—who is most discreet? SAY it is he
Who placeth not his affections on any one save the Creator."—*Æabd-ur-Raḥmān.*

385. II. Infinitives which totally reject the وُ in the past and aorist, also do away with it in the imperative, as—

يعقوب ؤد وِ تاسي دروميږي   دَ صحرا خوښي بيا موميږي
يوسف مه بيايږي له ما نه   دا وينا ده په ما گرانه

"Yakūb said, 'DEPART and ENJOY YOURSELVES by roaming in the forest,
But DO NOT TAKE Yūsuf from me; for this matter is afflicting to me.'"
—*Yūsuf and Zulīkhā.*

386. The imperative mood of compound infinitives also belong to this form, as—

پردي پريږده که په قطعَ مور و پلار وي   دَ ديچا و هيچا مه شه پيدا طمعَ

"The stranger LEAVE OUT of the question, for verily, even though it may be a mother or father.
Let it not happen that any one may be in need of the help of others."—*Æabd-ul-Ḥamīd.*

387. III. Like the corresponding forms for the aorist and future tenses, the infinitives derived from adjectives, etc. require the assistance of کړل or کول 'to do.' in forming the imperative. Example:

بيا دوباره بدره خاتون ويل اي خورِ   که څه حق په زړه لري شيرِ دَ مادر
يو ځل مخ و خپل گايل و ته څرگند کړه   محنتونه ئي دير کړي بحر و بر

"Again, for the second time, Badra'h Khātūn said, 'Oh sister!
If thou hast any gratitude for thy mother's milk,
One time, at least, SHOW thy face unto thy afflicted lover;
For he has performed many toils and troubles both by sea and land."—*Saif-ul-Mulūk.*

388. Some of these infinitives have also another form of the imperative, for the second person plural, in which the last radical letter of the regular imperative is changed into انړ, as will be seen in the following examples:

په شتابي ئي خبر راوانړئ ور دروميږي   راولئ ئي تر ما پورِ په تلوار

"Go to him quickly, and TRANSMIT information regarding him;
And with all possible speed bring him into my presence."—*Saif-ul-Mulūk.*

بادشاه وُ فرمايل نور خوراك راوانړئ   دا عفريت په ښه عنوان سرد موړ كانړئ

"The king commanded, saying, 'BRING YOU some more victuals,
And SATIATE this demon in a proper manner.'"—*Saif-ul-Mulūk.*

389. IV. The infinitive كول 'to do,' is somewhat irregular in the imperative, having كه, وُ كه, or كړه for the second person singular, and كړي with the necessary personal pronouns, for the third person singular and plural. كړه is changed into كړئ for the plural of the second person. Examples:

دَ سحر بادَ خوش نسيمَ خبر راوړه   دَ زړه گل مي خندان كه په بوستان كښي

"Bring tidings, oh fragrant zephyr of the morning!
GLADDEN the rose of my heart in the blooming garden!"—*Aḥmad Shāh, Abdālī.*

جنگ كړه له غليمانُ سره زويَ بيرته تيښت ور څني مه كړه دسي بويَ

"Do battle with the enemy, oh my son! do not retreat from them, so it behoveth."—*Ḥasan and Ḥusain.*

390. The prefixed وُ is sometimes retained and at times rejected.

THE POTENTIAL MOOD.

صيغهٔ امكاني *sīghah-i-imkānī.*

391. The Pushto has no regular potential mood, and the passive form of the verb is used instead, with a slight difference in the construction.

392. There are but three tenses—the present, past, and future.

INTRANSITIVES.

393. Intransitive verbs have no passive voice, but a passive form—the different past participles with the auxiliary 'to be'—is used for the potential of intransitives. The verb agrees with the agent, and the masculine or feminine form of the past participle must correspond accordingly; but the third persons of the past tense of the auxiliary, like all intransitive verbs, alone has a different termination for the feminine gender.

394. Therefore, whenever the passive form of an intransitive verb is met with in a sentence, it can be instantly recognised as the potential mood. The following are examples:

حال PRESENT TENSE.

ستا د عشق له موجَ په هيڅ لوري وتي نه شم   دواړه لاس مي پړوانه دَ عقل په لانبو كښي

"From the waves of thy love I CANNOT ESCAPE by any road:
Both my hands have become powerless for the swimming of wisdom."
—*Æabd-ur-Raḥmān.*

ماضي. PAST TENSE.

زه نه شوم تيريدي له يوه خسَ — ميني تير كړم هم ترسره هم ترمالَ

"I COULD NOT OVERLOOK even a straw or a splinter;
But love hath made me disregard both life and goods."—*Eabd-ur-Raḥmān.*

مستقبل. FUTURE TENSE.

كه ستاسي دَ مرتبي په جبت يو جهت مي معين شي چه سبب دَ جمعيت دَ زړه وي نور تر
عمرَ پوري له شكرَ دَ ذمه بهر به وتي نه شم

"If, through your rank, some mode of livelihood be established for me which may cause peace of mind, I SHALL not BE ABLE to emerge from the debt of gratitude as long as I live."—*Gulistān.*

TRANSITIVES.

395. The transitive form of the potential is easily distinguished from the passive voice, as both the agent and the object *must* be expressed for the former; whilst, in the latter, the agent is never expressed, or remains unknown. The verb also agrees with the object in gender and number for the former, and the agent must be in the instrumental or agent case in the past tense. The object is sometimes put in the dative, as is also the case with regard to a few infinitives which require it.

حال PRESENT TENSE.

لكه بي لاسَ لستوڼري څه كړيَ نه شي — هسي بي فضلَ بندد دي مضطرب

"In the same manner as an armless sleeve CANNOT DO anything,
So without grace and favour, man is confounded and perplexed."—*Eabd-ul-Hamīd.*

ماضي. PAST TENSE.

يو بزرګ ويليَ دي نن روځ چه كوليَ شي نه پوهيږي او چه پوهيږي نه شي كوليَ هر كله چه كوليَ
مي شه نه پوهيدم او چه وُ پوهيدم كوليَ مي نه شه

"A holy man hath said, 'To-day that you are able to do, you do not understand; and when you understand, you are unable to perform: and in the same manner, WHEN I COULD DO, I did not comprehend; and when I comprehended I COULD NOT PERFORM.'"—*Kalīlah wo Damnah.*

مستقبل. FUTURE TENSE.

ته به بار دَ امانت زغمليَ نه شي — دَ صلاح پر لار خړد څه نو آموز

"Thou WILT not BE ABLE TO BEAR the burthen of trust,
Therefore travel light on the road of integrity, thou inexperienced one!"
—*Mīrzā Khān, Anṣarī.*

THE PASSIVE VOICE.

صيغهٔ مجهول *sīg͟hah-i-majhūl.*

396. The passive voice of a verb is called مجهول, from the Arabic word signifying 'unknown,' as the agent is never mentioned.

397. Transitive verbs, alone, have a proper passive voice, which is obtained by prefixing the different forms of the past participle to the auxiliaries شول or كيدل 'to be' or 'become,' as in the following examples:

صيغهٔ حال PRESENT TENSE.

په حجة الاسلام کښي دي راوړي چه څوک رڼا کا مساجد په چراغونَ ور ببښلي شي همیشه گناهونَ
دَ اویا زره کالونَ

"It is stated in the Ḥujjat-ul-Islām, that if a person lighteth a place of worship with lamps, HE IS ever FORGIVEN the sins of seventy thousand years."—*Fawā'id-ush-Sharī'æa'h.*

هر سنگ کلوخ چه ليدد کيږي دَ دِ دهر واړه ککرۍ دي څوک دَ شاه څوک دَ گدا

"Every stone and every clod of earth of this world which IS SEEN,
All are skulls, some of kings and some of beggars."—*Æabd-ur-Raḥmān.*

ماضي استمرار IMPERFECT TENSE.

يو ورځ دَ دَغه په مجلس کښي شاه نامه دَ فردوسي په زوال دَ مملکت دَ ضحاك او په دور دَ
فريدون لوستِ شوه

"One day the Shāh Nāma'h of Ferdowsī WAS BEING READ in his assembly, on the subject of the decline of the dominion of Ẓoḥāk, and on the prosperity of that of Ferīdūn."—*Gulistān.*

ماضي مطلق PAST TENSE.

قضاكار دَ يوه ښهر په دروازه په تهمت دَ جاسوسۍ كښيوتل او دواړه سره په يوه كوټه كښي قيد شول
او وَر ور پسي وُ پښلي شه

"It so happened that they were apprehended at the door of a certain city on suspicion of being spies, and were placed together in a chamber, and its door WAS CLOSED UP on them."—*Gulistān.*

ماضي قريب PERFECT TENSE.

تر دَغه مړ شَوي نه يۍ پيش له مرگَ فقيري باطله وُگڼړه نادانَ خپل

"If thou HAST not BECOME DEAD to the world before death,
Count, oh fool! as false and futile, all thy devotion and austerity."—*Ḳāsim Æalī, Afrīdī.*

ماضي بعيد PLUPERFECT TENSE.

درويش لره په درست عمر کښي زوي ور کړي شَوي نه وُد وُ ويل كه څښتن تعالي زوي لا لره را كړي
بي له دي خرقي چه مي آغستيدة نور هر څه څما په مِلك كښي وي قربان دَ درويشانُ دي

"During the whole of the Darwes͟h's life no son HAD BEEN GIVEN unto him. He said, 'If the Almighty bestoweth a son on me, save this ragged garment which I have clothed myself in, whatever else may be in my possession is an oblation to the poor.'"—*Gulistān.*

مستقبل 2ND FUTURE TENSE.

دام دِ هيڅوک نه ږدي دَ دنيا ورد گذار ته　　ښکار به کړلئ نه شي دَ سيمرغ و دَ عنقا

"No one should (uselessly) place a snare on the highway of this world :
The griffin and the phœnix WILL NOT BECOME the PREY of any one."—*Eabd-ur-Raḥmān.*

مضارع AORIST TENSE.

پلار ور ته وُ ويل اي ځويَ په هر ځغه څه چه پوهيږي ته نيزوُ وايه وُ ئي ويل ويريږم چه وُ پښتيدئ
شَم له ځغه نه چه پرِ نه پوهيږم

"His father said unto him, 'Oh, son! whatever matter thou art acquainted with, do thou also state.' He said unto him, 'I fear I MAY BE ASKED concerning that with which I am not familiar.'"—*Gulistān.*

ماضي تشکيک DOUBTFUL PAST TENSE.

دريم ځغه سړي چه له خپلِ نوکرئ يستلئ شوي به وي او دو باره ئي اميد دَ نوکرئ بيا مندلو نه وي

"Third—that man who MAY HAVE BEEN REMOVED from his office or situation, and who may have no hope of obtaining it again."—*Kalīlah wo Damnah.*

ماضي شرطيه PAST CONDITIONAL TENSE.

کاشکي دا ځوي هيڅري له عدمَ په وجود راغلي نه واي او مينه محبت خما په ځغه باندِ نه واي
چه دَ دي دپاره دا نيولي په ناحق وَجلئ شوي نه ويَ

"Would to God that this son from non-existence had not come into being! that my love and affection had not been placed on him! and this weasel HAD NOT BEEN unjustly KILLED on his account!"—*Kalīlah wo Damnah.*

398. There is another method of forming the passive voice by using the imperfect tense of verbs with the auxiliaries, but it is peculiar to the transitive verbs, and is not used in forming the compound tenses of the passive. For the singular, the third person is used for all three persons, and the third person plural for the plural forms. The following are examples :

صيغه حال PRESENT TENSE.

ځنکندن که هرڅو ترښخ و تلخ وايه شي　　ستا دَ لبو په مدد آبِ حيوان دي

"The agony of death, although it IS CALLED so bitter and so sharp ;
Yet, by the help of thy sweet lips, it is the water of immortality."—*Eabd-ur-Raḥmān.*

دا اته وارِه صفات ذاتيه ور ته ويل شي تل له ذاتَ سره قديم وارِه بلل شي

"The whole of these eight qualities (of God) ARE CALLED natural, and together with the essence itself, ARE TERMED primitive and pristine."—*Fawā'id-us͟h-S͟harī'at'h.*

ماضي استمرار IMPERFECT TENSE.

تر ڊِ حدَ دوي کاته څو ښکاريدَ شه دَغه پس شه شاد و مصر ته ګردان

"They continued to look towards him as long as he WAS BEING SEEN,
After which the king set out on his return to Egypt."—*Saif-ul-Mulūk.*

2ND FORM FOR THE مدامي OR CONTINUATIVE TENSE.

دوي به وائي عملونَ څموږ دا وؤ چه په مسجد به موږ په دسي وقت حاضر شؤ چه اذانونَ به هلته واوريدَ شؤ

"They will say, 'Our practices were, that we used to be present in the mosque at such a time, that there WE always USED TO HEAR the calls to prayer."—*Fawā'id-ush-Sharī'æa'h.*

ماضي مطلق PAST TENSE.

پادشاه په غضب شه او دَ دِ خبري تحقيق ؤ فرمايه پس قاصد ؤ نيود شه او خط ؤ لوَستي شه

"The king became enraged and ordered a solution of the matter. So the messenger WAS SEIZED and the epistle WAS READ."—*Gulistān.*

مستقبل 2ND FUTURE TENSE.

پس له مرګَ به حساب له سړي غوښت شي په انداز او په مقدار دَ دِ دنيا

"After death an account WILL BE REQUIRED from every man,
According to the number of the sins of this world."—*Æabd-ur-Rahmān.*

مضارع AORIST TENSE.

که له چا دسي رنګ خبره واوريده شي چه پر کفر لازم کيږي حکم دَ کفر پر دَغه مه کولي بويه کند بي قصدَ ئي له ژبي وي وتلي يا په معني ئي نه پوهيږي په دا نه کافر کيږي

"If such a speech MAY BE HEARD from any person, on which certain blasphemy ariseth, it is not necessary to adjudge it as such on that account alone; for it may have fallen from him unintentionally, or perhaps he may not understand its signification; and therefore he does not become a blasphemer on that account."—*Fawā'id-ush-Sharī'æa'h.*

ماضي شرطي، PAST CONDITIONAL TENSE.

که په خوا تر آشنايي بيلتون ليدد شوي هيڅ بنده د خداي به نه ؤد په دا کار ګد

"Before friendship ariseth, WERE but absence TO BE SEEN,
No servant of God would become mixed up in the matter."—*Æabd-ur-Rahmān.*

399. Both forms of the passive are occasionally to be met with in the same sentence; thus—

يا دا دسي رنګ وائي چه په خريدن په فروختن څو دروغ ويلي نه شي نفع سود تر منده نه شي يا دا وائي له دروغ و خيانتَ چاره نه شته چه حرام دَ خداي تعالي سپک ګنړي کافر کيږي

"Or if he thus sayeth, 'In buying and selling until falsehood IS not SPOKEN no profit IS

OBTAINED,' or if he sayeth that 'there is no expedient save in falsehood and perfidy,' in order that that which is unlawful in the sight of God be considered trivial and trifling, he becometh a blasphemer."—*Farā'īd-ush-Sharī'æa'h.*

400. After this lengthened analysis of the Pushto verbs, it will be advisable to give a table of the moods and tenses according to the arrangement with which the European learner will be best acquainted; although the Arabic method, which is the same as the Hebrew, is by far the most simple; and I imagine that few will commence Pushto who are unacquainted with Persian, and the primary rules of the Arabic Grammar which are necessary in the study of it.

401. It will be more particularly requisite to give a table of all the moods and tenses of a few imperfect and irregular intransitive verbs, on account of the varieties which they assume, and in order that they may serve as models for others; but I shall retain the simpler method in the conjugations of the regular transitives and intransitives.

402. Conjugation of the irregular imperfect intransitive verb راغلل, *rāghlal*, 'to come.'

مصدر INFINITIVE.

راغلل 'to come.'

صيغه حال PRESENT TENSE.

SINGULAR.	PLURAL.
راځم I come.	راځو we come.
راځې thou comest.	راځئ you come.
راځي he, she, it comes.	راځي they come.

ماضي استمرار IMPERFECT TENSE.

	SINGULAR.		PLURAL.
	راتللم or راتلم I was coming.		راتللو or راتلو we were coming.
	راتللې or راتلې thou wast coming.		راتللئ or راتلئ you were coming.
M.	راته or راتٙ he, *or* it was coming.	M.	راتلهٔ or راتلل they were coming.
F.	راتلله or راتله she, *or* it was coming.	F.	راتللې or راتلې / راتللِ or راتلِ they were coming.

2ND FORM AS CONTINUATIVE TENSE.

	SINGULAR.		PLURAL.
	به راغللم or به راغلم I used to come.		به راغللو or به راغلو we used to come.
	به راغللې or به راغلې thou usedst to come.		به راغللئ or به راغلئ you used to come.
M.	به راغي he, *or* it used to come.	M.	به راغلهٔ or به راغلل they used to come.
F.	به راغلله or به راغله she, *or* it used to come.	F.	به راغللې or به راغلې / به راغللِ or به راغلِ they used to come.

ماضي مطلق PAST TENSE.

SINGULAR.		PLURAL.
	راغللم or راغلم I came.	راغللو or راغلو we came.
	راغللي or راغلي thou camest.	راغللي or راغلي you came.
M.	راغي he, or it came.	M. راغلهٔ or راغلل they came.
F.	راغلله or راغله she, or it came.	F. راغلل or راغلِ ; راغللي or راغلي they came.

ماضي قريب PERFECT TENSE.

SINGULAR. F.	M.	PLURAL. M. AND F.
راغلِ يَم or راغلي	راغلَي يَم I have come.	راغلي يو we have come.
راغلِ ئي or راغلي	راغلَي ئي thou hast come.	راغلي ئي you have come.
راغلِ ده or راغلي	راغلَي دي he, she, it has come.	راغلي دي they have come.

ماضي بعيد PLUPERFECT TENSE.

SINGULAR. F.	M.	PLURAL.
راغلِ وُم or راغلي	راغلَي وُم I had come.	راغلي وو we had come.
راغلِ وي or راغلي	راغلَي وي thou hadst come.	راغلي وئي you had come.
راغلِ وَه or راغلي	راغلَي وُه he, she, it had come.	F. راغلِ وِ M. راغلي وو they had come.

امر حاضر 1ST FUTURE TENSE.

SINGULAR.	PLURAL.
راشَم I should come.	راشو we should come.
راشي thou shouldst come.	راشي you should come.
را دِ شي or هَغه دِ راشي he, she, it should come.	را دِ شي or هَغه دِ راشي they should come.

مستقبل 2ND FUTURE TENSE.

SINGULAR.	PLURAL.
را به شَم or زه به راشَم I will come.	را به شو or مُنگا به راشو we will come,
را به شي or ته به راشي thou wilt come.	را به شي or تاسُ به راشي you will come.
را به شي or هَغه به راشي he, she, it will come.	را به شي or هَغه به راشي they will come.

مضارع SUBJUNCTIVE OR AORIST TENSE.

SINGULAR.	PLURAL.
راشَم I may, shall, etc. come.	راشو we may, shall, etc. come.
راشي thou mayest, etc. come.	راشي you, may, shall, etc. come.
راشي he, she, it, may, etc. come.	راشي they may, shall, etc. come.

ماضي تشكيك DOUBTFUL PAST TENSE.

SINGULAR. F.	M.	PLURAL. M. AND F.
راغلِ به يَم	راغلَي به يَم I may have come.	راغلي به يو we may have come.
راغلِ به ئي	راغلَي به ئي thou mayest have come.	راغلي به ئي you may have come.
راغلِ به وي	راغلَي به وي he, she, it may have come.	راغلي به وي they may have come.

ماضي شرطيه PAST CONDITIONAL TENSE.

	SINGULAR.		PLURAL.
	که راتلم or راتللم if I had come.		که راتلو or راتللو if we had come.
	که راتلې or راتللې if thou hadst come.		که راتلئ or راتللئ if you had come.
M.	که راتهٔ or راته if he, *or* it had come.	M.	که راتلل or راتلهٔ if they had come.
F.	که راتله or که راتلله if she, *or* it had come.	F.	که راتلئ or راتللئ / که راتلِ or راتللِ } if they had come.

امر IMPERATIVE MOOD.

SINGULAR.	PLURAL.
راشه ، راشَ ، راځه or راځَ come thou.	راشئ or راځئ come you.
را دِ شي or را دِ ځي and دَغه دِ راشي or دَغه دِ راځي } let him, her, it come.	را دِ شي or را دِ ځي and دَغه دِ راشي or دَغه دِ راځي } let them come.

صيغه امكاني POTENTIAL MOOD.*

حال PRESENT.

SINGULAR. F.	SINGULAR. M.		PLURAL. M. AND F.	
راتلِ شَم	راتلَي شَم	I can come.	راتلي شو	we can come.
راتلِ شې	راتلَي شې	thou canst come.	راتلي شئ	you can come.
راتلِ شي	راتلَي شي	he, she, it can come.	راتلي شي	they can come.

ماضي PAST.

SINGULAR. F.	SINGULAR. M.		PLURAL.	
راتلِ شوم	راتلَي شوم	I could come.	راتلي شوو	we could come.
راتلِ شوې	راتلَي شوې	thou couldst come.	راتلي شوئ	you could come.
راتلِ شوه	راتلَي شه	he, she, it could come.	F. راتلِ شوِ M. شول or راتلي شوو	they could come.

مستقبل FUTURE.

SINGULAR.

F.		M.		F.		M.	
راتلِ به شَم	or	راتلَي	or	راتلِ شَم	or	زه به راتلَي	I will come.
راتلِ به شې	or	راتلَي	or	راتلِ شې	or	ته به راتلَي	thou wilt come.
راتلِ به شي	or	راتلَي	or	راتلِ شي	or	دَغه به راتلَي	he, she, it will come.

PLURAL. M. AND F.

مُنږ به راتلي شو or راتلي به شو we will come.
تاسو به راتلي شئ or راتلي به شئ you will come.
دَغه به راتلي شي or راتلي به شي they will come.

* What I have here termed the Potential Mood is really the Passive form of the intransitive verbs, which is alone used to express power, will, or obligation. I have already described the peculiarities of the Passive and Potential form of the verbs in the analysis of the different moods and tenses, which see—page 132.

اسم فاعل The Agent.

SINGULAR.		PLURAL.	
M. راتلونکیَ or راتلونیَ F. راتلونکيِ or راتلونيِ ; راتلونکِ or راتلونِ	the comer.	M. and F. راتلونکي / راتلوني	the comers.

اسم مفعول Past Participle.

SINGULAR.		PLURAL.
F. راغلي or راغلِ	M. راغلیَ come.	M. and F. راغلي come.

اسم لیاقت Noun of Fitness.

دَ راتلو or دَ راتللو or دَ راتلْ or دَ راتللْ of, *or* for coming.

403. The imperfect and irregular intransitive تَلل *t'lal*, 'to go.'

مصدر Infinitive.

تَلل 'to go.'

صیغهٔ حال Present Tense.

SINGULAR.	PLURAL.
ځَم I go.	ځُو we go.
ځي thou goest.	ځئ you go.
ځي he, she, it goes.	ځي they go.

ماضي استمرار Imperfect Tense.

	SINGULAR.		PLURAL.
	تَلم or تَللم I was going.		تَلو or تَللو we were going.
	تَلي or تَللي thou wast going.		تَلئ or تَللئ you were going.
M.	تهَ or تَ he, *or* it was going.	M.	تَلل or تَلهٔ they were going.
F.	تَله or تَلله she, *or* it was going.	F.	تَللي or تَلي ; تَللِ or تَلِ they were going.

2nd Form as Continuative Tense.

	SINGULAR.			PLURAL.	
	به لارم or به وُ لارم	I used to go.		به لارو or به وُ لارو	we used to go.
	به لاري or به وُ لاري	thou usedst to go.		به لارئ or به وُ لارئ	you used to go.
M.	به لار or به وُ لار	he, *or* it used to go.	M.	به لارل or به وُ لارل به لارهٔ or به وُ لارهٔ	they used to go.
F.	به لاره or به وُ لاره به لارَ or به وُ لارَ به لارله or به وُ لارله به لارلَ or به وُ لارلَ	she, *or* it used to go.	F.	به لاري or به وُ لاري به لارِ or به وُ لارِ به لارلي or به وُ لارلي به لارلِ or به وُ لارلِ	they used to go.

ماضي مطلق Past Tense.

Singular.		Plural.	
لاړم or لاړلم وُ لاړم or وُ لاړلم	I went.	لاړوُ or لاړلوُ وُ لاړوُ or وُ لاړلوُ	we went.
لاړيْ or لاړليْ وُ لاړيْ or وُ لاړليْ	thou wentest.	لاړيِ or لاړليِ وُ لاړيِ or وُ لاړليِ	you went.
M. لاړ or وُ لاړ	he, *or* it went.	M. لاړل or وُ لاړل لاړهٔ or وُ لاړهٔ	they went.
F. لاړه or وُ لاړه لاړله or وُ لاړله لاړلَ or وُ لاړلَ	she, *or* it went.	F. لاړيْ or وُ لاړيْ لاړليْ or وُ لاړليْ لاړِ or وُ لاړِ	they went.

ماضي قريب Perfect Tense.

Singular. F.	Singular. M.		Plural. M. and F.	
تَلِ or ټَللِ يَم	تَلَيَ or ټَللَيَ يَم	I have gone.	تَلِي or ټَللِي يوُ	we have gone.
تَلِ or ټَللِ ئيْ	تَلَيَ or ټَللَيَ ئيْ	thou hast gone.	تَلِي or ټَللِي ئيِ	you have gone.
تَلِ or ټَللِ دد	تَلَيَ or ټَللَيَ دي	he, she, it has gone.	تَلِي or ټَللِي دِي	they have gone.

ماضي بعيد Pluperfect Tense.

Singular. F.	Singular. M.		Plural.	
تَلِ or ټَللِ وُم	تَلَيَ or ټَللَىَ وُم	I had gone.	تَلِي or ټَللِي ووُ	we had gone.
تَلِ or ټَللِ ويْ	تَلَيَ or ټَللَيَ ويْ	thou hadst gone.	تَلِي or ټَللِي وئِي	you had gone.
تَلِ or ټَللِ وَه	تَلَيَ or ټَللَيَ وُه	he, she, it had gone.	M. تَلِي or ټَللِي ووُ	they had gone.
			F. تَلِي or ټَللِي وِ or ويْ	they had gone.

امر حاضر 1st Future Tense.

Singular.		Plural.	
لاړ شَم	I should go.	لاړ شوُ	we should go.
لاړ شيْ	thou shouldst go.	لاړ شيِ	you should go.
هَغه دِ لاړ شيِ or لاړ دِ شيِ	he, she, it should go.	هَغه دِ لاړ شي or لاړ دِ شي	they should go.

مستقبل 2nd Future Tense.

Singular.		Plural.	
زه به لاړ شَم or لاړ به شَم	I will go.	مُوږ به لاړ شوُ or لاړ به شوُ	we will go.
ته به لاړ شيْ or لاړ به شيْ	thou wilt go.	تاسُ به لاړ شيِ or لاړ به شيِ	you will go.
هَغه به لاړ شيِ or لاړ به شيِ	he, she, it will go.	هغه به لاړ شيِ or لاړ به شيِ	they will go.

مضارع Subjunctive or Aorist Tense.

SINGULAR.	PLURAL.
لاړ شَم I may, shall, *or* will go.	لاړ شُو we may, shall, *or* will go.
لاړ شې thou mayest, shalt, *or* wilt go.	لاړ شئ you may, shall, *or* will go.
لاړ شي he, she, it may, shall, *or* will go.	لاړ شي they may, shall, *or* will go.

ماضي تشكيك Doubtful Past Tense.

	SINGULAR.		PLURAL.
M.	تَلَي or تْلَلَي به یم	I may have gone.	تَلِي or تْلَلِي به یُو we may have gone.
F.	تَلِ or تْلَلِ به یَم		
M.	تَلَي or تْلَلَي به ئې	thou mayest have gone.	تَلِي or تْلَلِي به ئي you may have gone.
F.	تَلِ or تْلَلِ به ئې		
M.	تَلَي or تْلَلَي به وي	he, she, it may have gone.	تَلِي or تْلَلِي به وي they may have gone.
F.	تَلِ or تْلَلِ به وي		

ماضي شرطيه Past Conditional Tense.

	SINGULAR.		PLURAL.
	كه تَلم or تْلَلم had I gone.		كه تَلو or تْلَلو had we gone.
	كه تَلې or تْلَلې hadst thou gone.		كه تَلئ or تْلَلئ had you gone.
M.	كه تهٔ or تَ had he, *or* it gone.	M.	كه تْلَل or تْلَهٔ had they gone.
F.	كه تَله or تْلَله had she, *or* it gone.	F.	كه تَلِ or تْلَلِ had they gone.

امر Imperative Mood.

SINGULAR.	PLURAL.
لاړ شه or ور شه or ځه go thou.	لاړ شئ or ور شئ or ځئ go you.
هَغه دِ لاړ شي or لاړ دِ شي, هَغه دِ ځي or ځي دِ let him, her, it go.	هَغه دِ لاړ شي or لاړ دِ شي, هَغه دِ ځي or ځي دِ let them go.

صيغه امكاني POTENTIAL MOOD.

حال Present.

SINGULAR. F.	M.	PLURAL.
تْلَلِ شَم	تْلَلَي شَم I can go.	تْلَلِي شُو we can go.
تْلَلِ شې	تْلَلَي شې thou canst go.	تْلَلِي شئ you can go.
تْلَلِ شي	تْلَلَي شي he, she, it can go.	تْلَلِي شي they can go.

ماضي Past.

SINGULAR. F.	M.		PLURAL.	
ټللِ شوم	ټللَي شوم	I could go.	ټللي شوُ	we could go.
ټللِ شوِي	ټللَي شوِي	thou couldst go.	ټللي شِئ	you could go.
ټللِ شوه	ټللَي شه	he, she, it could go.	F. ټللي شوِ M. ټللي شوُ	they could go.

مستقبل Future.

SINGULAR. — PLURAL. M. AND F.

M. ټللَي به شَم or زه به ټللَي شَم
F. ټللِ به شَم or زه به ټللِ شَم } I shall be able to go. — ټللي به شوُ or مُنږا به ټللي شوُ we shall be able to go.

M. ټللَي به شيِ or ته به ټللَي شيِ
F. ټللِ به شيِ or ته به ټللِ شيِ } thou wilt be able to go. — ټللي به شِئ or تاسُ به ټللي شِئ you will be able to go.

M. ټللَي به شي or هَغه به ټللَي شي he, or it will be able to go. — ټللي به شي or هَغه به ټللي شي they will be able to go.

F. ټللِ به شي or هَغه به ټللِ شي she, or it will be able to go.

اسم فاعل The Agent.

SINGULAR. — PLURAL.

M. ټلونکَي or ټلونَي
F. ټلونکِي or ټلونِي ; ټلونکِ or ټلونِ } the goer. — M. and F. ټلوني or ټلونکِي goers.

اسم مفعول Past Participle.

SINGULAR. — PLURAL.

F. تَلِ or ټللِ M. تَلَي or ټللَي gone. — M. and F. تَلي or ټللي gone.

اسم لياقت Noun of Fitness.

دَ ټلُ or دَ ټللُ ; دَ تَلو or دَ ټللو of, or for going, etc.

404. Conjugation of the irregular intransitive ختل *khatal*, 'to ascend.'

مصدر Infinitive.

ختل 'to ascend.'

حال Present Tense.

SINGULAR.		PLURAL.	
خېجم or خېژم	I ascend.	خېجُو or خېژُو	we ascend.
خېجِې or خېژِې	thou ascendest.	خېجِئ or خېژِئ	you ascend.
خېجي or خېژي	he, she, it ascends.	خېجي or خېژي	they ascend.

ماضي استمرار Imperfect Tense.

Singular.		Plural.	
ختلم or ختم	I was ascending.	ختلو or ختو	we were ascending.
ختلي or ختي	thou wast ascending.	ختلئ or ختئ	you were ascending.
M. خوت	he, *or* it was ascending.	M. ختاڼه or ختل	they were ascending.
F. ختله or خته	she, *or* it was ascending.	F. ختلې or ختې ختلِ or ختِ	they were ascending.

2nd Form as Continuative Tense.

Singular.		Plural.	
به ؤ ختلم or به ؤ ختم	I used to ascend.	به ؤ ختلو or به ؤ ختو	we used to ascend.
به ؤ ختلي or به ؤ ختي	thou usedst to ascend.	به ؤ ختلئ or به ؤ ختئ	you used to ascend.
M. به ؤ خوت	he, *or* it used to ascend.	M. به ؤ ختاڼه or به ؤ ختل	they used to ascend.
F. به ؤ ختله or به ؤ خته	she, *or* it used to ascend.	F. ختلې or به ؤ ختې ختلِ or به ؤ ختِ	they used to ascend.

ماضي مطلق Past Tense.

Singular.		Plural.	
ؤ ختلم or ؤ ختم	I ascended.	ؤ ختلو or ؤ ختو	we ascended.
ؤ ختلي or ؤ ختي	thou ascendedst.	ؤ ختلئ or ؤ ختئ	you ascended.
M. ؤ خوت	he, *or* it ascended.	M. ؤ ختاڼه or ؤ ختل	they ascended.
F. ؤ ختله or ؤ خته	she, *or* it ascended.	F. ختلې or ؤ ختې ختلِ or ؤ ختِ	they ascended.

ماضي قريب Perfect Tense.

Singular. F.	M.		Plural.	
ختلِ يَم	ختلَي يَم	I have ascended.	ختلي يو	we have ascended.
ختلِ ئي	ختلَي ئي	thou hast ascended.	ختلي ئي	you have ascended.
ختلِ دَه	ختلَي دي	he, she, it has ascended.	ختلي دي	they have ascended.

ماضي بعيد Pluperfect Tense.

Singular. F.	M.		Plural.	
ختل وَم	ختلَي وُم	I had ascended.	ختلي وُو	we had ascended.
ختلِ وئ	ختلَي وئ	thou hadst ascended.	ختلي وئ	you had ascended.
ختل وَه	ختلَي وُه	he, she, it had ascended.	F. ختلي وِ M. ختلي وُو	they had ascended.

امر حاضر 1st Future Tense.

Singular.		Plural.	
ؤ خيژم or ؤ خيجم	I should ascend.	ؤ خيژو or ؤ خيجو	we should ascend.
ؤ خيژي or ؤ خيجي	thou shouldst ascend.	ؤ خيژئ or ؤ خيجئ	you should ascend.
هَغه دِ ؤ خيژي or ؤ دِ خيژي هغه دِ ؤ خيجي or ؤ دِ خيجي	he, she, it should ascend.	هَغه دِ ؤ خيژي or ؤ دِ خيژي هَغه دِ ؤ خيجي or ؤ دِ خيجي	they should ascend.

مستقبل. SECOND FUTURE TENSE.

SINGULAR.		PLURAL.	
زه به وُ خيژم or وُ به خيژم زه به وُ خيجم or وُ به خيجم	I will ascend.	مُوږ به وُ خيژُو or وُ به خيژُو مُنگا به وُ خيجُو or وُ به خيجُو	we will ascend.
ته به وُ خيژې or وُ به خيژې ته به وُ خيجې or وُ به خيجې	thou wilt ascend.	تاسُ به وُ خيژئ or وُ به خيژئ تاسُ به وُ خيجئ or وُ به خيجئ	you will ascend.
دَغه به وُ خيژي or وُ به خيژي دَغه به وُخيجي or وُ به خيجي	he, she, it will ascend.	دَغه به وُ خيژي or وُ به خيژي دَغه به وُ خيجي or وُ به خيجي	they will ascend.

مضارع. AORIST TENSE.

SINGULAR.		PLURAL.	
وُ خيژم or وُ خيجم	I may, *or* shall ascend.	وُ خيژُو or وُ خيجُو	we may, *or* shall ascend.
وُ خيژې or وُ خيجې	thou mayest, *or* shalt ascend.	وُ خيژئ or وُ خيجئ	you may, *or* shall ascend.
وُ خيژي or وُ خيجي	he, she, it may, *or* shall ascend.	وُ خيژي or وُ خيجي	they may, *or* shall ascend.

ماضي تشكيك. DOUBTFUL PAST TENSE.

SINGULAR. F.	M.		PLURAL. M. AND F.	
ختلِ به يَم	ختلَي به يَم	I may have ascended.	ختلي به يُو	we may have ascended.
ختلِ به ئې	ختلَي به ئې	thou mayest have ascended.	ختلي به ئي	you may have ascended.
ختلِ به وي	ختلَي به وي	he, she, it may have ascended.	ختلي به وي	they may have ascended.

ماضي شرطيه. PAST CONDITIONAL TENSE.

SINGULAR.			PLURAL.		
	که ختم or که ختلم	had I ascended.		که ختو or که ختلو	had we ascended.
	که ختې or که ختلې	hadst thou ascended.		که ختئ or که ختلئ	had you ascended.
M.	که خوت	had he, *or* it ascended.	M.	که ختل or که خاتهٔ	had they ascended.
F.	که خته or که ختله	had she, *or* it ascended.	F.	که ختې or ختلې که ختِ or ختلِ	had they ascended.

امر IMPERATIVE MOOD.

SINGULAR.		PLURAL.	
و خيژه or خيژه ; وُ خيجه or خيجه	ascend thou.	وُ خيژئ or وُ خيجئ	ascend you.
دَغه دِ وُ خيژي or وُ دِ خيژي دَغه دِ وُ خيجي or وُ دِ خيجي	let him, her, it ascend.	دَغه دِ وُ خيژي or وُ دِ خيژي دَغه دِ وُ خيجي or وُ دِ خيجي	let them ascend.

صيغه امكاني POTENTIAL MOOD.

حال PRESENT.

SINGULAR. F.	M.		PLURAL. M. AND F.	
ختلِ شَم	ختلَي شَم	I can ascend.	ختلي شُو	we can ascend.
ختلِ شې	ختلَي شې	thou canst ascend.	ختلي شئ	you can ascend.
ختلِ شي	ختلَي شي	he, she, it can ascend.	ختلي شي	they can ascend.

ماضي Past.

SINGULAR.		PLURAL.	
ختليَ شوم or ختلِ شوم	I could ascend.	ختلي شوُ	we could ascend.
ختليَ شوي or ختلِ شوي	thou couldst ascend.	ختلي شوي	you could ascend.
M. ختليَ شه	he, *or* it could ascend.	M. ختلي شول or ختلي شوُ	they could ascend.
F. ختلِ شوه	she, *or* it could ascend.	F. ختلِ شوِ	they could ascend.

مستقبل Future.

SINGULAR.		PLURAL. M. AND F.	
M. زه به ختليَ شَم or ختليَ به شَم F. زه به ختلِ شَم or ختلِ به شَم	I shall, *or* will be able to ascend.	مُوږ به ختلي شوُ or ختلي به شوُ	we shall, *or* will be able to ascend.
M. ته به ختليَ شي or ختليَ به شي F. ته به ختلِ شي or ختلِ به شي	thou shalt, *or* wilt be able to ascend.	تاسُ به ختلي شئ or ختلي به شئ	you shall, *or* will be able to ascend.
M. هَغه به ختليَ شي or ختليَ به شي F. هَغه به ختلِ شي or ختلِ به شي	he, she, it shall, *or* will be able to ascend.	هَغه به ختلي شي or ختلي به شي	they shall, *or* will be able to ascend.

اسم فاعل The Agent.

SINGULAR. F.	SINGULAR. M.		PLURAL. M. AND F.	
ختونکِ or ختونِ	ختونکيَ or ختونيَ	the ascender.	ختونکي or ختوني	the ascenders.

اسم مفعول Past Participle.

SINGULAR.			PLURAL.	
F. ختلِ	M. ختليَ	ascended.	M. and F. ختلي	ascended.

اسم لياقت Noun of Fitness.

M. and F. دَ ختلو or دَ ختلُ ; دَ ختو or دَ ختٓ of *or* for ascending. S. and P.

405. The following is a paradigm of a regular intransitive verb, according to the system of the Arabian and Hebrew Grammarians, as referred to at paragraph 208. The active participle denotes the agent, and the passive participle the object acted on. The method of forming the different compound tenses by the aid of the auxiliary has already been explained in the analysis of the moods and tenses, which see.

مصدر Infinitive.

زغليدل *z'ghaledal*, 'to run.'

صيغه معروف ACTIVE VOICE.

ماضي Past Tense.

SINGULAR.		PLURAL.	
M. وُ زغليدَ or وُ زغليده	he, *or* it ran.	M. وُ زغليدل or وُ زغليدهُ	they ran.
F. وُ زغليده or وُ زغليدله	she, *or* it ran.	F. وُ زغليدِ or وُ زغليدلِ	they ran.
M. and F. وُ زغليدي or وُ زغليدلي	thou didst run.	M. and F. وُ زغليدئ or وُ زغليدلئ	you ran.
M. and F. وُ زغليدم or وُ زغليدلم	I ran.	M. and F. وُ زغليدوُ or وُ زغليدلوُ	we ran.

مضارع Aorist Tense.

Singular.	Plural.
وُ زغلي he, she, it runs, *or* may run.	وُ زغلي they run, *or* may run.
وُ زغلي thou runnest, *or* mayest run.	وُ زغلي you run, *or* may run.
وُ زغلم I run, *or* may run.	وُ زغلوُ we run, *or* may run.

امر Imperative Mood.

Singular.	Plural.
دَغه دِ وُ زغلي or وُ دِ زغلي / دَغه دِ زغلي or زغلي دِ } let him, her, it run.	دَغه دِ وُ زغلي or وُ دِ زغلي / دَغه دِ زغلي or زغلي دِ } let them run.
وُ زغله or وُ زغلَ, زغله or زغلَ run thou, *or* do thou run.	وُ زغلي or زغلي run you, *or* do you run.

اسم فاعل Active Participle.

Singular.	Plural.
M. زغليدونكَي or زغليدونَي } the runner.	M. and F. { زغليدونكي / زغليدوني } the runners.
F. زغليدونكِ or زغليدونِ	

صيغه مجهول PASSIVE VOICE (used as the POTENTIAL MOOD).

ماضي Past Tense.

Singular.	Plural.
M. زغليدَي or زغليدلَي شه he, *or* it could run.	M. زغليدي شول or شوُ } they could run.
F. زغليدِ or زغليدلِ شوه she, *or* it could run.	F. زغليدلي شولِ or شو
M. زغليدَي or زغليدلَي شوي / F. زغليدِ or زغليدلِ شوي } thou couldst run.	M. and F. زغليدي or زغليدلي } شوئ you could run.
M. زغليدَي or زغليدلَي شوم / F. زغليدِ or زغليدلِ شوم } I could run.	M. and F. زغليدي or زغليدلي } شوُ we could run.

مضارع Aorist Tense.

Singular.	Plural. M. and F.
M. زغليدَي or زغليدلَي شي he, *or* it can run.	زغليدي or زغليدلي شي they can run.
F. زغليدِ or زغليدلِ شي she, *or* it can run.	
M. زغليدَي or زغليدلَي شي / F. زغليدِ or زغليدلِ شي } thou canst run.	زغليدي or زغليدلي شئ you can run.
M. زغليدَي or زغليدلَي شم / F. زغليدِ or زغليدلِ شم } I can run.	زغليدي or زغليدلي شوُ we can run.

امر Imperative Mood.

Singular.	Plural.
M. دَغه دِ زغليدلَي شي or زغليدلَي دِ شي } let him, *or* it be able to run.	دَغه دِ زغليدلي شي or زغليدلي دِ شي } let them be able to run.
F. دَغه دِ زغليدلِ شي or زغليدلِ دِ شي } let her, *or* it be able to run.	
زغليدلَي شه or وُ شه be thou able to run.	زغليدلي شئ or وُ شئ be you able to run.

406. The following is the conjugation of the imperfect transitive verb كول 'to do,' 'to make,' or 'perform,' which is chiefly used as an auxiliary in forming the inflections of other verbs. The compound tenses are wanting.

مصدر INFINITIVE.

كول *kawul*, 'to do.'

صيغه حال PRESENT TENSE.

SINGULAR.	PLURAL.
كوم I do.	كوو we do.
كوې thou doest.	كوئ you do.
كاندِ or كا or كوي he, she, it does.	كاندِ or كا or كوي they do.

ماضي استمرار IMPERFECT TENSE (*Governing noun singular*).

SINGULAR.

F. كوله etc. ما M. كڼ, كه, كا, هِغِه كاوه or هَغه, تا, ما I, thou, he, it, she was doing.

PLURAL.

F. كوله etc. مُنگا M. كڼ, كه, كا, هُغو كاوه or تاسُ, مُنگا we, you, they were doing.

(*Governing noun plural*).

SINGULAR.

F. كولِ etc. ما M. هِغِه كول or هَغه, تا, ما I, thou, he, it, she was doing.

PLURAL.

F. كولِ etc. مورِ M. هُغو كول or تاسُ, مُورِ we, you, they were doing.

SECOND FORM—(*Governing noun singular*).

SINGULAR.

F. كوله etc. مي M. كڼ or كه, كا, ئي كاوه or دِ, مي I, thou, he, it, she was doing.

PLURAL.

F. كوله etc. مو M. كڼ or كه, كا, ئي كاوه or مو, مو we, you, they were doing.

(*Governing noun plural*).

SINGULAR.

F. كولِ etc. مي M. ئي كول or دِ, مي I, thou, he, it, she was doing.

PLURAL.

F. كولِ etc. مو M. ئي كول or مو, مو we, you, they were doing.

IMPERFECT USED AS CONTINUATIVE. (M. AND F.)

SINGULAR.

وُ كڼ or وُ كا, وُ كه به etc. ما or كڼ or كا, به كه هِغِه or هَغه, تا, ما I, thou, he, it, she used to do.

PLURAL.

وُ كڼ or وُ كا, وُ كه به etc. مُنگا or كڼ or كا, به كه هُغو or تاسُ, مُورِ we, you, they used to do.

SECOND FORM.

SINGULAR.

وُ كڼ or وُ كا, وُ كه etc. به مي or كڼ or كا, ئي كه or دِ, به مي I, thou, he, it, she used to do.

PLURAL.

به مؤ، مو or ئي كه، كا or كڼَ or به مؤ etc. ؤ كه، ؤ كا or ؤ كڼَ we, you, they used to do.

ماضي مطلق PAST TENSE (M. and F.)

SINGULAR.

ما، تا، هَغه or هِغِه، ؤ كه or ؤ كا or ؤ كڼَ or ما* etc. كه، كا or كڼَ I, thou, he, it, she did.

PLURAL.

مُنگا، تاسُ or هُغو ؤ كه، ؤ كا or ؤ كڼَ or مؤږ etc. كه، كا or كڼَ we, you, they did.

SECOND FORM.

SINGULAR.

ؤ مي، دِ or ئي كه، كا or كڼَ or مي etc. كه، كا or كڼَ I, thou, he, it, she did.

PLURAL.

ؤ مؤ، مو or ئي كه، كا or كڼَ or مؤ etc. كه، كا or كڼَ we, you, they did.

امر حاضر 1ST FUTURE TENSE.

SINGULAR.		PLURAL.	
ؤ كم	I should do.	ؤ كؤ	we should do.
ؤ كړْي	thou shouldst do.	ؤ كِي	you should do.
هَغه دِ ؤ كِي، دِ ؤ كاندِ or دِ ؤ كا ؤ دِ كِي، ؤ دِ كاندِ or ؤ دِ كا	he, she, it should do.	هَغه دِ ؤ كِي، دِ ؤ كاندِ or دِ ؤ كا ؤ دِ كِي، ؤ دِ كاندِ or ؤ دِ كا	they should do.

مستقبل 2ND FUTURE TENSE.

SINGULAR.		PLURAL.	
زه به ؤ كم or ؤ به كم	I will do.	مؤږ به ؤ كؤ or ؤ به كؤ	we will do.
ته به ؤ كړْي or ؤ به كړْي	thou wilt do.	تاسُ به ؤ كِي or ؤ به كِي	you will do.
هَغه به ؤ كِي، به ؤ كاندِ or به ؤ كا ؤ به كِي، ؤ به كاندِ or ؤ به كا	he, she, it will do.	هَغه به ؤ كِي، به ؤ كاندِ or به ؤ كا ؤ به كِي، ؤ به كاندِ or ؤ به كا	they will do.

مضارع AORIST TENSE.

SINGULAR.		PLURAL.	
ؤ كم	I may, *or* shall do.	ؤ كؤ	we may, *or* shall do.
ؤ كړْي	thou mayest, *or* shalt do.	ؤ كِي	you may, *or* shall do.
ؤ كِي، ؤ كاندِ or ؤ كا	he, she, it may, *or* shall do.	ؤ كِي، ؤ كاندِ or ؤ كا	they may, *or* shall do.

امر IMPERATIVE MOOD.

SINGULAR.		PLURAL.	
كه or ؤ كه، كوه or ؤ كوه	do thou.	كِي، ؤ كِي، ؤ كانږِي or كوئِي or ؤ كوئِي	do you.
هَغه دِ ؤ كِي، دِ ؤ كاندِ or دِ ؤ كا ؤ دِ كِي، ؤ دِ كاندِ or ؤ دِ كا	let him, her, it do.	هَغه دِ ؤ كِي، دِ ؤ كاندِ or دِ ؤ كا ؤ دِ كِي، ؤ دِ كاندِ or ؤ دِ كا	let them do.

اسم فاعل THE AGENT.

SINGULAR.			PLURAL.	
M.	كوونكَي or كوونَي	the doer.	M. and F. كوونكِي كوونِي	the doers.
F.	كوونكِ or كوونِ			

* The ؤ (the sign of the past) is omitted at times in this tense; but *only* when the verb is used as an auxiliary.

اسم لياقت Noun of Fitness.

دَ كوُ or دَ كوو ,دَ كولُ or دَ كولو of, *or* for doing.

مصدر Infinitive.

كړل *k'rral*, 'to do.'

صيغه حال Present Tense.

SINGULAR.		PLURAL.	
كړم	I do.	كړوُ	we do.
كړئ	thou doest.	كړئ	you do.
كړي	he, she, *or* it does.	كړي	they do.

ماضي استمرار Imperfect Tense—(*Governing noun singular*).

SINGULAR.

F. كړله or كړه or M. هغه كړ or هَغه ,تا ,ما I, thou, he, it, she was doing.

PLURAL.

F. كړله or كړه or M. هُغو كړ or تاسُ ,مُوږ we, you, they were doing.

(*Governing noun plural*).

SINGULAR.

F. كړلي or كړي or M. هغه كړل or هَغه ,تا ,ما I, thou, he, it, she was doing.

PLURAL.

F. كړلي or كړي or M. هُغو كړل or تاسُ ,مُنگا we, you, they were doing.

Second Form—(*Governing noun singular*).

SINGULAR.

F. كړله or كړه or M. ئي كړ or دِ ,مي I, thou, he, it, she was doing.

PLURAL.

F. كړله or كړه or M. ئي كړ or مو ,موُ we, you, they were doing.

Second Form—(*Governing noun plural*).

SINGULAR.

F. كړلي or كړي or M. ئي كړل or دِ ,مي I, thou, he, it, she was doing.

PLURAL.

F. كړلي or كړي or M. ئي كړل or مو ,موُ we, you, they were doing.

Second Form of Imperfect *as the* Continuative—(*Governing noun singular*).

SINGULAR.

F. به وُ كړله or به وُ كړه or M. هغه به وُ كړ or هَغه ,تا ,ما I, thou, he, it, she used to do.

PLURAL.

F. به وُ كړله or به وُ كړه or M. هُغو به وُ كړ or تاسُ ,مُوږ we, you, they used to do.

(*Governing noun plural*).

SINGULAR.

F. به وُ كړلي or به وُ كړي or M. هغه به وُ كړل or هَغه ,تا ,ما I, thou, he, it, she used to do.

PLURAL.

F. به وُ كړلي or به وُ كړي or M. هُغو به وُ كړل or تاسُ ,مُنگا we, you, they used to do.

SECOND FORM—(*Noun singular*).

SINGULAR.

F. وُ كړله or وُ كړه etc. به مي M. وُ كړ يې or دِ, به مي I, thou, he, it, she used to do.

PLURAL.

F. وُ كړله or وُ كړه etc. به مؤ M. وُ كړ يې or مو, مؤ به we, you, they used to do.

(*Noun plural*).

SINGULAR.

F. وُ كړلې or وُ كړې etc. به مي M. وُ كړل يې or دِ, به مي I, thou, he, it, she used to do.

PLURAL.

F. وُ كړلې or وُ كړې etc. به مؤ M. وُ كړل يې or مو, مؤ به we, you, they used to do.

ماضي مطلق PAST TENSE—(*For a noun singular*).

SINGULAR.

F. وُ كړله or وُ كړه or M. وُ كړ هِغِه or هَغه, تا, ما I, thou, he, it, she did.

PLURAL.

F. وُ كړله or وُ كړه or M. هُغو وُ كړ or مُوږ, تاسُ we, you, they did.

(*For a noun plural*).

SINGULAR.

F. وُ كړلې or وُ كړې or M. هِغِه وُ كړل or هَغه, تا, ما I, thou, he, it, she did.

PLURAL.

F. وُ كړلې or وُ كړې or M. هُغو وُ كړل or مُوږ, تاسُ we, you, they did.

SECOND FORM—(*For a noun singular*).

SINGULAR.

F. كړله etc. وُ مي or كړه etc. وُ مي M. يې كړ or دِ, وُ مي I, thou, he, it, she did.

PLURAL.

F. كړله etc. وُ مؤ or كړه etc. وُ مؤ M. يې كړ or مو, وُ مؤ we, you, they did.

(*For a noun plural*).

SINGULAR.

F. كړلې etc. وُ مي or كړې etc. وُ مي M. يې كړل or دِ, وُ مي I, thou, he, it, she did.

PLURAL.

F. كړلې etc. وُ مؤ or كړې etc. وُ مؤ M. يې كړل or مو, وُ مؤ we, you, they did.

ماضي قريب PERFECT TENSE—(*For a noun singular*).

SINGULAR.

F. كړِ دَه or M. هِغِه كړِيَ دي or هَغه, تا, ما I, thou, he, it, she have done.

PLURAL.

F. كړِ دَه or M. هُغو كړِيَ دي or مُوږ, تاسُ we, you, they have done.

(*For a noun plural*).

SINGULAR.

M. and F. هِغِه كړي دي or هَغه, تا, ما I, thou, he, it, she have done.

PLURAL.

M. and F. هُغو كړي دي or مُنگا, تاسُ we, you, they have done.

SECOND FORM—(*For a noun singular*).

SINGULAR.

F. کړِدَه or M. کړيَ دي, ئي or دِ, مي I, thou, he, it, she have done.

PLURAL.

F. کړِدَه or M. کړيَ دي, ئي or مو, مو I we, you, they have done.

(*For a noun plural*).

SINGULAR.

M. and F. ئي کړي دي or دِ, مي I, thou, he, it, she have done.

PLURAL.

M. and F. ئي کړي دي or مو, مو we, you, they have done.

ماضي بعيد PLUPERFECT TENSE—(*The noun singular*).

SINGULAR.

F. کړِوَه or M. هغه کړيَ وَه or هَغه, تا, ما I, thou, he, it, she had done.

PLURAL.

F. کړِوَه or M. هُغو کړيَ وَه or تاسُ, مُوږ we, you, they had done.

(*The noun plural*).

SINGULAR.

M. and F. هغه کړي وُه or هَغه, تا, ما I, thou, he, it, she had done.

PLURAL.

M. and F. هُغو کړي وُه or تاسُ, مُنګا we, you, they had done.

SECOND FORM—(*The noun singular*).

SINGULAR.

F. کړِوَه or M. ئي کړيَ وَه or دِ, مي I, thou, he, it, she had done.

PLURAL.

F. کړِوَه or M. ئي کړيَ وَه or مو, مو we, you, they had done.

(*The noun plural*).

SINGULAR.

M. and F. ئي کړي وُه or دِ, مي I, thou, he, it, she had done.

PLURAL.

M. and F. ئي کړي وُه or مو, مو we, you, they had done.

امر حاضر FIRST FUTURE TENSE.

SINGULAR.

وُ کړم I should do.

وُ کړې thou shouldst do.

هَغه دِ وُ کړي or وُ دِ کړي he, she, it should do.

PLURAL.

وُ کړو we should do.

وُ کړئ you should do.

هَغه دِ وُ کړي or وُ دِ کړي they should do.

مستقبل SECOND FUTURE TENSE.

SINGULAR.

زه به وُ کړم or وُ به کړم I will do.

ته به وُ کړې or وُ به کړې thou wilt do.

هَغه به وُ کړي or وُ به کړي he, she, it will do.

PLURAL.

مُوږ به وُ کړو or وُ به کړو we will do.

تاسُ به وُ کړئ or وُ به کړئ you will do.

هَغه به وُ کړي وُ به کړي they will do.

ماضي تشكيك DOUBTFUL PAST TENSE—(*Noun singular*).

SINGULAR.

F. به كړِوِي or M. ما, تا, هَغه or هِغِه به کړيَ وِي I, thou, he, it, she may have done.

PLURAL.

F. به کړِوِي or M. مُوږ, تاسُ or هُغو به کړيَ وِي we, you, they may have done.

(*Noun plural*).

SINGULAR.

M. and F. ما, تا هَغه or هِغِه به کړِي وِي I, thou, he, it, she may have done.

PLURAL.

M. and F. مُوږ, تاسُ or هُغو به کړِي وِي we, you, they may have done.

SECOND FORM—(*Noun singular*).

SINGULAR.

F. به مي etc. کړِ وِي or M. به مي, دِ or ئي کړيَ وِي I, thou, he, it, she may have done.

PLURAL.

F. به مؤ etc. کړِوِي or M. به مؤ, مو or ئي کړيَ وِي we, you, they may have done.

(*Noun plural*).

SINGULAR.

به مي, دِ or ئي کړِي وِي I, thou, he, it, she may have done.

PLURAL.

به مؤ, مو or ئي کړِي وِي we, you, they may have done.

ماضي شرطيه PAST CONDITIONAL TENSE—(*Noun singular*).

SINGULAR.

F. که ما etc. کړِوِي or واي M. که ما, تا, هَغه or هِغِه کړيَ وِي or واي if I, thou, he, it, she had done.

PLURAL.

F. که مُوږ etc. کړِوِي or واي M. که مُوږ, تاسُ or هُغو کړيَ وِي or واي if we, you, they had done.

(*Noun plural*).

SINGULAR.

M. and F. که ما, تا, هَغه or هِغِه کړِي وِي or واي if I, thou, he, it, she had done.

PLURAL.

M. and F. که مُنگا, تاسُ or هُغو کړِي وِي or واي if we, you, they had done.

SECOND FORM—(*Noun singular*).

SINGULAR.

F. که مي etc. کړِوِي or واي M. که مي, دِ or ئي کړيَ وِي or واي if I, thou, he, it, she had done.

PLURAL.

F. که مؤ etc. کړِوِي or واي M. که مؤ, مو or ئي کړيَ وِي or واي if we, you, they had done.

(*Noun plural*).

SINGULAR.

M. and F. که مي, د or ئي کړِي وِي or واي if I, thou, he, it, she had done.

PLURAL.

M. and F. که مؤ, مو or ئي کړِي وِي or واي if we, you, they had done.

امر Imperative Mood.

Singular.	Plural.
كرِ or وُ كرِ do thou.	كريُ or وُ كريُ do you.
وُ دِ كري or هَغه دِ وُ كري let him, her, it do.	وُ دِ كري or هَغه دِ وُ كري let them do.

اسم فاعل The Agent.

	Singular.		Plural.
M.	كرونكي or كروني } the doer.	M. and F.	كرونكي or كروني } the doers.
F.	كرونكې or كرونِ		

اسم مفعول Past Participle.

Singular.	Plural.
F. كرِ M. كړي done.	M. and F. كړي done.

اسم لياقت Noun of Fitness.

M. and F. دَ كړُ or دَ كرو دَ كرلُ or دَ كرلو of *or* for doing. S. and P.

صيغه مجهول PASSIVE VOICE.

حال Present Tense.

Singular. F.	M.		Plural. M. and F.	
كرِ شم	كړي شم	I am done.	كړي شو	we are done.
كرِ شې	كړي شې	thou art done.	كړي شئ	you are done.
كرِ شي	كړي شي	he, she, it is done.	كړي شي	they are done.

ماضي استمرار Imperfect Tense.

Singular. F.	M.		Plural. M. and F.	
كرِ شوم	كړي شوم	I was doing.	كړي شوو	we were doing.
كرِ شوې	كړي شوې	thou wast doing.	كړي شوئ	you were doing.
	كړي شه	he, *or* it was doing.	M. كړي شول or شو	they were doing.
كرِ شوله	كرِ شود	she, *or* it was doing.	F. كړي شو or شولِ	

Second Form for Continuative Tense.

Singular. F.	M.		Plural. M. and F.	
به وُ كرِ شوم	به وُ كړي شوم	I used to be doing.	به وُ كړي شوو	we used to be doing.
به وُ كرِ شوې	به وُ كړي شوې	thou usedst to be doing.	به وُ كړي شوئ	you used to be doing.
	به وُ كړي شه	he, *or* it used to be doing.	به وُ كړي شول or شو	they used to be doing.
شوله or به وُ كرِ شود		she, *or* it used to be doing.	به وُ كړي شو شولِ	

ماضي مطلق Past Tense.

Singular. F.	M.		Plural. M. and F.	
وُ كرِ شوم	وُ كړي شوم	I was done.	وُ كړي شوو	we were done.
وُ كرِ شوې	وُ كړي شوې	thou wast done.	وُ كړي شوئ	you were done.
	وُ كړي شه	he, *or* it was done.	وُ كړي شول or شو	they were done.
شوله or وُ كرِ شود		she, *or* it was done.	وُ كړي شو or شولِ	

ماضي قريب. PERFECT TENSE.

SINGULAR F.	M.		PLURAL M. AND F.	
كړِ شوِ يم	كړيَ شوي يم	I have been done.	كړي شوي يو	we have been done.
كړِ شوِ يې	كړيَ شوي يې	thou hast been done.	كړي شوي يئ	you have been done.
	كړيَ شوي دي	he, *or* it has been done.	كړي شوي دي	they have been done.
	كړِ شوِ ده	she, *or* it has been done.		

ماضي بعيد. PLUPERFECT TENSE.

SINGULAR F.	M.		PLURAL		
كړِ شوِ وُم	كړيَ شوي وُم	I had been done.	M. and F.	كړي شوي وُو	we had been done.
كړِ شوِ وې	كړيَ شوي وې	thou hadst been done.	M. and F.	كړي شوي وئ	you had been done.
	كړيَ شوي وُه	he, *or* it had been done.	M.	كړي شوي وُو	they had been done.
	كړِ شوِ وَه	she, *or* it had been done.	F.	كړي شوي وِ	they had been done.

امر حاضر 1ST FUTURE TENSE.

SINGULAR					PLURAL M. AND F.	
F.	وُ كړِ شم	M.	وُ كړيَ شم	I should be done.	وُ كړي شُو	we should be done.
F.	وُ كړِ شې	M.	وُ كړيَ شې	thou shouldst be done.	وُ كړي شئ	you should be done.
M.	وُ دِ كړيَ شي or هَغه دِ وُ كړيَ شي			he, *or* it should be done.	هَغه دِ وُ كړي شي or وُ دِ كړي شي	they should be done.
F.	وُ دِ كړِ شي or هَغه دِ وُ كړِ شي			she, *or* it should be done.		

مستقبل. 2ND FUTURE TENSE.

	SINGULAR		PLURAL M. AND F.	
M.	زه به وُ كړيَ شم or وُ كړيَ به شم	I will be done.	مُونږ به وُ كړي شُو or وُ كړي به شُو	we will be done.
F.	زه به وُ كړِ شم or وُ كړِ به شم			
M.	ته به وُ كړيَ شې or وُ كړيَ به شې	thou wilt be done.	تاسُ به وُ كړي شئ or وُ كړي به شئ	you will be done.
F.	ته به وُ كړِ شې or وُ كړِ به شې			
M.	هَغه به وُ كړيَ شي or وُ كړيَ به شي	he, *or* it will be done.	هَغه به وُ كړي شي or وُ كړي به شي	they will be done.
F.	هَغه به وُ كړِ شي or وُ كړِ به شي	she, *or* it will be done.		

مضارع. AORIST TENSE.

SINGULAR F.	M.		PLURAL M. AND F.	
وُ كړِ شم	وُ كړيَ شم	I may, *or* shall be done.	وُ كړي شُو	we may, *or* shall be done.
وُ كړِ شې	وُ كړيَ شې	thou mayest, *or* shalt be done.	وُ كړي شئ	you may, *or* shall be done.
وُ كړِ شي	وُ كړيَ شي	he, she, it may, *or* shall be done.	وُ كړي شي	they may, *or* shall be done.

ماضي تشكيک Doubtful Past Tense.

Singular F.	Singular M.		Plural M. and F.	
کړِشَوِ به یم	کړِيَ شَوي به یم	I may have been done.	کړِي شَوِي به یو	we may have been done.
کړِشَوِ به ئي	کړِيَ شَوي به ئي	thou mayest have been done.	کړِي شَوِي به ئي	you may have been done.
کړِشَوِ به وِي	کړِيَ شَوي به وِي	he, she, it may have been done.	کړِي شَوِي به وِي	they may have been done.

ماضي شرطيه Past Conditional Tense.

	Singular		Plural M. and F.	
M.	که زه کړِيَ شَوي وِي or واي	If I had been done.	که مُنگا کړِي شَوِي وِي or واي	If we had been done.
F.	که زه کړِشَوِ وِي or واي			
M.	که ته کړِيَ شَوي وِي or واي	If thou hadst been done.	که تاسُ کړِي شَوِي وِي or واي	If you had been done.
F.	که ته کړِشَوِ وِي or واي			
M.	که هَغه کړِيَ شَوي وِي or واي	If he, *or* it had been done.	که هَغه کړِي شَوِي وِي or واي	If they had been done.
F.	که هَغه کړِشَوِ وِي or واي	If she, *or* it had been done.		

امر Imperative Mood.

	Singular		Plural M. and F.	
M.	وُ کړِيَ شه or کړِيَ شه	be thou done.	وُ کړِي شِي or کړِي شِي	be you done.
F.	وُ کړِشه or کړِشه			
M.	هَغه دِ وُ کړِيَ شِي or وُ دِ کړِيَ شِي	let him, *or* it be done.	هَغه دِ وُ کړِي شِي or وُ دِ کړِي شِي	let them be done.
F.	هَغه دِ وُ کړِشِي or وُ دِ کړِشِي	let her, *or* it be done.		

اسم مفعول Past Participle.

Singular		Plural	
F. کړِشَوِ M. کړِيَ شَوي	become done.	M. and F. کړِي شَوِي	become done.

407. Conjugation of a transitive verb which rejects the prefix وُ.

مصدر Infinitive.

راوړل *rāw-ṟṟal*, 'to bring.'

صيغه معروف ACTIVE VOICE.

ماضي Past Tense—(*Governing noun singular*).

SINGULAR.

F. راوړه or راوړله M. راوړ or ما راوړ, تا, هِغِه, هَغه he, she, it, thou, I brought.

PLURAL.

F. راوړه or راوړله M. مُونږ راوړ or تاسُ, هُغو they, you, we brought.

(*Governing noun plural*).

SINGULAR.

F. راوړلِ or راوړِ M. راوړهٔ or راوړل ما or تا , هِغِه, هَغه he, she, it, thou, I brought.

PLURAL.

F. راوړلِ or راوړِ M. راوړهٔ or راوړل مُنګا or تاسُ , هُغو they, you, we brought.

SECOND FORM—(*Governing noun singular*).

SINGULAR.

F. راوړله or راوړه M. راوړ مي or دِ, ئي he, she, it, thou, I brought.

PLURAL.

F. راوړله or راوړه M. راوړ مُو or مو, ئي they, you, we brought.

(*Governing noun plural*).

SINGULAR.

F. راوړلِ or راوړِ M. راوړل مي or دِ, ئي he, she, it, thou, I brought.

PLURAL.

F. راوړلِ or راوړِ M. راوړل مُو or مو, ئي they, you, we brought.

مضارع AORIST TENSE.

SINGULAR.	PLURAL.
راوړي he, she, it may bring, *or* brings.	راوړي they may bring, *or* bring.
راوړې thou mayest bring, *or* bringest.	راوړئ you may bring, *or* bring.
راوړم I may bring, *or* bring.	راوړو we may bring, *or* bring.

امر IMPERATIVE MOOD.

SINGULAR.	PLURAL.
را دِ وړي or هَغه دِ راوړي let him etc. bring.	هَغه دِ راوړي let them bring.
راوړه or ته راوړه bring thou.	تاسُ راوړئ bring you.

اسم فاعل THE AGENT.

SINGULAR.		PLURAL.	
M. راوړونکي راوړونی F. راوړونکِ راوړونِ	the bringer.	M. and F. راوړونکي راوړوني	the bringers.

صيغهٔ مجهول PASSIVE VOICE.

ماضي PAST TENSE.

SINGULAR. F.	M.		PLURAL. F.	M.	
راوړِ شوه or شوله	راوړي شه	he, etc. was brought.	راوړې شوې or شولِ	راوړي شو	they were brought.
راوړِ شوې	راوړي شوې	thou wast brought.	M. and F.	راوړي شوئ	you were brought.
راوړِ شوم	راوړي شوم	I was brought.	M. and F.	راوړي شوو	we were brought.

SECOND FORM.

SINGULAR. F.	M.		PLURAL. F.	M.	
راوړه or راوړله شوه	راوړ شه	he, etc. was brought.	راوړِ or راوړلِ شولِ	راوړل شو	they were brought.
راوړه or راوړله شوې	راوړ شوې	thou wast brought.	راوړِ or راوړلِ شوئ	راوړل شوئ	you were brought.
راوړه or راوړله شوم	راوړ شوم	I was brought.	راوړِ or راوړلِ شوو	راوړل شوو	we were brought.

مضارع Aorist Tense.

SINGULAR. PLURAL.

F.	M.		M. and F.	
راوړِ شي	راوړي شي	he, etc., is brought, *or* may be brought.	راوړي شي	they are brought, *or* may be brought.
راوړِ شې	راوړي شې	thou art brought, *or* mayest be brought.	راوړي شئ	you are brought, *or* may be brought.
راوړِ شم	راوړي شم	I am brought, *or* may be brought.	راوړي شو	we are brought, *or* may be brought.

Second Form.

SINGULAR. PLURAL.

F.	M.		F.	M.	
راوړله شي or	راوړه شي or راوړ شي	he, etc. is brought, etc.	راوړلِ شي or راوړِ شي	راوړل شي	they are brought, etc.
راوړله شې or	راوړه شې or راوړ شې	thou art brought, etc.	راوړلِ شئ or راوړِ شئ	راوړل شئ	you are brought, etc.
راوړله شم or	راوړه شم or راوړ شم	I am brought, etc.	راوړلِ شو or راوړِ شو	راوړل شو	we are brought, etc.

امر Imperative Mood.

SINGULAR. PLURAL. F. and M.

M. راوړي دِ شي or راوړي شي هَغه دِ	let him, *or* it be brought.	راوړي شي	هَغه دِ let them be brought.
F. راوړِ دِ شي or راوړِ شي هَغه دِ	let her, *or* it be brought.	راوړي دِ شي	let them be brought.
F. ته راوړِ شه M. ته راوړي شه	be thou brought.	تاسُ راوړي شئ	be you brought.

اسم مفعول Past Participle.

SINGULAR. PLURAL.

F. راوړِ شَو M. راوړي شَوي brought. M. and F. راوړي شَوي brought.

408. Conjugation of a derivative transitive verb, formed from an adjective by the addition of وُل, which requires the aid of the verbs کړل or کول 'to do,' in forming its different inflections. See paragraph 285.

مصدر Infinitive.

دکول *ḍḍakawul*, 'to fill.'

صيغه معروف ACTIVE VOICE.

ماضي Past Tense.

SINGULAR.

F. دکه کړه or کړله M. دک کړ مـا or تا هِغه, هَغه he, she, it, thou, I filled.

PLURAL.

F. دکه کړه or کړله M. دک کړ مُنګا or تاسُ, هُغو they, you we filled.

(*Governing noun plural*).

SINGULAR.

F. دکِ کړِ or کړلِ M. دک کړل مـا or تا, هِغه, هَغه he, she, it, thou, I filled.

PLURAL.

F. دکِ کړِ or کړلِ M. دک کړل مُونګا or تاسُ, هُغو they, you, we filled.

SECOND FORM—(*Governing noun singular*).

SINGULAR.

F. کړله or دکه کړه   M. دکث کړ مې or بې, ئې he, she, it, thou, I filled.

PLURAL.

F. کړله or دکه کړه   M. دکث کړ مو or مو, ئې they, you, we filled.

(*Governing noun plural*).

SINGULAR.

F. کړلِ or دکثِ کړِ   M. دکث کړل مې or بې, ئې he, she, it, thou, I filled.

PLURAL.

F. کړلِ or دکثِ کړِ   M. دکث کړل مو or مو, ئې they, you, we filled.

مضارع AORIST TENSE.

SINGULAR. F.	M.	PLURAL. F.	M.
دکه کړي	دکث کړي he, etc., fills, *or* may fill.	دکثِ کړي	دکث کړي they fill, *or* may fill.
دکه کړې	دکث کړې thou fillest, *or* mayest fill.	دکثِ کړئ	دکث کړئ you fill, *or* may fill.
دکه کړم	دکث کړم I fill, *or* may fill.	دکثِ کړو	دکث کړو we fill, *or* may fill.

امر IMPERATIVE MOOD.

SINGULAR. / PLURAL.

M. دکث دِ کړي or ځغه دِ دکث کړي let him, *or* it fill.   M. دکث دِ کړي or ځغه دِ دکث کړي let them fill.

F. دکه دِ کړي or ځغه دِ دکه کړي let her, *or* it fill.   F. دکثِ دِ کړي or ځغه دِ دکثِ کړي let them fill.

F. ته دکه کړه   M. ته دکث کړه fill thou.   F. تاسُ دکثِ کړئ M. تاسُ دکث کړئ fill you.

اسم فاعل THE AGENT.

SINGULAR. / PLURAL.

F. دکوونِ or دکوونکِ   M. دکووني or دکوونکي the filler.   M. & F. دکووني or دکوونکي the fillers.

صيغهٔ مجهول PASSIVE VOICE.

ماضي PAST TENSE.

SINGULAR. / PLURAL.

M. دکث کړې شه he, *or* it was filled.   M. دکث کړي شو or شول they were filled.

F. دکه کړِ شوه or شوله she, *or* it was filled.   F. دکثِ کړي شو or شول they were filled.

F. دکه کړِ شوې M. دکث کړې شوې thou wast filled.   دکث کړي شوئ you were filled.

F. دکه کړِ شوم M. دکث کړې شوم I was filled.   دکث کړي شوو we were filled.

SECOND FORM.

SINGULAR. F.	M.	PLURAL. F.	M.
دکوله شوه	دکاوه شه he, etc., was filled.	دکولِ شولِ	دکول شول they were filled.
دکوله شوې	دکاوه شوې thou wast filled.	دکولِ شوئ	دکول شوئ you were filled.
دکوله شوم	دکاوه شوم I was filled.	دکولِ شوو	دکول شوو we were filled.

مضارع Aorist Tense.

Singular F.	Singular M.		Plural F.	Plural M.	
دکه کړِ شي	دک کړَي شي	he, etc., is filled, etc.	دکِ کړي شي	دک کړي شي	they are filled, etc.
دکه کړِ شې	دک کړَي شې	thou art filled, etc.	دکِ کړي شئ	دک کړي شئ	you are filled, etc.
دکه کړِ شم	دک کړَي شم	I am filled, etc.	دکِ کړي شو	دک کړي شو	we are filled, etc.

Second Form.

Singular F.	Singular M.		Plural F.	Plural M.	
دکوله شي	دکاوُد شي	he, etc., is filled, *or* may be filled.	دکولِ شي	دکول شي	they are filled, *or* may be filled.
دکوله شې	دکاوُد شې	thou art filled, *or* mayest be filled.	دکولِ شئ	دکول شئ	you are filled, *or* may be filled.
دکوله شم	دکاوُد شم	I am filled, *or* may be filled.	دکولِ شو	دکول شو	we are filled, *or* may be filled.

امر Imperative Mood.

Singular			Plural		
M.	دَغه دِ دک کړَي شي or دک کړَي دِ شي	let him, etc., be filled.	M.	دَغه دِ دک کړي شي or دک کړي دِ شي	let them be filled.
F.	دَغه دِ دکه کړِ شي or دکه کړِ دِ شي	let her, etc., be filled.	F.	دَغه دِ دکِ کړي شي or دکِ کړي دِ شي	let them be filled.
M.	ته دک کړَي شه or دک کړَي شه	be thou filled.	M.	تاسُ دک کړي شئ or دک کړي شئ	be you filled.
F.	ته دکه کړِ شه or دکه کړِ شه	be thou filled.	F.	تاسُ دکِ کړي شئ or دکِ کړي شئ	be you filled.

اسم مفعول Past Participle.

Singular	Plural
F. دکه کړِ شوِ M. دک کړَي شوَي become filled.	F. دکِ کړي شوي M. دک کړي شوي become filled.

409. Conjugation of a regular causal verb آلوزول *ālwuzawul*, 'to cause to fly,' formed from the present tense of the infinitive آلوتل 'to fly.'

صيغه معروف ACTIVE VOICE.

ماضي Past Tense—(*Governing noun singular*).

SINGULAR.

F. والوزوله M. والوزاوُه ما or تا, دِغه, دَغه he, she, it, thou, I caused to fly.

PLURAL.

F. والوزوله M. والوزاوُه مُونږ or تاسُ, دُغو they, you, we caused to fly.

(*Governing noun plural*).

SINGULAR.

F. والوزولِ M. والوزول ما or تا, دِغه, دَغه he, she, it, thou, I caused to fly.

PLURAL.

F. والوزولِ M. والوزول مُنګا or تاسُ, دُغو they, you, we caused to fly.

SECOND FORM—(*Governing noun singular*).

SINGULAR.

F. والوزوله M. والوزاوّه مې or دِ, ئې he, she, it, thou, I caused to fly.

PLURAL.

F. والوزوله M. والوزاوّه مو or مو, ئې they, you, we caused to fly.

(*Governing noun plural*).

SINGULAR.

F. والوزولِ M. والوزول مې or دِ, ئې he, she, it, thou, I caused to fly.

PLURAL.

F. والوزولِ M. والوزول مو or مو, ئې they, you, we caused to fly.

مضارع AORIST TENSE.

SINGULAR.	PLURAL.
والوزوي he, she, it causes to fly, *or* may cause to fly.	والوزوي they cause to fly, *or* may cause to fly.
والوزوې thou causest to fly, *or* mayest cause to fly.	والوزوئ you cause to fly, *or* may cause to fly.
والوزوم I cause to fly, *or* may cause to fly.	والوزوو we cause to fly, *or* may cause to fly.

امر IMPERATIVE MOOD.

SINGULAR.	PLURAL.
ځغه دِ والوزوي or وا دِ لوزوي* let him, etc. cause to fly.	ځغه دِ والوزوي or وا دِ لوزوي let them cause to fly.
والوزوه or آلوزوه do thou cause to fly.	والوزوئ or آلوزوئ do you cause to fly.

اسم فاعل THE AGENT.

SINGULAR.		PLURAL.	
M. آلوزوونکې or آلوزوونې; F. آلوزوونکې or آلوزوونِ	the causer to fly.	M. and F. آلوزوونکي, آلوزووني	the causers to fly.

صيغه مجهول PASSIVE VOICE.

ماضي PAST TENSE.

SINGULAR.		PLURAL.	
M. آلوزولې شه; F. آلوزولِ شوه or شوله	he, she, it was caused to fly.	M. آلوزولي شول or شو; F. آلوزولې شو or شولِ	they were caused to fly.
M. آلوزولې شوې; F. آلوزولِ شوې	thou wast caused to fly.	M. & F. آلوزولي شوئ	you were caused to fly.
M. آلوزولې شوم; F. آلوزولِ شوم	I was caused to fly.	M. & F. آلوزولي شوو	we were caused to fly.

* Infinitives similar to the one now conjugated, which have ا as the first letter, add that letter to the prefixed و in the second form of the imperative mood, and the دِ follows immediately after. In the same manner with regard to the other inflections, the prefix takes a (َ) instead of (ُ). See paragraph 284.

Second Form.

	SINGULAR.			PLURAL.	
M.	والوزاؤد شه	he, she, it was caused to fly.	M.	والوزول شول	they were caused to fly.
F.	والوزوله شوه		F.	والوزولِ شوِ or شولِ	
M.	والوزاؤد شوې	thou wast caused to fly.	M.	والوزول شوئ	you were caused to fly.
F.	والوزوله شوې		F.	والوزولِ شوئ	
M.	والوزاؤد شوم	I was caused to fly.	M.	والوزول شوُ	we were caused to fly.
F.	والوزوله شوم		F.	والوزولِ شوُ	

مضارع Aorist Tense.

SINGULAR. F.	M.		PLURAL. M. and F.	
آلوزولِ شي	آلوزولَي شي	he, she, it is caused to fly, etc.	آلوزولي شي	they are caused to fly.
آلوزولِ شې	آلوزولَي شې	thou art caused to fly.	آلوزولي شئ	you are caused to fly.
آلوزولِ شَم	آلوزولَي شَم	I am caused to fly.	آلوزولي شوُ	we are caused to fly.

Second Form.

SINGULAR. F.	M.		PLURAL. F.	M.	
آلوزوله شي	آلوزاؤد شي	he, she, it is caused to fly.	آلوزولِ شي	آلوزول شي	they are caused to fly.
آلوزوله شې	آلوزاؤد شې	thou art caused to fly.	آلوزولِ شئ	آلوزول شئ	you are caused to fly.
آلوزاؤد شَم	آلوزاؤد شَم	I am caused to fly.	آلوزولِ شوُ	آلوزول شوُ	we are caused to fly.

امر Imperative Mood.

	SINGULAR.		PLURAL.	
M.	دَغه دِ آلوزولَي شي or آلوزولَي دِ شي	let him, *or* it be caused to fly.	دَغه دِ آلوزولي شي or	let them be caused to fly.
F.	دَغه دِ آلوزولِ شي or آلوزولِ دِ شي	let her, *or* it be caused to fly.	M. & F. آلوزولي دِ شي	
M.	آلوزولَي شه	be thou caused to fly.	M. & F. آلوزولي شئ	be you caused to fly.
F.	آلوزولِ شه			

اسم مفعول Past Participle.

SINGULAR.		PLURAL.	
F. آلوزولِ شوِ. M. آلوزولَي شوَي	caused to fly.	M. & F. آلوزولي شوي	caused to fly.

NEGATION AND PROHIBITION.

نفي و نهي *nafī wo nahī.*

410. To signify negation and prohibition, the particles نه *nah* and مه *mah* are used with the verbs; but, as their position depends on the description of the infinitive with which they are used, it will be necessary to give a table of each. The third persons singular and plural of a few of the infinitives already conjugated will be sufficient for the purpose.

411. The particle of prohibition مه is alone used with the second persons of the imperative mood, and invariably precedes the inflection of the verb with which it is used, whatever its description.

412. Infinitives, such as راغلل 'to come,' پریوتل 'to fall,' راوړل 'to bring,' and پریکول 'to cut,' which have a prefixed particle, place the نه after the latter both in the past and present tenses.

مصدر INFINITIVE.

پریوتل *pre-watul*, 'to fall.'

ماضي مطلق PAST TENSE.

SINGULAR.		PLURAL.	
M. پري نه ووت	he, *or* it did not fall.	M. پري نه وتل پري نه واته	they did not fall.
F. پري نه وَته پري نه وَتِ پري نه وَتله	she, *or* it did not fall.	F. پري نه وَتلې پري نه وَتلِ	they did not fall.

مضارع AORIST TENSE.

SINGULAR.		PLURAL.	
M. & F. پري نه وُزي or ځغه پري نه وُزي	he, she, it may not fall.	M. & F. پري نه وُزي or ځغه پري نه وُزي	they may not fall.

امر IMPERATIVE MOOD.

SINGULAR.		PLURAL.	
M. & F. مه پریوزد	do not thou fall.	M. & F. مه پریوزئ	do not you fall.

اسم مفعول PAST PARTICIPLE.

SINGULAR.		PLURAL.	
F. نه پریوتل or نه پریوتِ	M. نه پریوتلي or نه پریوتي not fallen.	M. AND F. نه پریوتلي or نه پریوتي	not fallen.

413. Regular verbs, whether transitive or intransitive, take the نه after the prefixed وُ, but the participle مه as before stated, invariably precedes.

مصدر INFINITIVE.

زغلیدل *z'ghaledul*, 'to run.'

ماضي مطلق PAST TENSE.

SINGULAR.		PLURAL.	
M. وُ نه زغلیدَ وُ نه زغلیده	he, *or* it did not run.	M. وُ نه زغلیدل وُ نه زغلیدهٔ	they did not run.
F. وُ نه زغلیده وُ نه زغلیدله	she *or* it did not run.	F. وُ نه زغلیدِ وُ نه زغلیدلِ	they did not run.

مضارع AORIST TENSE.

SINGULAR.		PLURAL.	
M. & F. ځغه وُ نه زغلي	he, she, it may not run, etc.	M. & F. ځغه وُ نه زغلي	they may not run, etc.

امر IMPERATIVE MOOD.

SINGULAR.		PLURAL.	
M. & F. مه زغله	do not thou run.	M. & F. مه زغلئ	do not you run.

اسم مفعول PAST PARTICIPLE.

SINGULAR.		PLURAL.	
F. نه زغلیدلِ or نه زغلیدِ	M. نه زغلیدلي or نه زغلیدي not run.	M. AND F. نه زغلیدلي or نه زغلیدي	not run.

مصدر INFINITIVE.

راوړل 'to bring.'

ماضي مطلق PAST TENSE.

SINGULAR.		PLURAL.	
M. هغه را نه وَړ or ئي را نه وَړ	he or it did not bring.	M. هغو را نه وَړ or ئي را نه وَړ	they did not bring.
F. هغه را نه وّړه or را نه وّړله ئي را نه وّړه or ئي را نه وّړله	she or it did not bring.	F. هغو را نه وّړه or را نه وّړله ئي را نه وّړه or ئي را نه وّړله	they did not bring.

مضارع AORIST TENSE.

SINGULAR.		PLURAL.	
M. & F. هغه را نه وّړي	he, she, it may not bring, etc.	M. & F. هغه را نه وّړي	they may not bring.

امر IMPERATIVE MOOD.

SINGULAR.		PLURAL.	
M. & F. مه را وّړه	do not thou bring.	M. & F. مه راوّړئي	do not you bring.

اسم مفعول PAST PARTICIPLE.

SINGULAR.		PLURAL.	
M. نه راوّړیَ F. نه راوّړ	not brought.	M. & F. نه راوّړي	not brought.

414. When used with infinitives similar to ډکول 'to fill,' the نه follows the adjective or noun, and precedes the auxiliary; thus,

مصدر INFINITIVE.

ډکول <u>dd</u>*akawul*, 'to fill.'

ماضي مطلق PAST TENSE.—(*Noun singular*).

SINGULAR.		PLURAL.	
M. هغه ډک نه کړ or ئي ډک نه کړ	he, or it did not fill.	M. هغو ډک نه کړ or ئي ډک نه کړ	they did not fill.
F. هغه ډکه نه کړه or ډکه نه کړله ئي ډکه نه کړه or ډکه نه کړله	she, or it did not fill.	F. هغو ډکه نه کړه or ډکه نه کړله ئي ډکه نه کړه or ډکه نه کړله	they did not fill.

مضارع AORIST TENSE.

SINGULAR.		PLURAL.	
M. هغه ډک نه کړي	he, or it may not fill, etc.	M. هغه ډک نه کړي	they may not fill, etc.
F. هغه ډکه نه کړي	she, or it may not fill, etc.	F. هغه ډکې نه کړي	they may not fill, etc.

امر IMPERATIVE MOOD.

SINGULAR.		PLURAL.	
M. & F. مه ډکوه	do not thou fill.	M. & F. مه ډکوئي	do not you fill.

اسم مفعول PAST PARTICIPLE.

SINGULAR.		PLURAL.	
M. نه ډک کړیَ or کړلیَ F. نه ډکه کړِ or کړلِ	not filled.	M. نه ډک کړي or کړلي F. نه ډکې کړي or کړلي	not filled.

415. In the passive voice, the past participle or the imperfect tense used with the auxiliary as a second form (already described at paragraph 398) may precede, and the نه precede the auxiliary, or the particle of negation and auxiliary may precede, and the past participle and imperfect tense follow; as will be seen from the following paradigm.

مصدر INFINITIVE.

ويشتل *wis̱ẖ-tal*, 'to throw.'

ماضي مطلق PAST TENSE.

	SINGULAR.			PLURAL.	
M.	هَغه ويشتلَي نه شه هَغه نه شه ويشتلَي	he, *or* it was not thrown.	M.	هَغه ويشتلي نه شوّل or شوُّ هَغه نه شوّل or شوُ ويشتلي	they were not thrown.
F.	هَغه ويشتلِ نه شوّه or شوّله هَغه نه شوّه or شوّله ويشتلِ	she, *or* it was not thrown.	F.	هَغه ويشتلي نه شوّلِ or شوِ هَغه نه شوّلِ or شوِ ويشتلي	they were not thrown.

مضارع AORIST TENSE.

	SINGULAR.			PLURAL.	
M.	هَغه ويشتلَي نه شي هَغه نه شي ويشتلَي	he, *or* it may not be thrown.	M.	هَغه ويشتلي نه شي	they may not be thrown.
F.	هَغه ويشتلِ نه شي هَغه نه شي ويشتلِ	she, *or* it may not be thrown.	F.	هَغه نه شي ويشتلي	they may not be thrown.

امر IMPERATIVE MOOD.

	SINGULAR.			PLURAL.	
M.	ويشتلَي مه شه or مه شه ويشتلَي	do not thou be thrown.	M and F.	ويشتلي مه شئ مه شئ ويشتلي	do not you be thrown.
F.	ويشتلِ مه شه or مه شه ويشتلِ				

اسم مفعول PAST PARTICIPLE.

	SINGULAR.			PLURAL.	
M.	نه ويشتلَي شوَي or نه شوَي ويشتلَي	not become thrown.	M. and F.	نه ويشتلي شوي نه شوي ويشتلي	not become thrown.
F.	نه ويشتلِ شوِ or نه شوِ ويشتلِ				

416. The positions which the particles of negation and prohibition assume will also be seen from the following extracts:

يو به نسم مغلواله دَ رقيب ستا — که زو کړي يم ريښتيا له پښتني زه

"I WILL NOT BEAR with this Moghlā'ī (tyranny) of thy guardian,
If I am really born of an Afghān woman."—*Ʌabd-ul-Ḥamīd.*

هر خاکي چه خاکساري نکا ښه نکا — هر څوک ښه وي په خپل رسمو په رواج

"Every terrestrial being who PRACTISES NOT humility, ACTETH NOT rightly:
Every one will be excellent according to his own manners and customs."—*Ʌabd-ul-Ḥamīd.*

چه نه ؤ خوري نه ئې ورکړي مه ئې ويني — که په ګنج باندِ په څير دَ مار کښيني

"Who DOES NOT CONSUME himself, and DOES NOT GIVE to others, LOOK NOT towards him:
That sitteth like a serpent on a hidden treasure."—*Ʌabd-ul-Ḥamīd.*

بزرگانُ فرمايلي لويه لومه دَ شيطان ده چه توبه آخر كوينَ مومنانُ مه آخر كوئي

"Pious persons have said that the devil's great snare is, that you should put off repentance until the last hour; but POSTPONE IT NOT, oh, children of the true faith!"—*Fawā'id-ush-Sharī'æa'h.*

CHAPTER VII.

THE SEPARATE PARTICLES.

حروف *ḥurūf.*

417. Under this head are included adverbs, postpositions, prepositions, conjunctions and interjections. They contain, besides pure Afghān, a number of Arabic and Persian words.

ADVERBS.

418. The Adverbs may be divided into fourteen different classes; of place, time, number, quality, similitude, collection, separation, demonstration, interrogation, dubiation, exclamation, affirmation, negation, and prohibition.

419. They serve to qualify nouns, and are for the most part undeclinable; thus,

چه دِ زلفي دَ رحمان په زړه ور خرخ كړ   تر بنړوئي ځكه ځاځي اوښي سپيني

"Since thy ringlets have pierced the very heart of Raḥmān,
THEREFORE, from his eyelashes the white tears flow."

كه له خدايه دِ و خلقُ و ته مخ شي   له فردوسُ به دِ مخ شي و سقر ته
هميشه به دَر په دَر گرزي رټلي   دَ آستوگي ځاي به نه مومي هيچرته

"If thy face becometh turned from God unto the world, it will be also turned from heaven unto hell:
Thou wilt for ever wander driven from door to door: thou wilt NOWHERE find a resting or a dwelling-place."—*Æabd-ur-Raḥmān.*

چه پيدا شي يو ناكس په قبيله كښي   وړاندِ ورستو هيته كاند نسب

"When one degenerate being appeareth in a family,
He bringeth disgrace on his lineage both PRESENT and PAST."—*Æabd-ul-Hamīd.*

420. A number of adverbs are subject to the usual change in termination for the ablative case; as in the following example:

وزيرؤ ويل دا هلك لا تر اوسه دَ خپل روندانه له باغه ميوه نه ده خوړلي

"The Wuzīr said, 'As YET this boy has not eaten any of the fruit from the garden of his own existence."—*Gulistān.*

421. A few adverbs derived from nouns and adjectives are liable to the same

change in termination for gender, number, and case, as the nouns they qualify. Thus دير 'much,' becomes ډيره in the feminine singular, and ډيرئ or ډيرِ in the feminine plural and the oblique cases of the singular. The masculine plural is the same as the singular, and the oblique plural for both genders is ډيرو

مدعا دَ عاشقئ مشکله ډيره — رسيدلي په مطلب به طاق در طاق وي

"In love the (lover's) suit is an EXCEEDINGLY difficult one—
The object can only be obtained after many twists and turnings."—*Ḳāsim Æalī, Afrīdī.*

422. The adverbs of most frequent occurrence in the language, whether simple or compound, are as follows:

ADVERBS OF PLACE.

ظروف المکان *ẓurūf-ul-mukān.*

دلته, دلِ or هيسته	here, hither.	دي خوا or دي پلو	here, on this side.
هلته or هلته کي	there, thither.	پورته or لوړ	above, overhead.
کُورِ or کُورِ ته	there, thither.	ښکته or ږوره	under, below.
له دَغه or دي ځايَ or ځايه	from this place, from hence.	تر دَغه or تر دي پوري or پورِ	so far, to this degree.
له هَغه ځايَ or ځايه	from that place, from thence.	تر هغه پوري or پورِ	so far, to that degree.
		چرته	somewhere.
وړاندِ or وړاندي	before, in front, hitherto.	هر چرته or هر يو ځاي	everywhere.
ورسته or ورستو	behind, after.	هيچرته	nowhere.
دَغه or دي خوا	this side, hither.	نژدي or نږد	near, about.
هَغه خوا	that side, thither.	يو ځاي or چرته	somewhere or other.
هَغه خوا or هَغه پلو	beyond, there, on that side.	هر چرته	where, wherever.
		دننَ or دننه	inside, within.
خوا په خوا	side by side.	لاند باندِ	above and below.
دواړه خوا	on both sides.	نسکوره	upside down.
بل چرته or بل ځاي	elsewhere.	لري, له ورايه	far, at a distance.
دلته هلته	here and there.	چاپيره	round about.

ADVERBS OF TIME.

ظروف الزمان *ẓurūf-uz-zamān.*

اوس	now, at this time, presently.	کله کله	sometimes, frequently, occasionally.
کله	ever, sometime.		

هيچ كله never.
هر كله always.
هر كله چه whenever.
كله نه كله sometime or other,
هره روځ daily.
هره شپه nightly.
وار په وار or دم په دم } perpetually.
زر په زر instantaneously.
پايه په پايه gradually.
پله پسي successively.
په خوا or پيښس before, prior.
پس after, afterwards.
نن or نن ورځ to-day.
صبا to-morrow.
ورمه ورځ two days since.
لا ورمه ورځ three days since.
لا لا ورمه ورځ four days since.
سحرگاه at the dawn of day.
هرگز or هيچ كله ever.
لرغوني long since, long ago.
برائي بيگاه last night.
هر ځله as often, every time.
باري or آخِر once, at last.
ځو وار or ځو ځله often, repeatedly.

وار په وار repeatedly, often, frequently.
يو ځله or يوه پلا once.
دوه ځله or دوي پلا twice.
درِ ځله or درِ پلا thrice.
ژرت or سم له لاسَ instantly, quickly, without delay.
زر زر or مارد مار quickly, speedily.
نژدي or نژدِ shortly, soon.
ناگهان or نا ځاپه unawares, suddenly.
يک لخته all at once, suddenly.
رنبي or ورنبي first, in the first place.
دويَم secondly.
آخِر at last, at length, finally, at the end.
پرون yesterday.
نن صبا shortly, soon, to-day or to-morrow.
بل صبا the day after to-morrow.
وختي early in the morning, betimes, early.
تل or تر تلو always, ever.
تل تر تله or تل تر تله or هميشه } always, continually, ever.
تر اوسَ لا تر اوسَ as yet, up to the present time.
چري چري or چرِ چرِ sometimes.

ADVERBS OF QUANTITY.

حروف المقدار *ḥurūf-ul-miḳdār*.

هومبره or دهومبره . ځومبره so much.
هومبره قدر that much.
دغومبره قدر this much.
هر ځومبره as much as.
هر ځو howmuchsoever.

وبريا gratuitously.
ځو ځو a great number, several.
دير much, in a great degree, by far.
لږ, لږ or لكوتي a little, a few.

Adverbs of Similitude.

حروف التشبيه *ḥurūf-ut-tashbīh.*

دا or دَغه شان thus, in this manner.	دسي, دَغه سي or داسي or داسي thus, so, in this manner.
دا or دَغه رنگ thus, in this way.	مثلا for example.
لکه, شان, غندِ, دود, په دود, مخي or په څير like, as, as if, just as, for all the world.	يعني that is to say.
هَغه شان so, in that manner.	دسي شان thus, in this manner.
هَغه رنگ so, in that way.	

Adverbs of Admonition, etc.

حروف التنبيه *ḥurūf-ut-tanbīh.*

وُگورد or وُ وينَ or وُ وينه look out! have a care!	پود شه know! recollect!
بيدار شه be cautious!	خبر دار شه take care! mind!

Adverbs of Society and Separation.

حروف المعيت و المفارقت *ḥurūf-ul-maʿi-yat wo mufāraḳat.*

يوازي alone.	بيل, بيله or بيل بيل apart, separately.
مخا مخ face to face.	سره together.
لري or لرِ apart, at a distance.	بي له دي, سيوا له دي or پرته له دي besides, except.
لري لارغه far away, very far off.	تار په تار separately.
ارخ at the side.	وُچ په وُچه uselessly.
ارخ په ارخ side by side.	پوري را پوري on opposite sides, on both sides.
يو په يو singly, individually.	
شا په شا back to back.	
اوږد په اوږد shoulder to shoulder.	

Adverbs of Extremity and Termination.

حروف الغايت *ḥurūf-ul-ghā-yat.*

تر or پوري to, up to, until.	تر اوسَ پوري till now, as yet.
تر دي or دَغه پوري hitherto, up to.	تر هَغه پوري so far as.
څو or څو چه until, up to.	تر کله پوري till when? how long?
بي حدَ or له حدَ زيات beyond bounds.	تر آخرَ پوري to the end.
تر حدَ پوري to the last degree.	تر نهايتَ پوري to the last, to the extreme.

Adverbs of Interrogation.

حروف الاستفهام *ḥurūf-ul-istifahām.*

- چرته ,چري ,چرِ or کم ځاي where? whither?
- څنګه how? in what manner?
- څومبره or څومره how much?
- له کمَ or کومَ وقتَ since when?
- له کمَ or له کمَ / ځايَ or ځايه whence?
- کله when? at what time?
- لا تر کومَ how much longer?
- تر کله ,تر کله پوري / تر کمَ پوري or څو until when? how long?
- څومبره قدر how much?
- څو ځله how often?
- ولي به نه وي why not?
- څه لره ,څه له or په څه why? how? wherefore?
- ولي or څه دپاره for what? wherefore?
- څه رنګ ,څه شان or په څه توګه in what way? how?

Adverbs of Dubiation.

حروف التشکیک *ḥurūf-ut-tas͟hkīk.*

- ښائي ,ګوندِ or ګند perhaps, haply.
- نه دي وي perhaps not.
- خداي زده God knows.
- به وي may be.
- په ګمان سره probably.
- وي که نه وي may or may not be.

Adverbs of Affirmation and Emphasis.

حروف التاکید و الایجاب *ḥurūf-ut-tākīd wo ul-ījāb.*

- بي شکه ,لا چار certainly, doubtless.
- البته ,خو ,ضرور necessarily.
- هو yes, indeed, yea.
- جوړ merely, only, exactly.
- حق ناحق or کام نه کام right or wrong.
- هیڅري ,له سره or لسره by no means, never.
- په رښتیا or حقاً really, truly.
- خداي رو by God!
- بویه ,بایده or بوي necessarily, it behoveth.
- هر ګوره or یک لخته altogether, wholly, entirely.
- هدو or هڅ never, by no means.
- فقط only, simply.
- خواه نخواه at all events, whether or not, nolens volens.
- بیدو or هو به هو exactly, quite, the very same.

Adverbs of Prohibition and Negation.

حروف النفي و النهي *ḥurūf-un-nafī wo un-nahī.*

- نه or یه no, not, nay.
- مه do not.

CONJUNCTIONS.

حروف العطف و الموصول *ḥurūf-ul-ʿaṭf wo ul-mawṣūl.*

423. The conjunctions most in use are:

- که ,اګر if.
- اګرچه although.
- هم ,بل also, even, likewise.
- ولي or ولِ but, yet, however.

سیوا or پرته besides, except.

که نه or کنه if not, unless, otherwise.

له هَغه سبب then, therefore.

بلکه but, moreover.

سره له دي notwithstanding.

منگر, مگر unless.

او or و and, also.

پس or سکه therefore, then.

چه that, because, since.

بي له unless, if not.

څکه, له دي جهت or له دي سبب or ترو — then, because, therefore.

یا or.

EXAMPLE.

درویشي ترک دَ وجود دي ولي دوي په دودد غواړي چه په تورو په توبرو و بل ته زغلي

"The Darweshs' calling is to forsake all carnal and worldly desires; BUT they, through spitefulness, desire to rush on each other with swords and with arrows."—*Makhzan Afghānī.*

PREPOSITIONS AND POSTPOSITIONS.

حروف الجر یا معنوي *ḥurūf-uj-jarr yā maʻnawī.*

424. Besides the simple prepositions and postpositions used in forming the cases of nouns and pronouns, already described in Chapter III., there are other particles used in the same manner which require the noun, adjective, or pronoun, to be used in the genitive or ablative case when capable of inflection. Examples:

شریعت مثال ئې ونه چه ویخونَ ئې تر زمکي لاندِ تللي او که فهم دلیل ؤ کړي دَ سرښاخ ئې پورته تللي تر سما دي

"The Law is like unto a tree whose roots have gone UNDER THE GROUND; and (if thou shouldst make use of understanding and argument) the topmost branch of it has gone UP INTO THE HEAVENS."—*Makhzan Afghānī.*

پروانه یو څله سر بازي په عمر — که دا کار په یو شپي څو څله شمع

"The moth casteth away its life but once in its life-time;
But the candle doeth this several times IN ONE NIGHT."—*ʻAbd-ul-Ḥamīd.*

The chief prepositions and postpositions are:

دَ of.

ته, لره, له; وته, و لره or و له or و وته — to.

کښي or په کښي in.

تر لاندِ or دَ لاندِ below, under.

سره with.

دپاره for, for the sake of.

له or له نه or دِ or دِ نه from.

تر to, until.

پر or پر باندِ on, upon.

پرِ or پري from him, her, it *or* them.

دَ پاسَ or دپاسه over, above.

مخه before.

منز or مینځ in, between, betwixt.

په مینځ in between, in the middle.

425. INTERJECTIONS.

اصوات *aṣ-wāt.*

شاباش or شاباس .آفرین	well done! bravo!	افسوس	lackaday!
تم شه ,بیدار شه	have a care!	کشکي or کاشکي	would to God!
هي هي	alas! alas!	عجب ,هاي هوي	strange! good God!
دریغ	sorrow! alas!	هه	indeed! really!
چغه	avaunt! get away!	لري شه ,بیارته شه	begone! get away!
او ,اي or وهي	oh!	چپه ,چپ شه	hush! silence!
ؤوي ؤوي	dear! dear!	شوچه	hollo! oh! O!
واي واي ,آخ آخ	woe! woe!		

EXAMPLE.

دا یاران لکۀ گلونه دَ بهار دي   دَ خزان په تاو رژیږي دریغ دریغ

"These loved ones are like unto the flowers of spring,
For in the autumn they wither and fade. ALAS! ALAS!"—*Aḥmad Shāh, Abdālī.*

CHAPTER VIII.

THE DERIVATION OF WORDS.

426. There are a number of derivative and compound words in the Pushto language, formed from nouns, adjectives, and verbs, by prefixing, affixing, or inserting certain words or letters. They may be considered pure Afghān.

NOUNS.

427. Abstract nouns may be obtained from adjectives in eight different ways:

I.—By rejecting the final letter of the adjective and prefixing another; as, وږی 'hungry' لوږه or لوږَ 'hunger.' Example:

لوږه تنده پرِ غالبه شوه یک باره   په صورت ور پاتې نه شه طاقت توان

"HUNGER and thirst all at once overpowered him:
In his body no power or strength remained."—*Saif-ul-Mulūk.*

II.—Forms the noun by rejecting two letters of the adjective for three others; thus تږي 'thirsty,' تنده or تندَ 'thirst.'

لوږه تنده نه شته دَ قانع په قناعت کښې   دا کیمیا چه زده کا په خرقه کښې أمرا وي

"In the contentment of the contented man, there is neither hunger nor THIRST;
And they who acquire this alchemy will be nobles, tho' clad in rags."
—*Æabd-ur-Raḥmān.*

III.—Shortening the word by the rejection of و for (ـَ), and affixing ا ; as, رُونړ or رُوڼ ‘bright,’ رَڼا or رَڼا ‘brightness.’

په رڼا ئي دَ چا کار نه پوره کيږي — دَ آسمان برق و بريښنا ده دا دنيا

“By the LIGHT of it the business of this life cannot be perfected;
For this world is as the lightning and the light of the sky.”—*Ɛabd-ul-Ḥamīd.*

Sometimes the word takes ئي, as in the following example:

لکَ نمر په جهان وُ خيژي رڼائي شي — دم قدم هسي زنده کاندِ اخلاص

“As when the sun riseth on the world, LIGHT and BRIGHTNESS cometh,
So doth friendship and affection give life to both breath and footstep.”—*Ɛabd-ul-Ḥamīd.*

IV.—The middle letter of the adjective is rejected; يا inserted in its place; and ه (*hā-i-khafī*) or (ـَ) *fat'ha'h* affixed; as, تور ‘dark’ or ‘black,’ تيارہ or تيارَ ‘darkness’ or ‘blackness.’

کل جهان تورہ تيارہ شه له هَغه گرد و غبارہ — آسمان رعد بريښيدہ لکه شمشيران

“The whole world became filled with DARKNESS from this dust and vapour:
In the heavens thunder rolled, and lightning flashed as from swords.”—*Saif-ul-Mulūk.*

V.—The final letter of the adjective is inflected from ه or (ـَ) to ې (*yā-i-majhūl*) or (ـِ) *kasra'h*, and گړہ or گړ affixed; thus, ښه ‘good,’ ښيگړہ ‘goodness.’

يون گران په دَغه لاردي بوالبوس ته — مرد هَغه گڼړہ چه ښيگړي که بِنا

“Journeying on this road is difficult to the fickle and capricious:
Consider him a man who layeth the foundation of GOODNESS.”—*Ḳāsim Ɛalī, Afrīdī.*

The whole of the nouns of the preceding classes are feminine; and the following, with the exception of those formed by affixing تِيا, ستيا, گلوي, and ولي, which are feminine, are all masculine.

VI.—This form is something similar to the fourth, being formed from the same adjective (which however remains unchanged) and merely takes the affix والي; thus, تور ‘black,’ تور والي ‘blackness;’ کلک ‘hard,’ کلک والي ‘hardness.’ The final letter is changed to ي in the plural, similar to the first variety of nouns of 1st declension.

مخ دِ سپين لکه آفتاب وُد — تر آفتابَ ئي لا تاب وُد
ولي اوس دا هسي تور شه — په تور والي لکه سکور شه

“Thy countenance was white like unto the sun—yea! it was brighter than the orb of day:
But now, alas! it is become so black, that its BLACKNESS is like unto charcoal.”
—*Yūsuf and Zulīkhā.*

VII.—The nouns of this class are formed by dropping the final ي of the adjective, and affixing وُن; as, ژوندي ‘alive’ or ‘existing,’ ژوندُون ‘life,’ ‘existence;’

نښتيِ 'captive,' 'prisoner,' نښتؤن 'captivity,' 'imprisonment.' They are chiefly verbal nouns. Example:

کله ما و ته امید دَ خپل روندؤن شيِ په هجران به ئي روندؤن را ته زبون شيِ

"When shall I entertain hope for my own EXISTENCE?
Since separated from her, LIFE itself to me is infamous."—*Kāsim Æalī, Afrīdī.*

VIII.—This class is formed by the mere addition of the affixes تؤن, توب, and تِيا; thus, بيل 'separate,' بيلتؤن 'separation;' ځاي 'a place,' ځايتون 'a dwelling place,' 'a home,' 'a birthplace;' مَين 'affectionate,' مَينتوب 'affection,' 'love;' ليوني 'mad,' ليونتوب 'madness;' موړ 'satiated,' موړ تيا 'satiety;' خمسور 'impudent,' خمسور تيا 'impudence,' 'familiarity.' Those ending in تون and توب are masculine, and those in تيا feminine.

ناګاه ويښه شوه له خوبَ زړه ئي ډک له مَين توبَ
کښيناسته ګاه ئي ؤ کړه يار ئي نه ليد آه ئي ؤ کړه

"Suddenly she awoke from her slumbers, her heart filled with LOVE and AFFECTION.
She sat up and gazed around, but sighed; for she beheld not her beloved one."
—*Yūsuf and Zulīkhā.*

خداي دِ نه کاندِ بيلتؤن دَ دوؤ يارانو په بيلتؤن عاشق په روغ صورت بيمار دي

"God forbid that SEPARATION should be caused between two lovers;
For in SEPARATION the lover, though healthy in body, is sick at heart."—*Kāsim Æalī, Afrīdī.*

چه په ديدن دِ موړ تِيا نه شوه اوس د يار غمو کړې موړ

"Whereas from her presence thou didst not acquire SATIETY,
Grief on her account has now satiated thee."—*Ahmad Shāh, Abdālī.*

The whole of these derivatives, when capable of inflection, are subject to the same changes as other nouns.

428. Abstract nouns are obtained also from primitive nouns, by the mere addition of the affixes والِيَ, توب, تِيا or ستيا, ګلوي and ولي; thus, هلک 'a child,' هلک والِيَ 'childhood;' سړيَ 'a man,' 'a human being,' سړيَ توب 'manhood,' 'humanity;' ميلمه 'a guest,' ميلمستيا 'entertainment,' hospitality;' ورور 'a brother,' وروړګلوي 'brotherhood;' کام 'a clan,' کام ولي 'clanship.' The following are examples:

هر څوک چه له هلک والي په ادب نه کړي په لوي والِي نيکي ترِشي لاړه

"Whoever from CHILDHOOD may not have walked in the path of modesty and morality, in the years of MATURITY virtue and piety departeth from him."—*Gulistān.*

اي ځويه دَ تلو په وقت کښي در ته مي ويليَ نه ؤ چه دَ تش لاس خاوندانو لره دَ زړور توب لاس تړلي دي او منګله دَ مزري توب ماته

"Oh son! did not I say unto thee at the time of thy departure, that the hand of BRAVERY, if empty, is bound, and the paw of LION-LIKE INTREPIDITY broken?"—*Gulistān.*

ور ته وُد ویل اي بابا دَ بادشاد په میلمستیا څه دِ وُه نه خوړل زاهد وُد ویل دَ دوي په نظرکښي

هیڅ مي وُه نه خوړل چه په کار راشي

"He said unto him, 'O father! didst thou not eat of anything at the king's ENTERTAINMENT?' The devotee said, 'In his sight I did not make use of anything of consequence.'"—*Gulistān.*

Arabic and Persian words, when used in this language, as may naturally be supposed, are generally governed by, and subject to, their own rules of grammar; but in some instances the Pus̱hto affixes and prefixes may be found used with the words of those languages; thus, سخي 'generous, سخیتوب 'generosity;' شوُم 'niggard,' شوُم توب 'niggardliness;' بیګانه 'strange,' بیګانَ توب 'strangeness.'

429. Nouns of intensity are formed by prefixing adjectives to them; thus, تور 'dark,' prefixed to تم 'darkness,' becomes تور تم 'total darkness;' and in the same manner تور prefixed to تیاره signifies 'total darkness.' تم is not generally used without an adjective prefixed. Example:

که دِ مخ په زلفو پټ دي باك ئي نشته د حیات اوبه هم پټ په تور تم دي

"Of what consequence is it though thy countenance is enveloped in curls?
For the water of immortality itself is hidden in TOTAL DARKNESS."—*Æabd-ur-Raḥmān.*

430. The particles of exaggeration and diminution used with nouns have been already described under that head (page 27–29), and need no further notice here.

ADJECTIVES.

431. Adjectives may be formed from some nouns by the addition of ني and ي with its different modifications for gender, as described at paragraph 45; as, بیګا 'night,' بیګاني 'nocturnal;' پرون 'yesterday,' پروني 'yestern' or 'yester.' The following are examples:

دابشلیم پس له آرویدُ دَ دي خبري بیګاني خوب فقیر ته وُد و او دا راز و خپل یار ته ئي ظاهرکَ

"Dābs̱halīm, after hearing these words, related his NOCTURNAL dream to the Darwes̱h, and also mentioned this secret to his friend."—*Kalīlah wo Damnah.*

عبدُ الله دَ معاویه په لور روان شه دَ پروني خبرِ چه جویان شه معاویه وِ ښما لور وائي اي پلاره دَ دي عبدُ الله عورته خوش دیدارد زد به کله په نظر دَ دد ور شم وایم تا ته چه عبدُ الله نه قبولوم که دي خپله عورته کا طلاقه دغه پس به ئي قبول کړم له اتفاقه

"Æabdullah set out to see Muæā'wīyah, and when he inquired about the circumstances of the PRECEDING DAY (YESTERN), Muæā'wīyah said, 'My daughter says—Oh father! the wife of this Æabdullah is very handsome. When shall I appear to advantage in his sight? I declare unto thee that I will not have Æabdullah under these circumstances; but if he will divorce his wife, then I will accept him willingly.'"—*Ḥasan and Ḥusain.*

432. Adjectives of intensity may be obtained in the same manner as nouns of

intensity by the use of particles either prefixed or affixed to the word; thus, ړوند 'blind,' ټپ ړوند 'totally blind;' سپین 'white,' تک سپین 'perfectly white,' سپین سپیڅلي 'pure or spotless white.' They are subject to the same rules for gender and number as other adjectives. Examples:

ټپ ړانده دي عاشقان دَ يار په عيب ته ټپ ړوند دَ ګڼه يار په هنر مه شه

"Lovers are TOTALLY BLIND to the defects and blemishes of the beloved;
But do not thou also become WHOLLY BLIND to her virtues and merits."
—Æabd-ur-Raḥmān.

چه دِ زلفِ دَ رحمان په زړه ور څرخ کړ تر بانړو ئي اوبه څاځي تکِ سپینِ

"Since thou hast pierced the heart of Raḥmān with thy ringlets,
From his eyelashes the PURE WHITE water flows."—Æabd-ur-Raḥmān.

چا چه نوري وي په خپلو وينو وللي دَ شبنم په څير به تل وي سپین سپیڅلي

"Whoever may have washed his garments in his own blood,
Will, like the dew of the night, be ever SPOTLESS WHITE."—Æabd-ur-Raḥmān.

433. Several Persian, and a few Arabic adjectives also, are to be met with in Pus͟hto, differing but slightly from the originals in pronunciation; for example, غمژن 'aggrieved,' from the Arabic noun غم 'grief,' and Persian زن 'stricken;' and in the same manner مکر ژن or مکر جن 'treacherous,' 'malicious;' تپ ژن 'feverish;' اوتر or ابتر 'spoiled,' 'worthless,' from the Arabic word ابتر and Hebrew בתר, signifying 'cut short, etc.;' زړه ور 'intrepid,' 'brave,' from the Pus͟hto noun زړه 'the heart,' and the Persian particle ور signifying 'possession,' 'having;' تور زن 'warlike,' 'gallant,' from the Afg͟hān noun توره 'a sword,' and زن the active participle of the Persian infinitive زدن 'to strike,' 'to smite.' Example:

خلاص شي بيا لکه تور زن دَ تول له ميښځه که هر څو په غاښو ؤ نسم ژبان چپ

"The tongue again becometh liberated, like the WARRIOR from the thickest of the fight;
Although I may seize it with my teeth that it should remain silent."—Æabd-ul-Ḥamīd.

434. Another description of adjective is obtained by prefixing an adjective to a noun; as, نیمه خوا 'incomplete,' 'crude,' 'disappointed,' 'foiled,' etc., from the Persian adjective نیم 'half,' and the Afg͟hān noun خوا 'desire,' 'inclination;' thus,—

نیمه خوا دَ برق رڼرا ګوره هوښيار شه مه کړه کار دَ معطلي په شتاب ډير

"Behold the INCOMPLETE brightness of the lightning and be prudent!
The affairs requiring deliberation perform not with exceeding haste!"—Æabd-ul-Ḥamīd.

435. A few adjectives are obtained by affixing the Persian particle مند and the Pus͟hto corruption من, and the Pus͟hto particle يالي to Persian and Arabic nouns; thus, نیاز 'indigence,' 'poverty,' نیازمن or نیازمند 'indigent,' 'poor;' دولت 'wealth,' دولتمند or دولتمن 'wealthy,' 'opulent;' جنګ 'war,' 'battle.' جنګ يالي 'warlike,'

'martial;' ننګ 'honor,' 'reputation,' ننګ يالي 'honorable,' 'reputable.' The letter ن is also added to Persian and Pushto nouns indiscriminately in the formation of adjectives; thus, کرم 'a worm,' کرمن 'worm eaten;' ريم 'pus,' 'matter,' ريمن 'purulent,' 'mattery;' پم the Pushto for 'scab,' پمن 'scabby;' خيرن 'dirt,' 'filth,' خيرن 'dirty,' 'filthy;' ليچ 'blinking,' 'purblindness,' ليچن 'a blinkard,' 'purblind.'

436. A few adjectives can be formed by compounding two nouns, as in the Persian language, but they are not very common; thus, پيي مخي 'pretty,' 'delicate,' from پيي 'milk,' and مخ 'the face;' thus,—

ما يود بغدادي سري څخي چه خپل ځان په عربو کښي ګڼاوه ؤ مي پښتيدل چه دَ پيي مخو په باب کښي څه وائي

"I once made inquiry from one of those who accounted himself amongst the Arabs of Baghdād, saying, 'What sayest thou in respect to the HANDSOME!'"—*Gulistān.*

437. Relative or patronymical adjectives are for the most part obtained by affixing the different modifications of ي, (described at paragraph 45) in the same manner as the Persian '*yai-i-nisbut,*' to nouns; thus, کابلئ *kābulaey*, 'a native of Kābul;' پيښاوري *pekhāweraey* or *peshāweraey*, 'a native of Peshāwer;' کوهستانئ *kohistānaey*, 'a native of the Kohistān.'

The word پښتون now applied to the Afghāns as a nation, is really an abstract noun, derived from پښن the name of the old seat of the Afghāns in the Sūlimān mountains, west of the Indus, and تون a residence, a place of birth.

In the districts bordering on the Panjāb and Kashmīr, such as Buner and Paklī, the affix وال (a Hindī word) is generally used; thus, بنيروال *Bunerwāl*, 'a native of Buner;' پکليوال *Paklīwāl*, 'a native of Paklī.' At the same time it must be remembered that this affix cannot be always applied, for we could not call a native of Peshāwer, a Peshāwerīwāl; or a native of Kābul, a Kābulīwāl, and *vice versa.*

438. The past participles of verbs are extensively used as adjectives in this language, both alone and with a conjunction; thus, نازولي 'pampered,' obtained from the infinitive نازول 'to pamper,' formed by affixing ول, the sign of the infinitive of active verbs, to the Persian noun ناز, signifying 'delicacy,' 'softness,' etc.; and هم زولي 'of the same age,' 'cotemporary,' from the past participle of the verb زول 'to be born,' with the Persian conjunction هم 'together,' 'with,' 'similar,' 'mutual.' The following are examples:

آړولي بخت را ؤ کړي آړولئ چه غمخور يار و آشنا خما خونخور شَ

"INVERTED destiny made me ADVERSE and WAYWARD,
Since my sympathizing lover and friend became cruel and sanguinary."—*Æabd-ul-Hamīd.*

درخانۍ پلار ته سوال وُ کړ چه همزولي مې وارۀ لولي حکم را کړه چه زۀ هم لولم

"Durkhāna'ī made a request to her father, saying, "All THOSE OF MY OWN AGE learn to read; pray give directions that I also may learn to read.'"—*Adam Khān and Durkhāna'ī.*

It should be borne in mind that these derivatives are subject to the same changes for gender, number, and case, as other nouns or adjectives under whose classes they may come.

439. The حاصل مصدر *hāṣil-i-maṣdar*, called also the اسم مصدر *ism-i-maṣdar*, of the Pushto verbs, is derived from the infinitive (مصدر), the source or essence of the verb, by rejecting the ل, the final letter of the former, and substituting نه or نَ. It is subject to the same changes as feminine nouns of the first variety of the third declension, and changes the final ه (*hā-i-khafī*), one of the signs of the feminine gender, into ي (*yā-i-majhūl*), in the oblique cases; as, بېلېدل 'to separate,' بېلېدَنه 'separation;' تو کېدل 'to grow' (as a plant or grain), تو کېدَنه 'growth.' Infinitives terminating in وَل, are subject to the same rules.

The *hāṣil-i-maṣdar* of the preceding infinitives, which are intransitive, are used as nouns; but in case of making them transitive by changing the neuter sign or intransitive يدَل into the active or transitive termination of infinitives وَل, the *hāṣil-i-maṣdar* can then only be construed as a mode of action or manner of being, indefinite as to time, place, and sometimes even of person; thus, بېلول 'to separate,' بېلوَنه 'causing separation;' توکول 'to make grow,' توکوَنه 'causing growth or growing.' The *hāṣil-i-maṣdar* of a transitive infinitive terminating in يدَل, of which there are a few in the language and exceptions to the above rule, can be construed as a noun; thus, پښتېدل 'to ask,' پښتېدَنه 'inquiry.'

440. The اسم حاليه *ism-i-hāliah* or verb in its present state, similar to the present or indefinite participle of our language, is also occasionally used as a simple noun; but chiefly in the place of the infinitive. It forms the imperfect tense with the affixed personal pronouns, and appears to be the source of that form of the verb, and is obtained from the infinitive by substituting ه (*hā-i-ẓāhir*) for the final ل. It is masculine, and both singular and plural, and in the oblique cases the final ه is changed to ۀ or (ے), in the same manner as in the first variety of nouns of the 6th declension. Those infinitives, however, which lengthen the *ism-i-hāliah* by inserting ا in place of (ے), drop it for the imperfect tense, and in the oblique cases; as آلوتل 'to fly,' آلواته 'flight' or 'flying,' آلوته 'he was flying.'

This form of the verb cannot be obtained from infinitives terminating in وَل; and a few infinitives on the other hand, such as زغاستل 'to run,' and ناستل 'to sit,' form both the *ism-i-hāliah* and *hāṣil-i-maṣdar* by prefixing ه. In the former case, *hā-i-z̤āhir* which is masculine, and in the latter, *hā-i-k͟hafī* which is feminine; and both are subject to the same mode of inflection as nouns of the same description.

The verbal nouns of a few infinitives, both transitive and intransitive, instead of affixing نه or ه add ون to the root of the verb; as ډکيدل 'to fill,' ډکون 'filling;' ګډيدل 'to mix, ګډون 'mixing' or 'intercourse;' ترل 'to bind,' ترون 'binding.' They can also be formed by merely rejecting the ل of the infinitive; as ډکيدل 'to fill,' ډکيدون 'filling.' Both forms are somewhat rare. They can be used both as the *ism-i-ḥāliah*, and the *ḥāṣil-i-maṣdar*, and also as simple nouns. See page 173. The *ḥāṣil-i-maṣdar* cannot be used as the imperfect tense.

441. These forms of the verb—the *ḥāṣil* or *ism-i-maṣdar*, and the *ism-i-ḥāliah*, are subject to certain rules in construction which, although appertaining more to the syntax of the language, require explanation here.*

* "It now only remains to be observed that besides the infinitive, as above described, there is another species of noun in some measure resembling it, which the Arabian grammarians term اسم مصدر or the infinitive noun. Between these two nouns, namely, the مصدر and the اسم مصدر there is precisely the same distinction in point of sense as between the word 'drink' and the participial noun 'drinking,' when used as a general term in such an example as the following:—

'Bacchus, ever fair and ever young,
Drinking joys did first ordain;
Bacchus' blessings are a treasure,
Drinking is the soldier's pleasure.'

"In which lines the word 'drink' might be substituted for 'drinking' without much detriment to the sense, for 'drinking joys' mean the 'joys of drinking,' or 'drink,' and the same may be observed of all other words of the same classes; as 'grief,' 'grieving;' 'kiss,' 'kissing;' 'love,' 'loving,' etc. How, then, shall we ascertain the true character of these words? What, for instance, is 'love' as opposed to the general term 'loving?' It is certain that they are both general terms descriptive of certain sensations of delight or modes of pleasure in the mind, and as such may become either the subject or predicate of a proposition; but this explains nothing, and if we ask the Arabian grammarians for an explanation, they answer us by pointing out a mere distinction in their application. The اسم مصدر they say, has no other government than that of any common substantive noun, but this again is controverted by the grammarians of Koofah and Bag͟hdād, who bestow upon it the very same regimen as that of the مصدر; and even admitting the fact, which I believe to be just, it differs nothing in this particular from the infinitive of a neuter verb. The essential distinction then, for some essential distinction there certainly is, between the infinitive and the infinitive's noun or *ismo maṣdar*, is not in my judgment simple abstraction, that is, making the one an abstract noun in opposition to the other; for, as I have observed before, they are both general or abstract terms, but rather in the idea of action or energy conveyed by the infinitive; which action Locke observes, however various, and the effects almost infinite, is all included in the two ideas of thinking and motion. These are his words, 'For action, being the great business of mankind and the whole matter about which all laws are conversant, it is no wonder that several modes of thinking and motion should be taken notice of, the ideas of them observed, and laid up in the memory and have names assigned to them; without which, laws could be but ill made, or vice and disorder repressed. Nor could any communication be well had amongst men, without such complex ideas, with names to them; and, therefore, men have settled names and supposed settled ideas in their minds of modes of action, distinguished by their causes, means, objects, ends, instruments, time, place, and other circumstances, etc.'

"The real distinction, then, between the *maṣdar* and the *ismo maṣdar* seems to be this. The *ismo maṣdar* signifies simply the name of a mode, without any reference to action or energy; the *maṣdar* denotes a more complex idea and indicates indefinitely the action, energy, or being of that mode. Love, for example, is a name assigned to a certain feeling of delight, but loving is something more, being another name by which we indicate the action or efficacy of that feeling called love; and hence we perceive the real cause of its possessing an active or transitive government, in contradistinction to the *ismo maṣdar*, which, having no reference to action, has no other regimen than that of any common substantive noun.

"Action, indeed, is applicable to every infinitive, and this the Arabian grammarians acknowledge by dividing all the verbs in the language into two general classes, which they term متعدي and لازمي, that is, verbs denoting actions transitively (the *actio transiens* of Logicians); and verbs denoting actions inherent or inseparable (*actio immanens*) which we are accustomed to call neuter; and hence we perceive the propriety of the rule laid down in the Commentary, namely that the اسم الفاعل or active participle may be derived from either a transitive or intransitive verb, which is saying in other words that every action supposes an agent.

"This idea of action is conveyed in other languages by terminations, as beat-*ing*, etc., but in Arabic, with a few particular exceptions, there is no distinguishing mark by which we can discriminate the infinitive from the infinitive's noun, so that we

These forms of the verb are constructed in no less than nine different ways.

I.—The *ism-i-maṣdar*, as a noun, is connected as the مضاف *muẓāf* or governing word, in the relation of the genitive case with an agent, the object being at the same time expressed in the ablative case, and the verb agreeing with the governing noun. Examples:

له اغيارو سره گډون دي دَ يار هسي لكه څوك كا سره گډ پاك و نا پاك

"Thus, the INTERCOURSE of the sweetheart with the rival is,
As though one mix together pure and impure—holy and profane."—*Æabd-ul-Ḥamīd.*

له قسمتَ خلاصيدو دَ هيچا نه شي كه داخل شي دَ مكي په حرمونَ

"From destiny there is no ESCAPE for any one,
Though he enter the sacred plain of Mekka itself."—*Æabd-ur-Raḥmān.*

The entire construction changes, should the verb, which is intransitive in the preceding examples, be changed to a transitive in a past tense; the *ḥāṣil-i-maṣdar* then becomes the object, and يار and هيچا the مضاف اليه *muẓāf-illeh*, or words governed in each of the above examples, become the agents in the instrumental case; thus,

له اغيارو سره گډون وُ كړ يار هسي

"The beloved FORMED such INTERCOURSE with the rival."

له قسمتَ خلاصي هر چا وُ كړد

"Every one EFFECTED ESCAPE from destiny."

II.—The *ism* or *ḥāṣil-i-maṣdar* is used as the مضاف or governing noun, and also as the agent connected with the مضاف اليه or word governed, in the genitive case, the object being expressed in the ablative, and the verb, which is intransitive, being governed by the agent; thus,

دا دَ خداي ساتنه تيره تر دغه ده چه څوك په زغرو په خولونُ يا په لوي حصارونُ خوندي شي

"Although people be enclosed in armour or in helmets, or be defended by lofty fortresses; yet this PROTECTION of the Almighty hath surpassed all."—*Makhzan Afghānī.*

In the event of a transitive verb in a past tense being used instead of an intransitive, as in the above example, the *ism-i-maṣdar* as the مضاف would become

must trust entirely to the context for the sense of either. Every participle, however, in our language when used as a general term is the just representative of an Arabic مصدر or infinitive,—I mean every active participle formed by adding the termination *ing* to the imperative of a verb, which seems in this case to possess a similar power to the characteristic *to*, and therefore it may perhaps be said that we have two infinitives; as—

'Drink-*ing* is the soldier's pleasure, or *to* drink is the soldier's pleasure,'

formed by annexing *ing* and prefixing *to* to the imperative in one sense, and the اسم مصدر 'drink,' in the other. See 'THE MIUT AMIL,' by Capt. A. Lockett." Notes to page 207 to 211. Calcutta, 1814.

the agent in the instrumental case, connected with a مضاف اليه in the genitive, and the pronoun دا would refer to the object; as,

دا دَ خداي ساتني وُ ساته

"The PROTECTION of the Almighty protected him."

The *ism-i-ḥāliah* is also subject to the same rules as the *ism-i-maṣdar*, just explained; and although generally used as a mode of action, in this particular instance it may be used as a noun also. Example: *

دَ هَغه در و ديوار خضر دربان شي　　چه پرکيږي ستا واته ننواته

"May Khiẓr be the doorkeeper of that gate and wall,
By which thy COMING IN and GOING OUT—thy ENTRANCE and thy EXIT take place."
—*Æabd-ul-Ḥamīd.*

If the present tense of an active verb be substituted for کيږي, which is intransitive, the *ism-i-ḥāliah*, which was the مضاف, becomes a mere noun in construction with an auxiliary verb; and the مضاف اليه, which was in the genitive case, becomes the agent in the nominative, as in the following sentence:

چه پرکوي ته واته ننواته

"By which thou effectest EXIT and ENTRANCE."

The agent would of course assume the instrumental case with the verb in the past tenses.

III.—The *ism-i-ḥāliah* as the مضاف is used in conjunction with an object in the genitive case, with the agent expressed in the same sentence, the transitive verb being governed by the object; thus,

بد دِ نه مني دلبرَ خما کاته　　بلبلان کاندِ په گلو آلواته

"Thou shouldst not take amiss, beloved one, my LOOKING;
For the nightingales take flight round the rose."—*Æabd-ul-Ḥamīd.*

With an intransitive verb the *ism-i-ḥāliah* becomes the agent and the مضاف in the genitive case, and the former agent becomes the object in the ablative; as,

بد دِ نه لگي په دلبر خما کاته

"My SIGHT should not view the beloved one amiss."

IV.—The *ism-i-ḥāliah* is connected by the genitive case as مضاف to the object, an agent being neither expressed nor understood, having then a passive signification, and the verb agreeing with the مضاف. Example:

پيراندِ دَ محمد فرض دي په دا رنگ چه رسول دَ خداي دي چه مور ايمان دي په دد راوړي

* This example has been already given for the present participle, the *ism-i-ḥāliah*, for which see page 74.

"KNOWING (or KNOWLEDGE of) Muḥammad is a sacred duty, in this manner, that he is the Prophet of God on whom we have placed our faith."—*Fawā'īd-ush-Sharī'æa'h.*

With the present tense of a transitive verb used in place of the auxiliary دي, the *ism-i-ḥāliah* as the مضاف would become the agent, and the object would be necessarily expressed, as in the following sentence:

پېژاندهٔ دَ محمد مؤمنانٌ لره ايمان ور کوي

"KNOWLEDGE of Muḥammad giveth religion to the believers."

V.—The *ḥāṣil* or *ism-i-maṣdar* is the مضاف اليه joined to the object by the genitive case, the agent expressed in the vocative, and the object, which is the مضاف governing the verb, as in the following extract:

چه نمړئي دَ پاسلوني خوري حميده په يوه پرهر ږدي بل پرهر دپاسَ

"Since thou eatest the mouthful of DEPENDENCE, Oh Ḥamīd!
Over one wound thou placest another wound."

If an intransitive verb be substituted for the transitive in the preceding example, the object in that would become the agent, and the *ḥāṣil-i-maṣdar*, as the مضاف اليه, would convey the meaning of a simple noun; thus,

چه نمړئي دَ پاسلوني کلکه شي

"Since the mouthful of DEPENDENCE may become hard."

VI.—The *ism-i-maṣdar* as the مضاف اليه or word governed, is connected with the مضاف in the genitive case. The agent is not expressed, and the object governs the verb. Example:

دنيا ځاي دد دَ گټني چه دلِ ئي څه وُ نه کړ هغه ځاي دي دَ نتني هرڅوک ژاړئي عالمَ خپسر مه
کانړئي بي غمَ

"The world is the place of ACQUIREMENT, and he who has effected nothing in this, that world is the place of EJECTMENT and EXPULSION. Therefore, oh men! every one of you should weep, and not account yourselves free from sorrow and affliction."—*Fawā'īd-ush-Sharī'æa'h.*

VII.—The *ism-i-maṣdar* as the مضاف is connected with an object—the مضاف اليه grammatically,—in the dative case, but really in the genitive. The agent is also expressed. Example:

چه په زمکه په آسمان وو همګي ئي مټازان وو و ساتني ته ئي مينه د هر چا وُ شوه مبينه

"All who were on the face of the earth or in the heavens were hopeful of, and dependent on him; and for his NOURISHMENT the affection of all men became manifest."—*Tawallud Nāma'h.*

VIII.—The *ism-i-ḥāliah* or *ism-i-maṣdar*, may be used as a noun in construction with an auxiliary verb, the agent being expressed, and in the nominative case, if the verb be in any other than a past tense, and the object in the ablative; thus,

بد دِ نه مني دلبرَ څما کاته　　　بلبلان کاندِ په ګلو آلواته

"Thou shouldst not take amiss, beloved one, my looking;
For the nightingales take FLIGHT round the rose."—*Æabd-ul-Ḥamīd.*

With any past tense of a transitive verb used instead of the present tense, the agent بلبلان, which in the above example is in the nominative, would become بلبلو in the instrumental case.

Sometimes neither agent nor object is expressed, but is understood from something that has gone before or will transpire; as in the following example:

نه پوښتنه سرد کا نه مخ کتنه　　　شا په شا سره تيرېږي آشنا خلق

"They neither make INQUIRY of, nor cast a LOOK towards each other:
Back to back they pass along, the friends and acquaintances of this world."—*Æabd-ul-Ḥamīd.*

IX.—The *ism-i-ḥāliah*, or indefinite participle, is used as a mode of action indefinite as to time or place, in three different ways.

First.—When the agent is not expressed, but understood from something which has passed or which follows, and the *ism-i-ḥāliah* is placed in the ablative case, whether the verb be transitive or intransitive; as in the following extracts:

چه څوک حاضر شي په مسجد کښي په هر ګام به دوه لس نيکۍ کښي شي هم په تله هم په راتله

"Whenever a person may appear in a place of worship, for every footstep which he takes, twelve good actions will be written, both on COMING and on GOING."—*Fawā'īd-ush-Sharī'æa'h.*

ما ويل چه ځني ؤ ښتم کم پلو ته　　　دوي په زغاستي ؤ نيولم شتابان

"I said I should flee from these to some place or other;
But they by RUNNING seized me very quickly."—*Saif-ul-Mulūk.*

Second.—The *ism-i-maṣdar* and the *ism-i-ḥāliah* is the مضاف, or governing noun, in the relation of the ablative case to the مضاف اليه, the object in the genitive case: as in the following extracts:

شاهانه جشن ئي ساز کړ دَ خوښۍ　　　په راتله ئي دَ حسن ميمندي ځوان

"With much joy and delight he made a royal feast,
On account of the ARRIVAL of that youth—Ḥasan Mīmundī."—*Saif-ul-Mulūk.*

په خواست پورته کړه لاسونَ　　　په زړه تير کړه ګناهونَ
دواړه سترګي کړه نمناکي　　　په ريژون دَ اوښو پاکي

"When making thy supplication raise the hands, and recall to thy heart thy sins:
Moisten both thy eyes by SHEDDING tears of purity and innocence."—*Rashīd-ul-Byān.*

Third.—The *ism-i-ḥāliah* is (as I have already shown at pages 72—75) commonly used as a simple indefinite participle, at which time it is neither مضاف nor مضاف اليه, neither inflected nor used with an auxiliary. The following are examples:

په سراجي کښې هسي وائي سرسايه ياسته واجب دي په اصيل او په غنيانٌ

"It is stated in the Sirājī, that the PUTTING ASIDE of alms* is necessary and right, both to the freeman and to the rich."—*Fawā'īd-ush-Sharī'æa'h.*

که ئه زمکي و آسمان ته خاته گران دي دا سفر په يوه گام دي دَ اخلاص

"Although ASCENDING from earth to heaven is a weighty matter;
Yet this journey is attained with but one footstep of piety and sincerity."—*Æabd-ur-Raḥmān.*

442.—Another class of nouns is obtained from the third persons of the past tenses of verbs: as,

ورک څغه ناست ولاړ شه که په تخت وي چه مدام په ويار پاځي په ويار کښيني

"Confound that SITTING and RISING, though it may be on a throne,
Which ever riseth with jealousy, and sitteth with envy."—*Æabd-ul-Ḥamīd.*

443.—The imperatives of some verbs also furnish another description of derivative nouns, and of which the following is an example:

ورکړه راکړه ډمکي دَ بل په لاس دي دلته دخل نه خما دي نه دَ ستا دي

"TRADE and TRAFFIC, BUYING and SELLING, are all in the hands of others:
There is neither an opening or commencement here for me nor for thee."—*Æabd-ur-Raḥmān.*

CHAPTER IX.

THE PUSHTO NUMERALS.

اسماي عدد *is'mā'e æadad.*

444.—The Cardinal Numbers with the Pushto names and the Arabic figures which are used to represent them, are as follows:

The first number يو becomes يوَ or يوه in the oblique cases; and before a feminine noun it takes ه, and is liable to the same changes for number and case as other adjectives. The other numerals being plural, take the inflected form of the plural, and are not subject to any other changes for gender or number.

* The alms given on the Ædu-l-fitr, after the Muḥammadan Lent.

FIGURES.		
1	۱	یو or یود
2	۲	دوه or دوې (W)
3	۳	درې
4	۴	څلور
5	۵	پنځه
6	۶	شپګ (E.) or شپږ (W.)
7	۷	اووه
8	۸	اته
9	۹	نه
10	۱۰	لس
11	۱۱	یوُ لس
12	۱۲	دوه لس or دوولس
13	۱۳	دیارلس
14	۱۴	څوارلس or څورلس
15	۱۵	پنځه لس
16	۱۶	شپاړس
17	۱۷	اووه لس
18	۱۸	اته لس
19	۱۹	نولس or نونس (W)
20	۲۰	شل
21	۲۱	یو ویشت
22	۲۲	دوه ویشت
23	۲۳	درې ویشت
24	۲۴	څلیر ویشت
25	۲۵	پنځه ویشت
26	۲۶	شپګ or شپږ ویشت
27	۲۷	اووه ویشت
28	۲۸	اته ویشت
29	۲۹	نه ویشت
30	۳۰	دیرش
31	۳۱	یو دیرش
32	۳۲	دوُ دیرش
33	۳۳	درې دیرش
34	۳۴	څلور دیرش
35	۳۵	پنځه دیرش
36	۳۶	شپګ or شپږ دیرش
37	۳۷	اووه دیرش
38	۳۸	اته دیرش
39	۳۹	نه دیرش
40	۴۰	څلویښت
41	۴۱	یو څلویښت
42	۴۲	دوُ څلویښت
43	۴۳	درې څلویښت
44	۴۴	څلور څلویښت
45	۴۵	پنځه څلویښت
46	۴۶	شپګ or شپږ څلویښت
47	۴۷	اووه څلویښت
48	۴۸	اته څلویښت
49	۴۹	نه څلویښت
50	۵۰	پنځوس
51	۵۱	یو پنځوس
52	۵۲	دوُ پنځوس
53	۵۳	درې پنځوس
54	۵۴	څلور پنځوس
55	۵۵	پنځه پنځوس
56	۵۶	شپګ or شپږ پنځوس
57	۵۷	اووه پنځوس
58	۵۸	اته پنځوس
59	۵۹	نه پنځوس
60	۶۰	شپیته
61	۶۱	یو شپیته
62	۶۲	دوُ شپیته
63	۶۳	درې شپیته
64	۶۴	څلور شپیته
65	۶۵	پنځه شپیته
66	۶۶	شپګ or شپږ شپیته
67	۶۷	اووه شپیته
68	۶۸	اته شپیته
69	۶۹	نه شپیته
70	۷۰	اویا
71	۷۱	یو اویا
72	۷۲	دوُ اویا
73	۷۳	درې اویا
74	۷۴	څلور اویا
75	۷۵	پنځه اویا
76	۷۶	شپګ or شپږ اویا
77	۷۷	اووه اویا
78	۷۸	اته اویا
79	۷۹	نه اویا
80	۸۰	اتیا
81	۸۱	یو اتیا
82	۸۲	دوُ اتیا
83	۸۳	درې اتیا
84	۸۴	څلور اتیا
85	۸۵	پنځه اتیا
86	۸۶	شپګ or شپږ اتیا
87	۸۷	اووه اتیا
88	۸۸	اته اتیا
89	۸۹	نه اتیا
90	۹۰	نوي نوِ or نیوي
91	۹۱	یو نوي
92	۹۲	دوُ نوي
93	۹۳	درې نوي

FIGURES.			FIGURES.			FIGURES.		
94	٩۴	ځلور نوي	97	٩٧	اووه نوي	99	٩٩	نه نوي
95	٩٥	پنځه نوي	98	٩٨	اته نوي	100	١٠٠	سل
96	٩٦	شپږ or شپږ نوي						

100	١٠٠	يو صوَ	800	٨٠٠	اته صوَ	5,000	٥٠٠٠	پنځه زرد
200	٢٠٠	دوه صوَ	900	٩٠٠	نه صوَ	6,000	٦٠٠٠	شپږ or شپږ زرد
300	٣٠٠	درِ صوَ or تير صوُ	1,000	١٠٠٠	زر	7,000	٧٠٠٠	اووه زرد
400	۴٠٠	ځلور صوَ or څونصوُ	1,000	١٠٠٠	يو زر	8,000	٨٠٠٠	اته زرد
500	٥٠٠	پنځه صوَ or پونصوُ	2,000	٢٠٠٠	دود زرد	9,000	٩٠٠٠	نه زرد
600	٦٠٠	شپږ or شپږ صوَ	3,000	٣٠٠٠	درِ زرد	10,000	١٠٠٠٠	لس زرد
700	٧٠٠	اوود صوَ	4,000	۴٠٠٠	ځلور زرد			

100,000	١٠٠٠٠٠	لک	1,000,000,000	١٠٠٠٠٠٠٠٠٠	بيهند or الف
10,000,000	١٠٠٠٠٠٠٠	کرور	1,000,000,000,000	١٠٠٠٠٠٠٠٠٠٠٠٠	نيل

THE ORDINAL NUMBERS.

اسماي مشتقه *is-mā'e mushtaka'h.*

445. The ordinal numbers in this language are formed in a similar manner to the Persian ordinals, with the exception of the first, by affixing م. The changes to which they are subject for gender, number, and case, have been already described at paragraph 89.

رنبي or ورنبي or اول	first.	شپګم or شپږم	sixth.
دويم or دود يم	second.	اووم	seventh.
دريم	third.	اتم	eighth.
ځلورم or ځلرم	fourth.	نهم or نم	ninth.
پنځم	fifth.	لسم	tenth.

NUMERALS OF FRACTIONS.

اسماي کسور *is-mā'e kusūr.*

پاو	a quarter.	پنځه پاوَ or پاوه	one and a quarter.
نيم or نيمه	a half.	يو نيم or يود نيمه	one and a half.
درِ پاو or پاود	three quarters.	پاو کم دود	one and three-fourths.

THE DAYS OF THE WEEK.

اسبوع *isbūa'* or هفته *hafta'h.*

446. The Western Afghāns call the days of the week by the Persian names

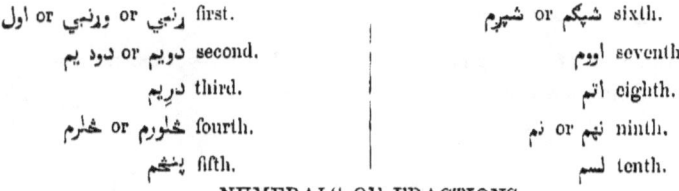

only, except Friday, which is Arabic. The Eastern names are derived from Arabic, Sanskrit, and Persian.

شنبه or خالي Saturday.	چار شنبه Wednesday.
يکشنبه or اتوار ,اتبار Sunday.	پنجشنبه or پان شنبه Thursday.
دو شنبه or پير ,ګل Monday.	جمعه Friday.
سه شنبه or نهٔ Tuesday.	

Amongst the tribes north of Peshāwer, Thursday is called دَ زيارت روځ 'The Day of Pilgrimage.'

THE MONTHS OF THE YEAR.

شهور *shuhūr.*

447. The Afghān tribes bordering on the Panjāb, who are, however, but a small portion of the children of Afghānah, use the months of the Hindū Calendar when referring to matters of agriculture. The names of the Afghān months are—

حسن حسين Ḥasan Ḥusain.	دَ شو قدر مياشت or دَ برات مياشت The Month of the Night of Destiny.
صفره Ṣafara'h.	
ړنبي خور The First Sister.	دَ روژي مياشت The Fast Month.
دوهيمه خور The Second Sister.	دَ واړه اختر مياشت The Lesser Feast Month.
دريمه خور The Third Sister.	ميانه The Intermediate Month.
څلورمه خور The Fourth Sister.	دَ لوي اختر مياشت The Greater Feast Month.
دَ خداي مياشت God's Month.	

The fifth month of the Afghān year—the Third Sister—commences on the 26th of the month of November of the present year 1859.

448. THE SEASONS.

فصول *fuṣūl.*

پسرلي Spring.	مني Autumn.
اوړي or دوبي Summer.	ژمي Winter.

ښايسته دَ پسرلي ګل دي   کل عاشقان لکهٔ بلبل دي
نه ګل بي بلبلَ ښهٔ وي   نه بلبل بي ګلَ ښهٔ وي

"Oh! beauteous are the roses of spring, And like nightingales are lovers:
The rose is useless without its nightingale, And Philomel without its rose."

— *Yūsuf and Zulīkhā.*

449. **THE CARDINAL POINTS.**

جهات *jahāt.*

خير طرف or نهي طرف North.	نمر خاته or نور East.
كينړ طرف South.	نمر پريواته or نور West.

طوطا وّد وِ اي كارغه دَ بيلتانه كشكي څما او ستا تر مينځه بيلتون دَ نمر خاته او دَ نمر پريواته وي

"The parrot said, 'Oh, raven of separation! would to God that between me and thee were as much distance as there is between the East and the West.'"—*Gulistān.*

CHAPTER X.

THE SYNTAX.

نحو *naḥo.*

450. I have generally fully explained the different peculiarities and exceptions of the various rules of each part of speech under their respective heads, and but little remains to be described beyond a few remarks peculiar to the idiom of the language.

As regards the order of words in a sentence, the chief circumstances to be borne in mind are, that the nominative should, properly, appear first in the sentence, and the adjective precede the substantive. Nouns in the different cases, as required, and a participle or adverb may follow, but the verb should terminate the sentence. In poetry, and in some styles of prose also, greater license is taken and allowed, the Afghān poets, like those of other nations, varying the dispositions of the words as they consider most suitable to the numbers and tendency of their poems.

The order and arrangement of words will be seen from the following extracts, as well as from the numerous examples already given, and also in the idiomatical tales inserted in the Appendix for this purpose.

بلبل ژبه دَ شكرګذاري پرانته شكر ئي دَ بارِ تعالي په ځاي راوړ نور ئي وّ وِ تا له ما سره نيكي وّ كړه البته پاداش دَ دي نيكي نيكي بويه وّ پوهيږد چه تردي وني لاندِ پټ وّ لاړي چلمچي دي دَ زرو وا ئي خله او په خپل كار ئي خرڅ كړه

"The nightingale opened the mouth of gratitude and gave thanks unto the Almighty. Then he said, 'Thou hast acted kindly with me, and certainly the return of such goodness should also be goodness. Know that beneath this tree there is concealed a vessel full of gold—take it and spend it in thy necessities.'"—*Kalīlah wo Damnah.*

میسره نومانډ قدیم دَ مُرتضي علي دَ خوني مریي عبد الصمد هم ور ته نوم وایه کیده مال متاع چه خپلو واړو سره ویش کړدي په ویش کښې بیا په بخره دَ حسین وُ رسیده ډیره مینه به کوله ده په لویو په هلکو

"Maiy'sarah by name, there was an old house-born slave of Murtaẓā Æalī, who was also called by the name of Æabd-us-Ṣamad. When the relatives divided the goods and chattels amongst themselves, this (slave) fell to the lot of Ḥusain in the distribution; and he used to show great affection both towards the elders and the juniors of the family."—*Ḥasan and Ḥusain.*

NOUNS.

451. When nouns of different genders occur in the same sentence, the adjective, the verb, or the participle, governed by them in common, must take the masculine form; as,

شاه زاده نشوربانو ملیکه واړه   په یوه محل کښې ناست وو سره واړه
درسته شپه ئي په خوښي کړه سره تیره   څو دَ ورځې روښنائي شوله برسیره

"The PRINCE, NASHŪRBĀNŪ, the QUEEN—all these were seated together in one apartment, The WHOLE NIGHT they passed together in pleasure, until the LIGHT OF DAY became APPARENT."—*Saif-ul-Mulūk.*

Whenever a noun is to be used in the same sentence with another, which is more immediately acted upon by a verb, the former must be put in the accusative case,* which in Pushto is the same as the nominative; thus,

دوي مکرونَ هسې کاندِ چه و خلق طعامونَ ور کوینَ او خپل څان ته خلقه مرجوع کوینَ

"These deceivers act in this manner—they give VICTUALS unto the people, and they bias THE WORLD towards themselves."—*Farā'id-ush-Sharī'æa'h.*

The particle دَ, which governs the genitive case, generally precedes the noun it governs, the مضاف or governing noun immediately preceding it likewise; but it may also precede the governing as well as the noun governed. Example:

یوه ورځ دَ باغ څښتن ناست وُه په تماشا دَ ګلونو بلبله ئي وُ لیده چه مخ به ئي په پانړیو دَ ګل مښل او په فریاد فریاد به ئي پرِ نارِ وهلِ ورق زرنګار دَ ګل به ئي په تیره مشوکه یو تر بله جدا کاوُه

"One day THE OWNER OF THE GARDEN was sitting amusing himself by viewing THE BEAUTIFUL ROSES, when he beheld a nightingale, which continued rubbing its face on the LEAVES OF A FLOWER, and uttering loud lamentations, was separating ITS golden leaves with its sharp beak."—*Kalīlah wo Damnah.*

When two nouns in the ablative case come together in a sentence, the (ـے) or ه, the sign of the case, is only used with the last; thus,

آزادي او کار و بار دي و بله لرِ   لاس له کار و بارَ وُ کاره که کار کړِ

* Called the حالتِ مفعول بهِ by the Arabian Grammarians.

"Freedom and independence, and the affairs of the world, are far distant from each other:
Take off thy hands from the BUSINESS OF THE WORLD, if thou doeth anything."
—*Æabd-ur-Raḥmān.*

In poetry, when the length of the rhyme requires it, the ablative sign may be altogether omitted.

ADJECTIVES.

452. The adjective must always agree with its noun in gender, case, and number, except with an uninflected masculine noun in the plural number, when the adjective is used in the singular. Examples:

تورِ سترګي تورِ زلفي تورِ ورځي دا همه تورِ بلا دي آدم خورِ

"BLACK eyes; SABLE locks; DARK eyebrows;
These are all GLOOMY calamities and MAN-DEVOURERS."—*Æabd-ul-Ḥamīd.*

دَ پسرلي ګلونه ډير دي په جهان کښ کٔ بلبل غندِ چغار کړي خما دلَ

"In the world the roses of spring are MANIFOLD in number,
If thou lamentest like the nightingale, oh heart of mine!—*Aḥmad Shāh, Abdālī.*

When any other than the first numeral adjective is used with nouns in the masculine gender, it is most generally inflected, and takes (ـے) or ﻩ; but occasionally the noun takes the plural form, and both forms may even be used in the same sentence; as in the following examples:

نور ما لښکر دَ خټک را وُ غوښت مهمندي اوريا خيل څلورسو پنځسو کسَ راغلل قصد مي وُد چه شاهي موشک به خانه کوچ خورِ لړ راولم ورغلم را مي وُ ليږداوه

"I then sent for the Khaṭṭak force, and the Muhmandīs and Aorīā Khels, to the amount of FOUR OR FIVE HUNDRED PERSONS, came to my assistance. It was my intention to bring along with me to Khwaṛṛ, the Shāhī Mūshak clan together with their families, so I went to them and made them march off."—*Afẓal Khān*; *Tārīkh-i-Muraṣṣaæ.*

په شمار سره اووه سوَ زرد آس اوښان هم هم يو لک ګورخرَ او ميښي غوا آهوان هم

"There were at a guess about SEVEN HUNDRED THOUSAND HORSES and CAMELS also;
ONE HUNDRED THOUSAND WILD ASSES too, with BUFFALOES, COWS, and DEER."
—*Saif-ul-Mulūk.*

When numeral adjectives are used with feminine nouns, the latter take the plural form without exception; as,

لس شپي ورځي شاهنه هسي مجلس وُد خوښٔ خورم په دا مجلس تمام الوس وُد

"In this manner for TEN NIGHTS and DAYS there was such a princely party:
The whole tribe were greatly delighted at this assembly."—*Saif-ul-Mulūk.*

When the first numeral adjective is used with nouns, it is subject to the same changes for gender, number, and case, as the noun it qualifies. The remainder take the plural inflected form in the oblique cases; thus,

که وعده دَ يو چارِ يو ساعت کړي دَ هَغي چارِ اميد مي په کال نه شته

"If she maketh a promise of ONE HOUR in any matter,
I have no hope of the fulfilment of the affair in a year."—*Æabd-ur-Raḥmān.*

PRONOUNS.

453. In the different tenses of intransitive verbs, and in the present, future. and aorist of transitives, in which the affixed personal pronouns (ضماير متصله) are used, the separate personal pronouns (ضماير منفصله) may be altogether omitted, as in Persian, Arabic and Hebrew, or may be used with them; and when the meaning is clear without them, they may be dropped in the third person singular and plural of intransitives also. Example:

دَ آشنا په ياد ژوندي يم زه به نه پايم بي خانَ الغياث

"I AM living merely on the recollection of my sweetheart:
Alas! I SHALL NEVER EXIST without my beloved."—*Aḥmad Shāh, Abdālī.*

In the following example, an affixed personal pronoun in the dative case has been joined to the past tense of a transitive verb, and the regular personal pronoun زه also used; and although it refers to the same object in the sentence, it is not inflected. The meaning would be complete and clear without the زه, and to put it in the dative form ما ته or ما لره would be incorrect, unless the affixed pronoun be removed. It must therefore be borne in mind, that in using a separate personal pronoun with an affixed one in the dative case, which it naturally assumes when used with the past tense of a transitive verb, the former must retain the uninflected form; thus,

زه دَ يار غمو بيمار کړم بيمار غمو دَ يار کړم
زړه به څه رنګ بيمار نه وي چه پر زړه زلفي تار تار کړم

"Grief on account of the beloved hath made ME wretched; anguish for her hath made ME ill indeed.
Why should not my heart be sad? when in my mind I think of her flowing tresses."
—*Aḥmad Shāh, Abdālī.*

It should also be remarked that the last word of this example, کړم is the first person singular of the *present tense*, although written precisely in the same manner as the past with affixed pronoun in the preceding line; and the affixed personal pronoun م is in the nominative case.

Personal pronouns may occasionally be met with in the inflected form of the dative case without the governing particles, and written in the same manner as the instrumental form of the pronoun. They are, however, comparatively rare.

هم توبه کړم هم گناه کړم — ته ما وینې کرد گارَ
زه عاجز بنده عاصي يم — پرده پوښ مې شې ستارَ

"I show contrition, yet I commit sin; but Thou seest ME oh Creator!
I am a poor weak mortal; oh concealer of faults, become Thou my screen!"
—*Khūshḥāl Khān, Khaṭṭak.*

A verb is often used in construction without any noun or pronoun expressed. Under these circumstances some such word as چار or حال 'point,' 'matter,' 'affair,' 'concern,' etc., is generally understood; as in the following example:

خواد ناخواد به دَ تقدير شَوې ور پيښ شې — که څوک هيچرې نظر په تقدير نکا

"At all events, WHATEVER hath been DECREED by fate will happen;
Although a person may have never cast his eyes on destiny."—*ʻAbd-ur-Raḥmān.*

If speaking of one's-self with another, preference is given to the first person in the first instance. The Afghāns being a plain spoken race, too, use the singular and not the plural form of the pronoun, as in English, when referring to one person only. Example:

زه او ته دواړه دَ يوَ څښتن غلامان يوُ — بندگان دَ بارگاه دَ سلطان يوُ
زه له خدمته يو دم نه يم په قلار — هر کله سر په صحرا يم

"*I* and THOU are both the slaves of one master, and the dependents of the audience hall of the Sovereign.
I am never at rest from my duty, for I am ever with my head in the desert."—*Gulistān.*

When a third person is mentioned, the words of the speaker himself must be repeated instead of using the third person, as in English; thus,

چه ور ته ياده شوه چه قعده مې کړِنه ده که و ناستې ته نژدې وِې دِ بيارته وَ جاروزې قعده دِ پرځاي کا

"When he recollects that 'the Ḳaʻda'h* has not been performed BY ME,' if he be near unto the sitting posture, he should return to that posture and perform the Ḳaʻda'h.—*Faʻā'id-ush-Sharīʻa'h.*

هيڅ په ځان نه پوهيده چه چرته دَرومو — نه يې زده وؤ چه کوم ملک دې کوم مکان

"They did not know at all in their minds as to 'where WE GO,'†
Neither did they distinguish what country it is, or what place."—*Saif-ul-Mulūk.*

The pronoun هغه is used for the third person, but generally in a demonstrative sense with reference to a distant object; and by way of discrimination, the pronoun

* A mode of sitting at prayer.

† Meaning, "Where they go."

دي, دِ, or دا must be used, in the same way as we use *this* and *that* in English. The following is an example :

معاويه وِ په زړکي مي غشي لګ شوُ په آخر به پرهار وُ کاندِ خوناب نه مي دا نه مي هغه شوُ نه
پوهېږم په قيامت به ځواب څه کړم دَ وهاب

"Muᵉā'wiyah said, 'An arrow hath pierced my heart, and in the end the wound will give forth bloody water. I have neither acquired THIS (world) nor THAT, and I know not what answer I shall make to the Giver of all good at the last day.—*Ḥasan and Ḥusain.*

When the use of a second pronoun is required to refer to the same thing as the subject of the sentence or nominative before the verb, the common or reflective pronoun خپل must be used. Examples :

ميرزا خپل ځان پخپله ستائي   په ميرزا ئي عنايت دي

"Oh! Mīrzā, He HIMSELF glorifieth HIMSELF,
And unto Mīrzā His favour and beneficence is extended."—*Mīrzā Khān, Anṣārī.*

وقت دَ نو بهار دي   بلبل په څو چغار دي
دَ بلبل په زړه غمونه   ګل مست په خپل خماردي

"It is the season of spring; the nightingale laments and bewails;
His heart is filled with anguish; the ROSE is inebriated with ITS OWN intoxication."
—*Aḥmad Shāh, Abdālī.*

When a pronoun in the second number of a sentence refers to the same subject or thing as the nominative or subject of the verb in the first, the personal and particular pronoun must be used instead of the reflective or reciprocal; thus,

اي کاشکي يوه ورځ په خوا له مرګه زه وَيَ را رسيدلَيَ دَ خپل زړه په مراد غسي يو نهر چه موج
وهلي ځما تر زنګونَ بتکَ مي وَيَ ډک کړي دَ زړه په مراد

"Alas! that before death I had once reached such a river, whose waves having flowed to MY knees, I had filled my water-vessel according to the wish of my heart.—*Gulistān.*

The common or reflective pronoun may also be used in a substantive sense, as in the following :

ور نه وُه وِ پرديو خپلو حضرت نه وُه دَ ليږلو خديجه ئي کړه لازمه تر حضرت پوري ملزمه

"The strangers and HER OWN (relations) also said unto her, 'The sending away of the Prophet was not necessary on thy part.' They rebuked Khadīja'h, and she stood reproved before him."—*Tawallud Nāma'h.*

خپل is also joined to nouns and pronouns by way of identity, peculiarity, or emphasis; as in the following extract :

خداي پخپله دا ويلي هرچه لاس ئي په قرآن دي لګولَيَ مباره‌کي باند کانړيِ مومنانُ

"God Almighty HIMSELF hath said, 'Whoever hath placed his hand on the Ḳur'ān, congratulate him, oh Faithful!'"—*Makhzan Afghānī.*

The pronoun څه, used both as an interrogative and an indefinite, although not applicable to persons generally, is often used to express scorn or astonishment; as in the following examples:

دَ حمید له فکره مه پوښته عام خلق   دَ زربفتو قدر څه زده بوریا باف

"Inquire not of the vulgar concerning the anxiety and care of Ḥamīd.
WHAT knoweth the mat-weaver regarding the value of cloth of gold?—*Æabd-ul-Ḥamīd.*

څه بلا سخته دانه یم نپوهیږم   چه کسیا نه شوم دَ هجر په آسیا کښي

"WHAT unfortunate hard grain I am, I cannot imagine;
Since I do not become ground in the mill-stones of absence."—*Æabd-ul-Ḥamīd.*

It may also be used in a discriminative or characteristic sense; thus,

څه حاکم څه رعیت څه غیر زیر   جهان واړه دَ بلا په لکئ سور شه

"WHETHER ruler or subject, or WHETHER foreign or strange;
The whole world is mounted on the tail of calamity and evil."—*Æabd-ul-Ḥamīd.*

The adverb چرته is used emphatically to denote dissimilarity, contrariety, and non-existence between matters or things; as,

چرته دَ یار شونډِ چرته غم دَ دل و جان   چرته کتي لعل او چرته لعل دَ بدخشان

"WHERE the lips of the beloved? WHERE the sorrow of heart and soul?
WHERE the nightshade's red berry? and WHERE the ruby of Badakhshān?"
—*Æabd-ur-Raḥman,*

واړه بي وقوف دي چه خوک دین په دنیا پرولي   چرته پنځه ورځ چرته عمرِ جاویدان

"Since people barter their faith for the world's wealth, they are fools;
WHERE is fifty days? and WHERE eternity and everlasting life?"—*Æabd-ur-Raḥmān.*

VERBS.

454. Transitive verbs in any past tense of the active voice *must* agree with the object in gender and number, whether it may or may not be put in the oblique case; as in the following extracts:

بهرام خلاصه هغه جنِ کړله له قیدد   له کوهي نه ئي را بیرته کړه بیرون

"Bahrām RELEASED THAT DAMSEL from confinement:
He drew her out from inside the well."—*Bahrām Gūr.*

شاه سلیمان جامه په خپل لاس پرانتله   ور ښکاره شه یو صورت دَ محبوبان

"King Sūlīmān OPENED the COVERING with his own hand:
To him became apparent a portrait of his beloved mistress."—*Saif-ul-Mulūk.*

In the preceding examples, the objects are feminine and the verbs also.

The agent, as already explained, is used in the instrumental case, and takes the inflected form when capable of inflection. The agents in the preceding extracts were not capable of change: in the following example the agent زمانه becomes زماني.

چه پرون ئې غم خورکي خما دَ غم کړه   زماني کړ ځغه يار خما خونخور نن

"He who yesterday commiserated and condoled with my sorrow and grief,
DESTINY to-day made that friend of mine sanguinary and cruel."—*Æabd-ul-Hamīd.*

Pushto nouns have no particular terminations for the objective case; it is distinguished merely by its position, which properly is after the agent and before the verb, when both agent and object are used in the third person. In all other instances the object may be known by the gender and number which the verb assumes to agree with it; and by the affixed personal pronouns, which, as in the Semitic dialects, point out the objective case. Examples:

چه اورنګ بهرام خبر که له دي حالَ   انديښنو ئې صورت تاو کړ شه پريشانَ

"When Aorang MADE BAHRĀM ACQUAINTED with this circumstance,
Care and anxiety excited HIM: he became perplexed and distracted.—*Bahrām Gūr.*

دَ غره په لمن کښي يو غار تاريک وُ ليد يو مردِ روشن دل دَ غار په خوله کښي ناست وُد له زحمتَ
دَ اغيار خلاص وُد

"At the skirt of the mountain HE PERCEIVED A dark CAVE; and a man of enlightened mind was seated at the mouth of the cavern, free from the disquietude of strangers.—*Kalīlah wo Damnah.*

مريي په خوا له دِ نه درياب ليدلئ نه وُد او خواري دَ بيړئ آزميلئ نه وَد ژړا او زاري آغاز ئې کړله

"The slave previous to this HAD NEVER BEHELD THE SEA, and had never experienced the annoyance and inconvenience of a boat. He commenced to weep and lament.—*Gulistān.*

Reverse the order in these examples and the meaning is also reversed. Thus, in the first, بهرام would be the agent and اورنګ the object; and in the last, درياب would be the agent and مريي the object.

There are some transitive verbs, such as ويل 'to speak,' and کتل 'to look at,' 'to observe,' with which it is absolutely necessary that the object be put in the dative case, without which the sentence would convey no meaning. The following are examples:

ملکي وَ خپلي مور و ته پټ وُد وِ   په دا حال ئې بدري هم کړه خبرداره

"The Queen SPOKE PRIVATELY UNTO HER MOTHER,
And with this circumstance she also acquainted Badrī."—*Saif-ul-Mulūk.*

آدم خان بلو ته وُړه وِ چه ور شه را ئي وَله چه دي ورغي راوست ملا ور ته وُړه وِ چه ښځي دِ بيرته شي هله به در شَم

"Adam Khān SAID TO BALO, 'Go thou and bring him;' and when he went and brought him, the Mullā said UNTO HIM, 'Let the women go away, then I will come to thee.'"—*Tale of Adam Khān and Durkhāna'ī.*

In sentences where there may be two objective cases, the one denoting the object and the other the person, the object of the transitive verb *must* be put in the dative case. Examples:

ما چه سترګي وګل رخ و ته وهلي   په هغو سترګو مي ويني وُ ژړلي

"Since I cast my eyes TOWARDS this ROSY-CHEEKED ONE,
With those eyes I shed tears of blood."—*Æabd-ur-Raḥmān.*

چه بهرام ته ئي جوړ واغوستولي   دَ ښايست شعلي زياتي شوي تر نمره

"When he caused BAHRĀM to be decked out in a suit of clothes,
The blaze of his beauty became greater than the sun."—*Bahrām Gūr.*

The dative case is sometimes used instead of the genitive to express relation or possession; as,

غه تحفه چه وَه پلار ما ته راستولي   را په يادد شوه هَغه ګړۍ هَغه زمان

"That curiosity which father had sent FOR ME,
Came to my recollection at that very hour and time."—*Saif-ul-Mulūk.*

اي مدام دَ نس په زيرمه مبتلا   ځان ته ولِ ويښوي اوده بلا

"Oh thou for ever fascinated and distracted with the cares of the flesh!
Why awaken FOR THY LIFE and SOUL sleeping calamity and misfortune?"
—*Æabd-ul-Ḥamīd.*

The infinitive form of the verb, besides its other uses already described, is also used to denote the absolute necessity of an action; thus,

بل حلال حلال ګڼړل دي   بل حرام حرام ګڼړل دي

"Moreover, that which is legal and right it is necessary to ACCOUNT lawful;
And that which is prohibited and unlawful it is necessary to ACCOUNT so."
--*Rashīd-ul-By'ān.*

The past tense of a verb is often used in a future sense, as in the following extracts:

که فراق په زړد زهير کړم   يا غم په غم شبګير کړم
زه به ستا نامه دستګير کړم   فرياد رس يا مصطفي

"If absence SHALL MAKE ME sad, or grief on grief SHALL at night ATTACK ME;
I WILL make thy name my helper, oh! thou Redresser of Wrongs! oh! thou Selected One!"
—*Aḥmad Shāh, Abdālī.*

بادَ که دَ یار خبر دي راوړ   له زړه بَ واخلي دَ هجران سَوي داغونَ

"Oh! gentle gale! if thou WILT BRING news of the beloved;
Thou wilt remove the absence-burned spots from the heart."—*Aḥmad Shāh, Abdālī.*

The present tense in many instances may also be used in a future signification; as,

دَ جنت نقشو نِگار ترِ پوري هیڅ شي   چه ښکاره کا یو نِگار نِگار له مخَ

"The rapture and bliss of Paradise WILL BE nothing in his eyes,
When the beloved displayeth one of the charms of her countenance."
—*Æabd-ul-Ḥamīd.*

شپږ رونړه کل لښکر به در سره شؤ   هر چه وائي موږ به کړؤ هَغه کارونه

"Six brothers, together with the army, we will all go with thee;
And whatever tasks thou WILT IMPOSE, those we will perform."—*Bahrām Gūr.*

هیڅ مي غم دَ څنکندن دَ تلخیِ نه شتهٔ   که مي یار په بالښت ناست وي سر طرف

"I SHALL HAVE no concern on account of the bitterness of death,
If my beloved may be seated by the pillow at the head of my bed."—*Æabd-ul-Ḥamīd.*

455. The past participles of Pushto verbs are sometimes used as past conjunctive participles, termed ماضي معطوف علیه, in the same manner as in the Persian language. This is a very useful form of the verb, although not very commonly used. It expresses the performance of something previous to another action, which is indicated by the verb following; and serves to conjoin the different members of a sentence. Example:

اوس به څهٔ د وطن کانړي بوټي ژاړم   د رخصت سلام مي کړيَ ترِ بدا شوم

"How shall I now weep after the rocks and the shrubs of my country?
HAVING MADE my parting salutation, I bade them farewell."
—*Ashraf Khān, Khaṯṯak.*

456. Two words which resemble each other in sound, are often adopted when one alone would be sufficient; but one of the words, generally the latter, has no signification, and is used merely for the sake of sound. Examples:

د دنیا دَ سود دپارد بایده نه دي   چه گریوان کړيْ دَ عزت په چا شوکَ پوکَ

"For the sake of the profit of the world, it behoveth not
That thou shouldest REND the collar of any one's fair fame."—*Æabd-ul-Ḥamīd.*

نښتيَ زړد ارجل برجل په دام دَ زلفو   په دروغ کا و پرهیز ته څان گواهي

"With the insnared heart in the noose of curly locks ENTANGLED,
The mind maketh false arbitration regarding discretion and caution."
—*Æabd-ul-Ḥamīd.*

APPENDIX.

I.—TRANSLATION FROM THE ARTICLES OF WAR.

Crimes punishable by General Court Martial with Dismissal or Suspension of Officers, or by General or District Court Martial with Dismissal, Reduction, Corporal Punishment, or Simple Imprisonment with or without Solitary Confinement, or Loss of Standing on the Roll of Non-Commissioned Officers and Soldiers.

بیان د دي ګناهونُ چه سزا دَ هُغو د لښکري عدالت دوړاندِ په دي شان سره دي یعني که سردار وي له نوکرۍ یا له عهدي نه وُ به یستي شي او که وړوُکي عهده دار یا سپاهي وي په حکم د جنرل یا دسترکت کورټ مارشل له نوکرۍ نه برطرف شي یا له وړي عهدي نه وُ ښکي شي او په ځاي د سپاهي به ئې وُ دروي یا به کړوړۍ وُ خوري یا به یوازي قید شي یا له نورُ سره یا نوم به ئې په دفتر کښي ورستي شي

Article 22.

Any Officer or Soldier who shall, in operations in the field, spread reports by words or letters calculated to create unnecessary alarm among the troops, or in the vicinity, or in the rear of the army; or

دوه ویشتم حکم

هر وقت چه لښکر په میدان کښي وي هر یو سردار یا سپاهي چه له ویلو د خبري او له ښکلُ د کاغذ داهسي خبره مشهوره کړي چه له ځغه نه په مینځ یا وړاندي یا دورستو یا چاپیره د لښکر کښي بیځایه ویره یا غوغا پیدا شي

Article 23.

Who shall in action, or previously to going into action, use words tending to create alarm or despondency; or

درِ ویشتم حکم

او هر څوک چه په وقت د جنګ کښي یا په خوا د تلو و جنګ ته داهسي خبري وائي چه له هُغو خبرو نه ویره یا نااميدي پیدا شي

Article 24.

Who shall be drunk when on, or for Duty, or on Parade, or on the Line of March; or

څلیر ویشتم حکم

او هر څوک چه د نوکرۍ د تیارۍ په وقت کښي یا په وقت د نوکرۍ کولو یا په وقت د قواعد یا په وقت د کوچ کښي شراب وُ څکي او مست شي

پنځه ويشتم حکم

Article 25.

او هر څوک چه پاره دار سپاهي ؤ وهي يا نيت د وهلو ؤ کړي

Who shall strike or force any Sentry; or

شپګ ويشتم حکم

Article 26.

او چه څوک عهده دار په خپله عهده بانډِ وي او په هغه وقت کښي که څوک سپاهي له بي ادبۍ د هغه عهده دار حکم نه مني يا د بي ادبۍ خبرد ور ته ؤ کړي يا څوک چه په لښکرِي عدالت کښي بللي شَوي وي او هلته ياغي شَوي له بي ادبۍ نه حکم نه مني

Any Soldier who shall be grossly insubordinate or insolent to his Superior Officer in the execution of his office; or grossly insubordinate and violent in the presence of a Court Martial; or

اووه ويشتم حکم

Article 27.

هر وقت لښکر د جنګ په ميدان کښي يا د پارد د جنګ د دښمن ولاړ وي هر څوک چه په جوړولُ د مورچي او د خندق يا په نورو کارونُ کښي مدد ور کولُ دپاره حکم نه مني—

Who, being on actual service, shall refuse to assist in making field works;

که ګناه ګار عهده‌دار وي په حکم د لوي کورټ مارشل له نوکرۍ د سرکار برطرف شي يا مرتبه او ماجب د هغه ګناه ګار به څو ورځو پورې بند شي

Shall, if an Officer, on conviction, be sentenced to be dismissed the service, or to be suspended from Rank and Pay and Allowances;

او که سپاهي وي او تقصير د هغه د جنرل يا دسترکټ يا ګاريسن لښکرِي عدالت دوراندِ ثابت شي پس موافق د دي لښکرِي آئين له حکمَ د جنرل يا دسترکټ يا ګاريسن لښکرِي عدالت پر هغه ګناه ګار باندِ سزا مقرره به شي

And, if a Soldier, shall, on conviction before a General, or District, or Garrison Court Martial, be sentenced to suffer such punishment as a General, or District, or Garrison Court Martial is by these Articles of War respectively empowered to award;

ولي له کولُ د دي مذکورُ ګناهونُ نه په ګناه‌ګار باندِ د وجلُ يا د ملک د يستلُ يا قيد له سخت مذدوري سره لښکري عدالت لره اختيار د حکم کولُ نه شته

Provided, that such Offender shall not be sentenced to Death, or Transportation, or Imprisonment with hard labour.

II.—IDIOMATICAL TALES, ENGLISH AND PUSHTO.

THE AFRĪDĪ AND THE MULLĀ.

A certain Afrīdī, being desirous of learning to read, went into a village to a Mullā and said it would be a great favour if he would teach him. The Mullā asked him whether he had learnt anything previously; but the Afrīdī told him that he had not as yet learned to read. The Mullā then asked him what he would like to commence with; and the latter replied, that he would do as the tutor might direct. The Mullā then told him that, in the first place, he should get the Alphabet by heart, and afterwards commence reading the first section of the Ḳur'ān; to which the Afrīdī having agreed, he was requested to come the following morning.

When the Afrīdī made his appearance the next day, the Mullā, taking the Alphabet in his hand, pointed out the first letter, and requesting his scholar to repeat after him, said "Alif." "*Alup*," repeated the Afrīdī. "That is not the pronunciation," said the teacher, "repeat exactly as I say, Alif." "*Alup*," says the Afrīdī again, with the greatest innocence possible. "Do not pronounce it so," said the Mullā, "call it Alif;" and the Afrīdī, like an obedient pupil, obeying his instructor to the letter, said, "Do not pronounce it so, call it *Alup*." The Mullā again said, "That is not correct, I say: call it Alif." "That is not correct, I say: call it *Alup*," said the Afrīdī. The Mullā, who was not a second Job, now losing all patience, said, "Oh! infidel, call it Alif," on which the Afrīdī replied, "Oh! infidel, call it *Alup*." The Mullā at this, becoming very angry, gave the Afrīdī a box on the ear. The latter now thought within himself, "Master commanded me to repeat whatever he said, and doubtless it is necessary that I should also do as he does;" so thinking this a part of the lesson, he dealt the Mullā a hearty box on the ear in return. At this specimen of *Afrīdiness*, the latter, becoming more enraged than ever, seized the Afrīdī by the throat; and the pupil, obeying his master to the letter, seized him by the throat also. In this state they both rose from their squatting position and commenced wrestling. At length the Afrīdī, having the advantage in strength, succeeded, with little trouble, in laying the Mullā at full length on his back, and seated himself on his breast, at the same time looking towards him in expectation that he would go on with the lesson.

In this unpleasant situation, it struck the Mullā that his amiable pupil might probably have taken his words, "to imitate him," in too literal a light, and that possibly he might be only imitating him in this instance; so, taking his hands off the Afrīdī, he exclaimed, "Oh! Infidel, let me go." The Afrīdī replied, "Oh! Infidel, let me go," and allowed the Mullā to get up; after which he said, "Master! that was not a good lesson by any means; it was a hard fight." The Mullā answered, "You speak truly; to-morrow it will come to swords." "If such is the case," said the Afrīdī, "I will go home and fetch mine," and he set out accordingly. The Mullā, glad of this opportunity, thought there was no time to be lost; and that very night he made himself scarce.

نقل د افريدي او د ملا

يو افريدي يوه کلي ته د لوستو دپاره ملا لره ورغي او وُ ئې وِ ديره مهرباني به دِ وي که و ما ته سبق وائي ملا وُ پښتيده چه ښخوا دِ څه لوستي دي که نه افريدي وُ وِ چه تراوسَ مي هيڅ نه دي لوستي ملا وُ وِ څه لولي افريدي وِ هر څه چه ته فرمائي ملا وِ ږنبي پټئ لوستي بويه پس له هغه سيپاره افريدي وِ ښه دي ږنبي به پټئ وايم پس له هغه به سپره ملا وُ وِ صبا را شه

بله ورځ چه افريدي په وعده راغي ملا پټئ په لاس کښي وُ نيوه او شاګرد ته ئې ږنبي حرف وُ ښو او وُ ئې وِ وايه الف افريدي وُ وِ الُپ ملا وُ وِ داسي مه وايه هرڅه چه زه وايم هغه وايه بيا ملا وُ وِ الِف افريدي وُ وِ الُپ ملا وُ وِ داسي مه وايه وايه الِف افريدي وُ وِ داسي مه وايه وايه الُپ ملا وُ وِ دا جوړه نه ده وايه الِف افريدي وُ وِ دا جوړه نه ده وايه الُپ ملا چه د ايوب په شان صبر نه لاره افريدي ته ئې وُ وِ اي کافره وايه الِف افريدي اتکل وُ کړ چه د استاد په شان ويلي بويه نور ئې وُ وِ اي کافره وايه الُپ له آرويدو د دي خبري ملا دير خپه شه او يوه څپيړه ئې افريدي پر غوږ وُ واهه افريدي فکر وُ کا چه استاد ويلي وه هرڅه چه زه وُ وايم ته هغه وُ وايه البته هرڅه چه استاد وُ کړي زه به هم هغسي کوم دا ئې هم سبق وُ ګاڼه او يوه مضبوته چپلاخه ئې استاد پر غوږ وُ واهه ملا له دي افريدي توبَ له حدَ زيات په قهر شه او افريدي ئې ترغاړه وُ نيوه افريدي هم د ملا په غاړه کښي لاس واچول دواړه له زمکي سره پاڅيدل او په غيږ و له ورغلل پس له لړه زوره افريدي ملا په زمکه وُ ويشت پر سينه ئې کښيناست او ور ته ئې کاته چه ګوندِ نور سبق به را ته وُ وائي

په دي حال کښي ملا فکر وُ که چه ما په خوا له دي و ده ته ويلي وه چه هرڅه زه وُ وايم هغه شان ته هم وُ وايه ښائي دي څما نقل کوي پس له هغه ئې افريدي ته وُ وِ اي کافره ما پريښوي او لاس ئې له افريدي نه لري کړ افريدي وُ وِ اي کافره ما پريښوي او د ملا له سيني پاڅيده ورته ئې وُ وِ چه دا سبق نه ود تيار جنګ وه ملا وُ وِ رښتيا وائي صبا به د تورو جنګ وي افريدي وُ وِ که داسي به وي زه څم چه له کوره تورد را واخلم پس افريدي لاړ شه او ملا په موندلو د دي فرصت دير خوشحال شه تلوار ئې وُ کړ وُ تښتيده

THE OLD MAN AND THE DOCTOR.

An old man complained to a doctor of bad digestion. "Oh! let bad digestion alone," said the doctor, "for it is one of the concomitants of old age." He then stated his weakness of sight. "Don't meddle with weakness of sight," replied the doctor, "for that also is one of the concomitants of old age." He complained to him of difficulty of hearing. "Alas! how distant is hearing," said the doctor, "from old men! difficulty of hearing is a steady concomitant of old age." He complained to him of want of sleep. "How widely separated," said the doctor, "are sleep and old men: for want of sleep is certainly a concomitant of old age." He complained to him of a decrease of bodily vigour. "This is an evil," replied the doctor, "that soon hastens on old men: for want of vigour is a necessary concomitant of old age." The old man (unable to keep his patience any longer) called out to his companions—

"Seize upon the booby! lay hold of the blockhead! drag along the ignorant idiot! that dolt of a doctor, who understands nothing, and who has nothing to distinguish him from a parrot, but the human figure, with his concomitants of old age, forsooth! the only words he seems capable of uttering." The doctor smiled, and said, "Come my old boy, get into a passion, for this also is a concomitant of old age."

نقل د زاړه او د طبيب

يوه زاړه سړي طبيب ته وُ وِ چه څما خوراك نه هضميږي طبيب وُ وِ پريږده خبره د بد هضمۍ چه دا علامه د زړوالي ده بيا هغه وُ وِ چه نظر مي كم شه طبيب وُ وِ چه دا هم له پيرۍ سره گډ دي بيا سپينګيري وُ وِ چه غوږونه مي درانه شوُ بيا طبيب وُ وِ چه د دي علاج مشكل دي له دي جهته چه دا لويه نښانه د پيرۍ ده بيا زاړه سړي وُ وِ چه خوب مي كم شه طبيب وُ وِ هاي هاي د خوب او د زړوالي تر ميانَ څومره بيتلون دي دا هم ملګري د پيرۍ دي پس له دي نه زاړه وُ وِ چه زور مي كم شه طبيب څواب وركه چه دا يود بدي دد چه په تلوار زړو ته رسيږي ولي دا كام نا كام نخښه د پيرۍ دد زاړه چه دا خبره واوريده ډير په تهر شه او خپل آشنايان ئي را وُ بلل او هغو ته ئي وُ وِ چه د خداي دپاره دا نادان وُ نسيۍ لاس واچوئ پر دي جاهل باندِ وُ باسيۍ له كوره دا احمق دا ګندد طبيب چه په هيڅ نه پوهيږي او په مينځ د ده او د طوطا هيڅ فرق نه شته بي له صورتَ نور هيڅ ويلي نه شي بي له دي خبري چه اثر د زړوالي دي طبيب وُ خندل او وُ ئي وِ چه شاباش اي سپين ږيري هلكَ به قهر وُ كړه دا لا له تولو نخښه د پيرۍ دد

UMBSUR—THE JOY OF HIS PARENTS.

I resided at Baṣrah, said a certain Arabian Yorick, as a parson and professor of humanity, and was one day a good deal amused by a strange fellow, squint-eyed, straddle-footed, lame of both legs, with rotten teeth, stammering tongue, staggering in his gait like a man intoxicated, puffing and blowing like a thirsty dog, and foaming at the mouth like an angry camel, who came up and seated himself before me. "Whence come you," said I, "Oh father of gladness?" "From home, please your worship," said he. "And pray where is your home?" I rejoined, "and what is the cause of your journey?" "My home," he replied, "is near the great mosque, adjoining the poor-house, and I am come for the purpose of being married, and to beg you will perform the ceremony. The object of my choice is this long-tongued, importunate, hump-backed, scarlet-skinned, one-eyed, pug-nosed, stinking, deaf, wide-mouthed daughter of my uncle." "Do you agree, Miss Long-tongue," said I, "to marry this Mr. Pot-belly?" "Ay," said the lady (with a great deal of Doric brevity). "Then accept, my friend," cried I, "this woman for your wife; take her home, cherish and protect her." So he took her by the hand and departed.

Now it happened that, about nine months after this event, they both returned to me rejoicing, and they had hardly seated themselves, when my old friend Adonis called out, "Oh, your worship! we have been blessed with a most sweet and fascinating child, and are come to request you will bless and give him a name, and offer up a prayer for his parents." Now, what should I behold but a little urchin, stone-blind, hare-lipped, without the use of its hands, splay-footed, bald-headed, ass-eared, bull-necked, not possessing one sense out of the five, and altogether frightful and deformed; in short, a perfect epitome of all the qualities of his parents. At this sight I said to them, "Be thankful for this darling boy, and call him Umbsur,* for truly he has all your perfections combined in himself, and that child is admirable indeed who resembles his parents."

نقل د هلک امبسر

يوه ملندي عرب ويلي دي په هغه وقت چه په بصره کښي خطيب وم او وعظ مي و خلقو ته کاوه ناګاه يوه ورځ يو کړستړګي ښځي ارتي ګډي ځنځا غاښونه تږي ژبه کوږ ووږ کيده په تلو کښي د ښکي په شان د ترږي سپي غندِ ئي ساه شړله په وقت د خبرو ئي ځکک لوست لکه مست اوښ هسي سړي ما له راغي او مخامخ را ته کښيناست ور ته مي وُ وِ اي پلارَ د خوښۍ له کمَ راځي هغه وُ وِ له کوره ته حضرت اره راغلم ما ور ته وُ وِ ستا کور چرته دي او سبب د سفر دِ څه دي هغه وُ وِ چه کور ځما د جمعي له جماعتَ سرد او په خيرات خانه پوري دي او دلته د واده د پاره راغلي يم غواړم چه ته مي نکاح وُ تړي له دي ژبه وري ډيره ښوښتونکي تيتۍ سور مخي کاڼري لند پژي بد بويه کنړه لوي خولي ترلي ځما سرد نور ما له هغي پښتنه وُ کړه چه اي بي‌بي ژبه وري څه وائي دا کيدد ور صاحب په نکاح قبلوي که نه هغي په تلوار وِ هو پس ما وُ وِ هرکله چه داسي دي وُ نسه اي ځما ياره دا ښځه چه دا ستا ارتينه ده کور ته ئي بوزه او ور سره نيکي کوه او ډيره خبر داري ئي کړه کيدد ور صاحب لاس د خپلي ارتيني وُ نيوه سره روان شول پس له نو مياشتو دواړه په ډيره خوشحلي سرد ما له بيا راغلل اولا ناست نه ووُ چه يوسف ثاني ځما په خواني دوست وُ وِ اي حضرتَ له فضلَ د خداي له مونکا يو ډير ښه او ښائيسته ځوي زيږيدلي دي او تاسو له راغلي يو چه نوم ئي کښيږدۍ او په غوږو کښي ئي بانګ وُ وائي او د مور و پلار د پاره ئي دعا وُ کاږۍ چه په طرف د هلک مي نظر وُ کړ څه وينم يو کچني هلک تپ ړوند په لاسو شل کړ پښي ګنجي د خره په شان غوږونه د جوانه غندِ ئي ځت او يو خوي د سړي توب په کښي نه ود ډير ويروونکي بد صورت ولي ټول ښائيست د مور و پلار په دد کښي ګډ ود پس له ليدلو ور ته مي وُ وِ دپاره د دي ډير ښکلي ځوي لوي شکر کوۍ او نوم د ده أمْبْسّرْ کيږدۍ چه په ريښتيا ټول ښائيست ستاسو دِ هلک په ځان کښي جمع کړي دي او هغه زُ زاد ډير ښه دي چه ټول صفتونه د مور او پلار لري

* Literally, "The joy of his parents," being compounded of ام "mother," اب "father," and سرور "joy."

THE END. تمه تمام شه

www.ingramcontent.com/pod-product-compliance
Lightning Source LLC
Chambersburg PA
CBHW031426020726
47499CB00005B/1611
9783743394346